SMALL GROUPS IN ORGANIZATIONAL SETTINGS

SMALL GROUPS IN ORGANIZATIONAL SETTINGS

Raymond S. Ross

Wayne State University

Jean Ricky Ross

contributing author
Former Chairman of the Board
VISITING NURSE CORPORATION
of Metropolitan Detroit

PRENTICE HALL, Englewood Cliffs, New Jersey 07632

Library of Congress Catalogue Card Number

88-43359

Editorial/production supervision
 and interior design: Virginia L. McCarthy
Cover design: George Cornell
Manufacturing buyer: Ed O'Dougherty
Business agent, Ross Enterprises: Ricky Ross

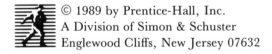
Printed in the United States of America

10 9 8 7 6 5 4 3 2 1

ISBN 0-13-814260-2

Prentice-Hall International (UK) Limited, *London*
Prentice-Hall of Australia Pty. Limited, *Sydney*
Prentice-Hall Canada Inc., *Toronto*
Prentice-Hall Hispanoamericana, S.A., *Mexico*
Prentice-Hall of India Private Limited, *New Delhi*
Prentice-Hall of Japan, Inc., *Tokyo*
Simon & Schuster Asia Pte. Ltd., *Singapore*
Editora Prentice-Hall do Brasil, Ltda., *Rio de Janeiro*

CONTENTS

4

PROBLEM SOLVING AND DECISION MAKING

60

5

COMMUNICATION: RULES AND PRACTICE

104

6 CONFLICT   139

---

9 | BOARDS: THE POWER GROUPS 281

PREFACE

Kaizen, quality circles, project teams, task forces, negotiation teams, commissions, boards, and other popular forms of group interaction point to a real effort by business, industry, labor, the voluntary sector, and government to involve people at all levels in the important business of planning, problem solving, and decision making.

This is not a new concept, but the efforts of the eighties are more determined, more specific, and, we think, more sincere that ever before. A better-educated population, newfound freedom and ambition for minorities and women, the success of foreign competition with involved workers—all these have helped with such motivations.

Since it is our view that all meaningful groups are related to some kind of organization in a world alive with organizations, our focus will be on group life in organizational settings: problem dynamics including conflict and communication, problem solving and decision making, leadership, and relational effectiveness.

All small groups are systems within systems, complete with all manner of external and internal dependencies and constraints. These matters including generic characteristics, structures, definitions, and perspectives from the psychodynamic to social exchange will be discussed.

The pragmatic dimension of this text may be seen in its analysis of organizational conflicts and its suggestions from G.R.I.T. and bargaining to rhetorical sensitivity and third-party interventions. More practical "rules" are found in the sections on leadership, language, rule sharing, and conversational effectiveness. The burgeoning numbers of boards, advisory committees, and consultative committees found everywhere in the public and private sectors will be addressed in Chapter 9 by an experienced professional, the past board president of the Visiting Nurse Corporation of Metropolitan Detroit, Jean Ricky Ross.

Since all organizational-group participants face the probability of being observed, analyzed, and even further trained in these matters, a final chapter has been included to give some orientation about what to expect if you are exposed to an encounter group, behavior therapy, consultant observers, microcounseling, and many more of the latest approaches.

This text is not meant to be an encyclopedia of current research on small groups. It is intended as a practical introduction for students concerned with small group communication in organizational settings. Difficult simplification has been risked in an attempt to make it readable, interesting, and practical. In our view students need to know the rules, skills, and practical communication concepts that will help them and their groups be more rhetorically sensitive and more effective in their small group deliberations in organizational settings.

An *Instructor's Manual* includes a test item file, cases and critical incidents, projects and games, rating scales, and lists of films and related learning packages.

We would like to thank Professor Dan Curtis, Central Missouri State University, and Professor Donald Springen, Brooklyn College/CUNY, for reviewing the manuscript and making helpful suggestions.

RSR

SMALL GROUPS
IN ORGANIZATIONAL
SETTINGS

1

THE IMPORTANCE OF ORGANIZATIONAL SMALL GROUPS

Two organizational consultants see a revolution on the horizon for American organizations.

> A combination of forces—from the rapidly changing business environment to the new work force to astonishing advances in technology—is forging a breakdown of the large traditional, hierarchical organizations that have dominated in the past. We think that this dismantling will result in highly decentralized organizations in which the work of the corporation will be done in *small*, *autonomous units* linked to the megacorporation by new telecommunications and computer technologies.[1]
>
> *Terrence E. Deal, Harvard University;*
> *Allan A. Kennedy, McKinsey & Company*

Not everyone is happy about such a small-group revolution. One classic, caustic comment heard frequently is "Committees are made up of the uninformed assigned by the unwilling to do the unnecessary." Even Boss Kett (Charles F. Kettering of General Motors Corporation) was heard to remark, "If you want to kill an idea, get a committee working on it." All of us have probably felt like that after a particularly boring or frustrating meeting. Yet the small group meetings go on and on. If you work in a corporate setting, you may spend over 3 hours a week in *formally* scheduled meetings and another 9½ hours in informal meetings. The numbers go up as you assume more organizational responsibility. These meetings take time and are not infrequently dominated by conflict and discord.

And they are expensive. It has been estimated that one 2-hour meeting attended by twenty executives would cost a week's salary of just one of them.[2]

Why do we do it? Why can't we just let people do their thing? For openers, their thing has changed. Since 1970 we have gone from a predominantly blue collar society to a 67 percent white collar society. Also, *we* have changed. There are 27 percent more of us in the work force and now we're 54.5 percent female, over half of whom are married.[3] We're also meeting first-rate, foreign competition from organizations who hold more meetings than we do. They relate their unique, often bizarre meeting formats to a more motivated work force and, of most importance, to higher-quality products and services. For all the strain, are proper group meetings the best way to insure informed decision making? We think so. So do Ford, RCA, Motorola, Xerox, and other giants. So do the Rotary, Kiwanis, Optimists, and Lions clubs. These clubs alone hold 20,000 meetings daily in Atlanta; 35,000 in Los Angeles; and 40,000 in New York.[4]

If you work in government, education, the health-care professions, or are seriously involved with a church, you know something about small groups in organizational settings. They will not go away, and they can work for us most of the time if we take the time to learn more about them. For some participants they can lead to growth, self-fulfillment, and even enjoyment.

It is time to prepare for a major change in the organization of the future, one that is already underway as we will show shortly. The two consultants who opened this chapter call this emerging structure the *atomized organization* to emphasize its small size and flexibility. The hallmarks of this new structure are

- small, task-focused work units (ten to twenty persons maximum),
- each with economic and managerial control over its own destiny,
- interconnected with larger entities through benign computer and communication links,
- and bonded into larger companies through strong (corporate) cultural bonds.[5]

PARTICIPATION AND PRODUCTION

LEARNING AND SATISFACTION

The notion of participation, or involvement, being related to motivation is not a new one to persuasion theory or social psychology. Successful, modern educators know that their students learn more when involved in the learning process and that they enjoy the experience itself more. These educators have devised creative strategies such as case studies, task forces, research groups, games, peer group evaluation, and class committees. As long as a clear learning outcome exists—a point to this participative fun—and as long as the activity doesn't run afoul of other organizational policies and rules, these group activities are productive.

EMPLOYEE PARTICIPATION

Business and industry, with some exceptions, have long felt that employee participation leads to higher productivity and higher morale. However, trouble usually follows when the character of the discussions and resulting decisions involve working conditions and rules that have been previously contracted. Unions are particularly sensitive about these matters. Ford of Europe had the popular Quality Circle (QC) technique (discussed in the next section) rejected in England primarily because it failed to advise and *involve* the unions in the early planning and design of the programs. If involving labor in policy matters through these groups is clearly anti-union in design or is perceived as union busting, it is doomed to failure in strong labor industries such as the auto industry and the United Automobile Workers Union (UAW). Unions have also been accused of using participative groups to their own advantage.

It is not easy to apply the notion of participation and production, yet it is obviously worth the strain. The Motorola Corporation has run its own version of the Japanese program called PMP, Participative Management Program, for over ten years and claims great success. Xerox Corporation has developed an elaborate program of employee group meetings; they range from problem-solving workshops to serious attempts at promoting labor–management relations through better understanding of work rules, company priorities, and standard procedures. The list of organizations that have tried or are trying to improve production and quality through employee participation is a long one. Successful or not, the programs are in vogue now and, given high-quality overseas competition, they are apt to remain so. "If it works for them, why can't it work for us?" With better understanding and training of our heterogeneous work force and better planning in the use of these small group techniques, perhaps it can. Ford, Sperry, Xerox, RCA, Motorola, and others claim just that. As of this writing, their production, quality, and profitability do seem to support their claims.

For years speech communication scholars have articulated a larger perspective on group discussion. The late James H. McBurney, Dean Emeritus of the School of Speech of Northwestern University, stated it well:

> . . . discussion is the essence of the democratic process. Whatever weakens discussion in America, weakens America. We need differing points of view, and we need articulate spokesmen for these points of view.[6]

Is this "discussion essence," this participatory kind of democracy, still alive and well and living in America? John Naisbitt, author of *Megatrends*, thinks so. He feels it is one of the major trends currently shaping America. "The ethic of participation is spreading bottom up across America and radically altering the way we think people in institutions should be governed. Citizens, workers, and consumers are demanding and getting a greater voice in government, business, and the market place."[7] Naisbitt concludes, "The guiding principle of this participatory democracy is that people must be part of the process of arriving at decisions that affect their lives."

What then are some of these trends, these participatory techniques and procedures found in organizational settings?

ORGANIZATIONAL SMALL GROUPS

Standard formats (e.g., panels, symposiums, brain-storming groups, and so forth) will be discussed in another chapter. In this chapter we will explain briefly some of the new, the unique, as well as the more standard activities found in modern organizational settings.

KAIZEN

Mazda's new auto plant in Flat Rock, Michigan (1986), has introduced us to still another new participative group concept. *Kaizen* means "improvement, or self-criticism." Workers suggest ways to make their work more productive and easier. With the help of management and trained group leaders, they follow problem-solving techniques and decide which suggestions might actually become part of the plant work rules. Four hundred and fifty workers were sent to the Hofu plant in Japan for four weeks of training, with one full week spent on learning Kaizen. The employees learned various techniques of defining, locating, analyzing, and solving problems and implementing solutions. We've heard of these techniques before, but rarely have they been incorporated with such intensity and with rank-and-file employees. Small monetary incentives are involved, and employees are given public credit on Kaizen boards found throughout the plant. These 450 trainees will then train the 3,500 employees hired for the 1987 plant opening in America. According to Kunio Fujii, training director for Mazda, last year 70 percent of the 3 million suggestions Hofu employees made were implemented.[8]

Flat Rock, Michigan, is not Hofu, Japan. Kaizen is set in a long cultural tradition with a homogeneous work force. Most of us are still having trouble distinguishing between sushi and sashimi*, much less Kaizen and *Karaoke*. *Karaoke* is an off-the-job, pub-like activity in which patrons take turns singing—once again, involved participation. Sushi houses have appeared in Flat Rock and the Japanese are encouraging the establishment of Karaoke clubs or bars. Even here culture intrudes. These clubs are male dominated in Japan. The point is that all of these involvement or participative group activities are culture and context bound. The Japanese know that very well. They also know that some firm pushing is often necessary. The UAW has already agreed to accept only 85 percent of their fellow workers' pay scale at Ford Motor Company,** rivaling only what Lee Iacocca has done at Chrysler Corporation. There is little room for the naive in attempting Kaizen.

QUALITY CIRCLES

In Japan the Japanese call them Quality *Control* Circles; in America we have dropped the word *control*. It is more than just semantics; "quality control" or "quality assurance" engineers have not always been well received by labor here.

Quality circles are small groups or circles of employees who meet regularly and discuss ways to improve methods of producing quality goods or delivering quality services, hopefully at lower costs. In addition this kind of teamwork is thought to improve morale and motivation. The groups are not chosen at random and include those people in the line or work unit that actually produces the product or part of the product or provides the service, including the foreman or supervisor.

Since their start in Japan in the early 1960s, quality circles have become a big business in themselves. The International Association of QCs Managers and Consultants has a membership of more than 7,000—a big leap from 1977 when only five American companies were known to have QC.

QCs are credited with saving the Verbatim Corporation of Sunnyvale, California, $100,000 by suggesting a better method for producing floppy disks; Blue Cross of Washington and Alaska claims savings of $430,000 in less than three years thanks to QCs suggestions regarding services and communication.[9]

What are these quality circles and where did they come from? Ironically, according to Professor Mitchell Lee Marks, they were introduced to post–World War II

Sushi is small, cold rice cakes topped with garnishes such as raw fish. *Sashimi* is thinly sliced raw fish.
**Ford has a 25 percent equity ownership of Mazda.

Japan (1948–1950) by Dr. Edward Deming, an expert in statistical methods and quality control. Deming's thesis was that production quality problems were best solved by the coordinated efforts of both labor and management.[10] In the 1960s the Japanese added their own special group dynamics and problem-solving techniques as well as generous government support. Something worked! By the 1970s Japan had lost its deserved reputation for shoddy goods; by the 1980s it had become famous for precision and high quality of goods. In 1973 Lockheed Corporation sent six employees to Japan to find the secret. They brought the QCs back to America and established their own program in 1974. Lockheed followed exactly the detailed Japanese problem solving format of " . . . problem generation and selection, causal analysis, solution generation and analysis, presentation to management, trial implementation, monitoring and feedback, and ultimately full implementation."[11]

Most early QCs followed the same sequence, at least until they could develop their own individual adaptation. Given our different management philosophy of the times, a more heterogeneous work force, and stronger labor unions, considerable adaptation was indeed in order. What if your QC group's suggestions were to cut costs and improve quality but in so doing would eliminate jobs or whole job classifications? Robots for welders, computer scanners for inspectors, plastic for steel, computers for inventory specialists, and so forth. Obviously, issues such as contract and job security also arise.

Chrysler opened the door for separate contracts with the United Auto Workers Union (UAW) in which benefits and salary were traded for job security, or really for jobs themselves. In the past we had the equivalent of industrywide bargaining. The contract was negotiated at the most successful company such as General Motors and then became the model for the rest of the industry. As mentioned earlier, Ford Motor Company, a 25 percent owner of Mazda U.S.A., made history with its 1982 negotiations when the UAW traded salary and benefits for bonuses and job security. This monumental change in industrial relations brought with it the kind of psycho-environment or psychological climate that allowed quality circles to become a reality.[12] At last look they were alive and well at Ford. Indeed, in 1987 Ford outprofited the GM colossus for the first time. Certainly that wasn't due entirely to quality circles or even the new labor contract; some creative engineering and styling together with marketing and training surely helped.

In the current American versions of quality circles, issues of pay, promotion, hiring, and firing are usually out-of-bounds as are other designated management prerogatives.

Training is still a critical element in quality circles and is perhaps, along with management commitment, the key to success. Problem solving, group dynamics, communication, and quality control itself are the major training elements. The first three are addressed in this book. QCs, Kaizen, or whatever—other things being equal—group decision making should lead to quality decisions with an increased motivation to carry them out. But does it? Tai K. Oh of California State University, Fullerton, says that more than 60 percent of American QC programs have failed. Perhaps these were the superficial ones, the band-aids that tried to cover problems too serious in scope. What does our limited research say?

In *Psychology Today* M. L. Marks reported a thirty-month research project that compared rates of productivity and attendance for an ongoing QC program. QC participants did raise productivity and did reduce absenteeism; nonparticipant (control) subjects did not change. An employee attitude survey produced mixed results. For example, attitudes toward group discussion improved but general job satisfaction did not. However, a recession occurred during the twenty months between the surveys, presenting a serious interviewing variable where attitudes were concerned.[13]

Marks reviews other research suggesting that employees who join a QC have positive attitudes going in and " . . . are satisfied by the experience if they see a direct link between QC activities and organizational change and if their QC has capable and productive people."[14]

Sud Ingle, quality control manager of Mercury Marine and author of *Quality Circles Master Guide*, states flatly that QCs can work "anywhere in the world . . . I can say without any hesitation that cultural difference does not interfere with the basic philosophy of the program. This philosophy is valid for all cultures, and a program will succeed anywhere as long as the people involved show continued determination, willpower, and commitment."[15]

Perhaps the jury is still out on some QC adaptations in our more heterogeneous work force because of the many prerequisites such as positive attitudes, capable people, commitment, and intercultural understanding. R. A. Dumas, a consultant on QCs thinks so: " . . . U.S. organizations have been largely unable to duplicate the Japanese success—as measured by impact on overall costs and quality, and the ability of the programs to survive on a long term basis."[16] Dumas reasons that our frequent failures are due to (1) our simplistic perceptions and applications of techniques that are, in reality, extremely complex, and (2) the lack of preparation of American managers to lead and participate in problem-solving groups—in short, *training*. We will review the need for training at the close of this chapter. A partial satisfying of that need is the goal of the chapters that follow.

CONVENTIONAL GROUPS

In the larger sense these include the prototype organizational divisions of marketing/sales, personnel, accounting, engineering, industrial relations, production, and so on. These divisions are usually linked together through some kind of management hierarchy and reporting system, involving groups made up of proximate representatives. Rensis Likert called this pyramidal, overlapping structure a "linking pin" arrangement of small groups.[17] The superior in one group is a participating subordinate in the next as shown in Figure 1.1.

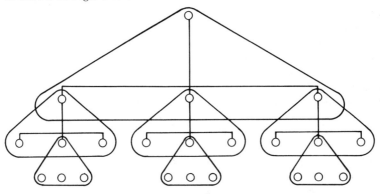

Figure 1.1   Linking pin arrangement.

Within these divisions and the administrative staff of the organization we find still more standard small groups: line and staff, standing committees, ad hoc groups, and, of course, many informal groups.

Line and Staff Groups

In the army, line personnel fired the weapons; staff supported them in every way from bullets and tactics to socks and rest and rehabilitation. A line officer might have a staff group that advised on intelligence, supply, personnel, even public relations. All were small groups linking the various elements and functions necessary to the operation of a successful line outfit. In industrial and business organizations, the production people or the people who actually perform the service or build the product are considered line. Those who support the line, usually at some distance, are considered staff: training, labor relations, research and development, and the like. The line–staff distinction is not always clear-cut. A company whose sole effort is research and development (R & D) would consider its researchers to be line. There is almost a built-in strain between line and staff groups. "The workers in the front office don't know what's going on in the field." "Engineering thinks I can put a four-inch pipe in a three-inch wall!"

Small departments can be line or staff or some combination, as can work crews, project teams, or airplane crews. All are conventional and very important small groups. Typically all have assigned missions, goals, rules, membership, and usually a designated leader. The formal leader or manager has discretion over task procedures, job assignments, and sometimes rewards.

Some of these conventional groups become very programmed or *prefabricated* as Cragan and Wright describe them.[18] Group cohesion is difficult when turnover is high; hence, highly prescribed work rules, scripted behaviors, and product control are the order of the day. Sales groups with high turnover rates such as book salespersons, fast food chain workers, amusement park employees, and even some real estate and car salespeople have highly structured training programs that in turn support a heavily prescribed set of work rules. The McDonalds Corporation maintains its Big Mac quality and uniformity through such techniques. Given the high turnover rate, this makes sense, but don't ask such fluid groups to solve unusual or unexpected problems. If it isn't a training-manual concern or a standard operating procedure (SOP), it will go unsolved until higher management is consulted.

Except for the structure and common goal, these loose collections of people are really not groups. A group of people on an airliner is not a true group either, but let a hijacker appear, a forced landing occur, or some other event happen that brings these people together; then the characteristics of a group begin to emerge: common, intense motivation; a spirit of comradery and togetherness; and, if panic hasn't set in, leadership comes forth. True groups attempt solutions and adapt to unique situations; programmed or prefabricated groups are usually limited to standard operating procedure.

Standing Committees

Standing committees are conventional groups that are long term. A large university department like mine, for example, will have a graduate committee, a personnel committee, an administrative committee, and a curriculum committee. Memberships in these committees are also long term; chairpersons may be permanently appointed or elected. Elected members usually represent the various functional areas of such a department: journalism, radio–television, speech pathology, theater, speech communication, and so forth. In some organizations memberships in these standing committees are mandated by rank, that is, membership must include representatives from the professorial ranks of graduate assistant, instructor, assistant professor, associate professor, and professor. In more conservative organizations, the committees are primarily composed of full professors. In some more liberal institutions, undergraduate student representation is required on some standing committees. As these standing committees, whether in academia or the business world, become more heterogenous, all of us must develop more group know-how, leadership, and sophistication than ever before. We need to know the federal and state laws on management and governance as well as the policies of our organizations. Laws such as affirmative action and equal opportunity often supersede and may affect the sex, color, and ethnicity of some standing committees. The Japanese have little concern with these matters given their cultural homogeneity and a long-standing and socially acceptable discrimination organizationally against women, minorities, and other "different" groups.[19] One wonders how Mazda in Flat Rock, Michigan, will fare.

To further complicate matters, some organizations have standing committees and procedures for "grieving" or complaining. Some are "organized," that is, unionized; others are not. When organized, specific steps are usually required, each with its own special small group. If the grievances aren't solved or adjudicated at the lower steps and if the labor agreement calls for it, they may go to arbitration. At this point we leave discussion and go to debate before an agreed-upon outsider who finally arbitrates. He or she *arbitrarily* decides what is to be done, such as "The employee has a legitimate grievance and shall be reinstated with back pay."

These small groups are complex, working with difficult issues. If the group you join is highly organized, you will discover industrial relations specialists, bargaining committees, shop stewards, business agents, jurisdictional fights (which union has the right to the work), and other surprises that usually result in a small group trying to define and solve a problem. One is often dealing with several organized groups, that is, more than one union. At Wayne State University in Detroit there were nine at last count. Sometimes they honor one another's strikes or work stoppages; sometimes they do not. When there is a choice, some employees are union members; others are not.

Enter still more groups: These are the "inter" groups and councils—interunion, intersorority, interdepartmental, and so on. Many of these become standing committees requiring the ultimate in small group dynamics. Once again we have proof of the importance of small groups in organizational settings. Add a turnover rate four to eight times higher than the Japanese and the challenge grows.[20] Clearly participation is related to production and not always in productive ways.

Ad Hoc Groups

These are temporary groups formed for specific or immediate problems or needs. *Ad hoc* means "for this particular end or case at hand without consideration or wider application." A senior partner takes early retirement, and an ad hoc committee is appointed to plan and effect a ceremony. A small firm needs to hire an engineer, and an ad hoc search committee is formed to do the legwork. A new work procedure is necessary or a new machine is purchased, and a special training group is formed. Some ad hoc groups become standing committees. One large organization had so many weddings, funerals, and births that the ad hoc flower fund committee became a permanent one, holding quarterly meetings. Large organizations may have whole divisions that handle training or personnel searches. What is ad hoc in one organization may be a line–staff or a standing committee in another.

Most ad hoc groups are relatively short lived and have zero history. That is, they are formed from scratch and often must generate their own motivation. Scratch usually means clarifying goals, establishing roles, even electing a chair, unless already appointed. Leadership can be difficult in ad hoc groups because it is short term, because members may be new to one another, and because they have special agendas that supersede what the group has in mind. One affirmative action officer on a search committee once announced that ''the next hire would be a black woman'' and that was that. The business of this ad hoc group suddenly became very complex legally and, for some, very difficult socially. One flower fund group decided to assess organization members according to salary. The organization came down on this group with a vengeance, screaming ''invasion of privacy.'' Nothing about small groups in organizational settings is easy; ad hoc groups are often the most difficult of all. The need for training is evident since one never knows when one will be called upon ad hoc. ''Ray, I'd like you to chair a committee of Barb, Bernice, and Ed whose purpose is to review and redo our faculty evaluation system.'' Look out!

Informal Groups

Informal groups are important social groups that emerge in any organizational setting. The brown bag group, the coffee break club, the bowling team—some, like the last, develop structure. Our brown bag club at Ohio State had only one rule: *no talking about university business*. Others can become clique-like with members who find their contacts highly satisfying and who tend to exclude those who don't think exactly as they do. A clique has been defined formally as a group where ''more than half of their communication is with each other, when each member is linked to all other members, and when no single link nor member can be eliminated and have the group break apart.''[21]

Some of these informal cliques become formal groups when they are strong enough or the situation fosters it. Our black theater students formed a club that eventually led to an autonomous black theater at Wayne State University. Other black awareness clubs eventually evolved into a very powerful black studies program. Religious groups, women's groups, and other ethnic and/or minority groups have similar histories. Whatever level of formality these informal groups achieve, they affect the organizational setting. Liaison between informal groups that develop the stature of a clique and the parent organization is critical for the organization to survive. A liaison person connects or links two or more cliques but is not a central member of any of them. Liaisons help tie an organization's communication system together if they are very special communicators; if not, they can aggravate the situation and really bottleneck communication flow.[22]

A liaison is more than a bridging person between cliques. A *bridge* person, unlike a more formal liaison person, *is* a member of a clique who just happens to have contact with members of other cliques. The more an organization depends on this kind of bridge for accurate communication linkages, the more message distortion it will encounter.[23] This is not to say that a bridge who is ''of the company'' cannot also serve a liaison function, but the distinction is a subtle one and not always easy to discern.

When informal cliques have long and strong ethnic or cultural heritages, they may be classified as *clans*.[24] Clans, when small yet part of a larger organization, may be viewed as informal groups. When of sufficient size and bonded together through economic activity, they quickly become quite formal and a force with which to be reckoned. Mutual support is a cornerstone of clans, at least until they are assimilated by the larger organization or dominant culture. Our nation's experience with early groups of Irish, German, Italian, Polish, Greek, Jewish, and similar groups illustrates this point. The clan groups of today are more apt to be Chaldean, Arab, Hispanic, Chinese, Japanese, and, to a lesser extent, Afro-American. Asian-Americans, for example, have a tradition of support through a kind of high-trust, informal credit union. The clans are called *Tanomoshi* by the Japanese and *Hui* by the Chinese. These are very tight, closed groups, and according to William Ouchi, " . . . one can only be born into *Tanomoshi* or *Hui*, and one can never escape from the network of familiar, communal, social, religious, and economic ties that bind those groups together."[25]

It is clear that organizations can be affected and shaped by these clan-like groups and the social environment in which they exist.

GROUPS OF THE FUTURE

Many of today's new participative groups (Kaizen, quality circles, and so on) are *concurrent* with or what Lawler and Mohrman[26] call *parallel* to the regular line–staff organization. These groups allow for participation without seriously conflicting with normal management channels and functions. If they should fail, they can be scrapped without disrupting the basic line of authority or decisions of policy. A natural extension of the quality circles is to give them more outright decision power in more management domains like design, organizational arrangement, and even policy. These expansions still represent a kind of concurrent structure. These groups are still more temporary than permanent and have been referred to as *task forces*.[27] They will probably include management personnel as well as production employees. Task forces are typically restricted to a single project or "task." Xerox Corporation is already using such groups.

To move beyond task forces, these groups will have to be delegated real not just joint authority to make production decisions including schedules, methods, leaders, and even pay scales. These groups are no longer just concurrent groups, but rather a regular part of the organizational structure. Lawler and Mohrman call them *work teams*. Work teams are not new in concept, nor are they necessarily natural extensions of quality circles. They have been used at companies such as Procter and Gamble and Johnson and Johnson. They represent a popular group of the future because they continue the participation and involvement concepts and represent a definable shift in management philosophy, a shift that is well underway and not apt to be easily deterred.

MOTIVATION AND ORGANIZATIONAL GROUPS

Now that we have learned something about the kinds of groups found in modern organizations, let us take an "other things being equal" look at what generally motivates, satisfies, and facilitates productive group effort. The emphasis is on the small group itself, not on the individual. As one group dynamicist stated: " . . . individuals work not in organizations, businesses, and industries, but in small groups that combine to form larger organizations, businesses, and industries."[28]

This is why knowledge of small groups is so critical for those who would function effectively in organizational settings. The systems nature of small groups and their specific characteristics will be detailed in Chapter 2.

GROUPS VERSUS INDIVIDUALS

Is it easier to change people individually or when they are in participating groups? Organizational persuasion seems to work better when people can discuss matters in groups. Kurt Lewin, a famous group dynamicist, clarified this during World War II. His research on convincing people to eat sweetbreads, kidneys, and other organ meats rather than the more desirable cuts of meat that were in short supply clearly showed that the group discussion approach was more effective than the lecture. Thirty-two percent of the discussants actually served the less desirable food while only 3 percent of the lecture group did.[29]

Another early field study showed the effectiveness of groups as agents of organizational change. Needed changes in production methods were being met with resistance, turnover was high, production was low. The researchers tried group participation training, ranging from the total work group to small groups representing the others. The nonparticipant control group improved very little. However, the participant groups accepted the changes, improved productivity, and turnover went to zero.[30]

Today most successful organizational development programs use the discussion group as a cornerstone of their training methods. The numerous studies reported by Rensis Likert and the Institute for Social Research point to the success of participative groups.[31] Some of the participating companies included Prudential Insurance, Aluminum Company of Canada, Detroit Edison, General Electric, Humble Oil, International Business Machines, Lever Brothers, the U.S. Navy, and many more. Esso Standard Oil and Texas Instruments clearly understood the value of group participation and teamwork (along with clear goals) as they built billion dollar enterprises.

GOALS, COHESION, AND PRODUCTIVITY

The Texas Instruments story is one of serious effort to build cohesive teams armed with clear, realistic goals and aspirations. If the goals are realistic the group can concentrate on its achievement—a positive direction. If the goals are unrealistically high, a group may get its motivation from simply trying to avoid failure, a behavior usually leading to frustration. If goals are too low or too easy, motivation is often lost and group dissatisfaction results. Success should be within one's grasp but not without reasonable team effort.

When purposes and goals are not clear, especially when information is weak or in error *and* if groups are experiencing a false sense of success (as the American automotive industry was in the early seventies), overoptimism and a lack of vigilance may occur. Big money is no problem so trivial things loom large. Perhaps Parkinson's *law of triviality* takes over: "The time spent on any item of the agenda will be in inverse proportion to the amount of money involved."[32] Millions of dollars for new big car production may be approved with relatively quick analysis and discussion while the issue of flying first or second class at company expense leads to long and acrimonious debate. Clear goals lead to productivity but only if productivity is one of the goals.

Cohesion refers to the forces that bind members of a group together. According to Clovis Shepherd, it refers also to the degree of closeness and warmth they feel for one another, their pride as members, their willingness to be frank and honest in their expressions of ideas and feelings, and their ability to meet the emergencies and crises that may confront them.[33] Cohesion—like clear goals—is a leg up on productivity, but again, only if the group is very aware of the productivity goal and if group norms encourage high productivity as well as cohesion.[34] This helps explain why some happy, cohesive groups may actually lead to poor productivity.

THE NEED FOR TRAINING

> . . . American supervisors are in dire need of more preparatory training to help them cope.
>
> *R. A. Dumas, Ph.D., management consultant*

The kinds of small group training Dr. Dumas specifically singles out are

- coping with disruptive behavior
- facilitator skills
- persuading and informing managers
- keeping meetings problem oriented
- adapting to member differences (education, experience, and so forth)
- group leadership skills

He comments knowledgeably: "'. . . *participants*—as well as supervisors—have an immediate need for training in basic group leadership, problem-solving, and decision-making skills.'"[35]

J. W. Dean, a professor of organizational development, in commenting about quality circles underscores the point that employee satisfaction and effective problem solving can be increased through appropriate training. He is, however, critical of most QC member preparation:

> . . . training is largely pro forma in most applications and not taken very seriously. Most people who go through training are bored to death because most of what is covered does not relate to their personal work situation. Training should be differentiated for engineers, blue-collar or clerical workers and others.[36]

The implied plea is for organizational and member adaptation. Early American QC programs used a detailed Japanese problem-solving model that didn't fit every American organization. These early American training programs were typically run from the top down with little feedback from the bottom up. In 1984 General Motors established a Corporate Training Priorities Committee, which was very important in that it gave line managers much more responsibility for identifying and meeting training needs of employees—a bottom-up process. Much of this training is directed at new technology, sophisticated tooling, and computer-generated data communications. Even here General Motors comments perceptively on the work force, "It must be well schooled in problem solving, process control, and interpersonal skills and techniques."[37] By 1986 GM had a program called "Quality of Work Life" (QWL) in most of its North American units. Key elements in making QWL work are open-mindedness, listening skills, trust, involvement, and teamwork.

> QWL has as its objective the creation of a stimulated, informed, problem-solving, and decision-making work force.
>
> *1986 General Motors Public Interest Report*

     These programs involve salaried and hourly employees, managers as well as nonsupervisory personnel. These are not easy changes to bring about, but the course is set. Participation and small group interaction are the order of the day and the times.

     Clearly, small group training is important and it is certainly big business. Whether it is called Quality of Work Life (QWL), Organizational Development (OD), Human Resources Development (HRD), Quality Circle Activities (QC), Kaizen Team Building, or even Small Groups in Organizational Settings, it has several common elements: group dynamics, problem solving, decision making, leadership, and interpersonal conflict. Add to these the research on special problem dynamics, language and relational effectiveness, communication systems theory, and the pragmatics of group discussion, and you have a synopsis of the material in the chapters that follow.

SUMMARY

     The decentralized organization of the future will result in work being done in small, autonomous groups linked to the megacorporation by new telecommunications and computer technologies. Since 1970 America has gone from a predominantly blue collar society to a 67 percent white collar society. The list of organizations trying to improve production and quality through employee participation is a long one. Some of the unique activities in modern organizational settings include *Kaizen* (improvement through self-criticism), *Karaoke* (off-the-job activities), and *Quality Circles* (small group discussions), all from Japan. More conventional groups include prototype organizational divisions, line and staff groups, standing committees, ad hoc groups, and informal groups such as cliques and clans. Participants have an immediate need for training in basic group leadership, problem solving, and decision making. Small group training is big business and has several common elements: group dynamics, problem solving, decison making, leadership, interpersonal conflict, language, relational effectiveness, systems theory, communication theory, and the pragmatics of group discussion.

PROJECTS AND CASES

PROJECTS

1. List all the organizational small groups of which you are a member (work, school, social, and so on). Prepare to compare and discuss your list with those of your classmates.

2. With two other classmates prepare a 9- to 12-minute informal group discussion, the purpose being to introduce your group members to the class.

3. Consider a specific organizational small group of which you are a member, and analyze the meeting format. Describe one positive and one negative behavior in which the group engages.

4. Do you think organizations are tending toward employee participation and power equalization? Give examples.

5. Do you belong to a clique or a clan as described in Chapter 1? Explain and prepare to report.

6. Keep a communication log. Guidelines are listed below.

   COMMUNICATION LOG

   The communication log is a record and analysis of your personal group communication experiences. Minimum standards (for a grade of *B* on the log) are as follows:

   a. *Number of entries.* Entries should be made on *at least* two days of each week. Date your entries.
   b. *Nature of entries.* Each week, at least one entry should describe something that occurred in class and at least one entry should be of something that occurred outside class. Some of the entries may be brief, for example, one sentence. Other entries should be much longer in order to demonstrate that you are growing in the ability to understand and analyze the communication problems of both yourself and others. In either case, try to explain why a speech interaction or discussion went well or poorly. Your efforts to explain what occurred in an interaction are the principal criteria for distinguishing between an *A* and a *B* log.
      In the first two weeks of the course, you *must* make one entry that describes your strengths and weaknesses in communicating in groups and that states what you expect to accomplish in this course. Be specific.
      During the last week, one entry *must* describe again what you think your strengths and weaknesses are and what you think you have accomplished during the term.
   c. *References to the textbook.* The log must show that you have read the text. This requirement can be met by making a *minimum* of ten references to the text in your log entries.

CASES

1. Mainstream Data Systems[38]

   Rick Rinaldi was happily employed as a software specialist at *Mainstream Data Systems*. At age twenty-four, he was earning more money and held more responsibility than he had anticipated at this stage in his career. Yet his contentment with MDS didn't stop him from at least listening to the scientific recruiter from International Communications Corporation. Both the recruiter and others at International Communications emphasized how much better off Rick would ultimately be at their company. As Rick's prospective boss put it, "I can understand how you enjoy the excitement of that little company you work for. Not a bad idea for a person getting started in his career. But don't you think you'd be better off playing in the big leagues? Don't forget, there's a very high ceiling here. No doubt, there's a very low ceiling at your little firm. Get my point?"
      Rick did get the point, and with mixed emotions, he accepted a systems analyst position with ICC. The decisive point for Rick was the jump in job responsibility, combined with a $2,750

annual salary increment. Rick began his new position with a burst of enthusiasm. He visualized himself as someday becoming a high-ranking management information systems executive at ICC. Yet as the weeks passed, Rick began to notice that he was having more trouble with what he perceived as red tape and overly cautious employees.

Rick's concern about a lack of organizational flexibility came to a head over an incident with a malfunctioning display terminal. Rick suggested to the department manager responsible for the terminal, "My opinion is that this broken terminal isn't worth fixing. My old company, MDS, has a terminal that works quite well and is underpriced in today's market."

"Hold on a minute," answered the manager. "We are not authorized to make new purchases in this department. You're stepping way out of line even making the suggestion. Before we could entertain the idea of using a new vendor, the problem would have to be studied quite carefully."

Several days after the incident involving the computer terminal, Ed McNabb, Rick's boss, called him into the office. "Rick, there is something we have to talk about. It seems that you are the high-talent guy we were looking for when we hired you. But you're just not allowing your talent to take hold here. Things aren't going as well as we planned in certain delicate areas."

"What delicate areas are you talking about?" asked Rick.

"Well, to be frank," said, Ed, "you're beginning to rub people the wrong way. You're too impatient. You overstep your bounds as a systems analyst. You seem to be having some trouble accepting the limits of your job description. We like your talent, but you're creating too many enemies by the way you try to get things done in a hurry."

"I hear what you're saying," responded Rick. "But I'm not so sure if I'm buying it. Back at my old firm, making waves was an asset. Here I feel like a fish out of water. Maybe I'm better suited for a free-swinging small company. Maybe I don't belong in a corporate behemoth like ICC."

"I'm glad we talked about this problem of your rounding off your rough edges. I think things will work out for you here now that you understand the problem."

Two weeks later Rick quit ICC and rejoined MDS in his former capacity.

QUESTIONS

1. Why did Rick quit? Was it a wise thing to do?
2. What did Ed McNabb, Rick's boss, do correctly or incorrectly?
3. What did Rick do wrong?

2. The Verysweet Candy Company

All of you work for the Verysweet Candy Company in the employee relations division. You have been constituted as a "problem-solving" group to consider and make recommendations (to the divison head) concerning the company's Christmas gift policy.

While Verysweet manufactures and packages chocolate-covered candies in a wide range of qualities and prices, the company had never offered its own product as a gift to its employees before last Christmas. Before then, the company had given very inexpensive but gaily colored jewelry (e.g., tie clasps, cufflinks, brooches, and so on). The reaction to these gifts was "neutral"— rarely had an employee thanked management for the gift, but there was no record of substantial complaints either.

On the afternoon before the previous Christmas, all employees were handed identical, colorfully wrapped packages, each apparently containing two pounds of Verysweet candy. Few employees showed surprise or interest in receiving the packages, and many returned to their work without opening them. A few did open their packages, however, and then the trouble began. The boxes contained one of the low-grade lines of filled chocolate candies. "The cheapskates!" one employee exclaimed. Several threw their packages into waste cans. A few even emptied their boxes and refilled them with high-quality candy when their supervisor's back was turned.

This reaction came to the attention of upper-level management during the weeks immediately following Christmas. Accordingly, your divison was assigned the task of seeking suggestions to avoid this sort of problem in the future. A survey of supervisors resulted in acquiring the five following frequently mentioned suggestions:

1. The company should never again give its employees material gifts.
2. The company should give essentially the same gift, but personalize it in some way, such as enclosing a personally signed card from the president.
3. The company should give a package of its highest-quality product.
4. The company should retain last year's policy, but steps should be taken to identify and discipline those employees who seem ungrateful.
5. The company should purchase the products of another company to distribute as Christmas gifts (e.g., jewelry or inexpensive pens).

Your group should consider these suggestions, but you may reach an entirely different recommendation to make to your supervisor.

NOTES

1. T. E. Deal and A. A. Kennedy, *Corporate Cultures: The Rites and Rituals of Corporate Life* (Reading, Mass.: Addison-Wesley, 1982), p. 177 (italics mine).
2. Donelson R. Forsyth, *An Introduction to Group Dynamics* (Monterey, Calif.: Brooks/Cole, 1983), p. 424.
3. Department of Commerce, Bureau of the Census; and Department of Labor, Bureau of Labor Statistics, 1985.
4. Carl R. Terzian, "PR for the Firm That Can't Afford It," *Sky Magazine*, March 1974, p. 18.
5. Deal and Kennedy, *Corporate Cultures*, pp. 182–83.
6. *SPECTRA*, March 1987, p. 6.
7. John Naisbitt, *Megatrends: Ten New Directions Transforming Our Lives* (New York: Warner Books, 1984), p. 175.
8. R. A. Ryan, "Americans Get Lesson in Raw Fish at Mazda Boot Camp," *The Detroit News*, June 22, 1986, sec. A, p. 15.
9. Mitchell L. Marks, "The Question of Quality Circles," *Psychology Today*, 20, no. 3 (March 1986), p. 36.
10. Marks, "Question of Quality Circles," p. 44; see also Sud Ingle, *Quality Circles Master Guide* (Englewood Cliffs, N.J.: Prentice-Hall, 1982), p. 8.
11. Marks, "Question of Quality Circles," p. 44.
12. William Ouchi, *The M-Form Society* (New York: Avon Books, 1985).
13. Marks, "Question of Quality Circles," pp. 38, 42.
14. Ibid., p. 44.
15. Ingle, *Quality Circles Master Guide*, p. vii.
16. R. A. Dumas, "The Shaky Foundations of Quality Circles," *Training*, 20, no. 4 (April 1983), p. 32.
17. Rensis Likert, *New Patterns of Management* (New York: McGraw Hill, 1961; Garland, 1987), p. 104.
18. John F. Cragan and David W. Wright, *Communication in Small Group Discussions*, 2nd ed. (St. Paul, Minn.: West, 1986), p. 266.
19. William Ouchi, *Theory Z* (Reading, Mass.: Addison-Wesley, 1981), p. 82.
20. R. E. Cole, *Work, Mobility and Participation* (Berkeley, Calif.: University of California Press, 1979).
21. R. V. Farace, P. R. Monge, and H. M. Russell, *Communicating and Organizing* (Reading, Mass.: Addison-Wesley, 1977), p. 186.

22. For more on liaisons, see I. C. Ross and F. Harary, "Identification of the Liaison Persons of an Organization Using the Structure Matrix," *Management Science*, 1 (April–May 1955), pp. 251–58; D. F. Schwartz, "Liaison Roles in the Communication of a Formal Organization," in *Communication in Organizations*, eds. Lyman W. Porter and Karlene H. Roberts (Middlesex, England: Penguin, 1977), pp. 255–71.

23. Farace, Monge, and Russell, *Communicating and Organizing*, p. 186.

24. Ouchi, *Theory Z*, p. 83.

25. Ibid., p. 86.

26. Edward E. Lawler III and Susan A. Mohrman, "Quality Circles: After the Honeymoon," in J. William Pfeiffer, ed., *The 1988 Annual: Developing Human Resources* (San Diego: University Associates, Inc., 1988), pp. 201–13.

27. Lawler and Mohrman, "Quality Circles," p. 205.

28. Forsyth, *Introduction to Group Dynamics*, p. 405.

29. Kurt Lewin, "Group Decision and Social Change," in *Readings in Social Psychology*, eds. Eleanor E. Maccoby, Theodore M. Newcomb, and Eugene L. Hartley (New York: Henry Holt, 1958), p. 202; see also Kurt Lewin, "Forces Behind Food Habits and Methods of Change," *Bulletin of the National Research Council*, 108 (1943), pp. 35–65.

30. L. Coch and J.R.P. French, "Overcoming Resistance to Change," *Human Relations*, 1 (1948), pp. 512–32.

31. Rensis Likert, *The Human Organization: Its Management and Value* (New York: McGraw-Hill, 1967), pp. 3–24.

32. C. Northcote Parkinson, *Parkinson's Law* (Boston: Houghton Mifflin, 1957), p. 24.

33. Clovis R. Shepherd, *Small Groups: Some Sociological Perspectives* (San Francisco: Chandler, 1964), p. 26.

34. Forsyth, *Introduction to Group Dynamics*, p. 409.

35. Dumas, "Shaky Foundations of Quality Circles," p. 33.

36. Marks, "Question of Quality Circles," p. 44.

37. *1986 General Motors Public Interest Report*, p. 7.

38. From A. J. DuBrin, *Foundations of Organizational Behavior* (Englewood Cliffs, N.J.: Prentice-Hall, © 1984), pp. 49–50.

2

THE NATURE
OF SMALL GROUPS

More and more we find ourselves interacting informally and formally in small groups. It is a sign of the times to participate in study groups, workshops, committees, boards, councils, buzz groups, case conferences, and the like. Our modern teaching methods call for subgroups of larger groups such as task forces, research groups, and role-playing groups. Our jobs often place us in very specialized work groups. Then there are the countless social and recreational groups that help occupy our time and efforts. We are asked to interact and to discuss cooperatively, sometimes systematically, sometimes for the vaguest reasons.

We do not always have a free choice about the world groups in which we find ourselves such as our nationality, racial, and ethnic groups. Organizationally one may be arbitrarily assigned to a given work group or committee. Off the job one theoretically has more choice—Weed and Feed Club, the Lions, Elks, Rotary, American Legion, and so on.

We all belong to many groups at the same time. It is clear that they overlap, as in the case of John Doe in Figure 2.1. The ellipses represent only a few of the groups of which he is a part. Some of these choices are simply collections of people who meet or associate yet never really come together as a group. Some professional associations are viewed as obligatory. They meet not really by choice but because they feel they must. Not all but certainly some unions, employers' associations, even church and school committees fall into this category. Some organizational units and committees never really jell as a group either. They meet, exchange information, make decisions, and adjourn. Perhaps in some ad hoc committees that's all that is necessary.

However, a group as a social and psychological entity is something special, something that goes beyond a mere collection of people. This something special is thought to energize, motivate, and facilitate the achievement of the purposes and goals of a given work unit, committee, or others in association for some reason.

How then does this sense of belonging, of identification, of unified purpose develop? What are the characteristics of this special entity where each person influences and is influenced by each other person?

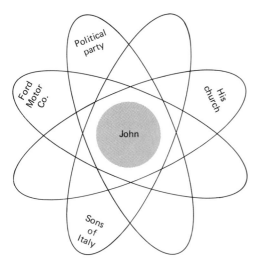

Figure 2.1

To continue further, why do we join the world groups we do? What are the large theoretical answers to such a broad question? How are small groups like systems? What are the characteristics of this groupness found in true small groups? What general constraints are part of organizational, small-group problem solving and decision making? These questions represent an outline of Chapter 2.

WHY WE JOIN: THEORETICAL PERSPECTIVES

There are some obvious reasons why we join most job-related organizational groups: It is required (the weekly meeting); it is necessary to coordinate with the rest of the organization; it is an integral part of organizational life. Those groups not *directly* job connected but still related offer more choice: trade associations, management clubs, company sports teams, even some unions. But what of the larger world groups that we join more or less voluntarily? Why do we do it? There are many theoretical perspectives that try to answer why we do it and why such arbitrary groups form. Donelson Forsyth, a group dynamicist, suggests four perspectives most worthy of consideration: psychodynamic, sociobiological, social comparison, and social exchange.[1]

PSYCHODYNAMIC

Sigmund Freud was the first person to discuss psychodynamic theory. His theory and others with the same perspective argued that people join groups because doing so satisfies basic biological and psychological needs. Two of Freud's interrelated notions are of most interest to us: identification and transference. The need to be part of, to *identify* with, a group is thought to be born of parental bonding that leads to a sense of belonging and dependency upon others. This early identification experience is thought to *transfer* to and influence one's later group needs and behaviors. Group leaders are subconsciously perceived as parents and group members as family. New groups *replace* family groups and membership regains the security of the family. This notion has been called *replacement theory*.

While perhaps an exaggeration of the role of unconscious needs in determining all group behavior, the theory does offer insights into emotionally intensive therapy groups such as Alcoholics Anonymous. These groups depend upon one another as members, and the group replaces whatever motive and control were lost. Veteran combat-group members who have seen many casualties may develop psychological inabilities to replace lost comrades with the new replacements. The pain of more loss is too great. Without enough of the old group, so-called combat fatigue may develop.

Some theorizers have rejected Freud's notions as being too poorly defined, too reductionist—that is, too concerned with only psychological variables. Others have attempted corrections, extensions, and improvements on Freud's original perspective. One well-known drive-motive theory is that of Abraham Maslow.[2] His categories of basic needs are physiological, safety, love, esteem, and self-actualization. The love or belonging need most pertains to group life. The assumption underlying the recognition of this need is that people must be loved and in turn must express their love. Sharing one's life with others is important to most people. They may react quickly to even a possibility that this need will be denied. We desire the approval and acceptance of our friends, our fellow workers, and the many groups of people with whom we associate and with whom we tend to identify. We are thought to alter our behavior and perhaps even our standards in order to belong to and be accepted by our chosen groups. Singles clubs may owe their existence to this need to belong and to give and share love.

David Krech and Richard Crutchfield postulated four principle motives that bridge our biological and social needs: survival, security, satisfaction, and stimulation.[3] These are grouped into deficiency motives (survival and security) and abundancy motives (satisfaction and stimulation). Krech and Crutchfield inventory four areas pertinent to the human experience: those relating to the body, to the self, to relations with the environment, and, of primary interest to us, to relations with other people. In this last area, the most important components are identifications with people and groups; enjoying other people's company; helping and understanding others; maintaining group membership, prestige, and status; being taken care of by others; conforming to group standards and values; and gaining power over others. These are plausible reasons for why we join—at least from this perspective.

Another popular extension of Freud's initial explanation is supplied by William C. Schutz's FIRO (Fundamental Interpersonal Relations Orientation). If you were attracted to a new group, a new organization, or just some new friends, it has been theorized that you would ask yourself three specific kinds of questions. Suppose you are attracted to a much needed part-time job in the college bookstore. The kinds of interpersonal questions with which you probably would struggle are diagrammed in Figure 2.2.

Assuming that everyone has some need for affiliation and association, it seems reasonable to contemplate questions of *inclusion* in the group that operates and works at the bookstore. Your need to both give and receive direction (and this varies with the person and the circumstances) prompts you to contemplate questions of *control*. Your interpersonal need to belong and to be liked generates questions of *affection*.

Schutz has postulated that inclusion, control, and affection are our primary social needs, and that they go a long way toward determining how we behave and relate to others.[4]

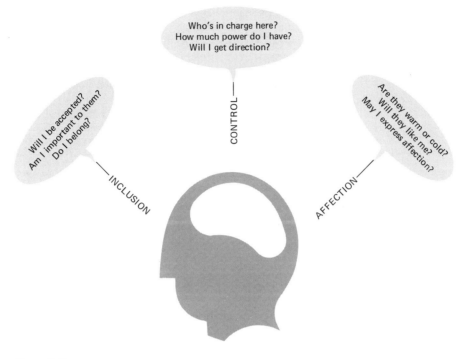

Figure 2.2

These three interpersonal needs are thought to operate on their own continua. For example, inclusion might have the following continua:

High affiliation————Low affiliation
High interaction————Low interaction
Much association————Little association
INCLUSION

According to Schutz, inclusion deals with things such as attention, acknowledgment, recognition, prominence, identity, and participation.[5] Other terms thought to connote positive or negative feelings of inclusion are associate, together, and involved (positive), and outcast, detached, and ignored (negative).

Control might have the following continua:

Strong authority————Weak authority
Much direction————Little direction
High achievement needs————Low achievement needs
CONTROL

According to Schutz, control is communicated by behaviors expressing leadership, power, accomplishment, and intellectual superiority (among others). When control is perceived as repressive, oppressive, or unfair—"The bookstore managers are slavedrivers"—then this side of the control need is typified by behaviors expressing rebellion, resistance, and in some cases, submission.[6]

If the bookstore managers give you appropriate direction but still let you exercise decision making over your small part of the organization, you approach a kind of optimal fulfillment of this powerful interpersonal need. This state of affairs is thought to enhance, or at least preserve, feelings of self-respect.

Affection might have the following continua:

Close (to others)———Distant
Intimate———Hostile
Acceptant———Rejectant
AFFECTION

According to Schutz, the flavor of affection is embodied in "situations of love, emotional closeness, personal confidences, intimacy. Negative affection is characterized by hate, hostility, and emotional rejection."[7]

If you perceive the bookstore group as a clique that couldn't care less about you or is downright discriminatory, your affection need is not going to be met in the bookstore. On the other hand, if the bookstore job turns out to be a real joy (you're part of the group, you meet genuine friends), you may have achieved an ideal or at least optimal state of affection (at least for the bookstore part of your life). In any event, this happy episode at the bookstore should promote the feeling of being loved.

It is possible, of course, to be high on affection and inclusion and low on control, such as you like the people but hate the boss. Ideally we will find some optimal fulfillment not only within each need, but also across all the needs.

Our success and comfort with this balancing act is thought to have much to do with our relating and interacting, so much so that Schutz provides a still stronger lens for observing these behaviors and feelings. The lens has four parts or "states": desired, ideal, anxious, and pathological. It looks at such things as being undersocial or oversocial, submissive or dominant, underpersonal or overpersonal, and also some of the pathological continua (e.g., obsessive and compulsive). This lens or system became so ponderous that Schutz called it an "elephant." The "elephant" is an attempt to relate all interpersonal behavior into all of the categories discussed above. It is worth reading if you are seriously interested in how and perhaps why you relate and interact the way you do. (See Table 2.1.)

For Schutz the compatibility of the members helps determine whether a true group forms or not. If all members wanted to be in control, it is unlikely a group would form. It takes members who wish to receive as well as originate inclusion, control, and affection. Schutz called this requirement *originator compatibility*.

A second type of compatibility for Schutz involves the ground rules by which the group will operate. He called this *interchange compatibility*. How much authority structure can be agreed upon? (Control) What amount of personal involvement will members agree to expend? (Inclusion) What degree of personal feelings and relationships is appropriate to the group and its individual members? (Affection)

Intermember compatibility is no small part of successful groups. Just as Freud's notions help us understand that individuals may join groups for no rational reasons, Schutz helps us understand how group formation depends on specific kinds of early perceptions of ground rules and member compatibilities.

SOCIOBIOLOGICAL

This speculation about why we join groups is based on the notion of a biological need, a herd instinct, or urge to affiliate. The sociobiologist extends the Darwinian work on evolutionary, biological fitness to the behavior of animals in social situations. The adaptive advantages of groups for some animals subject to predators is clear: better detection of danger, better defense, safety in numbers. In addition, hunting, feeding, nurturing, and reproduction are facilitated by group effort.

Affiliating in groups or *instinctive gregariousness* among humans is thought in this view to have enhanced our cave ancestors' survival through group protection and group hunting. Eons later the human need for groups was thought to become part of our biological nature, certainly a controversial and provocative theory. However, whether learned or innate, it seems clear that human beings are indeed social and that they do seek out others when frightened.

It's also clear that sometimes we need to escape the maddening crowd, the overactive group. "I'd give anything to escape this crowd of overachievers!" "All I want is to be alone on the pier with my fishing pole." "There ain't no privacy anymore." It is good to be alone . . . at times.

Real isolation and sensory deprivation have been studied in the laboratory and reported from real experiences. In one study students were paid to remain alone in a locked room. Of five students individually tested, one lasted two hours. Three made it for two days, one of whom said, "Never again." Only one student made it for the course of the eight-day experiment.[8]

In a survival study, Dr. Alain Bombard attempted a solitary Atlantic crossing in a life raft. His log records this chilling entry on real isolation:

> I had begun to understand the difference between solitude and isolation. Moments of isolation in ordinary life can soon be ended; it is just a question of going out of the door into the street or dialing a number on the phone to hear the voice of a friend. Isolation is merely a matter of isolating oneself, but total solitude is an oppressive thing and slowly wears down its lonely victim. It seemed sometimes as if the immense and absolute solitude of the ocean's expanse was concentrated right on top of me, as if my beating heart was the center of gravity of a mass which was at the same time nothingness. . . . It was a vast presence which engulfed me. Its spell could not be broken, any more than the horizon could be brought nearer. And if from time to time I talked aloud in order to hear my own voice, I only felt more alone, a hostage to silence.

Physical isolation can be a terrible thing. Solitary confinement in prison may indeed be the most sadistic of all punishments. We do know from experimental research and real-life episodes that real isolation makes us more anxious, less cogent, more suggestible, and prone to hallucinations.

TABLE 2.1 Nature of Relevant Interpersonal Data, "The Schutz Elephant"

		INCLUSION			CONTROL			AFFECTION		
		Self to Other (Actions)	Other to Self (Reactions)	Self to Self	Self to Other (Actions)	Other to Self (Reactions)	Self to Self	Self to Other (Actions)	Other to Self (Reactions)	Self to Self
DESIRED INTERPERSONAL RELATIONS (NEEDS)	Act	Satisfactory relation re interaction and inclusion behavior 1			Satisfactory relation re power and control behavior 19			Satisfactory relation re love and affection behavior 37		
	Feel	Satisfactory relation re feelings of mutual interest 2		Feeling that I am significant 15	Satisfactory relation re feelings of mutual respect 20		Feeling that I am responsible 33	Satisfactory relation re feelings of mutual affection 38		Feeling that I am lovable 51
IDEAL INTERPERSONAL RELATIONS	Act	Social 3	People include me 4		Democrat 21	People respect me 22		Personal 39	People are friendly to me 40	
	Feel	I am interested in people 5	People are interested in me 6		I respect people 23	People respect me 24		I like people 41	People like me 42	

TABLE 2.1 continued

		Over-social 7	Social-compliant 8		Autocrat 25	Rebel 26		Over-personal 43	Personal complaint 44	
ANXIOUS INTERPERSONAL RELATIONS (ANXIETIES) — Too much activity	Act	Over-social 7	Social-compliant 8		Autocrat 25	Rebel 26		Over-personal 43	Personal complaint 44	
	Feel	I am not *really* interested in people 9	People aren't *really* interested in me 10	I am insignificant (I don't know who I am; I am nobody) 16	I don't trust people 27	People don't trust me 28	I am incompetent (I am stupid, irresponsible) 34	*Really* I don't like people 45	People don't *really* like me 46	I am unlovable (I am no good, rotten bastard)
Too little activity	Act	Under-social 11	Counter-social 12		Abdicrat 29	Submissive 30		Under-personal 47	Counter-personal 48	
	Feel	I am not interested in people 13	People are not interested in me 14		I don't *really* respect people 31	People don't *really* respect me 32		I don't like people 49	People don't like me 50	
PATHOLOGICAL INTERPERSONAL RELATIONS	Too Much	17			Obsessive-compulsive 35			Neurotic 53		
	Too Little	Psychotic (Schizophrenia) 18			Psychopath 36			Neurotic 54		

(Reprinted by permission of the author and the publisher from William C. Schutz, *The Interpersonal Underworld*, reprint edition. Palo Alto, Calif.: Science and Behavior Books, 1966). p. 19.

WISHING FOR A WRONG NUMBER

Call me, anonymous drunkard, tell me
that you are God and can create in seven
hours a much better world. And call me, sell me
anything, everything, even
the rusty wheels of the sun, whoever you are—
merchant or minister, harlot or child,
but let the sound of a human voice compel me
to be reminded suddenly of life going on
for man and mountain and tree
for valley and wing and ocean
for all except me.

Yes, I have heard of flights from dawn to sunset,
of Europe meeting Asia in an hour,
of man and moon becoming
closer and closer, as close as a stem to a flower.
Why should it be so hard, then,
for man to remember man,
for you to let me hear the sound of your voice?

Call me, whoever you are, and tell me
whatever you please. Speak even
of wind and heaven
to a wounded eagle in the grass, of bread and fire
to a famished beggar in the snow.
Be cruel and be rude.
But talk to me and let me know
that I am not alone
in this my human solitude.

Joseph Tuisani

Some of the same results accrue to people who are *not* on life rafts or stranded like Robinson Crusoe. A form of social isolation may afflict all of us as we feel left out or in some way separated from others. These are serious matters, especially for some of our senior citizens who experience the very real pain of isolation from a lack of interpersonal communication.

It is clear that life is no good alone; we need others. We need people for love, reassurance, approval, a sense of reality, and, most critically, communication, even if it is simply a nonverbal presence.

SOCIAL COMPARISON

In this view people seek out others to compare themselves to appropriate others. It is a social reality test, a validating of their behaviors, attitudes, and belief systems.[9] We affiliate to gain and compare information. From the social comparison perspective, people seek others, even in fearful situations, to trade *information* rather than because of a basic instinct.

Social scientists have long referred to humans as *social* animals. Social tendencies have been called *gregariousness*, *companionship*, and *succorance*—that is, seeking *others* for help, encouragement, and sympathy. This urge toward sociability appears to be stronger in some people than in others. However, as we learned earlier, it does appear to affect us all, particularly in times of trouble or threat. When our beliefs are seriously threatened, we tend to seek out people of like mind as if to soften the hurt. It has also been theorized that some people socialize just for the sheer joy of it. Stanley Schachter said of affiliation, "Most of us have experienced occasional cravings to be with people, sometimes with good reason, frequently for no apparent reason: We seem simply to want to be in the physical presence of others."[10]

Schachter also found that anxiety heightened this need for companionship. Students were told they would be guinea pigs in an experiment involving painful but not dangerous electric shock. The experiment was interrupted, and the students were told that during the delay they could wait alone or wait with others; the majority preferred companionship.

In related experiments Schachter points out that anxious people seek out other anxious people. Misery not only loves company, it loves miserable company! Affiliation apparently provides much of its own communication. Just being with other people who have similar problems seems to reduce tension, even when no verbal communication takes place.

All of us like to hear our beliefs confirmed; we like to be reassured by others who share our opinions. This is an important insight. Our desires to hear what we want to hear, to think what we want to think, sometimes take over when feelings run high or when we are desperate to reassert a shaken belief or value. Many times people themselves, apart from the issues, become important to us because they provide approval, support, and a way of reducing anxiety (Figure 2.3).

Affiliation can be a fairly strong motive. Mayor Coleman Young of Detroit captured this meaning as he greeted two of Michigan's returned hostages from Iran, one white, one black. In a gesture of triumph, he raised the hands of the ex-hostages saying, "When the deal comes down, fate doesn't give a damn what color you are or where you came from."

In sum, people join groups to better understand their social reality through the information they trade while comparing themselves to others.

SOCIAL EXCHANGE

In this view people join groups because the rewards are higher and the costs lower than if they go it alone. Some rewards and goals can be realized only in groups. A baseball pitcher needs a team, a poker player needs a game, a sailor needs a crew. Groups can also reward us with reassurance, social support, and often afford us interaction with competent, attractive others. However, these advantages are not without some costs. Beliefs are not always confirmed; we may lose individual freedom; instead of social support we may get rejection; extremely competent, attractive others may make us feel less so; we may meet and confront very difficult personalities.

The motivation for joining a given group is thought to be based on how valuable such membership appears.[11] The value is determined by assessing rewards versus costs. It is a kind of economic model where one looks at cost estimates and compares them to projected profits. Some investment profits are realized only over considerable time;

Figure 2.3

Jean Rudolph Wyss

some personal investments in groups are equally complex. That we belong to many groups at the same time and with varying commitments also complicates specific applications of social-exchange theory.

Two special member characteristics or rewards are competence and social attractiveness. Competent people attract us because they can help us become successful, and we can identify with them. Sociable, attractive people make our joining more pleasant. We enjoy being with people who provide us with real or reflected status, position, and recognition. So much for rewards! Even here there are costs. Such social comparisons can be painful and lead to feelings of incompetence. Perhaps this explains why some people prefer groups of just friends, even incompetent ones. The costs of joining the first type of group are too high. Some highly competent people (or so perceived) may be subtly rejected by some groups. One much respected, professionally competent, nationally known professor felt discomfort when joining his colleagues in an informal luncheon club. Perhaps Elliot Aronson has captured what may have been happening: "Although we like to be around competent people, a person who has a great deal of ability may make us uncomfortable. That person may seem unapproachable, distant, superhuman."[12]

One day, at the beginning of a new term, this same professor went to the wrong classroom and delivered a brilliant lecture on organizational communication only to find that the class was composed of foreign students who were supposed to be learning English as a second language. When word leaked out about this human mistake, the halls of ivy rang with laughter. Interestingly, he was welcomed by the luncheon club after that, albeit not without a great deal of good-natured kidding. It wasn't that he was any less competent or less achievement oriented, rather that he was perceived as less perfect and more human.

Even physical attractiveness appears to have costs as well as rewards. It can foster group rejection particularly if coupled with aloofness and a lack of concern for others.[13]

GROUPS AS SYSTEMS

GENERAL SYSTEMS THEORY

As we have seen, a small group is more than the simple sum of its parts. Every member affects and is affected by every other member—in short, the group is a system. Some understanding of general systems theory is therefore useful.

The notion of system is not new. All systems have common elements. The solar system: a group of interacting bodies under the influence of related gravitational forces. The digestive system: a group of body organs that together perform one or more vital functions. A telephone system: a group of devices, objects, or an organization forming a network for communication. The new IBM personal computer is no longer a PC. It has become an IBM Personal System/2. How about a state-of-the-art system of stereo components? Will it integrate with the existing VCR and television systems? Why not use a solitary tape deck? Because then one is unable to capitalize on the synergistic benefits of a true system. A total operating system yields outputs that are somehow better, greater, or at least different from all the independent components.

A good example is our previous exploitive, mechanistic, piecemeal view of the natural environment. Individual actions to halt specific pollutants however necessary and praiseworthy were not enough. We now recognize that we are dealing with a complicated and often delicate ecosystem. Every part affects every other part, and we need a systems perspective to better order and prioritize the specific actions necessary.

The most basic notion of general systems theory is that every interacting component of any given system affects and is affected by every other component, leading to a synergy that is greater than the simple sum of its parts. The parts for hot-water heating in a modern home can be laid out part by part on the basement floor. At this point we have just a collection of pipes, radiators, boilers, pumps, gauges, and thermostats. Synergy and the status of a true system are attained when it all comes together. It is whole and it works—a case where the whole is greater than the simple sum of its parts. The system's interdependence with its own parts is illustrated by the thermostat component that interacts with the heating component, the water pump, and so on. The system is relatively closed but not completely. The thermostat interacts with the external environment for guidance and with the human systems that set it for the desired temperature. It must also interface and depend on other systems: the electrical system, the water system, the gas system, the ventilating system, and the plumbing system.

General systems theory makes practical, intuitive sense.[14] For example, it has great utility for better understanding how living organisms coordinate their chemical components and in describing how cybernetic mechanisms can be engineered to demonstrate artificial intelligence. It is considerably less precise as a theory for the social sciences. However, as a perspective and *analogy* for organizations and small groups, systems theory makes several important points.

1. Organizations (as systems) are related to and dependent on their component units or groups (subsystems) with these interdependencies constantly changing.
2. An intelligent combining and coordinating of these organizational, component units lead to a synergy that can accomplish far more than individual, disconnected units (or groups) can.
3. A small group as a subsystem of a larger organizational system develops synergy only when it interacts—that is, when individual members communicate with one another and when they become concerned with how their group fits into and interacts with the total organization.

Systems theory is characterized by two general principles: nonsummativity and openness. *Nonsummativity* means that simply summing or adding up the parts of a system doesn't tell the whole story. Adding up the weights, diameters, atmospheric components, and so forth of all the planets does not begin to explain what is happening. When we study all of the planets as a system, which is where this perspective helps, we look for the interactions, the gravitational and other interdependencies between the planets and their common sun. Eureka! The solar system: Each planet takes on new meaning.

Openness suggests that systems interact with and are affected by other systems, by the environment, and by many other forces. Even the total solar system is not a closed one. It interacts with its galaxy, with other galaxies, perhaps with other systems and forces still to be discovered. Yet some systems are clearly more open than others: a social or political system is more open than a weapons system. Some weapons systems are designed to be as closed as possible so that an enemy cannot interfere with the mission once the weapon is set in motion. To beat some systems you need a system. No physical system is completely closed whether natural or designed but few, if any, are completely open either. Unless you intend to talk about everything at the same time, the adjective describing your system suggests that you are limiting (or closing out) some other things.

The same is true for organizational or groups systems. The Secret Service, Strategic Air Command (SAC), Central Intelligence Agency (CIA), and similar groups attest to that.

Organizations and the small groups in them are essentially contrived social structures. Daniel Katz and Robert Kahn explicate this notion:

> People invent the complex patterns of behavior that we call social structure, and people create social structure by enacting those patterns of behavior. Many properties of social systems derive from these essential facts. As human inventions, social systems are imperfect. They can come apart at the seams overnight, but they can also outlast by centuries the biological organisms that originally created them. The cement that holds them together is essentially psychological, rather than biological. Social systems are anchored in the attitudes, perceptions, beliefs, motivations, habits, and expectations of human beings.[15]

Suppose your organization employs organized, skilled tradespeople such as in the plumbing trade. Some parts of the plumbing system are so specialized that they have divided into more than one union. The pipefitting trade and all of the special welding skills prompted that. It is another system or subsystem with which the contractor must deal. When sprinkler systems for fire protection became routine, another specialized subsystem and union came into being. Refrigeration is now so sophisticated that it too has its own union group. This is why one must be concerned with individual components in any organizational system and why it is so difficult to be expert in all of them. If this isn't complex enough, the trades themselves have a training and certification system that gets more open as one gains qualifications. For plumbers: apprentice, journeyman, and master. A journeyman plumber working on a large building needn't understand the whole mechanical system if he or she is primarily installing toilet bends. It takes an engineer to understand the sophisticated systems in a modern building. The master plumber needs to understand enough system to interact with the contractor and, frequently, the engineer. The contractor (or subcontractor) has to know enough of interacting systems to be able to talk to the architect as well as to the mechanical engineer.

This illustration points out that systems theory is complex in application and that systems are seldom completely open. Skills, or their absence, do not allow for it; design doesn't always allow for it (pipes must be in place before the concrete is poured); and people are jealous of the jobs that belong to their trades. Jurisdictional battles among the trades are common and inevitable. Roof sumps have piping. Are they part of the plumbing system or the roofing system? Do towel bars belong to the plumbers or to the tile setters?

While systems theorists are most interested in the interaction between components, the human components we have been discussing are groups of people made up of diverse individuals. Some individuals simply prefer component skill specialties to a system perspective. "You figure the mechanical; I'll do the welding." Some people apparently cannot think large systems. A brain surgeon must know something of the human body and its nervous system but once that surgeon becomes superspecialized, he or she is like a skilled tradesperson who must be able to relate to the other systems while depending on others to do their part of the job.

More will be said about individual motivations and leadership skills in future chapters. At this point we are concerned with the fact that the organizational groups that you join and perhaps lead are made up of individuals with various skills, interests, and commitments to the larger system of which they are a part. We need highly skilled people whether they like to think "system" or not. We also need highly skilled group facilitators to help fit such people into the system.

ORGANIZATIONAL CONSTRAINTS

Some otherwise "open system" small groups in organizational settings are saddled with a great many practical constraints such as policies, work rules, legal laws, and past practices. These constraints *close* off many avenues, even for discussion. A modern personnel committee is rarely a leaderless, zero-history group of peers freely adapting to the world. They are often secretive by the necessity of law (invasion of privacy), undemocratic (forced compliance), cavalier (poor leadership), and even deceptive (confused policies).

For these reasons most organizations are not completely open systems. To incorporate legally is to provide minimally a set of bylaws that initially at least constrains the system. Some organizations are more open systems than others, yet no organization nor the small groups in it are completely open systems.

When systems are relatively open with inputs, particularly informational ones, outputs can vary considerably as can the ways, the throughputs, by which the outputs come about. Systems theorists call this characteristic of an open system *equifinality*.

When systems are relatively closed as in the weapons system illustration, the initial inputs constrain, control, and largely determine the outputs. Systems theorists call this *equilibrium*. Computers are sometimes like that—garbage in, garbage out! The tendency of such programmed systems to be inflexible and often irreversible may lead to their own destruction over time. Systems theorists call this concept *entropy*. It can also refer to the steady disorganization and disintegration of an organization or group that becomes progressively more and more closed.

An organizational group is hopefully not so isolated, so programmed, nor so closed that it brings on its own destruction. Ideally it is an open system within a still larger open system, as an entity that attains and perceives its own groupness. It is a true system because of the clear interdependence of its members. It is mostly an open system because of its interdependence with the rest of the organization. Since all organizations are large systems, small groups in organizational settings may be considered subsystems.

Systems theory's overriding emphasis on the interdependent activities of functional organizational *units* has led to some criticism of its supporters since there appears to be "little concern for the organization member. . . ."[16] This apparent lack of concern for individuals is in part a response to the often myopic preoccupation of early classical and human-relations adherents with motives, attitudes, need-dispositions, unconscious complexes, role requirements, and other such factors that were used to study, analyze, and describe individuals. Individuals were studied *not* usually in groups or systems but rather as if they existed seemingly apart from the environment. In the more modern view, human action is directed through interaction with others and through resulting self-interaction by which one perceives and interprets his or her own words and constructs appropriate action.

For some systems-theory advocates to even analyze components individually is to deny the interdependence of those components.[17] Limiting or reducing your area or unit of analysis is always risky, especially if you lose sight of or deny the system variable of which it is a part. However, organizations will continue to analyze such components: psychological mechanisms such as motivation, morale, attitude; pragmatic components such as personnel, job descriptions, labor contracts, grievance procedures, message construction, and others. The hope is that the systems perspective is never lost in the doing. This call for an eclectic contingency blend is a tall order for the reductionist thinker and also for some confirmed system theorists who consider the two views incompatible.

In quick review, a group as an open system is capable of receiving and seeking inputs; setting or adjusting goals; responding to information and feedback from inside and outside of the organization. Through group effort, information is processed through internal communication and finally is outputted as a group decision or action. Each group must be aware of its interdependency with other groups in the system of which it is a part—a useful and healthy perspective for the study of small groups.

GROUPNESS CHARACTERISTICS

An aggregation of five young people on a basketball court is not necessarily a "group" or even a team, at least not in a group dynamics or groupness sense. The individuals would have to exhibit at least five interdependent characteristics to earn the title "team"—even a poor team.

THEY HAVE INTERDEPENDENT, INTERACTIVE COMMUNICATION

If we observe these five communicating with one another, we have a modest clue; chit-chat, however, is not enough. The communication, however subtle or nonverbal, must demonstrate that they are interacting in an interdependent way. Whether they have free choice in this matter is not always critical. If they have just been drafted by the Los Angeles Lakers, it is assumed they will interact, at least on the basketball court.

Work aggregations ("groups") may have even less choice, but if they are to achieve groupness or true teamwork, they will have to perceive themselves as interdependent, and their interactions and communications should exhibit this. This often takes time, effort, and coaching or training, which is not surprising since the number of dyadic communications possible in a small, coating force of eight people is 28 (see Figure 2.4). The total number of relationships and subgroups is something else—1099.*

THEY HAVE COMMON GOALS AND KNOW IT

Part of this group characteristic is realized and recognized whenever a small aggregate of people seek or find a common goal. That in itself is a decision and such behavior even at the most elementary level is a groupness characteristic.[18]

A good basketball team surely knows that one of its main goals is to win games through coordinated effort. One "bad news" player who is interested primarily in his

---

* The formula for predicting the total number of subgroup relationships may be expressed as follows:

$$R = \Sigma d \frac{n!}{d!(n-d)!} + 1 \quad \text{where } d = s(n-1), (n-2)(n-3) \ldots (2)$$

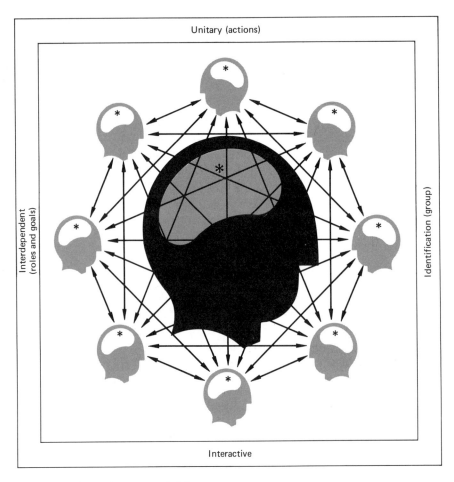

Figure 2.4   A coacting group of eight.

or her own individual fortune can sometimes disrupt and seriously ruin team effort. In organizational settings the common group goals are not always as obvious, and teamwork fails because people are only dimly aware of objectives. A quality circle certainly understands that its goal is to improve quality, but if it doesn't also understand that the subgoals—the practical objectives and practices—are also part of its collective, interdependent goal, it invites failure. If a member knows that he or she should be working toward a common goal but has a different version of that goal than others, *and doesn't know it*, teamwork can really flounder.

THEY HAVE STRUCTURE

A true group discovers or develops norms, rules, roles—a social structure. The basketball team develops floor leaders, captains, playmakers, and so on. In most organizational settings the norms, rules, roles, and leadership are assigned or strongly suggested, but not always. More and more freedom is being given to develop their own rules and practices as long as they support the larger organizational goals.

A case study involving eight young soldiers from three different Allied countries caught behind enemy lines illustrates some of the structures or networks that may emerge.[19] There were two Canadians, one British, and five Yanks, one a sergeant. After some initial fencing, a centralized network emerged with the sergeant assuming the leadership role. It can be diagrammed as a Y (see Figure 2.5).

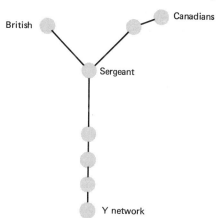

Figure 2.5 A Y network.

Within a day or two, the Canadian and British soldiers became a tighter subgroup and the communication network resembled a chain (see Figure 2.6).

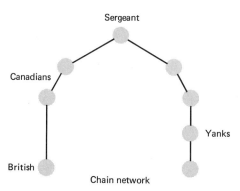

Figure 2.6 A chain network.

As the group seasoned and members developed more respect for each other, the necessity for even more central leadership seemed obvious. A wheel-type network developed (see Figure 2.7).

The dotted lines represent the interactions, now more egalitarian, between all of the men. The sergeant, given the diversity of the group, wisely encouraged this circle or all-channel network in their nightly strategy meetings, but was more autocratic when the bullets were flying.

These are the classic structures or networks that emerge. Many more are possible. Our basketball team has twelve different networks in which they can interact, as shown in Figure 2.8.

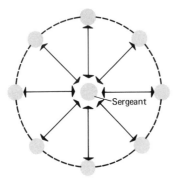

Figure 2.7 A wheel network.

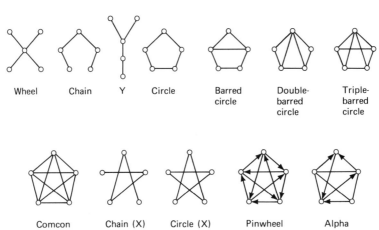

Figure 2.8 Five-person networks.

It seems obvious that the appropriate network, given the situation, is conditioned by the people, the group goals, and fast-changing events. Any network that works is a good one in the war context (and perhaps in others). In laboratory experiments dealing with simple tasks and no special life urgency, the centralized *wheel network* proved to be the fastest and best-organized network; a simple *circle network* (a wheel without a center) was the slowest and least well organized.[20] Indeed, many of the communications were suggestions on how to organize.

THEY EXPERIENCE PRESSURE TO CONFORM

"Shape up or ship out" is no idle saying. "Bad News" was not only a useless team player, he also fouled up the efforts of the remaining four. The team was better off without him even if they had to play shorthanded. "Bad News" did succumb to the pressure and was subsequently dropped from the team. Ideally this pressure is positive but it can be negative. "Bad News" did not respond to either one. This suggests that some people, at least in certain groups, are less teamwork-oriented than others.

At General Motors' Saturn plant and Ford's Mazda plant, cars are to be built using interdependent groups. Workers may even dress alike and exercise together on the job (see Figure 2.9). Note the uniforms; at Mazda even senior executives wear uniforms (see Figure 2.10). Their hiring practices now include screening out of applicants

Figure 2.9 Mazda workers in the body-metal finish section take a morning stretch near the assembly line.

Dale G. Young, The Detroit News, December 20, 1987.

Figure 2.10 Dennis Pawley, a manufacturing vice-president, holds a discussion with Takashi Itoh, senior advisor for manufacturing at Flat Rock.

Dale G. Young, The Detroit News, December 20, 1987.

judged incapable of teamwork.[21] So far the UAW union has taken a wait-and-see position.

Not all sports aggregations are full-fledged teams even though we call them that. Intense teamwork is necessary for successful basketball, football, baseball, and hockey teams. So-called golf, swimming, bowling, tennis, and ski teams are mostly efforts of individuals who pool their scores. They too need to coordinate and interact and they experience conformity pressure, though not in the same way that the intensive team sports do. Organizational small groups also vary in their need to conform and for many of the same reasons. Too much pressure may inhibit a designer, a stylist, or a research specialist. To feel zero pressure to conform suggests an individual who is not aware that he or she depends on someone else and that someone else depends on him or her . . . or has other problems.

THEY TAKE UNITARY ACTIONS

Team players tend to stick together, identify with one another, perceive a common fate, "We're in this thing together," and act with a single-minded purpose, especially if provoked. This does not mean that every member always agrees with the game plan or the group decision, but rather that members support the plan or action as a unit. In most cases consensus is the goal.

Because they are interdependent group members, aware of that fact, and have been participants in the deliberations, they tend to support and carry out the will of the group, clearly a strong characteristic of groupness or true teamwork (see Figure 2.11).

Figure 2.11   A Japanese Mazda employee finds a Japanese-English dictionary helpful during a recent meeting on metal fabricating.

Dale G. Young, The Detroit News, December 20, 1987.

DEFINITIONS

The late Aubrey Fisher said that "None of the definitions of a group is false or correct" and that "each definition is true and correct."[22] So much depends on your personal perspective, which aspect you happen to be examining, and how you construe and construct information from what you have discovered. With these admonitions in mind let's see what we can learn using different definitions from diverse viewpoints and also discover what common elements may exist.

PSYCHODYNAMIC AND SOCIOBIOLOGICAL

From the psychodynamic and sociobiological view we can infer that a group is

> A group of people who need each other to satisfy basic psychological and biological needs.

Sharing is a common denominator through these viewpoints. One needs to feel included, to find affection and security. There is even a herd instinct that fosters advantages in adapting to hostile environments.

SOCIAL COMPARISON

From the social-comparison view a group is

> A group of people who need each other to gain and compare information.

Such comparisons are thought to give us some understanding of social reality and to help us satisfy our need to better know who we are and frequently to help us reduce anxiety.

SOCIAL EXCHANGE

From the social-exchange view a group is

> A group of people who find affiliating more rewarding than being alone.

We will not join a group if the costs are too high or if the rewards are not sufficient. We are thought to weigh rewards heavily in favor of competent, socially attractive people.

SYSTEMS THEORY

From the systems-theory viewpoint a group is a system that behaves collectively as a group because of the interdependence of its members. A group as defined by Fisher is

> . . . A collection of individuals whose communicative behaviors—specifically, acts, interacts, and double interacts—become interstructured and repetitive in the form of predictable patterns.[23]

It is the interstructuring and interdependence of communication behaviors—the interactions—that characterize a group entity or system. The group system is thought to be always an open one, that is, freely interacting with other systems and the total environment.

GROUP DYNAMICS

From the very basic dimensions researched by those of the group-dynamics view, we find several notions held in common: interdependence, face-to-face, mutual influence, and interaction. Some illustrative definitions follow.

> For a collection of individuals to be considered a group there must be some interaction.[24]

> A group is a collection of individuals who have relations to one another that make them interdependent to some significant degree.[25]

> Two or more persons who are interacting with one another in such a manner that each person influences and is influenced by each other person.[26]

Remember that the group dynamicist is not particularly interested in pragmatics: how to organize groups, groups skills, rules, guidelines, participation, or even democratic leadership. "Group dynamics is an attempt to subject the many aspects of groups to scientific analysis through the construction of theories concerning groups and the rigorous testing of the adequacy of these theories through empirical research."[27]

SPEECH COMMUNICATION

Most speech communication professors are interested in the pragmatics as well as the basic dynamics and systems involved in small groups. Definitions of what we mean by group discussion show considerable basic agreement:

> . . . the process of verbal and nonverbal face-to-face interaction in a small group. A small group is a collection of individuals, from three to fifteen in number, who meet in face-to-face interaction over a period of time, generally with an assigned or assumed leader, who possess at least one common characteristic, and who meet with a purpose in mind.[28]

> . . . a few people engaged in communication interaction over time, generally in face-to-face settings, who have common goals and norms and have developed a communication pattern for meeting their goals in an interdependent fashion.[29]

> . . . one or more meetings of a small group of people who communicate, face-to-face, in order to fulfill a common purpose or achieve a group goal.[30]

> . . . a set of activities usually executed by a small group and directed toward determining appropriate answers to controversial questions of fact, conjecture, value or policy.[31]

. . . a small group of persons talking with each other face to face in order to achieve some interdependent goal, such as increased understanding, coordination of activity, or a solution to a shared problem.[32]

A student group summed it up well with, ''Discussion is a means of thinking together through cooperative conversation.''

Small group discussion in organizational settings can profit from all of these definitions. However, unlike the pure systems theorist or confirmed group dynamicist, we must also be concerned with individuals and the urgency of this very special and often constraining context. The processual nature of small-group decision making is considered extensively in Chapter 4.

SUMMARY

We all belong to many groups at the same time. A group as a social entity goes beyond a mere collection of people. This ''groupness'' energizes and motivates people to achieve and work toward goals. Psychodynamic theory argues that people join groups because it satisfies basic biological and psychological needs. William Schutz extends this theory through his FIRO (Fundamental Interpersonal Relations Orientation), which postulates three basic interpersonal needs: inclusion, control, and affection. Sociobiology argues a herd instinct or urge to affiliate directs people to groups. Social-comparison theory suggests that we affiliate to gain and compare information from appropriate others. Social tendencies have been called gregariousness, companionship, and succorance. Anxiety appears to heighten the need for companionship. Social-exchange theory postulates that we join groups because the rewards are higher and the costs lower than if we go it alone. We enjoy being with people who provide real or reflected status, power, and recognition—unless such social comparisons are painful and lead to feelings of inferiority.

The basic notion of systems theory is that every interacting component of any given system affects and is affected by every other component, leading to a synergy that is greater than the simple sum of its parts. Systems theory is characterized by two general principles: nonsummativity and openness. *Nonsummativity* means that simply adding up the parts of a system doesn't tell the whole story. *Openness* suggests that systems interact with and are affected by other systems, the environment, and many other forces. A group as an open system has *equifinality*, that is, it is capable of receiving and seeking inputs, setting goals, responding to information and feedback from within and outside the organization, and processing decisions. Closed, inflexible systems have *equilibrium*, that is, initial inputs control the outputs. Inflexibility can lead to *entropy*, or a group's steady disintegration. A small group as a subsystem of a larger organizational system develops synergy only when it interacts with its members and with the parent organization.

A small group has five basic characteristics: (1) they have interdependent, interactive communication, (2) they have common goals and know it, (3) they have structure, (4) they experience pressure to conform, and (5) they take unitary actions. Groups have patterns or networks. The classic ones are *Y*, *chain*, and *wheel*. In laboratory experiments the wheel was the fastest. Choice of network should be conditioned by the people, the goals, and the situation.

The definition of a group from the psychodynamic and sociobiological view is *a group of people who need each other to satisfy basic psychological and biological needs.* From the social-comparison view a group is *a group of people who need each other to gain and compare information.* From the social-exchange view a group is *a group of people who find affiliating more rewarding than being alone.* From the systems and group dynamics view a group behaves collectively as a group because of the interdependence of its members. A group (system) as defined by Fisher is *a collection of individuals whose communicative behaviors—specifically, acts, interacts, and double interacts—become interstructured and repetitive in the form of predictable patterns.*

Discussion may be thought of as a means of thinking together through purposeful conversation.

PROJECTS AND CASES

PROJECTS

1. List the groups you have joined voluntarily, and compare them with those to which you feel you belong for less than voluntary reasons. Prepare to discuss your reasons in terms of text explanations.

2. Discuss ''People join groups to better understand their social reality. . . . ''

3. Competent people are usually, but not always, perceived as attractive. Why is this so? Illustrate this phenomenon with a personal example, and prepare to report.

4. Study the definitions of ''group'' and prepare to discuss them in an effort to reach some kind of consensus about what a group really is.

5. Consider the five small-group characteristics discussed in the text and use them to analyze a group of which you are or were a part.

6. Attend two or three group meetings (clubs, fraternities, work groups, church committees, and so on), and try to diagram the type of communication *network* used in each. Discuss each network configuration in terms of effectiveness, group morale, efficiency, and the like (e.g., wheel, chain, Y).

7. With three or four others, set up two different networks in class and see which works better for two different kinds of message situations. Discuss your results in terms of the theory suggested in this chapter.

8. Select a group that you think is a mostly open or mostly closed system; prepare to discuss its characteristics.

CASES

1. Sprint Air Freight[33]

Sprint Air Freight is a multimillion-dollar commercial-freight forwarder, acting as an agent for various companies and arranging transportation for these organizations' industrial cargo. Sprint Air Freight is one of the pioneer companies in the air freight forwarding business. It handles primarily domestic and international cargo moving by air, but also handles some shipping (ocean) and trucking cartage.

Sprint's air-transport business is separated into domestic and international operations. Domestic air transportation is controlled by the Los Angeles main office, supervising its 17 branch offices in San Francisco, New York, Chicago, Dallas, Philadelphia, Pittsburgh, Boston, Atlanta, Denver, Detroit, Minneapolis, Miami, Tampa, Seattle, Phoenix, Portland, and Honolulu. The company also has a network of 30 independent air-freight agents in smaller American cities where it would be unprofitable for Sprint to set up its own offices. International air freight is controlled by the New York office (New York being the company's primary point of international cargo departure and arrival). The New York office supervises 30 overseas agents (15 in Europe, 5 in Asia, 5 in South America, and 5 in Africa and the Middle East). Additionally, the New York office handles any international freight originating at any of the Sprint domestic offices.

Sprint is a service organization. It arranges its customers' cargo pick up, storage, delivery to and pick up from carriers, delivery to final destination, preparation of all documents, payment of carriers, and insurance of cargo, and it keeps a written record of all shipped goods and costs. Sprint has stressed personalized service to its customers as one of its chief advantages over its competitors, and Sprint has lived up to its claim of personal service, even though the company's rapid growth sometimes has made this difficult.

In the early 1970s, Sprint Air Freight was at the peak of its organizational growth, making approximately $2 million profit per year. At this high point in Sprint's sales growth, it held a 14 percent share of the air freight forwarding market and was ranked as the third largest combined domestic and international air freight forwarder in the world (and was rapidly threatening to overtake the number 1 and 2 freight forwarders). Since the early 1970s, however, Sprint's sales growth and profits have steadily eroded and decreased. At the end of fiscal year 1979, it was running in the red by approximately $1 million and was considering either declaring Chapter 11 or bankruptcy, merging with another forwarder, or revamping its organizational structure and marketing approach.

Before taking any of these courses of action, Sprint's board of directors hired an external consultant to evaluate its organizational situation. The consultant provided the board of directors with a report that identified four major problems the company had faced since the early 1970s that may have been causing its financial problems:

1. Steady decrease in sales and loss of many large customers.
2. Increases in operating costs due to unionization of truck drivers, warehouse workers, and office personnel, who demanded pay raises with the threat of a strike in many of Sprint's larger offices (New York, Los Angeles, Chicago, San Francisco, and Miami). Additional higher operating costs due to inflation, causing increases in the price of fuel, loading equipment, and other supplies.
3. The long time lag between Sprint's appeals to the Civil Aeronautics Board to raise its rates (in accordance with airline rate hikes that the CAB had approved). Sprint had to absorb the additional costs of paying the airlines' higher rates while their freight-forwarding rates were frozen.
4. High international inflationary trend, upsetting the balance of international monetary values, made it difficult for many foreign markets to purchase American goods, which had been forwarded by air. This resulted in a decreased demand for international freight-forwarding services.

The consultant also noted that Sprint's chief competitor, Johnson Air Freight, the largest air-freight forwarder for the past two decades, had steadily increased its market share and profits since the early 1970s. For example, Johnson Air Freight's market share in 1970 was 21 percent, and by fiscal year 1979, its market share had increased to 27 percent of the domestic and international air cargo business. Sprint Air Freight and Johnson Air Freight had faced many of the same increases in operating costs and foreign market problems, yet Johnson had been able to enhance its sales in the private sector, selling air-freight services to many small customers and not depending so much on a few very large customers.

The Sprint board of directors evaluated the information available to them and pondered the best action to take.

QUESTIONS

1. How can systems theory help us analyze this problem?
2. Does Sprint demonstrate the principle of equifinality?
3. How open is Sprint to its environment?
4. How can Sprint resist entropy?

2. The Unbalanced Team[34]

Rob called his task force together for their first meeting. Cheerfully, he said to the group, "I hope the rest of you are as excited as I am about having been chosen to work on one of the Pure Waters Agency's most pressing problems. As explained to me by the director, the Pure Waters Agency has an image problem. People resent paying money for water pollution services. Part of their resistance is because they don't know what we do. They don't understand how important we are to their health. Our job is to develop some guidelines for informing the public. But first we have to learn how big a problem we really have. What are your thoughts, Ginger, Derek, Gil and Willie?"

Ginger spoke first: "So long as you mentioned my name first, I thought I would contribute before the good ideas were used up. It seems like a marketing research assignment to me. We have to go out into the field and find out how we are perceived by the public. After we get a clear picture of our strengths and weaknesses as the public sees us, we can plan some remedial action."

Willie commented, "I couldn't have said it better myself. But first we'll have to design a questionnaire and figure out whom we are going to interview. We have some experts in the department of statistics who can help us select the right kind of sample."

"I have a question, Rob," said Gil. "It sounds as if this task force will be pretty time consuming. Will we be getting enough time off from our regular jobs to do justice to this assignment?"

"The ground rules state that each member of this task force will be excused from twenty hours of regular work per week for up to three months," replied Rob. "I don't think we have to put that in writing."

Derek commented, "We haven't even begun and there goes Gil, trying to ensure that he's not overworked. For me, I couldn't be more pleased to be assigned to this project. I've done some depth interviewing for a course I took in consumer psychology."

"Good enough, team, let's make up a tentative list of questions right now. We still have a couple of hours till quitting time."

"Hey, I've got an idea," said Gil. "While you four are working on the questionnaire, I'll run over to the statistical department and see if they can help us draw up a sample."

Two weeks later the Public Relations Task Force was ready to begin field interviewing. Each member was assigned twenty-five interviews to be conducted in a ten-day period. After the interviewing project was one week old, Derek received a phone call from Willie:

"Derek, I've got something confidential to tell you."

"What is it, you're not in any trouble are you?"

"Not me exactly, Derek," said Willie. "But I think our team is headed for some trouble. I've just spoken to Ginger and she agrees. Gil has been goofing off since the start of the project. He finds the cutest ways to avoid work. He was supposed to meet me one day to do a group interview. Instead he left a message in my department that he was tied up with some urgent business matters."

"That's right, Willie, I remember the first day of our meeting, he took two hours to ask the statistical department a few questions. Have you noticed any other problem?"

"For sure. Not only is Gil behind in his interviews but I think he made up most of the ones that he plans to turn in. I think he is going to single-handedly ruin the output of the group."

"Okay, Willie, what are you telling me? What should we do about the problem?"

"That's why I've called you. Ginger doesn't have any good suggestions either. She thinks we should just let the issue ride. But if we turn in a mediocre or incomplete report, everybody on the task force will look bad. This is supposed to be a team effort. I'm afraid we're stuck with a team member who won't carry his weight."

QUESTIONS

1. What can the group do?
2. Is Gil being given a fair chance?

NOTES

1. Donelson R. Forsyth, *An Introduction to Group Dynamics* (Monterey, Calif.: Brooks/Cole, 1983), ch. 3, pp. 49–77.

2. Abraham H. Maslow, "A Theory of Human Motivation," *Psychological Review*, 50 (1943), 370–96.

3. David Krech and Richard C. Crutchfield, Norman Livson, Wm. A. Wilson, Jr., and Alan Parducci, *Elements of Psychology*, 4th ed. (New York: Alfred A. Knopf, 1982), p. 435.

4. William Schutz, *FIRO: A Three-Dimensional Theory of Interpersonal Behavior* (New York: Holt, Rinehart & Winston, 1958), p. 13.

5. Schutz, *FIRO*, p. 22.

6. Ibid., p. 23.

7. Ibid., p. 24.

8. Stanley Schachter, *The Psychology of Affiliation* (Stanford, Calif.: Stanford University Press, 1959), pp. 9–10.

9. G. S. Sanders, "Social Comparison as a Basis for Evaluating Others," *Journal of Research in Personality*, 16 (1982), 21–31.

10. Schachter, *Psychology of Affiliation*, 1.

11. See D. Brinberg and P. Castell, "A Resource Exchange Theory Approach to Interpersonal Interactions: A Test of Foa's Theory," *Journal of Social Psychology* 43 (1982), 260–69.

12. Elliot Aronson, *The Social Animal*, 4th ed. (San Francisco: W. H. Freeman, 1984), p. 290.

13. Dennis L. Krebs and Allen A. Adinolfi, "Physical Attractiveness, Social Relations, and Personality Style," *Journal of Personality and Social Psychology*, 31 (1975), 245–53.

14. L. Bertalanffy, "General Systems Theory: A New Approach to the Unity of Science," *Human Biology* (December 1951), pp. 303–61; see also L. Bertalanffy, *General Systems Theory: Foundations, Development, Applications* (New York: George Braziller, 1968).

15. Daniel Katz and Robert L. Kahn, *The Social Psychology of Organizations*, 2nd ed. (New York: John Wiley and Sons, 1978), p. 37.

16. Gary L. Kreps, *Organizational Communication* (New York: Longman, 1986), p. 106; see also B. Aubrey Fisher, *Small Group Decision Making: Communication and the Group Process*, 2nd ed. (New York: McGraw-Hill, 1980), p. 110.

17. Fisher, *Small Group Decision Making*, p. 110.

18. M. S. Poole, D. R. Seibold, and R. D. McPhee, "Group Decision-Making as a Structurational Process," *Quarterly Journal of Speech*, 71 (1985), 84.

19. Raymond S. Ross and Mark G. Ross, *Relating and Interacting* (Englewood Cliffs, N.J.: Prentice-Hall, 1982), pp. 228–44.

20. For more on networks, see M. E. Shaw, "Communication Networks Fourteen Years Later," in *Group Processes*, ed. L. Berkowitz, (New York: Academic, 1978).

21. Jan A. Zverina, "Teamwork Puts Applicants Ahead at Mazda," *Detroit Free Press*, December 17, 1987, sec. C, p. 8; see also Ann M. Job, "GM to Use Toyota's Production Methods," *The Detroit News*, October 4, 1987, sec. A, p. 1.

22. Fisher, *Small Group Decision Making*, p. 19.

23. Ibid., p. 22.

24. A. P. Hare, *Handbook of Small Group Research*, 2nd ed. (New York: Free Press, 1976), p. 4.

25. Dorwin Cartwright and Alvin Zander, *Group Dynamics: Research and Theory* (New York: Harper & Row, 1968), p. 46.

26. Marvin E. Shaw, *Group Dynamics: The Psychology of Small Group Behavior*, 3rd ed. (New York: McGraw-Hill, 1981), p. 454.

27. Forsyth, *Introduction to Group Dynamics*, p. 12.

28. Larry L. Barker, Kathy J. Wahlers, Kittie Watson, and Robert J. Kibler, *Groups in Process* (Englewood Cliffs, N.J.: Prentice-Hall, 1987), p. 8.

29. John F. Cragan and David W. Wright, *Communication in Small Group Discussions*, 2nd ed. (St. Paul, Minn.: West, 1986), p. 9.

30. Ernest G. Bormann and Nancy C. Bormann, *Effective Small Group Communication* (Minneapolis, Minn.: Burgess, 1980), p. 15.

31. Dennis S. Gouran, *Discussion: The Process of Group Decision-Making* (New York: Harper & Row, 1974), p. 5.

32. John K. Brilhart, *Effective Group Discussion*, 5th ed. (Dubuque, Ia.: Wm. C. Brown, 1986), p. 9.

33. From *Organizational Communication* by Gary L. Kreps, Copyright © 1986 by Longman, Inc., p. 107. All rights reserved.

34. From Andrew DuBrin, *Foundations of Organizational Behavior* (Englewood Cliffs, N.J.: Prentice-Hall, Inc., Copyright © 1984), p. 252.

3

SPECIAL PROBLEM DYNAMICS

DEINDIVIDUATION: THE LOSS OF INDIVIDUALITY

HYPERINTERSTIMULATION

Less than 10 years ago, eleven young Cincinnatians were stampeded to death in a tragic kind of group insanity while waiting for a rock concert given by the Who. Following are some randomly collected comments by psychologists who have tried to explain the incident.

> A blurring suggestibility occurs.
> The sense of self is lost.
> The mob becomes your identity.
> Regressive, impulsive behavior.
> Peer pressure is very strong.
> A sense of restraint is lost.
> Guilt is lost in anonymity.

This is a kind of mob mentality more likely to happen with large, polarized, hyperstimulated crowds than with small groups. However, the same mental mechanisms—*anonymity, contagion,* and *suggestibility*—appear to be involved. One who is lost in the press of a crowd or keyed up for an attack on an enemy gun position loses much of his or her sense of responsibility. This gives rise to a feeling of *anonymity* complete with inflated, irresponsible power. *Contagion* is evident in the description of the Cincinnati Who concert tragedy. It is a kind of high-speed, infectious mayhem. It is a perverted form of *social facilitation*. Individuals' desires are stimulated by the sight and sound of others making similar movements. A heightened state of *suggestibility* leads to hasty, thoughtless, and rash action. Many of one's restraining emotions are lost; fear is often missing in battle, and pity in a riot or a lynching.

This *groupthink* loss of responsibility and sense of anonymity is also called *deindividuation*, that is, a loss of individual or personal restraints. Evildoers wear masks or hoods not only to prevent identification, but because it also gives them a false courage born of deindividuation. In one experiment women were asked to discuss pornographic literature. Those with name tags and highly individual clothing were much more restrained in their language than those who were not so identified and who wore impersonal lab coats.[1]

No one person takes a rope and proceeds to lynch someone. It takes the dynamics of a group. However, deindividuation is not always a negative phenomenon. Battles have been won and countries have been saved by the power and courage of groups. According to one researcher, in some situations a deindividuated person " . . . might be more likely to donate a large amount of money to charity, might be more likely to risk his or her life to help another, and might be more likely to kiss friends—all behaviors that many consider laudatory."[2]

In organizational settings one sees near deindividuation and hyperinterstimulation in various sales motivation sessions. Some very articulate, evangelistic, animated speakers and facilitators attempt to stimulate people to work harder at their selling and to regain lost self-esteem. Certain programs are packaged complete with cassettes, pamphlets, filmstrips, and scripts for sales managers. Most of these ''hyper'' sessions are harmless, occasionally useful, and almost always entertaining. Selling engenders a great deal of frustration since even the most successful salesperson hears ''no sale'' over and over again. Self-concept often suffers and with it the motivation to press on. The dramatic motivators offer relief, catharsis, and regeneration for many salespersons whom I have observed and interviewed. Motivators should not be dismissed too quickly, especially if they don't torture the facts too badly *and* if most of the sales training program is more conventional and more concerned with the total system in which a salesperson operates.

Company retreats have been known to become so intense and ''open'' that deindividuation occurs, and people go beyond what their organizational norms will allow. This is not to deprecate retreats, but to suggest that a fine line exists between stimulation that leads to pro-social behavior and stimulation that leads to antisocial behavior.

Most strikes and work stoppages are orderly if not always quiet. A few that make the news turn ugly by accident. Rarely are they planned that way; often they are ''wildcats'' or unauthorized strikes, a case of negative deindividuation.

GROUPTHINK

Symptoms

This is a subtler form of losing one's critical thinking ability. Yoko Ono's paper dress act, which once stimulated nightclubbers to cautiously (at first) scissor off a piece of her dress and ended in a wild, mad spree that left her naked, was not really very subtle. The merrymakers who looked *individually* into their mirrors the next morning were probably experiencing some wonderment at their bizarre behavior the night before. We are usually retrospectively aware of our hyperinterstimulated behavior. However, when an amiable, cohesive group develops its own mentality and makes foolish or unfair decisions, it may not be aware of this fact for a long time, and perhaps never. This phenomenon is called *groupthink*. The Orwellian-sounding term was coined by Irving Janis, who defined it as ". . . a concurrence-seeking tendency that interferes with critical thinking . . . when members' strivings for unanimity override their motivation to realistically appraise alternative courses of action . . . a deterioration of mental efficiency, reality testing, and moral judgment that results from in-group pressures."[3]

For Janis the Cuban Bay of Pigs invasion was a decision fiasco caused by groupthink. Perhaps the American corporate auto executives became complacent in the early 1970s and talked only to each other about energy and car size. A failure to consider the full range of alternatives and a failure to work out contingency plans for possible setbacks now seem obvious. Were they, too, the victims of groupthink? Of course we had regulated gasoline prices, Ralph Nader, and many government regulations. These outgroups may have caused an even tighter Detroit ingroup, which in Janis's words ". . . fosters overoptimism, lack of vigilance, and sloganistic thinking. . . ."[4]

Groupthink is the tendency of a group to so vigorously strive for solidarity and unanimity that members systematically avoid questions or subjects that could lead to disputes. Their decisions then become ill-considered and unrealistic.

Some super-conservative or super-liberal groups have also been known to develop a group mentality that views anyone not of their persuasion as a "nut" or a dangerous character. They feed on one another, reinforce one another, and may eventually lose their ability to cope with reality. They obviously may have trouble coping with change.

At its worst, groupthink fosters an illusion of invulnerability, a holier-than-thou inherent morality, a stereotyping of opponents as evil, and a heavy pressure to conform to its group mentality. This is not to deprecate togetherness, dedication, loyalty, team effort, or even protest groups. In fact, we seek these virtues in our work and policy-making groups. It is however, a knife that cuts both ways. To make cohesion work for us, we need to constantly consider what we are about. We need feedback from other viewpoints. We should collectively consider as many alternate courses of action as possible. We have to consider contingency plans for things going wrong. We must do everything we can to protect independent, critical thinking whatever the pressures to conform. Every organization doesn't have to hire an obnoxious personality or a "nut" to keep it honest and to defend against groupthink, but perhaps a little eccentricity isn't all bad if it keeps us honest.

Prevention

If the Bay of Pigs invasion was a classic example of groupthink fiasco, then the Cuban missile crisis was an example of how the same Kennedy group prevented groupthink from happening again.

In all organizational settings, especially where crisis situations and decisions are involved, groups must guard against *premature agreement* about what is happening. Time is often short but that is precisely when groupthink emerges. Use as much time as you reasonably can. Sometimes no decision is better than a dumb one.

To avoid this pressure to conform, promote *open discussion* and inquiry. In some cases a person may even be assigned the role of *devil's advocate*. Robert Kennedy often played this role of one who actively tries to find fault and raise questions about any and all opinions and arguments. The role is best rotated through the group since it is not a way to gain popularity. This technique for preventing groupthink is presently used in a wide range of organizational settings with good results.[5] The technique and its name stem from deliberations by the Roman Catholic church over candidates for sainthood. To make sure that all negative evidence was heard, that nothing slipped through the screening process, one priest was specifically assigned the role of raising the questions the devil might ask—hence, devil's advocate. Of course the role doesn't always have to be assigned. Some people play it quite naturally, sometimes unfairly. If that is your healthy purpose, you can protect yourself and your group by giving a clue: "Let me play devil's advocate and ask . . . " or "just for the sake of argument" or "just so we don't miss something."

Avoiding emotional reactions can also help prevent premature agreement and groupthink. Don't go off half-cocked; if tempers and emotions flare don't be stampeded—cool it, but how? One way is to delay agreements, even if for only a short, cooling off recess. Then regroup and hold what Irving Janis calls a "second chance" meeting where members can raise nagging doubts and rethink the issues.[6]

Subgrouping or dividing your group in half and having each half discuss the same agenda is another way to lessen the pressures to conform. This technique often reveals differences that might otherwise go unnoticed had the group met as a whole. Where there are clear role and rank differences, subgroups can be designated in that way. Tenured faculty are frequently separated from the nontenured in some deliberations, junior staff officers from senior staff officers in the military, varsity from junior varsity, and so on. Lower-level peer groups often express themselves more openly with each other and when the groups are smaller. For subgrouping to work, individual efforts and decisions must be reported to the total group.

All of these groupthink preventions call for effectiveness in open leadership and open-system decision making. These two critical dimensions of organizational settings will be discussed in subsequent chapters.

RISKY-SHIFT PHENOMENON

RISKY DECISIONS

Risky decisions refers to the risks one is willing to take given the possible gains.[7] A ten-to-one longshot bet of $10 will return $100 *if* the horse wins. An eight-to-five bet is more *likely* to pay off (it says here), but you'll get only $16. Of course, how much you are into horse racing and how much the $10 is worth to you in the first place has a lot to do with this. A high-paying job with little security versus an adequate-salaried job with much security is another example. It has been said that risky decisions are harder to make when you are alone. Are they? Will a small-group decision be riskier, other things being equal, than the average of the individual decisions made privately?

Our intrepid Allied patrol was now three days and nights into their adventure. They were together and healthy. They saw numerous German support and supply troops and were able to avoid detection relatively easily. The group became more cohesive and was encouraged in the thought that they might get back after all. At the fourth day meeting in an abandoned stone silo, they were feeling bolder . . . "How much farther, Sarge?" "Who knows . . . twenty or thirty kilometers maybe." "Could be weeks the way we're playing hide." "Yeah, did you see the gas dump the Germans had outside Roermond . . . wasn't it?" This all-channel network was slowed when the Britisher said, "Sarge, we could have put a rocket in that German petrol real easy." After some

silence Sarge spoke, "You're right, Winnie . . . but our mission is to rejoin . . . ''
(interrupted) ''Our mission is to shoot up the Wehrmacht.'' ''What do you think,
Glover?'' On into the night eight young men calculated the risk of attacking large enemy
groups versus the less risky infiltration back maneuver in which they were involved.
Sarge spoke, "Hell, let's go after that gasoline. We'll be gone before they know what
hit 'em.''

The risky shift in strategy was made, one unlikely to be made by any single
individual, but one easier to make together. Not that everyone was gung-ho, but they
went along, which is what early risky-shift research would have predicted.[8] Oh yes, the
smoke from the explosion could have been seen for miles had the weather been clear.
Would this group, encouraged by this success, have taken on still more aggressive risks?
Probably . . .

Why did they do it? What factors are present in small groups that encourage
such risk taking? Sometimes a bold leader has a lot to do with it, but he or she needs
a cohesive, dedicated group with similar views to exert such influence. Our international
squad might come to that, but probably not in ten days.[9] On the other hand, a passive
leader might dampen such spirit.

The *values* one has about risk taking generally may have a lot to do with one's
behavior. The Yanks had the rags-to-riches reputation to uphold; we reward and admire
the bold risk takers. The same situation applied to the Canadians. Our British friend,
having seen his homeland almost lose it all in the Blitz, had a special motivation to take
some risks. All of these young soldiers wanted to look good to each other and be accepted.
This kind of *social comparison* probably promoted the risky decisions the little group continued to make.[10] Of course, these were experienced soldiers with a strong sense of duty.
A practical pooling of critical information and experience probably also bred confidence
and a greater willingness to gamble. The available weapons obviously helped. The pan-
zerfaust destroyed one immobilized tank before it could be repaired—not without considerable risk.

THE POLARIZATION HYPOTHESIS

More recent research suggests that the risky-shift phenomenon might better be called
the *polarization phenomenon*. That is, the direction of the group shift depends upon what
was initially the predominant view. The post-discussion decision will be more *extreme*,
but not necessarily toward the risk pole.

Cautious $\longleftrightarrow$ Risky

1 2 3 4 5 6 7 8 9

This phenomenon, supported by numerous research studies, has been called the *group-
polarization hypothesis*.[11] This reasonable notion does not deny the risky decisions' findings. It does, however, clearly extend the earlier explanation. We could then expect
more extreme shift from a group, but it could be in a more conservative or cautious
direction.

A creative study by Lamm and Myers clearly supports this broader explanation. ROTC cadets, army officers, and college students were asked to make decisions
about how the U.S. forces should deal with an armed conflict. The "hawks" shifted
to more forceful tactics than they had taken pre-discussion. The "doves" shifted toward

even less militaristic response than they had indicated before.[12] There is, of course, some semantic and some pragmatic argument about which is the riskier pole. A show of force and solidarity as in the Cuban missile crisis may have been *less* risky in a larger systems view than backing off and attempting negotiation. However, that the larger shift can go either way is clear and useful information for those in organizational settings. A very conservative business group might not make what could be viewed as a risky decision (i.e., modern changes in policy) after discussion, but rather could make decisions that are even more extreme in their conservatism (i.e., no change—back to the good old days). Some values and semantics intrude again. In terms of the company's survival, their decision (from a larger systems view) may have been the riskiest of all.

ECLECTIC EXPLANATIONS

There are several. None are entirely correct but all add insight. None are mutually exclusive nor do they seriously contradict one another. Some are generated by reductionist data (looking at smaller and smaller, isolated dimensions of a process or system). Some develop from a clearly stated but biased orientation (persuasive leadership, argumentation, and so forth).

If one can maintain the systems theory perspective—that is, everything is related to and affects everything else (nothing makes complete sense if one ignores the larger system of which it is a part)—*then* perhaps one can assemble all of the findings eclectically and evaluate them for what they are—pieces of a larger system. If one assembles enough pieces of a process or system, the character of the process or system emerges and allows one to make still more intelligent evaluations of the pieces themselves. Why then these shifts?[13]

The Responsibility Explanation   One can hide behind the group; if we're wrong the responsibility is spread around, and I can afford the risk.

The Leadership Explanation   Our leader is competent, charismatic, persuasive, and a successful risk taker; I'll go along. . . .

The Uncertainty Reduction Explanation   One gains more information from the group that breeds confidence and a willingness to take risks.

The Excitement of Risk Taking Explanation   Risk taking is a valued attribute of your organization; others are doing it; taking a chance is fun.

The Persuasive Arguments Explanation   More members equals more arguments; whether for or against they make extreme shifts more comfortable, perhaps more rational.

The Social Comparison Explanation   Being exposed to other opinions puts one into competition to demonstrate either greater risk or greater caution.

The ways of preventing risky or overly cautious shifts are not yet clear from the research available. However, knowledge of the phenomenon and the several non-exclusive theories about how it comes about should be of help in assessing your group's potential or tendency to be so afflicted. The general suggestions for preventing group-think discussed previously should also pertain. Whether you believe in systems theory or not, the system *orientation* or perspective should help you stand back and look at the larger message picture as well as the process in which you are involved. A large part of that process involves problem-solving techniques and decision making, which if done intelligently should help reduce the threat of all these special problem dynamics.

CLOSED SYSTEM REASONING

Still another problem dynamic is caused by groups that trap themselves into a single perspective, usually an analytical control-oriented one or a politically centered one. Harold Leavitt suggests that these styles of thought are too one-dimensional, and that groups, and especially their leaders, should take a broader, more eclectic perspective or what he calls a *pathfinder* attitude. This perspective includes a sense of mission, instinct, wisdom, and imagination.[14] Leavitt finds today's organizational types too interested in quantitative analysis and closed, rational reasoning or, if they are of the political school, too interested in the single perspective of teamwork, consensus, and other human and interpersonal concerns. Leavitt argues that these limited or closed styles of thought cause a lack of creativity and vision. He promotes a broader, more open, intellectual reasoning style. He suggests that the open, pathfinder style requires more of a liberal arts orientation than a business school one. It is a reasoning style that opens the mind to problems that might otherwise go unnoticed and to questions that might otherwise go unasked. We will have more to say about reasoning and the language style in which it is clothed in later chapters.

INTERPERSONAL CONFLICTS

Healthy differences of opinion on the issues do not usually represent a problem dynamic. Some researchers suggest that such exchanges are necessary for a group to reach quality decisions.[15]

Highly personal, affective conflicts are another matter. While one must pause on notions of "psychology of person" or "personality chemistry," some people do not seem to mix well with others, at least some special others. One senior member of an executive committee was so cantankerous and opinionated that the group's effectiveness was crippled for years. New members grew weary and left; old members grew weary and either gave in or simply voted against him even when he was making sense. I asked one member why he cast a vote against a proposition he had been supporting. "Because David was for it!" he responded. Now that's a problem dynamic. When personal feelings are running so high that they impede or even control intelligent problem solving and decision making, a group is in trouble. Only a strong leader with group support and a sick-leave taken by David allowed this group to regain its emotional equilibrium and do its job.

Thus there are relationships between such emotional conflicts and the messages group members exchange and process. In some cases *no decisions* result, policies stagnate, morale sags, and a vicious cycle has been started.

Gouran and Fisher give us their considered and chilling conclusions:

> Ambiguous and emotional language, personally oriented conflict, disruptions (especially those stimulated by the destruction of trust), irrelevancies, opinionatedness, lack

of direction, leaders' expressed preferences, inadequate collection and assessment of pertinent information, and rigidity all appear to reduce the probability that groups can execute their tasks effectively.[16]

David could plead guilty to all of the above and more—add poor listening— a very difficult person! More will be said regarding these matters in Chapter 6.

SPECIAL TYPES OF GROUPS

The same dynamics that often cause problems can also be put to positive use. Battles have been won by the synergistic cohesion of a group. Sports teams have pulled off the big upset by playing "over their heads" thanks to a new-found, almost mystical team-work.

The professional application of these powerful group dynamics to therapy and personal growth problems is an accepted procedure. They range from grief and family adjustment, drugs and alcohol, to improving one's self-concept and personal motivation. A few of the many available are briefly described here; they will be further detailed in Chapter 10.

ENCOUNTER GROUP

This special type of group started as the "t" (for training) group and was mainly interested in improving a person's "sensitivity" to others. It is a chilling experience for pragmatic, well-ordered (and sometimes insensitive) personalities. The heart of the sensitivity group process is to take away the task and the agenda. The only things left are the socio-emotional and interpersonal factors. Participants are then forced (theoretically) to face their own insensitivities in relating and interacting with others. This seemingly unstructured kind of group encounter appeared to be simplistic, and during the sixties a great many self-development programs got into the act. Some encounter groups were quite bizarre, often promising totally new personalities. By the seventies it was clear that encounter groups had the potential for self-destruction as well as for self-development and personal growth.[17] The apparent problem was a lack of professional leadership style (along with some charlatans). When a group turns on its members' personal habits, feelings, behaviors, and beliefs as the main agenda, a trained counselor or therapist is necessary to properly channel such often harsh feedback and personal evaluation. The encounter group is a fascinating dynamic, which in trained hands offers the promise of improving our human potential. Respected social psychologists from Maslow and Rogers to Elliot Aronson have endorsed it.

CONSCIOUSNESS RAISING (CR) GROUP

Early feminist groups seeking a strong, motivating identity discovered the synergy of an interacting group of people who possess *similar* motivations and characteristics. This discovery developed into a technique for raising one's consciousness about the women's movement. Other groups of the sixties also adopted CR sessions and claimed that such groups produced political and revolutionary commitment. By the seventies more conventional political and religious groups found adaptations of the CR techniques productive. In the eighties we find some business organizations holding CR-like sessions. I have observed them mostly among homogeneous sales, insurance, fund raising, and development groups.

The first requirement of this technique is that all group members have a common problem, attitude, and related identity. They must, for example, be all single mothers, all ex-priests, all gay, all Christian, and so forth. The double-edged assumption is that similar people are best able to help us in our personal growth.

The actual sessions may vary considerably. John Cragan and David Wright report four stages common to most CR groups: (1) self-realization of a new identity, (2) group identity through polarization, (3) establishment of new values for the group, and (4) acting out new consciousness.[18]

A typical session is leaderless and has six to twelve members of like mind, knowledge, and power. A subtopic may be chosen, but it is always part of the general attitude set. "Birth Control and the Modern Woman," "Fair Employment for Women," and "Equal Rights Amendment" can all be clearly related to and discussed in terms of the more general women's movement.

The group usually begins with short, uninterrupted, informal, personal-opinion and experience speeches. Each member gets a turn and when finished is subject only to questions of clarification or feedback that are clearly supportive. The heart of the process, at least at this point, is that *no* challenges, *no* arguments, *no* disagreements are allowed. A general discussion follows the last speaker, the next session is scheduled, and one's consciousness presumably has been raised.

On the negative side, when group synergy becomes too intense, consciousness and emotions may be raised so high that an elitist attitude demanding special privilege emerges.[19]

GESTALT GROUP

This type of group concentrates on a person's interpersonal inadequacies and emotional blocks to their resolution. The therapist leader works with one group member at a time. The observers are thought to help reinforce the training administered by the leader.

The Gestalt group is a less rigid application of psychoanalysis credited to Fritz Perls.[20] The method is often quite dramatic, concentrating on physical sensations, body awareness, and other nonverbal behaviors. It includes psychodrama,* role playing, group feedback, and other exercises all directed at helping one become aware of *how* one is responding rather than *why*. These existentially grounded techniques have also been associated with the Esalen Institute in Big Sur, California.

ASSERTIVENESS TRAINING

This is really a group therapy program usually advertised as an educational program for persons seeking social-skills training. Such training is now directed to like individuals with like interpersonal problems rather than to people who simply want to become more assertive and affirmative. Some interesting nontherapy applications emerged in the early eighties such as "Assertiveness Training for Women."

*Acting out a psychological drama based on a personal problem (e.g., grief, alcohol, obesity, fear, and so on).

"Assertive behavior is the skill to seek, maintain, or enhance reinforcement in an interpersonal situation through an expression of feelings or wants when such expression risks loss of reinforcement or even punishment."[21] This behavior is assessed and taught through structured group discussions and a role-playing procedure called *behavior rehearsal*. Group feedback on each participant's behavior and communication style is followed by suggestions from the therapist leader. Cornerstones of assertiveness training are a clear distinction between assertiveness and aggression and the firm refutation of irrational thinking.

ADDITIONAL FORMS

There are many special programs that use one or more of these methods and generally capitalize on the synergy and special dynamics of groups. They are utilized by therapists, counselors, and general trainers more interested in enhancing normal personal growth and development. Some examples follow.[22]

> Transactional analysis
> Synanon
> Existential/experiential
> Marathon
> Rational/emotive
> T-group
> Tavistock
> Reality
> Adlerian

SUMMARY

Hyperinterstimulation is more likely to happen with large crowds than with small groups, but the same mental mechanisms are present: anonymity, contagion, and suggestibility. This loss of a sense of responsibility and personal restraint is called *deindividuation*. *Groupthink* is a subtler form of losing one's critical-thinking ability, ". . . a concurrence-seeking tendency that interferes with critical thinking . . . when members' strivings for unanimity override their motivation to realistically appraise alternative courses of action . . . a deterioration of mental efficiency, reality testing, and moral judgment that results from in-group pressures [Janis]." To prevent groupthink one must guard against premature agreement, promote open discussion, avoid emotional reactions, and even play devil's advocate.

Risky decisions (or shift) refers to the risks one is willing to take given the possible gains. The risky decision is more apt to be made by a group than by any single individual. The *group-polarization hypothesis* suggests that the direction of a group's shift (Cautious ↔ Risky) depends upon what was initially the predominant view. A post-discussion may be more extreme but not necessarily toward the risk pole. Other explanations involve less personal responsibility, a charismatic leader, uncertainty reduction, excitement, persuasion, closed system reasoning, and social competition.

Closed system reasoning is another problem dynamic that causes a lack of group creativity and vision. Highly personal, affective conflicts, along with emotional language, opinionatedness, lack of information, and poor listening also qualify as problem dynamics.

Some special types of groups offer dynamics that can be put to positive use: encounter, sensitivity, consciousness raising, Gestalt, assertiveness training, and others such as transactional analysis, Synanon, T-group, and so forth.

PROJECTS AND CASES

PROJECTS

1. Remain near the center of an active group (for instance, a demonstration, a revival meeting, an athletic event, a fight, or a political rally) until you feel a sense of interstimulation (anonymity, contagion, suggestibility) or collective mind. Leave, and write the most detailed account possible of how you felt, what impulses came over you, what seemed to cause these impulses, and how the impulses might have been avoided.

2. Observe live or televised groups of people until you find two clear-cut examples each of (1) deindividuation and (2) groupthink. Describe each in a page or less.

3. Think of a time when you were a part of the *risky-shift* group phenomenon. Describe it in a page or less; be ready to discuss in class.

CASES

1. The Savage Corporation

For many years Mr. Peter Vallee, vice president of the Savage Corporation, has successfully combined the jobs of vice president in charge of production and labor relations manager. The firm's excellent record of good relations with the union has been due in part to the fact that Mr. Vallee knows in intimate detail every phase of production. He is the kind of executive who works with his sleeves rolled up and spends much of his time in the plant. In rate discussions with union representatives, he was completely master of the situation because he knew thoroughly the jobs on which rates were in dispute. And he was never a man to discuss a problem in the abstract. When a dispute arose with the union, he usually reached for his hat and said, "Let's go out and look at the job." This practical competence and his reputation for integrity, straightforwardness, and fairness had built up fine relations between union and management.

But at age 64 he found himself physically unable to handle both production and labor relations, and labor relations were turned over to Joseph Scoville. Scoville had not come up through the ranks, as Vallee had done. In fact, his previous experience had been with another firm. While he was in that firm his work had nothing to do with labor relations, but he had observed how disputes were handled. There had been prolonged wrangles and tough battles even over trivial issues; negotiations between labor and management were rather formal and marked by a good deal of hostility on both sides. It was from this observation that Scoville had formed his ideas of labor relations.

His first problem on the new job involved a dispute on the loading dock. The company contended that the loading crew was working at only 70 percent of pre-1985 efficiency, while the union insisted that there were differences now in the loading work due to differences in the design of the post-1985 models being loaded into freight cars. After one fruitless session Scoville prepared for the next by getting figures on comparable operations at the plants of competitors, which showed that the efficiency of the loading operation in his own plant was below that of competitors. When asked by the union for the source of his figures he refused to give it, saying that the information was given to him in confidence. This provoked a tirade from the union representatives, who accused him of underhanded methods and charged him with destroying good labor relations at the plant. After a stormy two hours, the session was adjourned without result.

QUESTIONS

1. What were the short- and long-range problems leading to this emotional meeting?
2. What can be done at this point in time?
3. How might this problem have been better handled?

2. The Company Picnic

Management began clamping down in certain plant areas in the interest of safety and economy. A memorandum was issued forbidding smoking in the women's washrooms because towels and lounges were sometimes burned through carelessness. This memo caused much resentment among the women employees, and they registered a complaint to management, who ignored it. Several weeks later, when invitations requesting attendance at a company picnic were sent out to employees, few even returned the reply card.

WHAT IS THE LESSON?

1. One of the strongest deterrents to upward communication is the failure to react to previous complaints.
2. Where safety and economy are involved, management must ignore complaints against a regulation.
3. Employees should have a voice in deciding what fire-safety measures should be taken.
4. Employees' complaints should be listened to sympathetically, even when nothing can be done.
5. In the interest of plant safety, management has to ignore some complaints.

NOTES

1. J. E. Singer, C. A. Brush, and S. C. Lublin, "Some Aspects of Deindividuation: Identification and Conformity," *Journal of Experimental Social Psychology*, 1 (1965), 356–78.
2. E. Diener, "Deindividuation: The Absence of Self-awareness and Self-regulation in Group Members," in *Psychology of Group Influence*, ed. P. B. Paulus (Hillsdale, N.J.: Erlbaum, 1980).
3. Irving L. Janis, *Victims of Groupthink* (Boston: Houghton Mifflin, 1982), p. 9.
4. Ibid., p. 12.
5. T. T. Herbert and R. W. Estes, "Improving Executive Decisions by Formalizing Dissent: The Corporate Devil's Advocate," *Academy of Management Review*, 2 (1977), 662–67.
6. Janis, *Victims of Groupthink*, p. 270.
7. This is also referred to as the *risky-shift* or *risky-choice phenomenon*. See Dorwin Cartwright, "Risk Taking by Individuals and Groups: An Assessment of Research Employing Choice Dilemmas," *Journal of Personality and Social Psychology*, 20 (1971), 361–78.
8. See N. Kogan and M. Wallach, *Risk-taking: A Study in Cognition and Personality* (New York: Holt, Rinehart & Winston, 1964). See also K. Dion, R. Baron, and N. Miller, "Why Do Groups Make Riskier Decisions than Individuals?" in *Advances in Experimental Social Psychology*, vol. 5, ed. L. Berkowitz (New York: Academic, 1970), pp. 306–78.

9. M. Wallach, N. Kogan, and R. Burt, "Are Risk Takers More Persuasive than Conservatives in Group Discussion?" *Journal of Experimental Social Psychology*, 4 (1968), 76–88.

10. For more on social comparison theory, see J. M. Suls and R. L. Miller, eds., *Social Comparison Processes* (New York: Halsted Press, 1977).

11. H. Lamm and D. G. Myers, "Group-induced Polarization of Attitudes and Behavior," in *Advances in Experimental Social Psychology*, vol. 11, ed. L. Berkowitz (New York: Academic, 1978).

12. Ibid.

13. For more on these matters, see Franklin J. Boster and Michael E. Mayer, "Differential Argument Quality Mediates the Impact of a Social Comparison Process of the Choice Shift," (unpublished paper from the International Communication Association convention, May 1984); also Jerold L. Hale, "The Effect of Ambiguity on Polarity Shift Processes," (unpublished paper from the International Communication Association convention, May 1984).

14. H. J. Leavitt, *Corporate Pathfinders* (New York: Penguin, 1987).

15. Kristin B. Valentine and B. Aubrey Fisher, "An Interaction Analysis of Verbal Innovative Deviance in Small Groups," *Speech Monographs*, 41 (November 1974), 413–20.

16. Dennis S. Gouran and B. Aubrey Fisher, "The Functions of Human Communication in the Formation, Maintenance, and Performance of Small Groups," in *Handbook of Rhetorical and Communication Theory*, eds. Carroll C. Arnold and John Waite Bowers (Boston: Allyn and Bacon, 1984), p. 631.

17. M. A. Lieberman, J. D. Yalom, and M. B. Miles, *Encounter Groups: First Facts* (New York: Basic Books, 1973), p. 264.

18. John F. Cragan and David W. Wright, *Communication in Small Group Discussions* (St. Paul, Minn.: West, 1986), pp. 44–50; see also James W. Chesebro, J. F. Cragan, and P. McCullough, "The Small Group Technique of the Radical Revolutionary: A Synthetic Study of Consciousness-Raising," *Communication Monographs*, 40 (1973), 136–46.

19. Ibid., p. 49.

20. See Fritz Perls, *Gestalt Therapy Verbatim* (Lafayette, Calif.: Real People Press, 1969).

21. A. Rich and H. Schroeder, "Research Issues in Assertiveness Training," *Psychological Bulletin*, 83 (1976), 1082.

22. See J. Hansen, R. Warner, and E. Smith, *Group Counseling: Theory and Process* (Chicago: Rand McNally, 1980).

PROBLEM SOLVING AND DECISION MAKING

DEFINITIONS

Problem solving involves a combination of recurring phases and/or sequential stages directed toward resolving the difficulty under consideration. Decision making occurs within this process whenever reasonably clear alternatives emerge and choices must be made. They are both part of the same system where interacting groups are charged with resolving problems and taking or recommending action.

INDIVIDUAL VERSUS GROUP SUCCESS

Should I join a study group or prepare for the big exam alone? A decision is necessary even if I do both, but the emphasis and effort may be directed mostly on the problem or question. This leads to the general question of whether or not some decisions might better be pondered and worked out *alone* rather than by a group. Mixed evidence exists. Much depends on *who* is making the decision. How much expertise is involved? How much time is available? While medical second opinions make good sense, most of us would prefer the best-qualified surgeon available to remove our appendix fast and without a group meeting.

To further confound the alone-versus-group question, one prominent social psychologist suggests that in some difficult tasks the presence of others only interferes with learning. R. B. Zajonc advises students to study alone, preferably in an isolated cubicle.[1] He then states that a group publicly observing you take the exam will exert a beneficial, social-facilitating effect.

Medical schools emphasize facts acquisition usually achieved by cramming students full of information in lectures, followed by testing. As a learning tool this format has recently been challenged. Not only is it inefficient, but it also suggests "one right answer" and does not teach a physician to "make decisions in light of uncertainty."[2]

A new problem-solving pedagogy has emerged. David Holzman describes this approach currently being used at six medical schools in the United States and Canada:

> Students solve real medical problems, instead of scribbling lecture notes. In these so-called problem-based tracks, lectures are reduced to less than five hours a week or eliminated entirely. Instead, students meet several times a week with a faculty member in groups of a half-dozen or so. Typically, the faculty tutor presents a fictitious case such as "an old man short of breath," sometimes with an actor specially trained to simulate the symptoms.
>
> The students must figure out what subject matter they need to know to diagnose the case, and then divide responsibility for learning that subject matter among themselves. They each spend one to two days in the library, and at the following meeting, they synthesize the material into a diagnosis. The students share their newly acquired knowledge through discussions and questions.[3]

The goal we are seeking and the type of task we are attempting clearly make a difference in how we judge group success. We may, for example, be seeking the goal of better group cohesion or member satisfaction with less interest in the task itself, whatever its nature. In most organizational groups, however, we are very much interested in productivity.

Group dynamicist Ivan Steiner[4] has usefully classified tasks by analyzing *divisibility* (can it be broken into subparts?), *task goal* (are we seeking quantity or quality?), and *member inputs* (what is their character, and how do they affect group product?).

I've discovered that my garden is a divisible task (planning, tilling, planting, weeding, and harvesting) and therefore, a group is an asset. A single flower pot on the patio or deck, however, is a unitary task that a single person can usually handle.

When the task goal is to see how many widgets a group can produce or maximize, then the more the better (quantity). If we are trying to build a car that matches the *quality* of a specific European sportscar, we are dealing with preset standards, and we are judged in terms of how closely we meet them.

Steiner divides member or individual inputs into five types of tasks that relate to group behavior and group product:

1. *Additive.* Group product depends on adding up individual inputs (stuffing envelopes).
2. *Compensatory.* Group product depends on averaging individual inputs (how many beans in the jar?).
3. *Disjunctive.* Group product depends on one specific yes/no, either/or answer (negotiate or strike).
4. *Conjunctive.* Group product depends on the contributions of all (an airplane crew).
5. *Discretionary.* Group product and methods are left to the free choice of the group (delegate, vote, debate, average, seek consensus, and so on).

In the Steiner typology of tasks, any particular task can be classified theoretically as to type. However complex, it does make clear that group effectiveness covaries with the type of task it has undertaken.

While there are other variables such as good communication that affect group productivity, certainly the type of task and the resources of the group are critical to small groups in organizational problem solving. While Steiner's typology and generalizations are the result of some very close and mostly closed-system reasoning, and the problems used to generate data are somewhat plastic (hypothetical puzzles, paradoxes, and quan-

TABLE 4.1 A Summary of the Potential Productivity of Groups Working on Various Types of Tasks

TYPE OF TASK	PRODUCTIVITY EFFECT	DESCRIPTION
Additive	"Better than the best"	Group outperforms even the best individual member
Compensatory	"Better than most"	Group outperforms a substantial number of the individual members
Disjunctive (Eureka)	"Equal to the best"	Group performance matches the performance of the "best" member
Disjunctive (non-Eureka)	"Less than the best"	Group performance can match that of the "best" member, but often falls short
Conjunctive (unitary)	"Equal to the worst"	Group performance matches the performance of the "worst" member
Conjunctive (divisible with matching)	"Better than the worst"	If subtasks properly matched to ability of members, group performance can reach high levels
Discretionary	"Variable"	Group performance is substantially dependent on the performance process adopted by the group

daries), the typology is very creative. A summary of his generalizations is shown in Table 4.1. Note that in the disjunctive (non-Eureka) and the conjunctive (unitary) group efforts do not fare very well. "Eureka" refers to those case problems where once someone figures it out, it is patently clear to all (e.g., the missionary/cannibal).

ASSETS AND LIABILITIES OF GROUPS

With the support of a U.S. Public Health Service grant, Norman Maier was able to sort out the forces operating in small groups that are assets and liabilities and some that can be either, depending largely on the communication and leadership skills of the members. A summary of his report follows.[5]

GROUP ASSETS

More Information Is Available   When a broad range of knowledge is required, a group should have an advantage over individuals.

More Approaches Are Available   More people usually represent more ways of analyzing a problem. Groups should help individuals prevent tunnel vision and closed system reasoning.

Participation Increases Acceptance   When decisions require strong acceptance, group involvement with the issues should enhance comprehension and support, other things being equal.

Better Communication of the Decision Relaying the decision to those who must act on it is improved. This is particularly true if the executors are also part of the decision group.

GROUP LIABILITIES

Unreasonable Social Pressure All of the problem dynamics (groupthink, risky shift, and so forth) fit here. Agreement may become more important than a quality decision based on the facts.

Premature and/or Noncritical Agreement Maier calls this "valence of solutions." Groups that quickly reach what seems like an obvious solution often do not critically evaluate it. This interruption of the critical-thinking process can also be aided and abetted by a vocal minority or a skilled manipulator.

Individual Domination Unreasonable influence is controlled by one person through excessive and intense participation or stubborn persistence (fatiguing the opposition).

Debate Supersedes Discussion Winning the argument or case for your particular solution becomes an end in itself. Finding the *best* solution no longer matters—you've found it!

MIXED FACTORS

Disagreement Healthy disagreement can lead to better, more innovative group solutions. Unhealthy disagreement can lead to emotional, personal animosities, irrelevant arguments, and low-quality decisions. How emergent or assigned leadership reads the signs of such disagreement (and deals with them) is critical.

Single Problem Perspective Maier calls this "conflicting interests versus mutual interests." Limiting the problem by first gauging the range of opinions and perspectives and locating mutual interests is usually an asset. Otherwise a group may overlook the fact that there may be separate problems deserving separate decisions. At its worst each person is discussing his or her own "single problem perspective" without really being aware of it: "I'm sorry; I thought birth control and abortion were the same problem."

Risk-Taking That groups sometimes are polarity prone was discussed previously. That a group might take necessary and acceptable risks that an individual would not is the asset dimension.

Time Elapsed Group decisions usually take more time than those made by an individual but not always. A procrastinating, confused, conservative, or uncourageous leader can delay a decision for a very long time. How a group uses its allotted time can also make time an asset or a liability.

Attitude Shift Who changes and in what direction is the critical point for Maier. If an unconstructive minority prevails in its persuasion, it is considered a liability. If persons with the most constructive views prevail, attitude shift is an asset. One's perception of "constructive view" is in itself a mixed factor.

PROCESSUAL NATURE OF GROUP COMMUNICATION

PHASE/STAGE MODELS

We are interested here in how groups change and how they develop ideas. Process implies dynamic, ongoing change. Small group experts have typically taken one of two basic approaches in describing these developmental changes. The *recurring phase* model suggests that certain aspects, themes, issues, or parts of the process regularly prevail during the life of a group but not necessarily in any consistent order or sequence. The *sequential stage* model suggests again that certain aspects, themes, or parts dominate the discussions and that they *do* tend to follow a typical step order during the group's developmental life. The latter model has been the starting point for most of the extant agenda recommendations.

RECURRING PHASES

Therapy Groups

The therapy-type groups discussed in Chapter 3 are an illustration of this process notion. Change and development in these groups are usually described in terms of three distinguishable and prevailing *but not* necessarily sequential aspects or themes: (1) leader dependency, (2) pairing for emotional support, and (3) fight-flight responses.[6] These are distinguishing peculiarities (phases) that regularly recur in such groups. There are no ordinal priorities among them.

Interaction Process Analysis (IPA)

A better example for our purposes is the equilibrium model of Robert Bales called *Interaction Process Analysis*, which delineates two major distinguishing-theme categories: (1) *socio-emotional* and (2) *task*. The socio-emotional aspect refers to the interpersonal-relating problems the group experiences, the task to the content or job of the group apart from personalities.

Later Bales and fellow researcher Fred Strodtbeck added a third aspect, *control*.[7] This included communications about possible directions and ways of action for the group to take. This third aspect or phase was based on their "Interaction Process Analysis" of problem-solving groups. They further found that in the *socio-emotional* or interpersonal phase, the communications pertained to *orientation, information, repetition*, and *confirmation*; in the task phase, the interactions were seeking *analysis, evaluation*, and *communications*, or giving *opinions* and *feelings*. Bales and Strodtbeck also indicate that as a group approaches the *control* phase, it experiences increasing strain on the members' solidarity and social-emotional relationships. Both positive and negative reactions tend to increase. The reduction of tension and conflict is apparent as differences are resolved and agreement is reached. The Bales' model is really a system for classifying communicative acts and will be discussed in Chapter 10.

TABLE 4.2 Five Stages of Group Development

STAGE	MAJOR PROCESSES	CHARACTERISTICS
Forming	Development of attraction bonds; exchange of information; orientation toward others and situation	Tentative interactions; polite discourse; concern over ambiguity; silences
Storming	Dissatisfaction with others; competition among members; disagreement over procedures; conflict	Ideas are criticized; speakers are interrupted; attendance is poor; hostility
Norming	Development of group structure; increased cohesiveness and harmony; establishment of roles and relationships	Agreement on rules; consensus-seeking; increased supportiveness; we-feeling
Performing	Focus on achievement; high task orientation; emphasis on performance and productivity	Decision making; problem solving; increased cooperation; decreased emotionality
Adjourning	Termination of duties; reduction of dependency; task completion	Regret; increased emotionality; disintegration

Source: From D. R. Forsyth, *An Introduction to Group Dynamics*, p. 20. Copyright © 1983 by Wadsworth, Inc. Reprinted by permission of Brooks/Cole Publishing Company, Pacific Grove, Calif. 93950.

SEQUENTIAL STAGES

Tuckman 5 Stage

Bruce W. Tuckman found the same two *recurring* phases that Bales discovered. In addition, he reported five *sequential stages* in most of the fifty studies he reviewed. That is, these distinguishable steps (stages) appear typically in a 1, 2, 3 order and recur throughout the group's five-stage development. The five stages are shown in Table 4.2.

Simon Stages

Most of these studies and models are primarily interested in the social and psychological dimensions of group development. The problem or task in such research groups was mostly a means to such an end or interest. H. A. Simon, however, is mostly interested in the task from a management view.[8] His four stages* or four-step process is thought to fit either an individual or a group faced with a problem needing a solution or decision. They are

1. *Intelligence activity*. Seeking information about the problem, as in "military intelligence."
2. *Design activity*. Inventing, developing, and analyzing possible courses of action.
3. *Choice activity*. Selecting a specific course of action.
4. *Review activity*. Assessing choices made in the past.

*Simon calls these four ingredients sequential phases.

PROGRESSIVE PHASE MODELS

These explanations of how groups solve problems, develop ideas, and approach decisions might better be called progressive *cycle* models. A cycle in this context may be defined as (1) "a course or series of events or operations that recur regularly and usually lead back to a starting point," and (2) "an interval of time during which a sequence of a recurring succession of events or phenomena is completed." (Webster)

Reach-testing

A pioneering study by Thomas Scheidel and Laura Crowell[9] using an improved system of interaction analysis[10] found a cyclical or "spiral-like" phenomenon in which ideational backtracking and reaching out recurred regularly. They called this reaching out for new ideas *reach-testing*. Once a group has reached some ideational agreement or anchoring position, members then reach out and test still more ideas. If the new idea is group approved, they progress forward to a new anchoring position; if the idea is rejected, the group backtracks to its former position and starts the cycle anew. Ideas slowly progress and build on previous agreements. Therefore, at the end of the cycle there is a diminishing need to backtrack. It is a cumulative, progressive phase or cycle phenomenon. This spiraling, cyclical model has been described as a "Slinky" toy (see Figure 4.1). The spirals of steel may be more compressed at the end of the spring in the same way as ideas are compressed when a group finally nears agreement.

After studying idea development in ten discussions, Scheidel and Crowell concluded that members devoted one-fourth of their comments to confirming statements and another fourth to clarifying and substantiating them. The latter function is represented by the outward movement of this spiral model. The progress toward decision is represented as the onward movement.

Decision Emergence

Fisher's descriptive research is an expansion of the spiral reach-testing model discovered by Scheidel and Crowell.[11] Fisher concentrated on the task dimension and found that decisions appeared to *emerge* in a gradual, cumulative process. The groups studied tended to confirm decisions *after* they had already been made. Fisher then describes and postulates four progressive phases that groups go through: orientation, conflict, emergence, and reinforcement. Distinctions among these phases blur and Fisher considers the phases cumulative (what I call progressive) rather than linear. However, the model is generally sequential, and even Fisher has commented that "Decisions appear to emerge in four progressive stages."[12] These provide much insight into the processual nature of group communication.

Orientation Phase   This is an early, typically first phase in which the group tentatively searches for ideas and directions. Attitudes expressed are generally am-

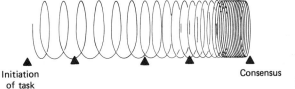

Initiation
of task

Consensus

Figure 4.1

biguous in this phase, becoming more forthright as issues become better clarified and the social climate is better understood. It is a period of uncertainty reduction and getting acquainted.

Conflict Phase   The group now progresses into ideational argument and debate over the emerging issues and decision proposals.[13] Data and evidence usually come forth, coalitions often form, and interaction analysis suggests that a polarization of attitudes takes place. These ideational conflicts (Fisher's main interest) have been described as *innovative deviance*. Valentine and Fisher in 1974 discovered that innovative deviance serves different functions during the four phases.[14] In this phase it produces a healthy, "salutary" effect. In the orientation and reinforcement phases (or is it stages?), their study suggests that it is detrimental. This seems reasonable—to come on too strong, too soon, whether on the ideas or interpersonally is usually disruptive. Clearly, to refight and rehash the issues and preliminary decisions *after* they have been agreed to earlier is also a good way to slow down the process and become unpopular as well. This is not to say that some last minute review or a "last look" isn't a good idea. The context, the special organizational setting, the urgency for decision, and the issue or issues may seriously alter the character and intensity of conflict in this phase. More will be said of conflict in Chapter 6.

Emergence Phase   In this phase ambiguity toward decision proposals appears again while dissent and conflict decline. The ambiguity is less tentative than in the orientation phase. However, dissent appears to be seeking some accommodation, and opposition attitudes weaken. Coalitions weaken or disappear in this phase as the consensus for decision emerges, often with considerable help from an emergent task leader.

Reinforcement Phase   Assuming all has gone well in the previous three phases, that is, the group didn't fall apart because of unresolvable ideational or interpersonal conflict, then a spirit of unity appears. Members positively reinforce one another's favorable opinions and foster decision consensus and commitment.

The emphasis in Fisher's research that led to this useful model was on task behavior. Fisher concedes that the task and interpersonal (socio-emotional) dimensions are interdependent. The recurring phases described earlier, while more likely to occur in Fisher's conflict phase, can appear anywhere in a group's development. Sometimes, as we shall see in Chapter 5, these more personal and emotional phases reach such a high intensity that interaction ceases and the group disintegrates.

METHODS OF DECISION MAKING

CONTINGENCY ANALYSIS

In organizational settings, unlike some of the one-time, zero-history groups studied in the previous pages, subsequent decisions are affected by previous decisions, ongoing developments, policies, assigned leaders, and the place where your group fits into the total system. Systems are not only quite different from one organization to another but also may change internally while you're still working on a decision. A new and unexpected union contract, a takeover, a merger, suprasystem managerial changes, new legal and governmental constraints or demands—these and more confound and complicate decision making.

One needs a middle or contingency view between natural or universal phases and sequences and the view that each decision (or organization) is so unique that no generalizations are helpful. Knowing one's own organization and how its system works and relates to its environment is a good first step.

Fremont Kast and James Rosenzweig suggest at least two general organizational forms or styles one might encounter. They describe (1) a *stable-mechanistic* form where stable, uniform operations exist as in a refrigerator assembly line with precise planning and control, and (2) an *adaptive-organic* form where dynamic technologies and an uncertain environment exist such as one might find in an advertising agency.

Systems that may lead to *stable-mechanistic* styles of management and decision making are described as follows:

1. The environment is relatively stable and certain.
2. The goals are well defined and enduring.
3. The technology is relatively uniform and stable.
4. There are routine activities and productivity is the major objective.
5. Decision making is programmable and coordination and control processes tend to make a tightly structured, hierarchical system possible.

Systems that may lead to *adaptive-organic* styles are characterized by the following:

1. The environment is relatively uncertain and turbulent.
2. The goals are diverse and changing.
3. The technology is complex and dynamic.
4. There are many nonroutine activities in which creativity and innovation are important.
5. Heuristic decision-making processes are utilized and coordination and control occur through reciprocal adjustments. The system is less hierarchical and more flexible.[15]

In the ongoing evolution and development of organizational theory, a more eclectic view based on systems theory combined with analysis of the contingencies found in specific situations has emerged. Decision making becomes still more complex. Dennis Moberg and James Koch put it well:

> An applier of contingency views must recognize more and different kinds of goals and needs for his organization, consider more factors bearing on a decision, employ a wider variety of ways of making and carrying out decisions, and evaluate decisions not on a one-by-one basis, but in relation to each other. Therefore, practitioners must be made aware that they must learn new approaches to solving organizational problems if they choose to use contingency views.[16]

Kast and Rosenzweig attempt to model this organizational development. Their model shown in Figure 4.2 suggests still another more specific systems application of decision theory.

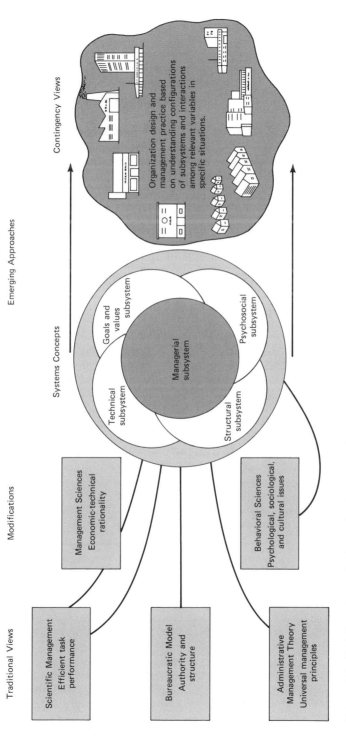

Figure 4.2 Evolution of organization and management theory toward systems concepts and contingency views.

By permission of Fremont E. Kast and James E. Rosenzweig, Organization and Management, 1979, and McGraw-Hill Book Company.

METHODS

Consensus

Consensus implies decision agreement and commitment. It need not be unanimous agreement nor total commitment. However, it is one that *all accept* as probably the best solution or compromise they are going to get, which will evoke some kind of support beyond toleration.

Unanimity is a rare phenomenon. "Unanimous group endorsements" are typically voted by the majority on a parliamentary resolution. "We offer our unanimous congratulations to the new chairperson by a vote of 13 yes, 12 no, and 10 abstentions." To seek 100 percent consensus is a time-consuming, frustrating, however noble, search. Except in very homogeneous groups, such efforts usually result in either no decision, decisions so late in coming that they make little difference, or a phony commitment just "to get it over with."

For some experts it is primarily commitment rather than agreement that defines consensus:

> . . . even though some members might disagree with the decision on principle, they will accept it and personally carry out their part.[17]

Except for resolutions that are majority voted "unanimously," consensus decisions are not typically unanimous nor voted nor need they be. Some leaders and groups that know and "read" one another very well (or that are being hoodwinked) may infer implicit agreement from group silence or inaction. "May I presume consensus and move on?" "Hearing no objections . . . " These kinds of experiences have led some people to use the word *consensus* in this informal and limiting way.

The search for consensus as described in the first paragraph of this section should allow and encourage all members to be heard, to listen, and to feel involved in the decision process. It is an idealistic, laudatory, and sometimes slow method of decision making. Many of the roadblocks to consensus decision making are procedural as well as interpersonal and task in character. Here are some guidelines that cover all three:

1. Maintain flexibility; listen for ideas better than your own; be tolerant of substantive conflict.
2. Seek out and *listen* to differences of opinion.
3. Restrain emotionality; concentrate on substantive issues (the task).
4. Beware of false consensus; ask for reasons behind sudden opinion changes.
5. Vote only as a last resort; seek a manifest acceptance of and commitment to the solution.

Vote

Like consensus, voting is not always a simple concept or even a simple behavior. In organizational settings the voting rules and procedures themselves are often debated before they are used to effect a decision.

In a democratic classroom situation with no bylaws, past practices, policies, or constitution to complicate your voting, it's easy to understand that *majority vote* (one more than half) decides. Not so in situations where constitutions, bylaws, and policies are in place. If, for example, your group is to legally transact business, you may first have to decide if you have a *quorum*. Who *decides* a quorum for a subcommittee is often very clear but not always. Even boards typically cannot decide their own quorum; it is usually the prerogative of the parent body. If no rules pertain, parliamentary law suggests a simple majority of the members. Most organizations do specify quorums for transacting business ranging from 90 percent for a fraternity or sorority to perhaps 20 percent for a church. Where the decisions by vote are controversial, one may also have trouble defining a *voting member*. To further complicate voting, all members may not be equal. In one university, department members had from one-half to four votes each depending upon their rank.

All decision votes then are not simple majorities. To change some policies or rules such as bylaws and constitutions may take a three-fourths majority. To suspend the rules may take a two-thirds majority. If you're electing someone, it may take a two-thirds majority to close nominations.

Some decision voting must be done by ballot. One encyclopedia of parliamentary rules devotes six technical pages explaining how to do it.

More will be said of the criticality of understanding organization voting rules in the next section on process planning.[18] For now let the lesson be that decision by vote is often a very complex procedure, and that members are well advised to study the rules, policies, and past practices of their particular group.

Leader Prerogative

Even the most democratic of organizations usually reserve some decisions for the designated leader. In some cases where policy does not intrude, it may be such simple *sounding* things as office or work space, schedules, and committee assignments. Of course a group may also simply defer a decision to its leader: ''Do what you think is best—we trust you.''

Most organizations in the private sector reserve still more areas for leader prerogative. Manager leaders are paid more because they are assigned more responsibility. If their groups foul things up, it is the leaders' heads that higher management will seek. Managers are therefore given more authority to get the job done, often including the right to reject their groups' or staffs' decisions and go their own way.

Some organizations are formally set up in a line–staff arrangement where *all* critical decisions are left to the line person in charge. The military is a good illustration and not necessarily an atypical one. For example, a high ranking air force commander (line) may have three problem-solving staff groups reporting to him or her (see Figure 4.3).

Command decisions are *never* made by a staff officer. Staffs only recommend courses of action. The commander is given a thorough appraisal of the problem, a suggested course of action, and an explanation of why the staff believes such action will achieve a satisfactory solution. The commander may accept, reject, return to staff for more consideration, or, in rare cases, choose a personal solution. The commander makes the decision.

Most modern organizations (including the military) have a range or continuum of leader prerogative. In moments of crisis there is usually less democracy in the decision making. Policy and issue may also decide leader prerogative; so too might the particular style of the individual leader. Some styles allow for more emergent leadership and subsequent decision power. More will be said of these matters in Chapter 8.

Robert Tannenbaum and Warren Schmidt described leadership decision behavior years ago in a manner that has stood the test of time. It characterizes seven kinds

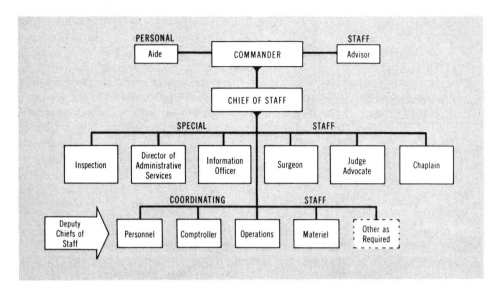

Figure 4.3 A typical "multiple directorate" staff organization, showing the position of the chief of staff and a common interpretation of the terms "personal staff," "special staff," and "coordinating staff."

of leader prerogatives ranging from a simple announcement of his or her decision, "This is it group; implement it" (when such power is policy), to a democratic group decision "within limits defined by superior."[19]

In more recent times, many upper-level managers still have near "command" power and depend on their staffs to initiate and implement action on decisions. Many lower-level managers still tend to have more decisions initiated for them and are more often required to consult with a superior before making a decision.

Much of the leader prerogative emphasis is directed at saving time. Perhaps some group meetings are long and dull because a leader, in an attempt to be democratic, is avoiding decisions that are within his or her own job description to make. On the other hand, for a leader to assume such power when it is not clearly granted and understood by all is to invite decision disaster, particularly at the implementation stage.

Delegation, Referral, and Delay

Some decisions a group deals with may be delegated to a subgroup such as a standing committee, an ad hoc committee, or even an expert individual. This may be done democratically or autocratically, depending upon your organization and the nature of the issues involved. Unless it has been delegated out of policy demands, the responsibility remains with the parent group—only the authority has been granted. Your superiors will hold you and your group accountable, not the subcommittee to whom you have delegated the job or decision. Of course that group is accountable to your group.

Some organizational structures are so devised that certain decisions *must* be referred to special groups. A labor problem often must be referred to the industrial relations group, a safety problem to the safety group, or a financial decision to the accounting group. In some organizations there is even a "committee on committees" that must be consulted in special cases. When the decision involves grievances, it may be necessary to refer it to a formal grievance committee.

No decision, postponement, or delay for whatever reason is still a decision, not always problem related or intended but a decision nevertheless. And not always a bad one! Some group decisions are better delayed. In heated, emotional group interactions, one might better cool it or seek a viable solution of the moment, a much used technique by university groups during the antiwar protests and other periods of student unrest.

Suppose your group follows some kind of parliamentary rules but has no policy that *demands* delegation, referral, and delay of a given problem needing solution. And yet you wish to delegate, refer, or delay. Voting rules may now pertain. Someone wishing to force a decision may move ''the previous question.'' This stops discussion and forces a vote, which, if seconded, typically requires a two-thirds vote. Another member who wishes to defer or delay action may move ''to table,'' which takes only a majority vote. Still other motions are available for specifically postponing or referring to committees. (See the Appendix, Parliamentary Rules.) More will be said of parliamentary forms of discussion in Chapter 5.

Negotiation, Mediation, and Arbitration

Some decisions that involve very divergent goals on the part of factions in a given group may necessitate compromises that are brought about by *bargaining* rather than by some kind of consensus seeking. ''Labor will back off on wage demands if management will loosen the work rules.'' Negotiations sometimes call for third-party interventions: experts, lawyers, ombudsmen, consultants, fact-finders, and mediators. These people or groups try to help your group negotiate and finally reach a compromise agreement. They do not make the decision for you. There are Federal and State Mediation Services available when the problems involve labor agreements. In the larger area of labor contracts, when bargaining breaks down we are faced with strikes, lockouts, and other forceful efforts to bring about good-faith bargaining and agreement decisions.

When a work group and its leader cannot solve day-to-day differences of opinion over work rules, contract interpretations, or general perceptions of unfairness, most contracts provide for a three-step grievance procedure. This procedure is designed to

Figure 4.4   B.C. by Johnny Hart.

By permission of Johnny Hart and Creators Syndicate, Inc.

solve problems and make decisions at the lowest level, that is, as close to the "rub" as possible. When this fails the grievance goes up to higher levels and higher authority.

When bargaining breaks down at all steps of the grievance procedure, some organizations have an arbitration clause in their agreement (at least for specified kinds of grievances). The grieving parties agree on a referee, an umpire, or an arbitrator who hears the case or debate and makes a decision, one that all parties agree to abide by in advance.

Conflict is involved in all of these negotiation and intervention methods of decision making. Some conflict is unavoidable in organizations and often useful in avoiding complacency and groupthink. However, when such conflict is uncontrolled, one may spend more time in grievance procedure and in preparation for arbitration than on the job the organization was designed to do. Chapter 6 will deal with interpersonal and intergroup conflicts in more detail.

IMPLEMENTING A DECISION

Good decisions are often lost or diminished because groups and their leaders fail to establish a procedure for putting them into effect. "Well, we really solved things; let's go home." It happens especially when another group (or groups) is responsible for carrying out the decision. If your group is responsible for the implementation as well as the decision, make sure everyone knows his or her specific role or task and has a timetable for completion of the task.

If other groups are to act on decisions already made, make sure they have adequate information and an opportunity to interact with the decision makers. Communication between decision groups and implementation groups is critical. Don't assume that implementation is automatic and is always S.O.P. (standard operating procedure). It takes time, coordination, and communication to break work down into manageable, accountable units, but it is well worth it.

When two or more groups need to coordinate, information must not only be carefully sorted out and coded by the senders but also verified by the receivers. Implementation procedure is only as good as the communication that affects it.

In some long-range, very complex implementation cases, elaborate, computer-assisted programs are utilized. PERT (Program Evaluation and Review Technique), first devised to assist the Navy Polaris missile program, has been used by many industries from defense to heavy construction. PERT allows a group to review its implementation flow plan in diagram form. It reveals time schedules, impending bottlenecks, personnel requirements, and, most important, the character, kind, and time frame of future decisions that may have to be made. It helps locate and define the *critical path* that very specific implementation must follow. A review of the PERT procedure follows.

STEPS IN PERT[20]

1. Discussion is completed. Group has defined problem, discovered facts, made statement of causes, determined authority, limitations, and goals, suggested solutions, selected a solution, phrased the solution as a program.
2. Group specifies final event that signals completion of its program.
3. Group lists events that must happen before the final event and assigns reference numbers.
4. Immediate, necessary, precedent events are determined for each event.

5. A blank PERT diagram is drawn showing connection of events. Extraneous and redundant events are deleted.

6. Activities are listed between each pair of events.

7. Group makes best, worst, most likely time estimates for activities, and time estimated in days (t_e) is calculated for each track. Variances are calculated for each event.

8. Expected completion time is calculated by summation for each event. Where activities converge, maximum expected completion time (T_E) is used.

9. Scheduled completion date is determined. Latest allowable time is calculated for each event. Where activities converge, minimum latest time allowable (T_L) is used.

10. Slack time is calculated for each track to final event. Critical path is drawn based on path with least slack.

11. Probability estimate of satisfactory completion is made based on critical path.

PROCESS PLANNING

IMPORTANCE

It seems obvious that planning or "thinking ahead" about *what* one is to do and *how* one is to do it makes good sense. Perhaps that's one reason why it is so uncommon, at least among unstructured small groups. Perhaps it's the overload of structure our society has already put on us. Try the amount of preplanning and planning headaches necessary to pay your income tax or to get into the college of your choice. "Order but not structure" is still a plea from students today.

For whatever reason, there is evidence that small discussion groups of students rarely plan strategies or procedures they will follow. In one study of 100 task-group discussions only one and one-half comments about the planning process were made per group.[21] Yet when groups in the same study did discuss process, that data was positively related to improved performance.

In another experiment where groups were encouraged to discuss the process, plan, or strategy they would follow, their task requiring intermember coordination was clearly improved.[22] In a group communication study by Hirokawa, the main factor that distinguished successful student groups from failing ones was the number of process-planning remarks made during the discussions.[23]

Still we resist process planning. The task overpowers us and process takes a lower priority. It seems like a waste of time: "We'll proceed as we always do." Clearly, knowledge about process and the planning of how you will proceed are superior to plunging into the task and hopefully letting the process evolve.

PROBLEM SOLVING PATTERNS

Prescriptions and Systems

These patterns, or what some small group people call *agendas**, are thought to follow some kind of a natural system of phases or sequences as previously discussed. Many, as we shall see, are thought to be extensions of our natural thinking process.

*We will refer to them as patterns or procedural formats to distinguish them from specific business agendas.

In truth they are mostly prescriptive, but there is nothing wrong with prescriptions if they are good ones and if they allow for reasonable flexibility.

Some would not agree. "Probably the greatest reason to dismiss the use of agendas [Problem Solving Patterns]* is that they just don't work."[24] Even Professor Fisher doesn't fight the "comfort" some people feel with the order inherent in generic-type patterns: "...I shall take the position that the group members themselves should decide whether an agenda is used."[25] Some organizational settings will not permit such freedom in planning. Written business agendas are often requested in advance, and meetings of busy people are expected to run according to some acceptable, problem-solving pattern.

Some of the research does partially support Fisher, but usually only when other strong forces such as emotions, cliques, and special interests offset or overcome orderly problem solving.[26] The bulk of the research clearly supports the value of some sort of orderly, rational problem solving.[27] That orderliness pays off in agreement is shown in a study of seventy-two conferences by Collins and Guetzkow. They report: "Those meetings in which discussion is orderly in its treatment of topics, and without backward references to previously discussed issues, tended to end in more consensus. . . . When participants discussed but one issue at a time, instead of simultaneously dabbling in two or three, it was more possible for the group to reach consensus."[28]

A medical prescription is a written direction for a therapeutic or corrective agent or, more commonly, a written direction for the preparation and use of a medicine. As a system such prescriptions are pretty much closed, at least where the medicine is concerned. Closed systems do what they do, at least theoretically, regardless of what goes on around them. The danger and harm resulting from using a bad or negligently advised medical prescription is real and often irreversible. The comparison is not totally fair for socially based recommendations and so-called prescriptions. These order-based agenda recommendations have considerably more built-in flexibility and, from a systems theory perspective, they are nowhere near as closed.

We also find closed systems (or nearly so) operating as part of open systems in other, comparative illustrations. Given the driver, the road, and the fuel requirements, an automobile is a relatively open system. However, consider the closed (or nearly so) systems within the suprasystem (the car)—parts that are now replaced in toto when they fail: electronic ignitions, fuel monitors, speed controls, inertial switches, and many more.

Small groups in organizational settings must realistically face many rules, policies, time frames, computer interfaces, and so forth, which also prescribe and to that extent close an otherwise open system. One must be ever vigilant against letting these forces close down the creative freedom of an open system. It is a serious concern and rightly so.

Just as medical prescriptions, electronic ignitions, policies, and rules when intelligently and properly applied have a beneficial and salutary effect, so too with problem-solving patterns or formats. Keep your open-system perspective, insist on flexibility, but remember the recurring phases, the progressive phases, the sequential stages that frequently appear. This is how an open-systems orientation can accommodate not only problem-solving patterns but also the inevitable restrictions and constraints found in organizational settings.

*Brackets ours.

Reflective Thinking

Most of the problem-solving patterns that follow owe their existence to philosopher John Dewey and also to speech communication pioneers like James H. McBurney, Kenneth G. Hance, Henry Lee Ewbank, and J. Jeffery Auer.[29] These men were among the first to adapt Dewey's reflective-thinking explanations of individual problem solving to group problem solving.

Reflective thinking was defined by John Dewey as "active, persistent, and careful consideration of any belief or supposed form of knowledge in the light of the grounds that support it, and further conclusions to which it tends,"[30] as opposed to nondeliberate, everyday thinking. Dewey thought of reflective thinking as a scientific habit, one that consisted of acquiring the attitude of *suspended judgment* and mastering the various methods of searching for materials. Maintaining an intelligent state of doubt and practicing systematic inquiry are the essentials of reflecting thinking.

Dewey's view of general education is also pertinent to group discussion, both as problem-solving patterns and in the way we conduct ourselves. He thought of the aim of education as the establishment of a kind of *self-discipline* in students. This self-discipline consisted of *systematic observation, thorough examining*, and, most important to us, the *methodical arrangement of thought*. The *Dewey system of reflective thinking* contains five steps.[31]

1. The occurrence or awareness of a *felt difficulty*. You know something is wrong, unexpected, or unidentified.
2. The *definition* of the felt difficulty to see what kind of problem you have and how serious it is. Look carefully, don't misdefine, suspend your judgment regarding solutions.
3. The formulation of alternative suggestions, explanations, and hypotheses as *possible solutions*. Inference and analysis take place here.
4. The rational working out of the possible solutions by gathering facts, evidence, and inferences—further analysis of the consequences of alternative solutions.
5. Further testing, rejecting, or confirming of the solution chosen in step four by observation, measurement, hypothetical case or model building, or actual experiment if applicable. You now have a reasoned solution in your thoughts.

Our pioneers referred to earlier adapted reflective thinking to what they described as the "logical pattern of discussion." The major headings of their detailed applications follow.

MCBURNEY AND HANCE[32]

1. Definition and delimitation of the problem
2. Analysis of the problem
3. Suggestion of hypotheses or solutions
4. Reasoned development (appraisal) of the hypotheses or solutions
5. Further verification

EWBANK AND AUER[33]

1. Locating and defining the problem
2. Exploring the problem, research, analysis, evidence, argument, fallacies

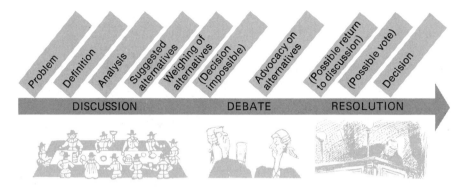

Figure 4.5 Discussion/debate continuum.

3. Examining suggested solutions
4. Choosing the best solution
5. Securing acceptance of the chosen solution: persuasion

Our early writers also saw discussion and debate as part of the same process typically described as a flexible continuum. What follows is our interpretation of their thinking.

The term *discussion* is derived from the Latin *discussus*—to strike asunder, to pull apart, to separate and subordinate the elements and ideas that make up a question or topic. Discussion is many sided. Debate is competitive; discussion, cooperative. If decision is impossible through discussion, then discussion may very well lead to debate. Debate may then lead to resolution. If it does not, the group very possibly will return to discussion. Premature or unnecessary debate has interfered in many group discussions. A discussion/debate continuum is illustrated in Figure 4.5.

Ewbank and Auer thought of *discussion and debate* as synonomous with *investigation and decision*. For them *problem solving* was the business of discussion; *decision making* was the purpose of debate. They defined discussion as " . . . the activity of problem solving, through purposeful talk by a group, with or without an audience."[34]

For McBurney and Hance, discussion was " . . . the cooperative deliberation of problems by persons thinking and conversing together in face-to-face or coacting groups under the direction of a leader for purpose of understanding and action."[35]

Procedural Formats

(1) **FOUR STEP (LARSON AND GOLDBERG)[36]**

1. Are we all agreed on the nature of the problem?
2. What would be the *ideal solution* from the point of view of all the parties involved in the problem?
3. What conditions within the problem could be changed so that the ideal solution might be achieved?
4. Of the solutions available to us, which one best approximates the ideal solution?

(2)

SEVEN STEPS (BORMANN AND BORMANN)[37]

1. Define terms
2. Set goals
3. Nature of problem
4. Possible solutions
5. Advantages and disadvantages
6. Best solution
7. Implementation

(3)

FIVE STEP (BRILHART)[38]

I. Problem description and analysis
II. Generation and elaboration of possible solutions
III. Evaluation of possible solutions
IV. Solution decision (emergence of consensus decision)
V. Planning for implementation of the solution.

(4)

SIX STEP (WOOD, PHILLIPS, PEDERSEN)[39]

1. Understanding the charge
2. Understanding and phrasing the question
3. Fact-finding
4. Setting criteria and limitations
5. Discovering and selecting solutions
6. Preparing and presenting the final report

(5)

TEN STEP (WRIGHT)[40]

1. Ventilation
2. Clarification of problem and establishment of group goals
3. Analysis of the problem
4. Establishment of general criteria
5. Suggestion of general solutions
6. Evaluation of solutions according to steps 3 and 4
7. Development of situational criteria
8. Evaluations of solutions according to step 7 criteria
9. Selection of solution(s)
10. Implementation of solution(s)

(6) | **ROSS FOUR-STEP PROBLEM-SOLVING PROCEDURE**

I. Definition and limitation: a concise but qualified statement of the felt difficulty, problem, or goal
II. Analysis: the determination of the nature of the problem and its causes
   a. Questions of fact
   b. Questions of policy
   c. Questions of value
III. Establishing criteria: a group consensus on the standards to be used in judging solutions
   a. Minimum and/or maximum limits
   b. Rating the criteria in importance
IV. Solutions
   a. Evaluation in terms of the criteria
   b. Decision and suggested implementation or action

Elaborations   Using the *Ross four-step problem-solving procedure* as a point of reference, but with the understanding that what is said here will apply for the most part to all the formats shown, let's look at some of the finer points of a problem-solving procedure.

The Definition Step   In most problem-solving discussions, a suggestion to take stock of the felt difficulty, to ventilate it fully, is pertinent. It helps remove emotional heat, if any, from the topic; it allows a quick audit of feelings (for example, there may be more than one felt difficulty in the group). It helps the group formulate the problem and determine goals.

The definition step consists of the *definition* and, if pertinent, the *limitation* of the problem. Our little combat squad had all kinds of felt difficulties such as a division of German tanks on the offensive. After the eight met for the first strategy meeting, you will recall they did define several limited goals: stick together, get back to friendly lines. In a sense they had limited their problems to these two (later to be reevaluated). In a less violent example, a group may talk about unemployment as a national problem or limit the problem to unemployment in Detroit.

If members of a group define a problem in several different ways, and worse, are not aware of the differences, confusion and irritation are sure to follow. Had our GIs each decided differently (and silently) about "friendly lines," the Canadians might have headed one way, the Americans another, and so on. Discussion time is well spent on the definition step. Agree on the problem and/or goal *before* you proceed.

In some cases (for example, medical diagnosis) a thorough discussion of the problem and a knowledge of previous identical situations may make the solution obvious. Most often, however, a group is now ready to *analyze* its accepted problem. Agenda suggestions range from fact finding and problem restatement to a systematic determination of the *nature* of the problem.

The nature of a problem is usually determined by *fact*, *policy*, and *value*, or, in the Ross system, by *puzzle*, *probability*, and *value*. A proposition of fact is one that asserts something about observable phenomena that can be judged true or false. "Mark was at the meeting or he was not." "Is there agreement about what was observed?" "I didn't see him." "I did. He was behind a post." Can the phenomenon under discussion be verified to the satisfaction of group members? *Policy* is concerned with the possibility or desirability of a future course of action. Of course, facts will probably also be a part of this kind of deliberation. *Value* is concerned chiefly with judgments about attitudes, beliefs, and feelings—very often the thing most difficult to measure. More will be said about value shortly.

    The Analysis Step—Puzzles   In our division of the nature of a problem, the *puzzle* dimension refers to questions of *fact*. This dimension is easier to apply than the fact dimension, though it may be less comprehensive. As an illustration consider a common jigsaw puzzle. No one would deny that a jigsaw puzzle can be difficult or frustrating (or capable of solution by group effort). Yet there is definitely a solution, and only one solution. Better yet, the solution is recognizable when you achieve it. It *is* the canals of Venice! Early detection of and agreement on a problem, as with a puzzle, can save much time and aggravation. If we were to view the jigsaw puzzle as a question of value— perhaps as a threat to our intelligence—then the problem would become more difficult, and the solution (putting the pieces together) would probably be delayed.

    Some puzzles are complicated. We use computers to solve engineering problems, and we use cash registers in supermarkets. But such problems are still puzzles, and we are well advised not to involve our emotions, morals, or value systems too quickly.

    Our combat patrol did go after the puzzles first. (Oh, they talked about staying alive.) Recall the attempts to locate their position from reports of last-known positions. The analysis continued by collecting facts on the whereabouts of the enemy. These were events observed by each of the soldiers hopefully in some definable place. Many probability decisions were involved here as well.

    Military policies that pertained could also be considered puzzles in this case— such things as ''Codes of Conduct,'' prearranged military strategies, the Geneva Convention, and so forth. They could also be viewed as criteria the soldiers' behaviors should meet.

    Probability   The *probability* dimension of the nature of a problem refers to common sense reduced to calculation. The suggestion here is that certain problems can be solved according to probability theory or according to the laws of chance. Although the word *probability* itself indicates that such problems may never be solved with certainty, the mathematical chance of a solution being correct may often be treated as an operational fact. Gamblers can predict their odds with relative certainty. They know that they have a 50 percent chance of getting a head in flipping a coin. Even in simple games, however, determining probabilities can quickly become complicated. If your winning number is 5 in a dice game with two dice, you have only four possible combinations: 1-4, 4-1, 3-2, and 2-3 (see Figure 4.6). Since theoretical probabilities are multiplied— two 6-sided dice give 36 (6 × 6) possible combinations—the odds of your winning are 4/36 or 1/9. The six combinations yielding the number 7 have a probability of 6/36 or 1/6. The number of rolls is, of course, a significant variable. In general, the larger the number of rolls, the greater the likelihood that the theoretical probability will become an established fact.

    Not all probability and prediction problems have odds that are as theoretically absolute as those in a coin flip or a dice game. An insurance company never knows exactly how many accidents, deaths, and fires will occur among its policyholders, but it can make predictions on the basis of past experiences. Our allied squad tried some of the same thing. Should they head north toward the British Second Army, south toward the American Seventh Army, west toward Patton's retreating Third Army

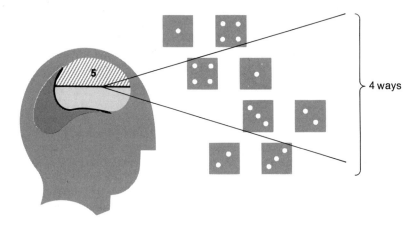

Figure 4.6

or . . . ? All decisions are to be decided on the probability of a successful journey. They didn't have any extremely reliable data to analyze statistically as insurance companies do.

This science of probability prediction is called *statistics*. From statistics we learn not only to ask "What caused the difference?" but also how to test whether the difference is merely a random variation or indicates some known or unknown factor at work. *Significance tests* make it possible to express and interpret the difference mathematically. This number may be considered an indicator of the "level of confidence" we may justifiably have in the data, or it may reflect our chances of being wrong. Discussants need not be statisticians, but they should be aware of probability problems and of how theory can influence decisions about problems of large masses of data.

Values   The *value* dimension of the nature of a problem concerns desirability rather than probability or certainty. Value systems held by group members are commonly considered as deriving from their past experiences. It is in this light that questions of value must partly be evaluated. In retrospect the army squad had no cowards; they felt the war was morally justified; they wanted to survive to fight again. No one suggested surrendering. That would have involved some value analysis.

Your general value system is determined by your past experiences; your understanding and acceptances of the concept of law as natural, universal, and/or pragmatic; and your interpretation of various concepts such as good and bad, pleasure and pain, noble and ignoble, and loyal and disloyal; as well as by a multitude of minor preferences that often defy any search for an underlying principle (preferences for certain foods, colors, architecture, and so on). By knowing the experiences, interpretations, and preferences that make up a person's general value system, it is often possible to make fairly reliable nonnumerical predictions and analyses of questions of value.

To the extent that preferences and attitudes (a form of preference) may be considered as values, it is possible to measure attitudes toward many things, from the size of next year's cars to the latest fashions.

Although the *value* dimension of analysis is the part most resistant to numerical measurement, this does not mean we should not try to measure, objectify, and analyze problems. It does mean that we must know our own intelligently derived values and how they may be applied to the group's decision. This kind of analysis should lead to better and more prudent group decisions regarding questions of value.

In the Larson and Goldberg system, analysis also includes calm analysis of what an ideal solution would or should look like. It can help you find criteria that your perhaps less than ideal solution should at least try to meet.

The Criteria Step Whether one thinks of this step as really a continuation of analysis or as the beginning of the solution step is of no great importance. There sometimes are *givens*—as in the case of "codes of conduct," "duty," or the Geneva Convention—which are with you right from the definition step. A *criterion* is a single standard or yardstick by which we may measure or evaluate something (see Figure 4.7).

In the case of group discussion, criterion refers to an *agreed-upon standard*. The three nations involved in our military group might discover three different policies (criteria) regarding surrender or the taking of prisoners of war. This can present real difficulties. Fortunately, thanks to Eisenhower's previous coordination of these matters, this was not the case. If a group has reasonably clear and agreed-upon criteria in mind, the evaluation or testing of suggested solutions is a lot easier, or at least more systematic.

If in a less crisis-prone situation a social group were discussing the problem of a clubhouse for their organization, they would want to clearly establish the criteria of cost, size, location, new or old, and so on. The concept of *limits* could help the group at this point. If they are talking about cost in terms of $100,000, what do they really mean? Is that the top limit or the bottom? If the group really means $75,000 to $110,000, it should state this, at least to itself. The same can be said for size and location. Criteria can also be negative. The group could, for example, name locations that it would not consider under any conditions.

The concept of *weighting* your criteria in terms of importance should also be considered. If size is the single most important criterion, then the group should agree on that point. Say, for example, that the old clubhouse is crowded; unless the next place is X amount larger, however beautiful a bargain, it won't solve the problem. If location is next most important (say the facilities must be close to where the members live), and then cost, parking, architecture, and so on, they have the beginnings of a subagenda for evaluating solutions. The list of criteria should then appear in some kind of rank in terms of importance. *Weighting* may be used profitably by a group if some of the criteria are close together in importance. Assuming a 100-point weighting scale and the determination that both size and location are very important, the group might assign 90 points to size, 80 points to location, 50 points to cost, 20 points to architecture, and

Figure 4.7

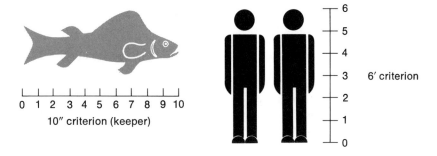

0 1 2 3 4 5 6 7 8 9 10
10″ criterion (keeper)

6
5
4
3 6′ criterion
2
1
0

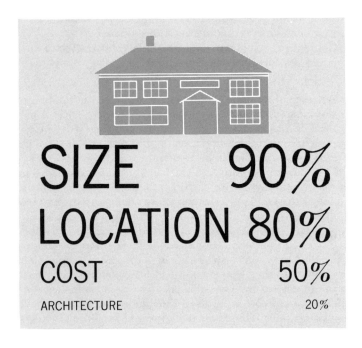

SIZE   90%
LOCATION 80%
COST   50%
ARCHITECTURE   20%

Figure 4.8 Weighting criteria.

so on, along with specific upper and lower limits for each criterion (see Figure 4.8). Such a scale gives the group considerably more insight into the distances among its ranked criteria. Furthermore, it gives the group a more logical, systematic approach to the solution step.

The Solution Step   To continue the illustration of the clubhouse under the criteria step, the group may now consider solutions that individuals may offer. If Steve A. offers pictures and real estate data on a building he's found, but the building fails the criterion of size because it doesn't meet the lower limit (and no plan for enlargement is provided by the contributor), then the group is quickly and systematically ready to go on to the next possible solution. It is possible that a group may come up with several solutions that meet the major criteria; the discussion may then focus on the less heavily weighted criteria. This is progress, and the group is aware of it. Without stated criteria to follow, the group might engage in lengthy argument over minor aspects of a problem while virtually ignoring the major aspects.

You may wish to discuss and evaluate your alternate solutions further according to the puzzle-probability-value analysis suggested earlier. Or you may wish some additional firsthand observation or action testing. But, in any case, the group is ready for *decision*.

Remember that discussion may sometimes be called upon to solve inappropriate questions. We do not need a group to solve most questions of fact or even some questions of probability. The library, the computer, the map—these solve some problems without group discussion. Nor does discussion solve the unsolvable. Some questions of value belong here. Once past the educational value, we sometimes may be well advised to adjourn. We should, of course, always look for viable solutions of the moment, if not for all time.

It seems clear that no one format is a perfect fit for all occasions. In a group that meets over time, one might switch to another or perhaps combine them.

INFORMATION

> I keep six honest serving men
> (They taught me all I knew);
> Their names are What and Why and When
> And How and Where and Who.
>
> *Rudyard Kipling*

Sources

Conversation and Interview   An obvious way to gather materials is to talk with the people in your group. Inventory group information. If somebody has firsthand or secondhand experience with the problem, you may be in luck. If there are knowledgeable people on your topic who are available for consultation on your campus or in your locality, you may be able to turn from conversation to a more formal interview. Before you interview someone, always do some preliminary research, inventory your own knowledge, observe or poll your friends. Then you will be prepared to ask clear and brief questions of your subject. Explain early in the conversation why you want this person's opinion or information. Avoid loaded or biased questions (even though you may have a bias) and try to be objective. Note any sources mentioned. Listen carefully, letting your subject do most of the talking.

Conversations with knowledgeable people can be very valuable. However, any serious interviewing or corresponding should usually follow some reading and observing. The purpose of starting your research early is to help you understand what the important questions are. If, for example, you were going to interview a professor of electrical engineering on problems of information theory, you would be well advised to browse through one or two of the classic books or articles in the field in order to obtain maximum value from the interview. The same would be true if you were going to interview a business professor on a subject such as arbitration, grievance procedure, or organizational psychology.

Once you are ready for your interview appointment, be sure you have the right place, day, and time. Briefly review your purpose and listen to the informant. He or she should do most of the talking. Don't argue, and do respect your informant's time. Be on time and stop on time. Say thanks, and find a quiet place to review and rewrite your notes while you can still remember what you heard.

Observation and Experience   Studying the engineering drawings of a production-line problem makes sense, but most managers will want a first-hand look as well. If you had a group project involving computer-assisted information flow in a modern office, one excellent method of securing information would be to spend a few hours observing such an organization. Make your observations systematic; time things; record things; list operational steps; double check; if possible, compare notes with a second observer from your group.

If you've had previous experience with such information flow, be it good or bad, inventory your own knowledge. Try some intrapersonal communication. Ask yourself to reflect on your experiences. Were they objective or prejudiced going in? Were they complete and fair or partial and suspect? Write these down and compare notes with others in your group who may have had similar experiences. See where your group comes up short, and consider dividing the chore of finding out what you still need to know.

Reading   Often the largest source of information is your library card catalog or its computerized version. This source is a vast treasure house of information, so take advantage of it. A library is built for random access, that is, for finding information about a topic that you have already worked on in advance. It is for filling in holes in your previous preparation.

Almost every library has the *Reader's Guide to Periodical Literature*. This source lists magazine articles by author, title, and subject. It is bound into volumes by year and is found in the reference section of the library. You should use it much as you would the library card catalog. *Magazine Index* is an automated system indexing 400 general-interest magazines using a special microfilm terminal. You might also look through *Books in Print*, the *Cumulative Book Index*, and its predecessor, *The United States Catalog*; these sources do for books what the *Reader's Guide* does for magazines. The *Book Index* is arranged according to author, title, and subject. *Forthcoming Books* lists books that have just been released or will be released within five months. While you are in the library, see if it has *The New York Times Index*. This is the only complete newspaper index in the United States; it can be a real timesaver. There is also an *Index to the Times of London*.

A good selection of general encyclopedias (such as *Britannica*, *Americana*, *New International*, *World Book*) and special ones (such as *International Encyclopedia of the Social Sciences*, *New Catholic Encyclopedia*, the *Jewish Encyclopedia*, and the *Encyclopedia of Religion and Ethics*) is found in many libraries. Very often, these sources present the best short statement on a given subject to be found anywhere. These encyclopedias are usually kept current by annual supplements called yearbooks; however, they should not be the sole source of your information.

For descriptions of cultural and political events, see *The Official Associated Press Almanac* or *Facts on File*; for geographical topics, see *The Information Please Almanac*. The *Reader's Digest Almanac* offers facts and household hints and advice. When you need statistics and short statements of factual data, see *The Statesman's Yearbook*, the *World Almanac and Book of Facts*, and the *Statistical Abstract of the United States* from the U.S. Bureau of the Census. This last source covers social, political, and economic facts of a wide range. Smaller general encyclopedias, such as *Columbia* or *Everyman's*, also contain compact statements and facts. Finally, an atlas can provide political facts as well as detailed maps. Try *The Hammond Citation World Atlas*, the *National Geographic Atlas of the World*, or the *Rand-McNally Commercial Atlas and Marketing Guide*. Check the date of publication on all of these sources; the world has changed dramatically in the last few years.

To learn more about famous individuals, you can consult some of the better-known directories and biographical dictionaries, such as *Current Biography*, *Who's Who in America*, *Who's Who in American Education*, *Who's Who in Engineering*, *American Men of Science*, and the *Directory of American Scholars*. For information on prominent Americans of the past, see *Who Was Who in America*, *Dictionary of American Biography*, *Lippincott's Biographical Dictionary*, and *The National Cyclopedia of American Biography*.

Most professional or trade associations publish journals of their own. Some of these organizations are the American Bar Association, the American Bankers' Association, the American Medical Association, the Speech Communication Association, the American Psychological Association, and the AFL–CIO. Many of the articles in the journals published by these organizations are indexed by special publications often available in your library: *Biological and Agricultural Index*, the *Art Index*, the *Index to Legal Periodicals*, *Index Medicus*, *Psychological Abstracts*, *Encyclopedia of Associations*, *Business Periodicals Index*, and many more.

In addition to the *Statistical Abstract of the United States*, mentioned earlier, other government publications can be excellent sources of speech materials. The *Commerce Yearbook*, the *U.S. Government Manual*, and the *Monthly Labor Review* provide much valuable information. The *Congressional Record* is an especially fruitful source for speech students. It includes a daily report of the House and Senate debates—indexed according to subject, name of bill, and representative or senator—and it has an appendix that lists related articles and speeches from outside of Congress.

Other sources of speech materials are the thousands of organizations that issue pamphlets and reports, often at no cost. You can write directly to these organizations for information; in some cases (for example, Planned Parenthood, the World Peace Foundation, the American Institute of Banking, and the AFL–CIO), you may receive a speech outline or manuscript in return. If you would like to know the addresses of these or other organizations, refer to *The World Almanac* under the heading, "Associations and Societies in the United States."

If you cannot find enough information in these sources, or if you would like to start out with a printed bibliography on your subject, some libraries provide an index of bibliographies called the *Bibliographic Index*. Online databases such as *ERIC*, *NEXIS*, and *LEXIS* are also available. Many college and community libraries have a computerized information service, with a search being done for the reader by library personnel. Information searches that would have taken eight hours just a few years ago can now be done in seconds. A fee is charged to the person requesting the search with the amount depending on the cost per minute of the database being searched. Other libraries are installing microcomputers for cardholders to use. Check with your librarian for these sources.

Now you are ready to start taking systematic notes. The emphasis is on the word *system*. As long as you have done some rough sorting and are not taking notes without purpose, you may use any system that works for you. The most common system in library searches is the use of file cards. You should write only one subject, source, classification, and note on each card. The big advantage of file cards over a notebook is that you can rearrange the file cards and thus reclassify or subclassify your material very easily. This shuffling of cards becomes very useful when you prepare for discussion.

Evidence

Essentially, the sources of evidence are objects or things that are observable or reports about things that are observable. For our purposes, the most useful sources of evidence are (1) statements by authorities, (2) examples, and (3) statistics.

Authority This type of evidence is usually in the form of quoted testimony from a person better qualified than the group to give a considered opinion about something. However, the value of an authority depends on how expert that person is. Perhaps the testimony simply supports the observations of the group.

The idea or statement being supported determines in part who the experts are. If you are trying to prove that the man who crashed into your car ran a red light, the expert is the lone person who was standing on the corner and saw the whole thing. With this kind of nonprofessional testimony, you often need more than one witness. If you are trying to prove that you have observed a bird considered extinct such as the passenger pigeon, you will need the testimony of a qualified ornithologist. This expert will insist on firsthand observation of the bird in this exceptional case.

Authorities are qualified to give expert testimony by their closeness to a first-hand observation and by their training in observing the phenomenon in question. The authority should be an expert on the *topic under discussion*. You would not ask a maestro to diagnose a problem in an airplane engine!

Another aspect is your group's knowledge and opinion of the person quoted. The bias the group assigns your expert may be very troublesome. When the group simply does not know who John Doe is, then you must explain why his testimony is authoritative (for example, "John Doe is professor of economics at Cornell University and a member of the U.S. Tax Commission").

Examples   An example is a specific illustration, incident, or instance that supports a point you are trying to make. A hypothetical example may be a real aid to clearness and is often very persuasive, but it is *not* proof as we are discussing it. We are concerned here with *real, factual* examples.

To prove that a person can operate normally in a state of weightlessness, you can cite one example of an astronaut who has done so successfully. However, in some situations *one* factual example, though proving its own case, may be so exceptional that it does not truly support a generalization. If you were arguing that Volkswagens are assembled poorly and carelessly, and you supported this statement with only one example of a car that was defective, then your proof would become suspect. The question in the latter case becomes, "How many specific examples do I need?" This involves the question of inductive proof, which we will discuss shortly.

Statistics   Using statistics as a method bewilders many people. You do not have to be a statistician to realize that the *mean* (an average) is not always the most representative measure. To illustrate, let's consider eleven hypothetical educators and their yearly incomes:

TABLE 4.3

	SALARY		SALARY
Educator A (Administrator)	$45,000	Educator G	$20,000
Educator B (Administrator)	40,000	Educator H	18,000
Educator C	30,000	Educator I	17,200
Educator D	25,500	Educator J	16,000
Educator E	22,500	Educator K	15,000
Educator F	20,000		

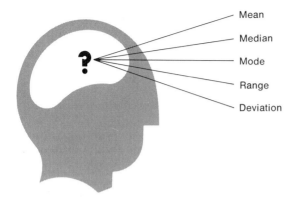

Figure 4.9

The mean income of these eleven educators in $24,472. The problem is obvious: two educators (the administrators) make the figure unrepresentative, particularly if you are more concerned with teachers than with administrators. Counting halfway down the list of salaries, we find $20,000. This is the *median*, in this case a much more meaningful and representative figure. If we do not include the two administrators, the average income of the teachers is $20,466, and the median is $20,000. You could then figure the amount by which each income differs from the average; the average of these differences is the *average deviation*. If you were to translate these deviations from the average onto a so-called normal distribution, you could then determine the *standard deviation* (also known as *sigma*).

Divorce statistics are frequently distorted. The dramatic statistics—sometimes cited as high as one in two marriages ending in divorce—are generated by a one-year sample. For example, if your city showed records of 100,000 marriages and 33,000 divorces, you might say that the divorce rate was 33⅓ percent or "one in three." However, if you judge the statistics *over time*, perhaps there will be one million marriages in the city. The divorce rate then becomes 3 percent! The statistics on the average duration of marriage are something like 6.9 years; however, the median duration is 43 years.

It should now be evident that statistics can quickly become complicated, capable of many applications, and (if you are not careful) meaningless. The lessons are (1) select the most appropriate statistics for your problem, and (2) make sure your group will understand them.

Forms of Reasoning

From Cause   If we were to see a man accidentally shoot a live man and then see the victim fall dead with a bullet in his heart, we could say the *effect* was death and the *cause* was the bullet or the man with the gun. Even this simple, observed, cause-to-effect relationship is full of problems. If the shooting were deliberate, would it in any way change the relationship? Let us suppose you found a dead man (the effect of something) with a bullet in his heart. Can we conclude absolutely that the bullet is the cause? This is reasoning from effect to cause—*a posteriori* reasoning. The bullet is certainly a possible cause, but as any Simon and Simon fan knows, the man might have been killed by arsenic poisoning, then shot after his death as a means of hiding the real cause. We should expect causes to be complex and interrelated.

One more example: Suppose a man dashes into your classroom, shoots a gun at your professor, and dashes out. Your professor falls to the floor and everyone runs out screaming. You observed the case and concluded that the effect was murder or attempted murder. (Perhaps it was a role-play instead.)

Your car battery is weak, you observe that it's ten degrees below zero, and you conclude that your car isn't going to start. This is before-the-fact, or *a priori*, reasoning. The conclusion is based upon circumstances you observed before the disputed fact. You are reasoning from *cause to effect*.

If when you get up tomorrow morning you say, "It's ten below zero; my car won't start; I'll be late for school," you are reasoning from *effect to effect*. Both your faltering battery and your tardiness (as well as the thermometer reading) are the effects of a common cause—low temperature. In arguing from effect to effect, you must first sort out the effect-to-cause and cause-to-effect elements and then apply the general requirements for arguments based on causal relations. These requirements are as follows:

Effect to cause

1. Is the attributed cause able to generate the particular effect?
2. Is the claimed cause the only possible cause of the effect?
3. Has coincidence been mistaken for cause?[41]
4. The alleged cause must not have been prevented from operating.

Cause to effect

1. Is the alleged cause relevant to the effect described?
2. Is this the sole or distinguishing causal factor?
3. Is there reasonable probability that no undesirable effect may result from this particular cause?
4. Is there a counteracting cause?
5. Is the cause capable of producing the effect?
6. Is the cause necessary and sufficient?
7. How does a new cause affect the system?[42]

From Generalization   Reasoning from generalization involves inducting from fair and sufficient samples or examples. *Induction* is the process of reasoning by which we arrive at a conclusion or generalization through observing specific cases or instances. "Properly conceived [it] may be thought of as the synthetic process used in moving from particulars to probable conclusions."[43] If you were to observe 500,000 spiders and if each one had eight legs, it would be reasonable to conclude that spiders have eight legs. The induction is perfect for the 500,000 cases, since there were no exceptions. To be intolerably scientific, however, our induction is merely a prediction (although a highly probable one) when applied to all spiders in the world. Assuming we are happy with the generalization, "All spiders have eight legs," we can then conclude *deductively* that this particular eight-legged thing in our garden is a spider. In sum, induction starts with particular cases and proceeds to a generalization, whereas in deduction we start with a generally accepted observation or principle and apply it to a particular case. Here are some tests for good generalizing:

1. Is the example relevant?
2. Are there a reasonable number of examples?

3. Do the examples cover a critical period of time?
4. Are the examples typical?
5. Are the negative examples noncritical?[44]

From Analogy   Analogies can make things clear, vivid, and interesting. Some analogies are figurative or emotive, others more literal. All offer support, but the literal are thought to be the more logical.

A *literal* analogy is open to less argument but is nevertheless always imperfect proof. Its effectiveness depends on how close the comparison really is. In arguing for gun control, Senator Edward Kennedy tried a *literal* analogy:

> Opponents of firearms laws insist that gun licenses and record-keeping requirements are burdensome and inconvenient. Yet they don't object to licensing automobile drivers, hunters, or those who enjoy fishing. If the only price of gun licensing or record-keeping requirements is the inconvenience to gun users, then the public will have received a special bargain. Certainly sportsmen will gladly tolerate minor inconvenience in order to protect the lives of their families, friends, and neighbors.[45]

George Ziegelmueller and Charles Dause analyzed this analogy as follows: "Senator Kennedy asserts that gun licensing is like automobile, hunting, and fishing licensing in an essential characteristic (inconvenience), and he suggests that it will be like the other forms of licensing with regard to the characteristic (tolerance) known in the other forms but not known in the instance of guns."[46]

Figurative analogy is often persuasive but not always very logical! (See Figure 4.10.)

"The parallel you drew between the rewards awaiting the pure of heart and an unending supply of Sanders' tin-roof sundaes was beautiful."

Figure 4.10

Cliff Wirth, cartoonist. The Detroit News.

From Sign   We reason from circumstances or clues that act as signs. Some are better at doing this than others. Sherlock Holmes was an expert at reasoning from subtle signs. Consider his assessment of Dr. Watson:

> "But do you mean to say," I said, "that without leaving your room you can unravel some knot which other men can make nothing of, although they have seen every detail for themselves?"
>
> "Quite so. I have a kind of intuition that way. Now and again a case turns up which is a little more complex. Then I have to bustle about and see things with my own eyes. You see I have a lot of special knowledge which I apply to the problem, and which facilitates matters wonderfully. Those rules of deduction laid down in that article which aroused your scorn are invaluable to me in practical work. Observation with me is second nature. You appeared to be surprised when I told you, on our first meeting, that you had come from Afghanistan."
>
> "You were told, no doubt."
>
> "Nothing of the sort. I *knew* you came from Afghanistan. From long habit the train of thoughts ran so swiftly through my mind that I arrived at the conclusion without being conscious of intermediate steps. There were such steps, however. The train of reasoning ran, 'Here is a gentleman of a medical type, but with the air of a military man. Clearly an army doctor, then. He has just come from the tropics, for his face is dark, and that is not the natural tint of his skin, for his wrists are fair. He has undergone hardship and sickness, as his haggard face says clearly. His left arm has been injured. He holds it in a stiff and unnatural manner. Where in the tropics could an English army doctor have seen much hardship and got his arm wounded? Clearly in Afghanistan.' The whole train of thought did not occupy a second. I then remarked that you came from Afghanistan, and you were astonished."
>
> "It is simple enough as you explain it," I said, smiling.[47]

Some tests that Holmes always applied are useful for all of us:

- Are the signs reliable?
- Are they in sufficient number?
- Do any contradict one another?

Fallacies

Fallacies represent reasoning too far removed from the facts or a tangle of generalizations based on inadequate facts. Aristotle devised a classification of fallacies that has been the springboard for all classification systems to this day. He divided fallacies into two principal types: those in the *language* of the argument and those in the *content* or matter of the argument. There are seven fallacies of matter, or "beyond the language." Aristotle himself admitted that there were problems in his system, so we may presume to rearrange his list. For our purposes we shall examine four major types of fallacies, together with their respective subtypes. The four are *overgeneralization* ("They're all dumb."), *false cause* ("The dance caused the rain."), *begging the question* ("Still cheating?"), and *ignoring or ducking the issue* ("What discrimination?").

Overgeneralization

"They're all dumb."

Snap judgments or generalizations based on insufficient evidence or experience belong in the category of overgeneralization. We are not talking here about language and the dangers of the word *all*, but rather the concept of *allness* itself. This fallacy results in our going from the general case to a specific case or vice versa. It is similar to the problems of induction and deduction.

It is in the *exceptions* to generally accepted rules that overgeneralization causes the most trouble. We would all agree that it is wrong to kill a person. However, a specific case of killing in self-defense can be an exception to this rule. To take another example, there could be exceptions to the rule, ''Alcohol is harmful.''

Sampling   A group of star high school football players was being oriented to a certain Big Ten campus when they observed a dozen devastatingly chic females coming out of a campus building. To a man, the generalization was, ''Wow! What coeds this place has!'' The coach did not bother to tell them that these women were all professional fashion models who had just come from a faculty wives' program.

Consider the size and representativeness of your sample before generalizing. A rash of teenage delinquencies may cause some people to conclude that all teenagers are juvenile delinquents, but this would be an unfair generalization. The most treacherous part of this fallacy is that it does start with facts. There *were* twelve stylish females on a given campus; teenage delinquency *has been* recorded. It is the lack of objective analysis of the sample of experiences or subjects that causes the trouble.

Extrapolation   This fallacy is also known as the ''camel's nose in the tent.'' It too is a form of sampling trouble (as are all overgeneralizations), except that this one is keyed to *prediction* and *probability*.

Space scientists extrapolate or they do not predict at all. This is also true of economists and weather forecasters. Scientists usually know the dangers of extrapolation; to offset these dangers, they generally phrase their predictions in terms of *statistical chance* or *confidence*. Scientists draw predictive curves only when they have found enough points to make a qualified prediction. We are well advised to do the same.

False Cause

''The dance caused the rain.''

This is the fallacy of assigning a wrong or false cause to a certain happening or effect. It also is refutation with irrelevant arguments. Superstitions belong here. If you blow on the dice and win, was it the blowing that brought you luck? Rabbits' feet are still being sold; and most hotels still have no thirteenth floor. Debaters call it *non-sequitur* (it does not follow).

After This, Therefore Because of This   Superstitions fit here. In our saner moments we are aware of this fallacy. It arises from the subtle misuse of time sequence. For example, if a new city government comes into power after a particularly rough winter and is faced with badly damaged roads, you may hold them responsible as you survey one ruined $70 tire: ''We didn't have roads like this until after their election.'' The great Roman Empire fell after the introduction of Christianity—care to try that one? You will hear it in Latin as *post hoc ergo propter hoc:* after this, therefore because of this.

Thou Also   This fallacy consists of making a similar, but essentially irrelevant, attack upon an accuser. A discussion between a Brazilian student and several Americans about Communist infiltration in Latin America became quite heated. Suddenly, the Brazilian said, ''Communists? How about segregation in your country?'' The retort was equally brilliant: "How about Nazis in Argentina?" A classic instance of this fallacy occurred in an army basic training mess line a few years ago. The mess steward put a perfectly good salad right in the middle of a soldier's mashed potatoes. When told what an ignoramus he was, the steward retorted in a most effective (if illogical) way, "Yeah, what about those poor guys in the Persian Gulf?"

Consequent   This fallacy simply is the corruption of the reasoning or inferential process used in conditional syllogisms. The problem in conditional syllogisms is with possible, partial, or even probable truths. If he lies, he will be expelled from school; he was expelled; therefore, he lied. (In actuality, he may have been expelled for poor grades.) When we use conditional reasoning and argue from the truth of the consequent (what happened: he was expelled) to the truth of the antecedent (what preceded: he lied), or when we argue from the falsity of the antecedent to the falsity of the consequent, we are committing the fallacy of the *consequent*.

Either/Or   Certainly, there are things in this world that are either one way or another. You are either living or dead; the lake is frozen or it is not. There is no such thing as being slightly pregnant. However, when a statement or problem with more than two possible solutions is put in an either/or context, we have a fallacy. "The fight is either Jan's or Jim's fault." It may be neither's fault, or it may be the fault of both. There are shades of gray in most things. All too often, we hear either/or arguments that only slow real solutions: science versus religion, capitalism versus socialism, suburban versus city living, and so forth.

Loaded Question   This trick assumes something has already happened; it usually asks two questions as if they were one. You're in trouble no matter how you answer. In a discussion it may take the form of a great many questions, the combination of answers leading to fallacious reasoning. The answers sought are *yes* or *no*. "Have you stopped drinking? *Yes* or *No*?" If you answer *no*, you are an admitted drinker. If you answer *yes*, you are an admitted former drinker. Either way, the loaded question stacks the deck against you. "Heads I win, tails you lose."

Begging the Question

"Still cheating?"

This fallacy assumes the truth or falsity of a statement *without proof*. A common form is the use of two or more unproved propositions to establish the validity of one another. Other forms are simple, unwarranted assumptions or statements. It is related to loaded questions.

Arguing in a Circle   This is the classic form of using two or more unproved propositions to prove one another. "Professional boxing should be outlawed because it is inhumane; we know it is inhumane because it is a practice that should be outlawed." "Detroit is to blame for the smog in Los Angeles since they make the cars we drive." This assumes cars are the major source of pollution, and that all the cars are made in Detroit—a vicious circle. We might just as easily accuse the Japanese car makers.

Direct Assumption   In this form of question begging, language is carefully selected to conceal unsupported assumptions. Many statements may be used, or perhaps just a word or two are subtly inserted. In a discussion of big-time college football, an opposition speaker started with the words, "It is my purpose to show that buying professional players is not in the best interest of college football." This statement begged the whole proposition by assuming at the outset that colleges buy professional players. Unless the statement is proved, it remains an assertion.

Ducking the Issue

"What discrimination?"

This fallacy can be a subtle, treacherous, and often vicious process. It almost always uses apparently relevant but objectively irrelevant arguments to cloud or duck the real issue or argument. This fallacy has several types, and each is worthy of a word of warning.

Attacking Personalities　This fallacy is also known as *ad hominem*. When a person attacks the personal character of an individual rather than the issue at hand, that person is guilty of *ad hominem* argument. The purpose of *ad hominem* is to change the issue from an argument on the proposition to one of personalities. To argue the stage and screen abilities of Burt Reynolds by referring to him as "that self-centered, woman-chasing louse" is a good example of *ad hominem*. Mr. Reynolds's stage and screen *abilities* have no direct logical connection to his alleged off-stage pursuits. This is not to say that every personal attack is unfair or illogical. If Mr. Reynolds were being evaluated on his public relations abilities, it might be a different matter.

Appeals to Prejudice　This is an appeal to the people through their biases and passions. The symbols of motherhood, the flag, race, and sin are typical themes. Vicious and often unsupported attacks have been made against liberal Americans in the name of un-Americanism, Romanism, Zionism, racism. The "ist" words—sexist, racist, feminist, abortionist, socialist—are often misused in this type of appeal. *Ad populum* appeals should become less successful as the general population becomes better educated and more sophisticated.

False Appeal to Authority　This type of fallacy is an appeal to authority and dignity. When the authority is legitimately connected to the subject, as Aristotle is to logic, we have no problem. However, if in our reverence of Aristotle we use him to oppose modern probability theory, we are guilty of false appeal. Sparky Anderson and Reggie Jackson are highly paid experts in their specialized fields. They are probably not authorities on laser theory or even beer or shaving cream. If you are impressed because Dr. Whosis says that alcohol causes cancer, find out if Whosis is an M.D. or an English professor!

Appeals to Ignorance　This is a mean trick, hiding weak arguments by overwhelming a group with impressive materials about which they know little. A twelve-cylinder vocabulary can screen many a feeble argument. Improper use of statistics (or even proper use) for people ignorant of the theory or the numbers involved is a good example of an appeal to ignorance. This is not to say that vocabulary and statistics are the problem; the problem is the intent of the user.

SUMMARY

Group problem solving involves a combination of recurring phases and/or sequential stages directed toward resolving the difficulty under consideration. Decision making occurs within this process whenever reasonably clear alternatives emerge and choices must be made.

Effective group problem solving covaries with the type of task it has undertaken. Five types (Steiner) are (1) additive, (2) compensatory, (3) disjunctive, (4) conjunctive, and (5) discretionary. The weakest are the disjunctive and the conjunctive. Group assets (Maier) are more information, more approaches, more acceptance, and better decision action. Group liabilities (Maier) are social pressure, premature and/or noncritical agreement, individual domination, and debate supersedes discussion.

Group communication is processual. The *recurring phase* model suggests that certain aspects, themes, issues, or parts of the process regularly prevail during the life of a group, but not necessarily in any consistent order or sequence. The *sequential stage* model suggests again that certain aspects, themes, or parts dominate the discussions and that they *do* tend to follow a typical step order during the group's developmental life.

Three recurring themes in therapy groups are (1) leader dependency, (2) pairing for emotional support, and (3) fight-flight responses. Interaction Process Analysis (IPA) suggests that normal groups go through three phases: (1) socio-emotional, (2) task, and (3) control. Socio-emotional refers to the interpersonal experiences, task to the content or goal of the group, and control refers to communications about possible directions and causes of action for the group to take.

Tuckman's research suggests that groups go through a five-stage development sequentially: (1) forming, (2) storming, (3) norming, (4) performing, and (5) adjourning. H. A. Simon offers a four-step or stage-management view: (1) intelligence activity, (2) design activity, (3) choice activity, and (4) review activity.

Progressive phase models of how groups solve problems should be called progressive cycle models. *Reach-testing* (Scheidel and Crowell) is a cyclical explanation in which ideational backtracking and reaching out for new ideas occurs regularly. Ideas slowly progress and build on previous agreements.

Decision emergence (Fisher) is a belief that decisions emerge in a gradual, cumulative process. These progressive phases are (1) orientation, (2) conflict, (3) emergence, and (4) reinforcement.

In decision making one needs a middle or contingency view between natural or universal phases and sequences and the view that each decision (or organization) is so unique that no generalizations are helpful. Knowing one's own organization and how its system works and relates to its environment is the first step. Five methods of decision making are (1) consensus, (2) vote, (3) leader prerogative, (4) delegation, referral, delay, and (5) negotiation, mediation, and arbitration. *Consensus* need not be unanimous, but it is one that all accept as the best solution they are going to get, and that it will evoke support beyond mere toleration. The *voting* method of decision making involves the complexities of defining majority, quorum, voting member, ballot, related bylaws, and other technical and/or parliamentary rules. The *leader's prerogative* or power to make the decision apart from what the group thinks or recommends is a function of organizational policy. Some decisions may be *delegated* or *referred* to a standing committee, an ad hoc group, or an expert individual. Sometimes there are decisions that must be referred to special groups (e.g., safety, budget, union contract, and so on). A *delayed* decision is still a form of decision and not always a bad one.

Decision making by *negotiation* involves compromises by divergent factions, which are brought about through bargaining. Negotiation assistance by mediators, fact-finders, or other third parties is sometimes required or desirable. If bargaining still breaks down and grievances go unsolved, some contracts call for arbitration where decisions so rendered are binding on all parties.

Communication between decision groups and implementation groups is critical. It takes time and effort to break work down into manageable, accountable units. PERT (Program Evaluation and Review Technique) allows a group to review its implementation flow in diagram form. It helps locate and define the *critical path* that very specific implementation must follow.

Research supports the value of some orderly, rational problem-solving patterns (or agendas). *Reflective thinking* (Dewey) is a scientific habit of problem solving that consists of acquiring the attitude of suspended judgment and mastering the various methods of searching for materials. These five steps have been adapted to logical patterns of discussion. A typical pattern is (1) awareness, (2) definition, (3) possible solutions, (4) testing solutions, (5) accepting final solution. Criteria by which to test solutions are agreed upon in the first three steps. Other specific, problem-solving procedural formats are offered by Larson/Goldberg, Bormann and Bormann, Brilhart, Wood/Phillips/Pedersen, Wright, and Ross. The Ross four-step procedure is: (1) definitive and limitation, (2) analysis (fact, policy, value), (3) establishing criteria, and (4) solutions. In the Ross procedure, criteria should be weighted and ranked in order of importance.

Three major sources of information are (1) conversation and interview, (2) observation and experience, and (3) reading. A library is often the largest source of information. It is designed for random access, that is, for finding information about a topic that you have already thought through in advance. Its use is for filling in holes in your early preparation.

The sources of evidence are (1) statements by authorities, (2) examples, and (3) statistics. Four forms of reasoning are (1) from cause, (2) from generalization, (3) from analogy, and (4) from sign. Four major types of fallacies are (1) overgeneralization, (2) false cause, (3) begging the question, and (4) ducking the issue.

PROJECTS AND CASES

PROJECTS

1. Describe two group experiences: one where the group proved to be an asset and one where the group proved to be a liability.

2. Research the words *phase*, *stage*, *sequential*, and *progressive*. Prepare to discuss your findings and opinions.

3. Research the words *negotiation*, *mediation*, and *arbitration*. Prepare to discuss their differences and to cite examples.

4. In a small group try to get a consensus on what a ''consensus'' is.

CASES

After being assigned to a group of three to six people, assess the following problems and prepare for a 10- to 15-minute panel discussion in which you spend the first few minutes setting an agenda and the remaining time following it toward a solution.

1. One of your instructors, who has tenure, appears to be an alcoholic. He keeps coming to class somewhat drunk, and, because of his drinking, he misses 25 percent of the class meetings. Most of the students like him, and he is a qualified instructor. The material is taught if the students want it, but they end up learning most of it from the text. The instructor doesn't push his students and gives just one test during the semester. Your success in future courses in this field depends on how well you grasp the material and basics in this course.

    YOUR COURSE OF ACTION SHOULD BE TO

    1. Go straight to the dean and ask that disciplinary action be taken against the professor.
    2. Drink with your professor in order to get a good grade in his class.
    3. Boycott his class and try to get the other students to do the same. This way you would draw attention to the situation.
    4. Talk to the professor, explain your feelings, and ask for an explanation.
    5. Inform the department chairperson of your suspicions, after checking with other students.

2. Doris has been one of the best operators in your department, but recently a large portion of her work has been defective. She works on a repetitive job requiring intermittent attention in order to avoid the formation of scrap. This unsatisfactory work began at about the same time as the introduction into the department of a new, unmarried male employee.

    WHAT SHOULD YOU DO?

    1. Without referring to the man, reprimand Doris for her poor work.
    2. Ask Doris why the quality of her work has fallen off.
    3. Solve the problem by transferring one employee or the other to another department.
    4. In a friendly way, give Doris advice about not letting her interest in another employee interfere with her work.
    5. Discuss the problem with each of them separately.

3. Mr. Davis, electrical supervisor of the plant, decided that an electrical conduit would have to be run from one section of the plant to another distant section. He planned to run it through the ventilating system. The ventilating system consisted of square metal pipes large enough for a person to crawl through and drag the conduit after him. The job would be disagreeable but in Mr. Davis's opinion, not dangerous. He asked Reid, one of the electricians, to do the job. Reid refused, and the following conversation took place:

    Davis: Why won't you do it?
    Reid: It's too dangerous.
    Davis: Where's any danger involved?
    Reid: It gets mighty hot in those ventilators. A guy could pass out in there and you'd never get him out. And another thing—it's easy for you white collar fellows to sit in your cool offices and dream up these jobs. I don't see you ever doing anything to get your clothes messed up.

Davis: Reid, I do my job as I'm told and I expect you to do the same. But since you have made that last statement, I'll tell you what we'll do. You and I are going through that ventilator with the conduit, and I'm going to lead the way. If you refuse to follow me, you are through with this company. If you do follow me, you will be suspended from work for three days for forcing me to get the job done this way.

Reid followed him through the ventilator and was suspended for three days.

HOW SHOULD DAVIS HAVE HANDLED THIS SITUATION?

1. He should have repeated the order and immediately suspended Reid if he still refused to obey.
2. He should have simply asked another electrician to do the job.
3. He should have offered some incentive (e.g., half a day off) to get the job done, *if* the head of the safety department said the job was not dangerous.
4. He should have called in the head of the safety department to discuss whether the job was dangerous. If the head said the job was not dangerous, Davis should then have repeated the order and disciplined Reid unless he obeyed it.
5. His solution of the problem was a very satisfactory one.

4. "What Are Word Processors Really Doing for Our Company?"

Barry Rogers, president of NATCO Insurance, called Irv Chandler, vice president of human resources, into his office. Starting the conversation, Rogers said, "I know you've been busy grappling with the problem of investigating our program of creating the right opportunities for handicapped employees. That's a project we certainly think is important. But I have something else in mind that might represent another interesting problem for you to investigate.

"As you know, Irv," Rogers continued, "our firm has invested substantial sums of money in word processing centers in our regional offices. Right now, I'm not concerned about the larger word processing centers that have replaced the steno pools in the home office. Each work station complete with the electronic typewriter, computer, and built-in software costs about $10,000. We decided to take this step as a way of improving productivity in our branches. But lately, we're beginning to wonder what we have bought for our money."

"What specific reservations do you have?" asked Irv.

"The word processing work stations sure look impressive, but what are they really accomplishing for NATCO? Are we investing our money wisely, or are we spending money on a frill? I want to know if employees are any happier or more productive using word processing than they were when using the previous equipment. Maybe electric typewriters combined with the old dictating equipment were just as good.

"Another problem to ponder is that some of the office supervisors think that age seems to make a difference. Younger employees may be more favorably inclined toward word processing than older employees.

"Other members of the executive committee and I would like the human resources department to provide us some answers to the questions I've asked."

After thinking for a moment, Chandler replied, "Barry, you're asking the right questions. This is just the kind of assignment our people in personnel research should be tackling. I'll have some preliminary thoughts about our approach in a couple of weeks."

QUESTIONS

1. What problem-solving pattern should the research team follow? Why?
2. What should be done?

5. McCormick and Sons

J. R. McCormick and Sons, General Contractors, is a small highway construction company specializing in bridges and drainage. The three owners of the firm are J. R. himself; William, a 29-year-old son and a graduate civil engineer who has been a member several years; and John, a 23-year-old son who has recently joined the firm.

The firm employs from five to thirty men, depending on the phase of a job they are in at any particular time. In compliance with state law regarding construction work, all of them are union workers hired through the local unions (carpenters, iron workers, and so on). J. R. has close personal friends among the union workers, and the firm's relations with the local unions have always been excellent. Recently, Joe Carter, a new and very demanding young union leader, has become head of the iron workers union. In a small firm of this kind the owners occasionally work along with the men. The state law exempts the owner from the requirement that all workers must belong to a union, but most contractors do belong to one of the unions and limit their manual activities to the type of work appropriate to the union of which they are a member. J. R. and William are union members. When John joined the firm he called his father's attention to the exemption clause in the law and said that he would prefer not to join a union. He was in fact rather hostile toward unions. His father questioned the wisdom of this, but it was agreed by the three partners that John would not join a union.

William and John were jointly in charge of the next job undertaken by the firm, a $175,000 bridge job. As John was still learning the ropes, William acted as superintendent and John spent most of his time working with the men sent out by the local iron workers union. When Carter visited the job and saw John at work with the men, he told John that he should get an iron workers union card and that he would be admitted to the union at once. John ignored the suggestion.

A few days later, when the firm asked the union for more iron workers, the men sent out proved to be so inefficient that it was necessary to discharge them and ask the union for another crew. The second group of men proved even more inefficient than the first, and it seemed obvious that the union was attempting to pressure the firm into requiring John to join the union.

QUESTIONS

1. Could this be a communication problem?
2. If it's union pressure . . . what are six possible solutions?

6. Apply the various tests of reasoning to the following article by William Raspberry, and be prepared to discuss your observations in class.[48]

"ALL YOU HEAVIES: TAKE HEART" by William Raspberry

WASHINGTON. I've finally licked my weight problem.

For a year, I've been assaulting my bathroom scale to the tune of 175 pounds—a blubbery 15 pounds more than the charts say I should weigh for my height and build.

I am now pleased to report I am some 25 pounds underweight. Moreover, it required no jogging, no starvation, no diet books, or liquid protein. All it took was Dr. Reubin Andres, that brilliant Johns Hopkins professor.

I still weigh 175 pounds, mind you. Andres's brilliance rests in his discovery that the charts are wrong.

Hear this genius:

"The results (of his review of 40 studies, covering six million people around the world) all point in the same direction: The desirable weight if you want to live longer has been underestimated. The current charts on doctors' walls, and our own idea of desirable weight fixed by a sense of esthetics, are not desirable if you want to live longer."

Particularly encouraging is his finding that the highest longevity for one group of middle-aged workers (employees at a Chicago utility company) was for men who were 25 to 32 percent over their "desirable" weight.

What that means is that instead of the 160 pounds the charts mandate, my best weight is actually between 200 and 211 pounds. The 175 pounds that once had me 15 pounds overweight now leaves me practically svelte. Brilliant man, that Andres.

Actually, Andres isn't the first person to discover that the power to define is the power to cure. Several years ago, the American Psychiatric Association cured the problem of homosexuality—not by changing anyone's sexual behavior but by deciding that homosexuality is not really a problem.

More recently, there is a phenomenon called "the new chastity." Adherents, including a fair number of newlyweds, simply decide to abstain from sex. What these pioneers have created, though they seem not to be aware of it, is a cure for sexual dysfunction. If sexual dysfunction is defined as the inability to perform normally, then it can be cured by the simple device of changing the definition of normal. If chastity becomes normal, there is no such thing as sexual dysfunction.

Any careful newspaper reader can think of other examples: school districts that cure the problem of nonlearning not by improved teaching but by setting lower standards, social statisticians who cure poverty not by improving income but by reassessing the assets of the impoverished.

Marijuana use is no longer a social problem but a normal, if illegal, activity of the young. What used to be marital infidelity—a problem—is now "open marriage"—a new "lifestyle."

I remember seeing (in the *New York Times*, I believe) a feature on "natural gardens." The idea was to declare a truce with bindweed, thistle, chickweed and plantain: to stop calling them weeds, which is a declaration of war, and make peace with them as part of a "natural" landscape.

Your scraggly, unkempt lawn is transformed, like magic into nature's own garden, and you don't even have to cut the grass.

The prospects are endless. Joblessness could be redefined as full-time leisure. Racial animosity could become ethnotension.

We've got a hostage crisis? No, sir. We've got 52 people on indefinite foreign assignment.

The beauty of the approach is that it doesn't cost anything, neither money nor exertion. Problems simply evaporate, like dew in the August sun.

So, pass the butter, sell the lawnmower, and let's light up a joint. And, please, not tonight, dear.

NOTES

1. R. B. Zajonc, "Social Facilitation," *Science* (1965), p. 274.
2. David Holzman, "Med Schools Test Problem-Solving," *Insight* (April 21, 1986), p. 60.
3. Ibid., p. 60.
4. I. D. Steiner, "Task-performing groups," in *Contemporary Topics in Social Psychology*, eds. J. W. Thibaut, J. T. Spence, and R. C. Carson (Morristown, N.J.: General Learning Press, 1976).
5. Norman R. F. Maier, "Assets and Liabilities in Group Problem Solving: The Need for an Integrative Function," *Psychological Review*, 74 (1967), 239–49.
6. See W. R. Bion, *Experiences in Groups* (New York: Basic Books, 1961); D. S. Whitaker and H. A. Thelen, "Emotional Dynamics and Group Culture," in *Group Psychotherapy and Group Function*, eds. M. Rosenbaum and M. M. Berger (New York: Basic Books, 1975).
7. Robert F. Bales and Fred L. Strodtbeck, "Phases in Group Problem-Solving," in *Group Dynamics: Research and Theory*, eds. Dorwin Cartwright and Alvin Zander (New York: Harper & Row, 1960), pp. 624–38.
8. H. A. Simon, *The New Science of Management Decision*, (Englewood Cliffs, N.J.: Prentice-Hall, 1977).
9. Thomas M. Scheidel and Laura Crowell, "Idea Development in Small Discussion Groups," *Quarterly Journal of Speech*, 50 (1964), 140–45.
10. Laura Crowell and Thomas M. Scheidel, "Categories for Analysis of Idea Development in Discussion Groups," *Journal of Social Psychology*, 54 (1961), 155–68.

11. Dennis S. Gouran and B. Aubrey Fisher, "The Functions of Human Communication in the Formation, Maintenance, and Performance of Small Groups," in *Handbook of Rhetorical and Communication Theory*, eds. Carroll C. Arnold and John Waite Bowers (Boston: Allyn and Bacon, 1984), p. 623.

12. Ibid., p. 623.

13. B. Aubrey Fisher, *Small Group Decision Making*, 2nd ed. (New York: McGraw-Hill, 1980), p. 146.

14. K. B. Valentine and B. A. Fisher, "An Interaction Analysis of Verbal Innovative Deviance in Small Groups," *Speech Monographs*, 41 (1974), 413–20.

15. Fremont E. Kast and James E. Rosenzweig, *Organization and Management* (New York: McGraw-Hill, 1979), p. 116. For a Japanese view see Lea P. Stewart, William B. Gudykunst, Stella Ting-Toomey and Tsukasa Nishida, "The Effects of Decision-Making Style on Openness and Satisfaction Within Japanese Organizations, *Communication Monographs*, 53, no. 3 (September 1986), 236–51.

16. Dennis J. Moberg and James L. Koch, "A Critical Appraisal of Integrated Treatment of Contingency Findings," *Academy of Management Journal* (March 1975), p. 121.

17. Abraham Zaleznik and David Moment, *The Dynamics of Interpersonal Behavior* (New York: John Wiley and Sons, 1964).

18. See also Appendix: Parliamentary Rules, text p. 335.

19. Robert Tannenbaum and Warren H. Schmidt, "How to Choose a Leadership Pattern," *Harvard Business Review* (March–April 1958), p. 96.

20. Gerald M. Phillips, *Communication and the Small Group* (Indianapolis: Bobbs-Merrill, 1973), p. 130; see also G. M. Phillips, "PERT as a Logical Adjunct to the Discussion Process," *Journal of Communication*, 15 (1965), 89–99; H. Lloyd Goodall, *Small Group Communication in Organizations* (Dubuque, Ia.: Wm. C. Brown, 1985), pp. 235–53.

21. J. R. Hackman and C. G. Morris, "Group Tasks, Group Interaction Process, and Group Performance Effectiveness: A Review and Proposed Integration," in *Advances in Experimental Social Psychology*, vol. 8, ed. L. Berkowitz (New York: Academic, 1975).

22. J. R. Hackman, K. R. Brousseau, and J. A. Weiss, "The Interaction of Task Design and Group Performance Strategies in Determining Group Effectiveness," *Organizational Behavior and Human Performance*, 16 (1976), 350–65.

23. R. Y. Hirokawa, "A Comparative Analysis of Communication Patterns Within Effective and Ineffective Decision-Making Groups," *Communication Monographs*, 47 (1980), 312–21.

24. Fisher, *Small Group Decision Making*, p. 246.

25. Ibid., p. 133.

26. John T. Lanzetta and B. Roby Thornton, "The Relationship Between Certain Group Process Variables and Group Problem-Solving Efficiency," *Journal of Social Psychology*, 7 (1960), 135–48.

27. Edward R. Mabry and Richard E. Barnes, *The Dynamics of Small Group Communication* (Englewood Cliffs, N.J.: Prentice-Hall, 1980), p. 78.

28. Barry E. Collins and Harold Guetzkow, *A Social Psychology of Group Processes for Decision-Making* (New York: John Wiley & Sons, 1964), p. 111; see also Carl Larson, "Forms of Analysis and Small Group Problem Solving," *Speech Monographs*, 36 (1969), 452–55; Jay Hall and Martha S. Williams, "Group Dynamics Training and Improved Decision Making," *Journal of Applied Behavioral Science*, 6 (1970), 39–68; Harry Sharp, Jr. and Joyce Milliken, "The Reflective Thinking Ability and the Product of Problem-Solving Discussion," *Speech Monographs*, 31 (1964), 124–27; Hirokawa, "Comparative Analysis of Communication Patterns," p. 312.

29. James H. McBurney and Kenneth G. Hance, *Discussion in Human Affairs* (New York: Harper and Brothers, 1939, 1950); Henry L. Ewbank and J. Jeffery Auer, *Discussion and Debate* (New York: Appleton-Century-Crofts, 1941, 1951).

30. John Dewey, *How We Think* (Boston: D. C. Heath, 1910), p. 68.

31. Ibid., pp. 68–78.

32. McBurney and Hance, *Discussion in Human Affairs*, pp. 65–84.

33. Ewbank and Auer, *Discussion and Debate*, p. 57 and Ch. 4, pp. 5–9, 10–11, 14.

34. Ibid., pp. 4–5.

35. McBurney and Hance, *Discussion in Human Affairs*, p. 10.

36. Alvin A. Goldberg and Carl E. Larson, *Group Communication* (Englewood Cliffs, N.J.: Prentice-Hall, 1975), p. 149. See also Larson, ''Forms of Analysis,'' pp. 452–55.

37. Ernest G. Bormann and Nancy Bormann, *Effective Small Group Communication* (Minneapolis, Minn.: Burgess, 1980), p. 95 (key phrases only).

38. John K. Brilhart, *Effective Group Discussion* (Dubuque, Ia.: Wm. C. Brown, 1986), p. 307.

39. Julia T. Wood, Gerald M. Phillips, Douglas J. Pedersen, *Group Discussion: A Practical Guide to Participation and Leadership* (New York: Harper & Row, 1986), p. 55.

40. David W. Wright, *Small Group Communication: An Introduction* (Dubuque, Ia.: Kendall/Hunt, 1975), p. 43; see also John F. Cragan and David W. Wright, *Communication in Small Group Discussions*, 2nd ed. (St. Paul, Minn.: West, 1986), p. 78.

41. The first three items of this list are taken from Craig R. Smith and David M. Hunsaker, *The Bases of Argument* (Indianapolis: Bobbs-Merrill, 1972), pp. 88–89.

42. This list is taken from Austin J. Freeley, *Argumentation and Debate*, 6th ed. (Belmont, Calif.: Wadsworth, 1986), pp. 139–44.

43. George W. Ziegelmueller and Charles A. Dause, *Argumentation: Inquiry and Advocacy* (Englewood Cliffs, N.J.: Prentice-Hall, 1975), p. 88.

44. Freeley, *Argumentation and Debate*, pp. 134–36.

45. Quoted in ''Tighter Gun Controls—Both Sides of the Dispute,'' *U.S. News and World Report*, July 10, 1972, p. 69.

46. Ziegelmueller and Dause, *Argumentation*, p. 98.

47. A. Conan Doyle, *A Study in Scarlet* (New York: Harper & Brothers, 1892), p. 14.

48. © 1981, The Washington Post Company. Reprinted with permission.

5

COMMUNICATION: RULES AND PRACTICE

All organizations operate according to some kind of rules—written, unwritten, and those based on precedent and past practices. They also operate in context and an environment, both physical and psychological and hopefully ethical. These matters, as well as the forms small groups might take, are the content of this chapter.

COMMUNICATION CONTEXT

CONTEXT INTERRELATIONSHIPS

Hierarchy of Contexts

According to Stephen Littlejohn these various contexts all overlap, and they should be viewed " . . . as a hierarchy of nested contexts in which the higher level includes the lower but adds some additional constraints and qualities."[1] His diagram (see Figure 5.1) illustrates how interpersonal communication cuts through, or is a diminishing part of, the larger contexts.

Interpersonal communication and contexts are clearly a large part of what goes on in small-group interactions. Figure 5.2 suggests that 80 percent of such contexts may be interpersonal communication. Most small groups are face-to-face, interactive, oral exchanges.

Organizational contexts are thought to be largely involved with small-group communication. The pyramidal structure of most organizations is thought to be one of overlapping or "linking" group memberships. The superior in one group is a participating subordinate in the next. The structure has been referred to as a "linking pin" arrangement as diagramed in Chapter 1.[2]

Since interpersonal communication is a large part of group communication, it is clearly a major part of all organizational contexts. We suggest that it is 50 percent

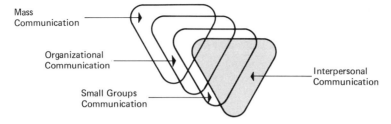

Figure 5.1 The hierarchy of communication contexts.

of organizational contexts with some trepidation, since organizations vary widely in their goals, size, importance, and the like. A large part of organizational communication is quite obviously dependent upon special knowledge in areas such as planning, organizing, accounting, contracting, and so on. Nevertheless, managing is basically a process of getting work done through people, and that takes human communication.

The last context shown (there are others) in Figure 5.2 is public communication or ''relating to audiences.'' A public speech to a large audience is obviously quite different from an intimate, dyadic interaction. However, most of the basic speech communication processes are involved. Language is still critical (sometimes more critical). Voice is special; so are all of your nonverbals. Listening (especially if you're in the audience) is involved; so are all the problems of messages, attitudes, perception, attraction, and so on.

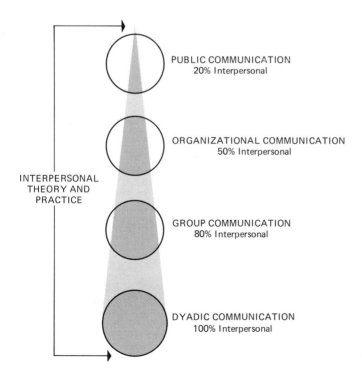

Figure 5.2 Interpersonal communication contexts.

Levels of Communication

Another way of looking at this interrelationship is in terms of *levels* of communication. Jurgen Ruesch and Gregory Bateson start with the intrapersonal and carry us through four contexts, which again are interrelated (see Figure 5.3). Their insights into the communication networks involved at the various levels shown are found in their text.

Place and Ritual

Our communication at whatever level is often limited by *where* we are. Some places may restrict communication, whereas others may aid it. In addition, place may have a ritualistic aspect. Much of our communication is dictated by the place and ritual alone. Observe the impact on communication of a church, an elevator, a commuter bus, a 400-seat Boeing 747; study their rituals.

Now let's illustrate the often awesome impact of place. Visualize an impressive church complete with stained-glass windows, exquisite statues, and a high arched ceiling. In it we feel close to our creator. There is a temptation to whisper. People seem to alter their voices, their language, and their dress to meet the communication requirements of this powerful setting. The ritual associated with this setting also dictates much of the verbal as well as the nonverbal communication. Even an empty church is a powerful communication setting, and we adjust our signals accordingly.

Reacting and interacting always occur somewhere at some level in some context. The place in which communication and its ritual occur is important for it affects both senders and receivers of messages. We may not always like or approve of certain surroundings, but sensitive human interaction demands that we take them into account. We should take the setting into special account when we evaluate a person's social adjustment. A ''nut'' may not be a ''nut'' when he or she is out of the special situation you are observing. A berserk football fan may be calm and collected when we find him or her in church.

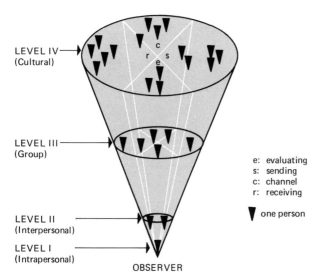

LEVEL IV (Cultural)
LEVEL III (Group)
LEVEL II (Interpersonal)
LEVEL I (Intrapersonal)
OBSERVER

e: evaluating
s: sending
c: channel
r: receiving

▼ one person

Figure 5.3   Levels of communication.[3]

The ambient environment in which your group meets—that is the lighting, heating, air, noise level, room size, even color—is thought to have the potential to affect group behavior. Lighting has been studied in group situations from conference rooms to industrial settings.[4] We learn to live with and accommodate less than perfect lighting arrangements if there are good reasons, as we shall see in the next section.

Extremes in temperatures (below 60 degrees or above 80 degrees) in experimental research conditions have produced group feelings of irritability, discomfort, and reduced productivity.[5] Even interpersonal attraction is thought to suffer under extremes of temperature.[6]

Research suggests not only that extremes and unexpected types of noise are disruptive to groups but also that people make amazing *adaptations* when motivated.[7] This helps explain how students study with a blaring stereo or how athletic teams overcome crowd noise. It also reminds us of the value of a systems orientation when evaluating single variable research. Clearly the ambient environment is only part of a larger and more important system of group interaction.

Still the lessons are clear. Place, ritual, and even the ambient environment have an influence upon group behavior, and we are well advised to take them into account.

THE PSYCHO-ENVIRONMENT

A near poverty-stricken family finds happiness, high morale, and a certain amount of self-realization. How can this be in view of their physical environment? Because a poverty-stricken *physical* environment need not be a poverty-stricken psycho-environment, any more than a rich physical environment necessarily leads to a rich and happy psycho-environment. This is not to deprecate the importance of animal comforts and the ambient environment, but rather it is to make clear that the psychological climate in most things is a more critical context than the physical climate.

Psychological climate refers to *all* of the influences that affect group communication. It includes all of the *environmental dimensions*, both physical and psychological, and particularly those human aspects of climate variously described as *accepting*, *understanding*, *facilitating*, and so on. These aspects could also be negative—that is, strongly *judgmental*, *evaluative*, *defensive*, *dogmatic*, and the like.

All human communication and interaction take place in some kind of psychological climate. Our surroundings and our involvement with them may or may not lead to motivation and better human relations. The attitudes that people hold about their organizations and the style of leadership they encounter (or express) in them are critical to the communication climate. The subtlety and importance of appropriate human interactions and transactions are often lost in a sea of organizational or environmental requirements.

Elton Mayo and F. J. Roethlisberger taught the lessons of the psycho-environment and human relations years ago. Too few of our organizational leaders, they argued, were alert to the fact that it is a human social problem and not an economic problem that they face.[8]

It took the Hawthorne studies of the 1930s, starting out in quest of knowledge about physical environment, to make very clear that it was the *human* environment that offered most in terms of motivated effort and moral conscience. The widely growing industrial unions of the thirties made quick note and quick demand not only for wage adjustments but also for human considerations. Today the fringes are truly misnamed psychologically as well as economically.

A horrendous amount of pseudosophisticated, naive, sometimes opportunistic manipulating of human relations and the work environment have undoubtedly slowed the emergence of a unified theory of human relations and the psycho-environment. In any event, it is now clear that a person's motivation depends to a large extent upon how he or she relates to his or her organizational group environment and the important people in it—those people and arrangements that affect a person's life, attitudes, and perception of the psychological climate.

Human Relations Theory

It is doubtful that any efforts parallel in human relations impact the studies done from 1924 to 1932 at the Chicago Hawthorne plant of the Western Electric Company. Mayo and his Harvard associates did not join the Western Electric team until 1927. In 1924 Hawthorne in collaboration with the National Research Council initiated a study with the purpose of determining the relationship between illumination intensity, or lighting, and worker efficiency as measured by production or output. The results were to confound the engineers, delight the socal psychologists, and usher in a new age of human relations and involvement.[9]

The assumption of this early study was that the better the lighting, the better the production of induction coils. With one group of workers the light intensity was held constant. With the experimental group the light intensity was varied, first made higher and then made lower than with the control group. When the lights went up production went *up*; when the lights went down production went *up*! To confound things even more, in the control group with which the lights remained constant the production also went *up*! In near desperation the lights were brought down even more. It was not until near moonlight that production slipped even a modicum. Obviously, something more than lighting was operating here. The researchers did not rule out a relationship between work and light, of course, but they did become dimly aware of another variable running wild in their experiment. They labeled it psychological. They then devised an expectation study with light in which they replaced bulbs of equal, rather than more, wattage. The workers, living up to expectations, commented favorably on the increased illumination. These early researchers were disturbed by the extraneous psychological variables and attempted to design a way of eliminating them. They thought they might isolate and control some of them, such as fatigue, rest periods, equipment, and the like. It was decided that if a small group of workers could be isolated in a specially partitioned-off room and asked to be their normal selves, then some of these psychological variables would be suppressed. Output could finally be correlated to physical conditions. At this point, Mayo and others from the Department of Industrial Research of the Harvard Graduate School of Business Administration became involved. Earlier studies by Mayo in a Philadelphia textile mill had prepared him for assessing the psychological and human variables. He had found that it was not so much rest periods that helped production, morale, and turnover as it was the workers' *involvement* and attention in *scheduling* the rest periods.

In this special room partially described above, the now famous "Relay Assembly Room" experiment was started. In the spring of 1927 six women were chosen as average representative workers of the 100 persons who assembled telephone relays. Moving these six workers into the test room made it possible to accurately tabulate the number of relays produced literally from one moment to another. Records were kept from 1927 to 1932. The plan was to get a normal output number and then vary payment, rest breaks, days off and company lunch and quitting times to see the effect of each under these controlled conditions. To keep things scientific, a very attentive observer was also present to maintain records and counsel with the women.

The results made the dimly emerging lesson of the lighting experiment much brighter. In brief review of a mountain of data, the following general findings can be reported: When wages were varied production went up; when breaks were varied production went up; free snacks, production went up; variations in quitting time, production went up. After 18 months of this, the researchers decided to take away all of these special conditions and go back to the first day in the special test room—let output return to normal, as it were. No one was quite prepared for the result! Production set an all-time high! It was also found that the usual fatigue curve did not pertain, nor did the one for absenteeism. Everything was better. Perhaps this is what Thomas Wolfe meant when he wrote, ''You can't go home again,'' or what Heroclites meant when he said, ''You can't step in the same river twice.'' No one could ever go back to day one; ''Nothing, nothing is the same.''

The research staff saw the light. People had begun to feel important. Stuart Chase's interpretation of what happened goes a long way toward defining human relations in its very best sense.

> What was this X? The research staff pulled themselves together and began looking at it. They conferred, argued, studied, and presently they found it. It wasn't in the physical production end of the factory at all. It was in the girls and their group. By segregating them into a little world of their own, by asking their help and co-operation, the investigators had given the young women a new sense of their own value. Their whole attitude changed from that of separate cogs in a machine to that of a congenial team helping the company solve a significant problem.
>
> They had found stability, a place where they belonged, and work whose purpose they could clearly see. And so they worked faster and better than they ever had in their lives. The two functions of a factory had joined into one harmonious whole.[10]

Another dimension of the psycho-environmental influence was found in an extension of the Hawthorne studies in a giant employee interview program. After some 2,000 interviews it was concluded that (1) complaints are often coverups or symptoms of personal and social problems; (2) a persuader should look upon wages, goods, work hours, and physical events as conveyers of social value; (3) a worker's social status or position should be taken into account in handling grievances; (4) the meaning a worker assigns his or her position is related to his or her perception of the extent to which that position permits a fulfilling of the social demands needed in his or her work; (5) the organization as a social unit is a value system from which an employee derives satisfaction or dissatisfaction based upon his or her expectations and perceived social status in the unit; (6) the significance of work as a motivator is defined by social experience off as well as on the job.[11]

Still further elaboration of the human relations element and the social organization that develops in work groups was gained observing and interviewing a small group of employees in the Bank Wiring Room. Some of these findings give insight into the psychology of environment reminiscent of what was discussed earlier concerning interpersonal needs and helping relationships. For example, the group quite effectively set its own standards for output, how supervision was to be treated, and interpersonal relations in general. There was great pressure to conform to these norms. The social organization and group spirit that developed were based primarily on sentiments, status, customs, behavior codes, and human interactions.

The student of communication, especially a would-be leader, is poorly trained if he or she is unaware of these informal social units that develop within the environment of any formal organization. It was Mayo's contention that the spirit of such groups should be a communication and leadership objective.

Psychological Safety

A healthy communication climate might be described as a *cohesive* context and environment in which the discussants, through *interaction*, achieve a mental state of relative psychological safety and freedom. *Interaction*, in this context, is communication behavior directed toward another person or persons when their reactions or mutual behavior are taken into account. It pertains directly to our interpersonal responsibilities in group communication.

What is being discussed is obviously a large part of the psychological climate. If we are faced with bad news, deserved criticism, necessary evaluation, or generally unhappy feedback, some cold or even defensive psychological climate is perhaps unavoidable. This is precisely the time when we must be our very best communicative selves, or we may make an already difficult psychological climate really impossible.

"Left lane, Jane. Left lane! *Left lane, Jane!!* Damn, we make left turns from the left lane. That's three bad mistakes." If you remember your driver-training group, you probably recall at least a few bad days during which criticism of your driving behavior seemed harsh (to you) or threatening, however necessary it may have been in the name of highway safety and your own driving skill. The way in which such criticism is given as well as taken is what is known as psychological climate.

If an English professor objectively criticizes a bad essay of yours line by line (as professors are paid to do), it is easy to become defensive. The voice and articulation teacher has to really consider psychological climate and safety. Correcting someone's diction, articulation, or pronunciation can be very threatening in group situations. "No, Leroy, it's [ASK] not [AX]."

Human interaction is, of course, a knife that cuts both ways. Someone may lack *sensitivity* as a message sender, but be too sensitive as a receiver. If on a given day Leroy is feeling superdefensive about his race, national origin, or some other large dimension of his personality, his group may find communication very difficult indeed. At this point Leroy has a considerable communication obligation to avoid being overly sensitive in his role as a receiver and to strive to reestablish a healthier group climate. It is as if we must have both thick and thin skins at exactly the same time. We need to develop a tolerance for conflicting information, beliefs, and perceptions, as well as a general tolerance for doubt and uncertainty.

The group climate and our assessment of and contribution to it are truly essential to how we learn, communicate, and grow. A flippant, sexist, or cute remark is sometimes all it takes to put your foot in your mouth.

We probably feel less safe psychologically in group situations pertaining to evaluation than in most other kinds. Where there is good rapport and basic respect for one another, a group may achieve a kind of *psychological freedom*, a happy climate in which a person's status is not unreasonably threatened, in which he or she feels accepted as a person, in which he or she has the freedom to be wrong and to become involved. Both psychological safety and freedom involve being accepted as an individual of some worth in a climate in which the individual is not persistently evaluated as a person.

When the group is tense and angry, emotional voices are heard and we are put to a real communication test. When our feelings are out of sync or out of balance with our beliefs, we are apt to ruin the psychological climate. Our emotions may affect the way we think in a given situation or communication episode, but the reverse is also true—the way we think affects the way we feel.

We cannot stop people from being human, which means any of us may occasionally let anger get the best of us. We will have more to say about anger and conflict in Chapter 6.

Shadow Groups

These are the informal, behind-the-scenes, often powerful groups that provide unstated rules and practices that allow bureaucracy to be expedited. It has been described as the "Inner Face" by *Time-Life Books* and sociologist Charles Page, and "consists of rules, groupings and sanctioned systems of procedure . . . they are never recorded in the codes or official blueprints . . . they are clearly and semipermanently established, they are just as 'real' and just as compelling on the membership as the elements of the official structure, and they maintain their existence and social significance throughout many changes of personnel."[12]

Shadow groups depend on close contact and usually limit themselves to one or two levels in the hierarchy. People come and go, roles change, power changes, but the shadow groups persevere. Their rules range from the social—youngest members get the coffee—to regulations of job swaps and even sanctions of the lazy. Their unofficial rules can be changed only by consensus, and are thus difficult to change by either the shadows or the official organization, the outer face.

These powerful groups occur at all levels including the executive. Some cross over, at least partway, into the formal organization. The Caucus Club in the General Motors building is well named; large banks buy loan officers multiple country-club memberships. The most dramatic example is the *zaibatzu* of prewar Japan, composed of four huge business groups that dominated the economy. The postwar occupation authorities broke up the zaibatzu and purged their leaders or so they thought. This shadow group continued to meet and make unofficial decisions that were faithfully followed. According to *Time-Life*, Mitsubishi is clearly under the control of this Inner Face. This informal group of about thirty meets once a month and " . . . decides on major new investments by member firms, approves large foreign deals, chooses the companies to help out brother firms in trouble and generally determines policy for the entire combine."[13]

Newcomers to organizational groups need to learn the unofficial as well as the official rules. Until one learns these rules, communications can be confusing. Some impossible-sounding directives are unofficially recorded by the shadow group so that the job is done with minimal strain. Without their help life can be complicated indeed. Are shadow groups getting weaker? Do they often create conflict? These questions will be explored in Chapter 6.

RULES AND PAST PRACTICES

In organizational settings not all group communication is concerned with the psycho-environment or even problem-solving strategies. There are more mundane announcements, reports, old business, and so forth in short business agendas with which we must live. To live with them comfortably, one must know something of the specific, official organizational rules that apply and how past practices often make or interpret them.

COMMON PARLIAMENTARY LAW

> Where there is no law, but every man does what is right in his own eyes, there is the least of real liberty.
>
> *Henry M. Robert*

History and Principles

Parliamentary law evolved from the rules and customs of the English Parliament. General or *common parliamentary law* came out of adaptations made by legislative bodies of the United States. It is widely adopted in deliberative organizations everywhere. It has become the common rule for groups engaging in consequential decision making. When such a group has *not* formally adopted any procedural rules, that group " . . . is commonly understood to hold itself bound by the rules and customs of the *general parliamentary law*—or *common parliamentary law*. . . . "[14]

Of course all small groups aren't always seriously deliberating, nor are they always democratic, but they all operate under some kind of formal or informal rules based on anything from Robert's Rules of Order to past practices. Nothing in common parliamentary law prohibits a group from confirming, adding to, or deviating from such law if they so decide. That is why bylaws, if a group has any, vary as they do.

As precise as parliamentary law is, it is basically designed to protect democratic principles and the rights of the group members. They are based on a regard for the rights of

- the majority,
- the minority, especially a strong minority—greater than one third,
- individual members,
- absentees, and
- all these together.[15]

A seventeenth-century manual prepared for the convenience of Parliament lists rules still useful to any deliberative group today:

- one subject at a time,
- alternation between opposite points of view,
- call for the negative vote also,
- avoidance of personalities in debate,
- confine debate to the merits of the question,
- divide questions that allow for split opinions.[16]

Committees and Small Groups

Committee rules are much less formal in the parliamentary sense and are often similar to those that control many small groups in the organizational settings that interest us. Ordinarily committees are of two types: *standing* and *special*. In a business or professional organization many committees have a continuing existence and are considered *standing*: personnel, administration, policy, finance, and so forth. Other committees are temporary or *special* purpose: entertainment, housing, retirement, training, library, and United Fund. In larger organizations some special committees become standing.

As always, *Robert's* is formal in describing the informality of the rules and procedures for committees. These are directed at groups of twelve or less where business might be hindered by excessive formality:

- Members are not required to obtain the floor before making motions or speaking, which they can do while seated.
- Motions need not be seconded.
- There is no limit to the number of times a member can speak to a question, and motions to close or limit debate generally should not be entertained.
- Informal discussion of a subject is permitted while no motion is pending.
- Sometimes, when a proposal is perfectly clear to all present, a vote can be taken without a motion's having been introduced. Unless agreed to by general consent, however, all proposed actions of a board must be approved by vote under the same rules as in other assemblies, except that a vote can be taken initially by a show of hands, which is often a better method in such meetings.
- The chairperson need not rise while putting questions to vote.
- The chairperson can speak in discussion without rising or leaving the chair; and, subject to rule or custom within the particular board (which should be uniformly followed regardless of how many members are present), usually can make motions and usually votes on all questions.[17]

In addition to those procedures quoted above, others are suggested throughout the fifty-four pages of Chapter 16 of *Robert's Rules of Order* (1981). Some of the more pertinent ones follow:

- The chairperson need not abstain from speaking and voting. He or she may be the most active participant.
- A committee chairperson may be appointed by the parent organization or elected by the committee members. If neither action is taken or specified, the first person named is the chairperson.
- A quorum, unless otherwise specified, is a simple majority.
- "Straw" votes are permissible.
- "Consent" votes are allowable. "Hearing no objections, may I presume we agree?"
- The chairperson is responsible for the minutes but may delegate the chore.

The last rule on *minutes* can be a very important one should there be disagreements at a later date about just what business was discussed or decided. Minutes when distributed also assure that those members who were absent will be informed of the group's action and generally be brought up to date. They are the rule and/or practice in most small groups in organizational settings.

Order of Business and Agenda

Parliamentarians make a distinction between agendas and the order of business. The order of business is the overall procedure of a meeting; an agenda is a list of items of business to be brought before a group for consideration at a specific meeting.[18] What follows is a standard order of business for a formal group meeting.

ORDER OF BUSINESS

1. Reading and Approval of Minutes
2. Reports of Officers, Boards, and Standing (that is, permanently established) Committees
3. Reports of Special (Select or Ad Hoc) Committees (that is, committees appointed to exist only until they have completed a specific task)
4. Special Orders (that is, matters which have previously been assigned a type of special priority)
5. Unfinished Business and General Orders (that is, matters previously introduced, which have come over from the preceding meeting)
6. New Business (that is, matters initiated in the present meeting)[19]

The *agenda*, or the list of items of business to be discussed, is normally circulated in advance of the meeting and may fit the *order of business* in several places. If matters of business were left undone at the last meeting they could be brought up under item 5, Unfinished Business. If matters of business are related to the reports or special orders of committees (or subcommittees), they could be brought up under item 2, 3, or 4. In these cases the committee chairpersons may provide the agenda for the meeting chairperson. Obviously, an agenda of new business would come up under that category.

An organization's agenda might be very detailed and show the entire order of business with one or more of the specific agendas inserted in the appropriate places. It might also be a simple list of the new business to be discussed.

AGENDA

1. Job descriptions
2. Home care accreditation
3. Escort service
4. TV advertising
5. Parking lot

The group tackling the heavy agenda above decided, after discussion, that there were solutions needed in item 1, Job descriptions; item 3, Escort service; and item 5, Parking lot. Items 1 and 2 were referred to appropriate standing committees for action; item 3 was retained for their immediate and further consideration; item 4, TV advertising, was postponed indefinitely since no pressing problem was discovered. The group spent the rest of their meeting time discussing the parking lot, concluding that there was a very real problem. They then appointed a *special* committee to study the problem further and recommend solutions. We'll come back to this *special* problem-solving small group and its own agenda shortly.

ORGANIZATIONAL NORMS

Common Group Practices

Common group practices or norms or rules while not in written form still have considerable influence over members' conduct and behavior.

The way in which the parent organization conducts business, solves problems, and makes decisions implies norms and practices for the subgroups to follow. A subgroup may, of course, modify, amend, or even challenge these rules in the conducting of its own business. It is important to review such norms and practices occasionally to see if they still make sense. Perhaps they are blindly accepted simply because they have been the "rule" for so long.

Some of these norms cover mostly social behavior. Is it "strictly business" or can we "joke around"? Does it matter where we sit? Is smoking allowed? Can we argue with the boss? Some norms involve mostly procedures: Do we follow some kind of common parliamentary rules? Is the agenda sacrosanct? Do we formally vote on things? Does leadership move with the topic or is it guarded by the chairperson? Are there punishments? Can new members speak up?

Policy and Past Practices

Policies are more definite rules that govern group behavior, especially communication and decision making. They should be in written form but frequently are not. They may emerge from long-standing practices or, in some cases, are the will (or whim) of the boss. Contracts, job descriptions, labor agreements, and promotions are usually matters of policy, not to be taken lightly.

When matters of policy are being challenged or subjected to revision, small groups as well as larger ones in organizational settings typically (normatively) become more formal in their deliberations. Just the discussion of personnel policy matters may cause an otherwise informal group to suddenly revert to common parliamentary rules. Seconds to motions are required, votes are carefully counted, and voting qualifications and quorums may be challenged. Frequently there is some written guidance in these matters; old timers know the rules and procedures by heart. Newcomers are advised to review such policies and also ask what practices have been followed in the past. In the case of labor contracts, past practices are critical in that, for an arbitrator at least, they interpret the contract. All manner of policies outside of your organization may supersede your own. These are such things as accrue from EEOC (Equal Employment Opportunity Commission), Title VII (affirmative action laws), IRS (Internal Revenue Service), and the EPA (Environmental Protection Agency).

Problem-Solving Formats (or Agendas)

The question of fitting your business agenda into the order of business was discussed briefly under "Order of Business and Agenda." Here we are concerned with how one fits the problem-solving format (or agenda) into the business agenda.

First, you must decide which of the formats is most appropriate for the problem you are to discuss. Sometimes the procedural leader decides the format; other times (check your norms) the group itself decides and makes that decision an agenda item.

Some groups have a kind of S.O.P. (standard operating procedure) for these matters. The group in our previous illustration has one procedure for problems that are apt to be quickly referred to others (or rejected as problems) and another for those with which they will wrestle themselves.

The first is a two-step procedure:

1. Is it a problem?
   a. Does it involve policy?
   b. Is it technical?
2. Is there a related standing committee or organizational group?
   a. Should it be referred?
   b. Should it be referred with recommendations?

If discussion could quickly determine that the matter was of little concern because someone had overreacted, or perhaps it was recently solved (as was the case with ''TV advertising''), then step 2 was unnecessary. If, on the other hand, a problem was readily apparent or had a probability of becoming so, and if it was technical (as in the cases of ''Job Descriptions'' and ''Escort Services''), then the question of standing committees arises. Since there were important standing committees responsible for ''Job Descriptions'' and ''Employee Safety,'' these matters were appropriately referred.

The ''Parking Lot'' item was given enough general discussion to decide that a *special* committee should be appointed for further consideration and decision. The two-step format allowed them to attach a recommendation that their solution be limited to $100,000 in cost since that was all the line item budget provided.

The *special* group charged with the ''Parking Lot'' responsibility now knows it has a *problem* in need of a solution. Perhaps more than one good solution is possible. Perhaps policy expects them to recommend more than one solution for the parent group or board to decide.

After such preliminary ''rules review'' or ''past practices'' review, the group decided its business agenda, which in this case is the same as the problem-solving format. This is why these patterns or formats are often referred to as agendas.

The charge handed down from the parent group and the group's inventory of their own information led to the following agreement (agenda or format) for procedure.

AGENDA
PARKING LOT PROBLEM

1. Definition
   a. User complaints
   b. City inspector's report
2. Analysis
   a. Shared use policy
   b. City code violations
3. Criteria
   a. Satisfy users
   b. Meet city codes
   c. Improved safety
   d. $100,000 budget

4. Solutions
   a. Contractors A, B, and C
   b. Evaluate against criteria
   c. Recommend Contractor B
   d. Recommend budget and plan of implementation

FORMS OF DISCUSSION

Some meetings in organizational settings call for special arrangements and procedures—for example, when your group has guests, observers, a trainer, a debate, or perhaps a guest speaker. There is general agreement about what these forms are, but their applications vary widely. Parts of the standard forms and special techniques may be combined to facilitate problem solving. Brainstorming may be used as an opener when many ideas are wanted in a short period of time. If some members give short speeches or reports utilizing their particular expertise or experience with a problem, you are engaging in a partial symposium. It is therefore useful to be aware of these standard forms to enrich your agendas and to know what to expect should you be invited to participate in one of them.

STANDARD FORMS

The basic forms of group discussion are *dialogue, panel,* and *symposium.* A *forum* is simply that part of a discussion in which guests or observers may speak. It can be and often is included in any of the discussion forms. Forums are *open* groups. When there is neither audience nor observers, it is considered a *closed* group.

Dialogue

A *dialogue* is a two-person interaction that may be simple conversation, an interview, or counseling. If a dialogue is held before a group and they are invited to participate, the interaction becomes a dialogue forum (see Figure 5.4).[20]

Figure 5.4 Dialogue forums.

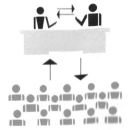 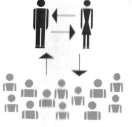 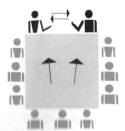

Panel

The *panel* discussion is most often composed of three to seven persons pursuing a common goal in an informal climate that aids spontaneous interaction (see Figure 5.5). An audience may or may not be present. A panel discussion generally calls for a procedural leader—one who plans, starts, and ends the meeting—and some *agenda*.

Figure 5.5   Panel forums.

Symposium

A *symposium* is a small, open group (three to five persons) that has special knowledge of different aspects of a broad topic (see Figure 5.6). Each individual makes an uninterrupted speech before an audience. A procedural leader controls the order of speakers and the time limits. A forum usually follows except when an audience is not physically present (as with radio or TV broadcasts). Frequently the symposium speakers then relate to one another more informally in a panel discussion.

These forms of discussion—dialogue, panel, and symposium—may be used for information sharing, problem solving, or decision making, as well as for instructional purposes. Examples of information-sharing groups are *staff meetings, study groups*, and *workshops*. The overlap among these groups is evident and probably unavoidable. A workshop, for example, may be thought of as a study group that has concentrated its work into a couple of days, or even a few hours. Problem-solving groups include

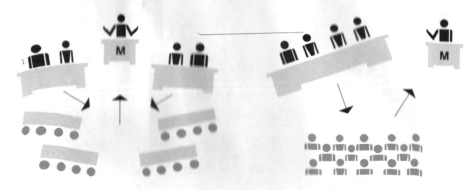

Figure 5.6   Symposium forums.

committees, *conferences*, and *governing boards* or *councils*. These discussion groups have the power of decision, or at least the power to recommend action based on their collective problem solving. Their group discussions are sometimes closed to nonmembers.

SPECIAL TECHNIQUES

Instructional Formats

Instructional formats of discussion include case conferences, role playing, and to some extent all the forms and techniques of discussion. A *case conference* is a discussion of a real or hypothetical incident that is meant to have a learning outcome for the participants. It may or may not be conducted with an audience present. It can be evaluated according to participant interaction, leadership, agenda setting, and the solution.

The extemporaneous acting out of assigned roles, or dramatic parts in a group—often in a case conference—is known as role playing (see Figure 5.7). As a technique role playing is often a good preliminary to the other forms of discussion.

Figure 5.7 Role playing.

Large groups in which wider forum participation is desired may be divided into subgroups of four to six persons for more intimate, informal discussion. This technique is known as *buzz*, ''Phillips 66,'' or ''Discussion 66'' (see Figure 5.8). The numbers refer to subgroups of six that discuss a carefully worded question. The results of the individual buzz sessions are reported to the larger group by a spokesperson. The number of people in the subgroups seems to be important: A person is more apt to speak up in a group of six than in one of sixty.

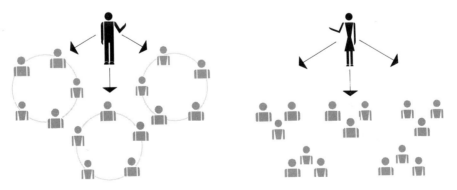

Figure 5.8 Buzz groups.

Brainstorming

This technique operates in an arbitrary psychological climate complete with penalties, the purpose of which is to prohibit immediate criticism of ideas (see Figure 5.9). Brainstorming permits more creative ideas to come to light in a short period of time than the more traditional climate.[21] This technique also can be combined with other forms and used for purposes other than instruction. It can be particularly useful when a great many ideas are wanted from a group in a short period of time. It is a good technique for screening attitudes and opinions. Take the question "What should this class use as a topic for a project discussion?" Under brainstorming rules this question regularly produces sixty or seventy topics in 10 minutes. No evaluative discussion of the topics is allowed until later. Using buzz groups to screen the list more systematically is a good follow-up.

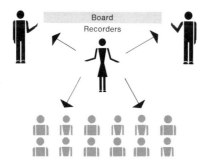 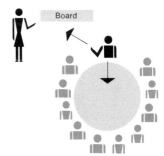

Figure 5.9 Brainstorming.

If your organization were the marketing group for the local telephone company and your problem was to think up creative ways to increase the sale of extension phones, *brainstorming* might be a good way to open your meeting. The Industrial Relations Center of the University of Chicago as well as the advertising agency of Batten, Barton, Durstine and Osborn (BBDO) recommend rules similar to those which follow.

1. *Criticism is ruled out.* Adverse judgment of ideas must be withheld until later.
2. *"Free-wheeling" is welcomed.* The wilder the ideas the better; it is easier to tame down than to think up.
3. *Quantity is wanted.* The greater the number of ideas, the more the likelihood of good ones.
4. *Combination and improvement are sought.* Panel members should hitchhike on suggestions by others and try to turn two or more ideas into still another idea.

A visual aid also states these rules. The chairperson explains that he or she will ring a bell whenever any panelist violates any of the rules.

A list of idea-spurring words and questions is thought useful for brainstorm leaders.

IDEA-SPURRING QUESTIONS

Put to other uses? New ways to use as is? Other uses if modified?

Adapt? What else is like this? What other ideas does this suggest?

Modify? Change meaning, color, motion, sound, odor, taste, form, shape? Other changes?

Magnify? What to add? Greater frequency? Stronger? Larger? Plus ingredient? Multiply?

Minify? What to subtract? Eliminate? Smaller? Lighter? Slower? Split up? Less frequent?

Substitute? Who else instead? What else instead? Other place? Other time?

Rearrange? Other layout? Other sequence? Change pace?

Reverse? Opposites? Turn it backward? Turn it upside down? Turn it inside out?

Combine? How about a blend, an assortment? Combine purposes? Combine ideas?

Nominal Group Technique (NGT)

There are several adaptations of the brainstorming technique. One that purports to better balance the task and socio-emotional dimensions of small groups is called *nominal group technique* (NGT).[22] Four steps are involved: *First*, a silent brainstorm is held, that is, members write their ideas privately. *Second*, there is a round-robin reporting or sharing. *Third*, a discussion is held to better clarify the ideas. *Fourth*, ideas are ranked and averaged mathematically. Sometimes more steps are added to discuss the vote and perhaps revote.[23] The thesis is that people will have less fear of sanctions while working alone (step 1) and therefore have better ideation.

LISTENING

COMMON ERRORS

Consider this group interaction between Jane and Jim from Jim's perspective.

Jane:	In my thinking I've come to the conclusion that certain narcotic drugs should be legalized in the same way alcohol is legal. I guess what I'm really talking about are marijuana derivatives.
Jim:	(thinking) *How can she possibly argue that?*
Jane:	Furthermore, I think . . . (talk, talk, talk).
Jim:	(thinking) *THC (active ingredient in marijuana) is a central nervous system depressant and as such is the functional equivalent of other CNS depressants . . .*
Jane:	But you know . . . (talk, talk, talk).
Jim:	(thinking) *. . . like barbiturates . . .*
Jane:	My argument seems to be losing . . . (talk, talk, talk).
Jim:	(thinking) *. . . seconal, phenobarbital, amytal . . . dangerous stuff.*
Jane:	So anyway, I guess I really have to come off my initial argument.
Jim:	(talking) How can you make such a claim? THC is a CNS depressant, the functional equivalent of barbiturates. We might as well make seconal legal. Could you imagine that? A bunch of seconal ''heads'' running down everything in sight with their cars.
Jane:	(puzzled) Yeah, I know. In fact that's just what I'm saying. Weren't you listening?
Jim:	(embarrassed) Oh, sorry . . .
Jane:	Really . . .

In this example Jim has failed to be a good listener, but what happened to him is common. We get so *ego-involved* with an argument that we spend the lion's share of our nontalking time in developing and rehearsing our counter-arguments. In doing so we sometimes fail to grasp the texture or logic or history of the initial argument. We don't listen; we may not even be hearing.

Failure to listen adequately has relational implications. In the example, Jim is telling Jane nonverbally that he didn't listen. Jane might interpret this as insulting or condescending on Jim's part (a one-up move). With the characteristics of the relationship gone awry, much of the real message may be lost. An unproductive and unwanted conflict may even result—all this because of Jim's listening mistake. Therefore, listening has clear message and relationship implications. We can unintentionally "put someone down" by our failure to listen. Sometimes we fail to realize this when we are insensitive to relational cues and find ourselves in a real communication bind.

The key to communicative competence and good listening is in being a *participant observer*. In our example Jim was participating; he certainly had a *line* to say. But he put himself in *wrong face* because the line was inappropriate. Jim uttered an inappropriate line because he failed to *observe* the interaction. He lacked reflexive listening skills. Had Jim been both participating and observing his interaction, he would have seen that Jane was working her way out of her initial claim. If Jim had listened more carefully, the interpersonal encounter would have been better coordinated and he probably would not have the relationship problems that he now has.

A survey of training directors indicated that poor listening was one of the most important problems they faced. Among the causes was their finding that, like Jim, most people mistakenly believe that they *are* good listeners.[24] If that's not enough, listening was ranked most perplexing during (1) meetings, (2) performance appraisals, and (3) superior–subordinate communication.

LISTENING MODEL

If we can become better listeners by understanding the listening process, the following four-step model may help.

The messages entering the model in Figure 5.10 illustrate that some messages are never heard because they never reach the sensations level, circle 2. They may be in the environment, circle 1, but they are not being attended to by the listeners. Other messages may reach only into sensation circle 2, never be totally understood, and then ignored. Even the messages that penetrate the intrapersonal response circle (message

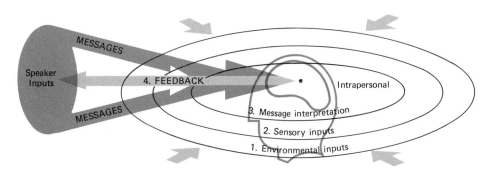

Figure 5.10   Ross perceptive listening model.[25]

interpretation) may be disregarded. The arrows also remind us that we are often dealing with several messages simultaneously or at least in very close succession. They may compete with and distort one another. Because of their complexity or perhaps emotionality, some of the messages may need more time to go through the steps and overcome the specific barriers.

If, as listeners, we finally process all of these inputs—and they can be affective, cognitive, behavioral, verbal, and nonverbal—then we achieve some kind of intrapersonal response and *interpretation* (step 3). *Feedback* (step 4) to the sender and to one's own understanding (after self-observation) is the final step. ''I don't think I heard you.'' ''Did I say (or do) that?'' ''What did you call me?'' ''That's heavy; run it by me again.'' This feedback must go through the same circles for the sender who has now also become a receiver.

Since all of the steps can be operating at the same time with more than one message and with distractions possible at each step, it is no surprise that we often have listening problems.

Environmental Inputs

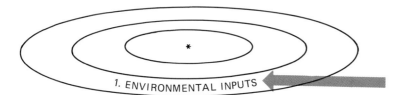

The place, the setting, the auditorium, or the room are all environmental variables and inputs. Other environmental inputs can be more subtle: psychological climate, cultural differences, social standing—your personal perceptions of the group members and their messages. All of these affect what you hear and interpret. Any of them can cause listening to suffer or cease. Part of that syndrome is also caused by intrapersonal inputs—evidence that the four steps are processual, but not always sequential.

Sensory Inputs

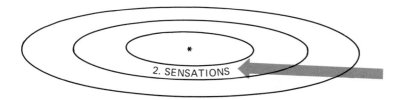

Step 2 deals with more than hearing. Since all of your sensory inputs relate to each other, your hearing is affected by your other senses.

Some sensory barriers are reasonably obvious. If someone is operating a jack hammer or beating a drum, you may lose the verbal signal because of sheer noise. You have learned that you hear poorly when you are tired. Sensory distraction could be competing noises, other verbal messages, or distractions by the other senses. A really foul smell, temperature extremes, an attractive face—any of these can be barriers to hearing. Assume you have overcome the barriers and are willing to remain attentive; you are finally auding (or hearing) but may not be seriously listening.

Message Interpretation

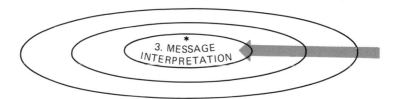

      Message interpretation and reconstruction depends on *intrapersonal* inputs. It is the most important step in effective listening.

      Your knowledge, past experience, attitudes, emotional blocks, and so forth start to interpret the group's messages; critical decoding has begun. A listener's motivation, intelligence, cognitive complexity, and personal constructs greatly affect what meaning that listener will finally deduce from all of the inputs.

      In step 3 we are talking about your *understanding* of what you are listening to. Understanding is really the link between people's direct perspectives and metaperspectives on experience. To the extent that you understand my direct experience of you and vice versa, we have understanding.

      With understanding we are better able to sense the characteristics of the episodes within which our speech acts occur. Understanding helps us determine when our groups are asking for advice, help, or just looking to "blow off some steam" communicatively. With an understanding of the episodes from which people are working, we better coordinate our communication behaviors. Listening is therefore a key to understanding.

Feedback

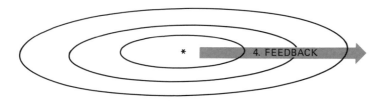

      In step 4, *feedback*, we are talking about the things you do and say while you are listening (or right after). Feedback is both verbal and nonverbal, obvious and subtle.

      After a terrible budget meeting, Ross emerges:

           Bernie: I'd like you to look at this new . . .
     Ross (angrily):   What the heck is wrong now?

Bernie: Is this a bad time?

Ross: I'm sorry Bernie; it really is. Can we . . .

Ross responded honestly (if emotionally), and Bernie wisely tested the waters to see if Ross was in a listening mood.

Sometimes we try to avoid difficult listening situations by trying to repress feedback. After silently listening to a group member unfairly and emotionally rail about her budget director, the group sat stunned.

Railer to group: I'm certainly glad you agree with me!

Group member: (startled) Hold on, where do you get that idea?

Had the group elected not to react at all, they could have been grossly misunderstood by the ''railer'' and perhaps the budget director as well. Clearly, we must react somehow, and we must consider the context and situation when we do. Perhaps there are times when we should sharply interrupt or at least reflect the message back to the sender.

TABLE 5.1   10 Keys to Effective Listening

KEYS TO EFFECTIVE LISTENING	THE BAD LISTENER	THE GOOD LISTENER
1 Find areas of interest	Tunes out dry subjects	Opportunitizes; asks ''What's in it for me?''
2 Judge content, not delivery	Tunes out if delivery is poor	Judges content; skips over delivery errors
3 Hold your fire	Tends to enter into argument	Doesn't judge until comprehension complete
4 Listen for ideas	Listens for facts	Listens for central themes
5 Be flexible	Takes intensive notes using only one system	Takes fewer notes. Uses 4–5 different systems, depending on speaker
6 Work at listening	Shows no energy output; fakes attention.	Works hard, exhibits active body state
7 Resist distractions	Is easily distracted	Fights or avoids distractions, tolerates bad habits, knows how to concentrate
8 Exercise your mind	Resists difficult expository material; seeks light, recreational material	Uses heavier material as exercise for the mind
9 Keep your mind open	Reacts to emotional words	Interprets color words; does not get hung up on them
10 Capitalize on fact that thought is faster than speech	Tends to daydream with slow speakers	Challenges, anticipates, mentally summarizes, weighs the evidence, listens between the lines to tone of voice

Source: ''Your Personal Listening Profile,'' p. 9. © Sperry Corporation.

Do we hear you saying . . . ?
Are you assuming that we . . . ?
Let me ask you this . . . ?

A responsible listener tries to be a participant observer. Being able to observe allows us to review our previous listening behaviors. Being able to see our behavior in terms of the total group interaction allows us to better coordinate, relate, and respond to other members.

The Sperry Corporation program is concerned mainly with improving listening skills. They, and their listening consultant, Dr. Lyman Steil, have developed ten rules or "keys" to effective listening shown in Table 5.1.

ETHICAL NORMS: RESPONSIBLE GROUP COMMUNICATION

Organizations are required by regulatory agencies and consumer groups to meet specified ethical practices and standards. This fact of life has motivated most organizational managements to take ethics more seriously than ever before. The penalties for noncompliance are too great, and, perhaps more importantly, business has learned that in modern society with its instant communication media, ethical behavior is pragmatically the best policy. In 1980 Ford Motor Company set things right for 14,000 women and minorities giving them $13 million in back pay. In 1983 General Motors Corporation worked out an agreement with the EEOC and the UAW to settle job discrimination charges, which cost the corporation $42 million.[26] Clearly, ethical norms are in. Many MBA programs and most organizational communication programs require some training in ethical norms. Many training programs across the spectrum of organizations are including sessions and even seminars in ethical behavior.

LIES AND MENTAL RESERVATIONS

A communicator is morally responsible for telling the truth and for the social consequences that result if the truth is not told. This critical statement is meant to include not only our words but all the nonverbals as well. "He tells a lie who has one thing in his mind and says something else by words or by any signs whatsoever [St. Augustine]." To some moral philosophers the natural end of speech is to communicate our thoughts, and a lie is evil because it frustrates the very end and purpose of speech.

Being honest and fair to the facts are obvious moral obligations. We must play by the game rules and obey the law. Using outright lies, manufactured facts, and "dirty tricks" is clearly unethical. Even here we encounter some problems.[27] Prudence is a virtue. Can the ethical person be honest without being unkind? Can he or she be both tactful and forthright?

Are some broad mental reservations allowed? Yes, say the ethicians, in the same way that a defendant pleads not guilty, or a doctor, questioned about professional secrets, replies I don't know. Yes, they say, because there were fair and sufficient *clues* within the special contexts and situations. A courtroom would not allow for any kind of mental reservation (a very special context). According to moralists, the common good is at stake here superseding the private good of the individual.

A strict mental reservation without any clue is a lie in any context. So too are all communications that are grossly unfair to the facts, or so subtle that they give the receiver no clue about possible alternatives.[28]

Honest clues protect the receiver's fundamental right of choice. Even in social compliance situations there is usually some choice. When choice is minimal, at least there are some alternatives (the courts when necessary). The ultimate decision of how to behave, act, interpret, or believe must in some way, however small, be left to the receiver. That choice must be a viable one. "Your money or your life" is no real choice.

SPECIAL SITUATIONS

If moral law permits some concealing of the truth, to what situations does this pertain? What are some guidelines? First, some generalizations with wide ethical acceptance in a democracy are the following:

> We have a right to do what is necessary or helpful to preserve our own personal dignity and independence.
>
> We have a right to keep our private affairs secret.
>
> We should do that which promotes mutual trust among people. (Doctors, lawyers, and others should not reveal secrets except in extraordinary circumstances in which the common good demands it.)

All of these generalizations deal with situations in which trust and some kind of *secret* put us in a double bind.

Joseph Sullivan, S. J., deals forthrightly with the ethical principles that should govern the keeping or revealing of secrets. We offer them for your consideration.

DEFINITIONS

Secret—is a truth which the possessor may (right) or ought (duty) to conceal.

Natural Secret—is a truth, which *from its own nature*, gives the possessor said right or duty.

> *For example:* One's own or one's neighbor's private affairs, the revelations of which, at least in ordinary circumstances, would cause reasonable offense or injury.

Secret of Promise—is a truth, which, *because of a promise made*, possessor has a duty and therefore a right to conceal.

Secret of Trust—is a truth, which, because of the fact that it was confided to one by another on the express or tacit agreement that having been communicated for a serious purpose it be held in trust, possessor has a duty and right to conceal.

> *For example:* Knowledge communicated to a lawyer or doctor, or even in some circumstances to a mere friend.

At times permits—i.e., man sometimes has the *right* to keep a secret.

At times commands—i.e., man sometimes has *more than a right*, he has a *duty*.

Question: When are these times?

Answer: a. *Man has a duty* to keep:

1. a *natural* secret—as long as
   a. the truth is not made common property by someone else;
   b. he cannot reasonably presume the leave of those concerned, to reveal it;
   c. concealing the truth works no serious harm to a community;
   d. he is not questioned about the matter by legitimate authority;
   e. it can be kept without serious inconvenience to himself or another.
2. A secret of *promise* as long as
   a, b, c, d, as above.
   e. it can be kept without serious inconvenience to himself or another, and even at the cost of such inconvenience, if he has *expressly promised* to do so.
3. A secret of *trust*—as long as
   a. *revelation is not necessary* to avert serious and impending harm from
      (1) the community,
      (2) the holder of the secret,
      (3) a third and innocent party who is endangered by the person who has confided the secret in another.
      (4) the one who confided the secret.
   The reason why the obligation of keeping a secret, even of promise, ceases in the circumstances mentioned above, is because, even when assuming obligations of a strict contract, no man can reasonably be thought to intend to bind himself in such circumstances. Cf. approved authors in Moral Theology.
   b. *Man has a right* to keep all secrets
      (1) in all the above-named cases where he has a duty;
      (2) in some of the cases mentioned where he has no duty.[29]

CULPABLE IGNORANCE

The intent of the sender is, of course, critical to an evaluation of the morality of his or her message. Equally important is the *role*, or *status*, of the sender. A person qualified to serve and serving in a leadership role has special ethical obligations. We expect our political and religious leaders and our professional people to be responsible, regardless of intent. A doctor convicted of malpractice rarely *intended* to do harm. An incompetent teacher may have *good intentions*. We judge such people harshly and hold them ethically responsible, even though their intent may have been good. Our laws accommodate this notion, not just for professionals, but for political leaders as well. Senators, Congressmembers, and other public figures have less protection from libel and slander than does the average citizen. (They, of course, do have their protective immunities, however.)

All of us have some ethical obligations beyond intent. Many people have been hurt by those who "meant well." All of us have some obligation to get our facts straight before sending messages that might capriciously misinform or injure the receiver. Moralists call this *culpable ignorance*—that is, ignorance usually from carelessness deserving blame.[30]

Most often we have an ethical responsibility to rhetorically analyze our receivers. For one not to care how people are apt to decode a message borders on immorality. A child may decode a message quite differently from a mature adult. How a particular person will interpret a particular message is an ethical consideration.

Nilsen challenges communicators to take into account the special circumstances, the intent, the feelings behind questions, and to combine honesty with respect for sensitivities. He goes on to say,

> Morally good communications are those which best preserve the integrity of the ego, contribute to personal growth, and harmonize relationships. These ends are served by communications which, in addition to providing the information needed in a given situation, permit and encourage the expression of thought and feeling, and reveal respect for the person as a person.[31]

UNSUPPORTED PERSONAL ATTACKS

When a member attacks the character of an opponent rather than the issue at hand, that person is guilty of *ad hominem* argument (unless the character of the person *is* the issue). When *ad hominem* is used solely to change the argument from one of issues to one of personalities, as a rule it is considered unethical. Our legal system calls it *slander* if the personal charges are unsupported, and *libel* if the charges are put in writing— clearly serious matters of ethics (and legality) for responsible people. To quote Ewbank and Auer: "It is unethical for a speaker to divert attention from weaknesses in his or her argument by unsupported attacks on an opponent or by appeals to hatred, intolerance, bigotry and fear."[32]

Let us not forget our ethical responsibilities as receivers.[33] As receivers we have a moral obligation to give *fair hearing* once we have committed ourselves to some legitimate interest in the issue. We must make an effort to understand the sender's biases and intent. We should show *tolerance* and work at understanding intent. Fair hearing replaces force in a free society.

To give fair hearing we must also analyze our own *range of acceptance*. Are we really stuck with a "hard" attitude? Is there some latitude in our position? To give a fair hearing also means allowing the other person some chance to talk. Ethical interpersonal communication doesn't outlaw aggressive arguing, but it does outlaw excessive monologuing; it does necessitate giving the sender some chance to make and explain his or her point. Fair hearing also calls for fair fighting. Sandbagging or setting people up for an obvious embarrassment borders on unethical entrapment. Dragging in every superfluous issue to deliberately confuse is another question of ethics. These unfair interpersonal conflict techniques will be discussed in Chapter 6. We have a moral obligation to ourselves and the society we represent to stubbornly protect our own independence and dignity.

T. J. Larkin, borrowing from Kant, reminds us that morality doesn't exist where the treatment of people is indistinguishable from the treatment of objects. "Act so that you treat humanity, whether in your own person or in that of another, always as an end and never as a means only." Larkin admonishes organizations " . . . to treat people as humans and not solely as things is not only a useful pluralistic exercise, revealing yet another perspective, but is in fact a moral imperative."[34]

SUMMARY

All organizations operate according to some kind of rules—written, unwritten, and those based on precedent and past practices. Some settings restrict communication while others aid it. Interpersonal communication cuts through all of the larger contexts. Some of these are mass, organizational, group, and public communication. Various levels of communication in ascending order are described by some as intrapersonal, interpersonal, group, and cultural.

Much of our communication is dictated by the setting. Time, place, ritual, and purpose have great influence on communication. Some general purposes for communicating are social, ventilation, seeking help, bargaining, and evaluation.

Motivation depends in large part upon how we relate to our psycho-environment, our organizations, and the important people in them. Human relations theory teaches us that a would-be leader is poorly trained if unaware of the informal communications and social units that develop within the environment of any formal organization.

The group studies done from 1924 to 1932 at the Chicago Hawthorne plant of the Western Electric Company ushered in a new age of human relations. The spirit of such groups should be a communication and leadership objective (Mayo).

A healthy communication climate is a cohesive context in which interactants achieve a state of psychological safety and freedom. The climate and the interactants' assessment of and contributions to it are essential to how they each learn, grow, and communicate. Psychological freedom is a climate in which our status is not unreasonably threatened, in which we feel accepted as people, in which we have the freedom to be wrong and to become involved.

Shadow groups are the informal, behind-the-scenes, often powerful groups that provide unstated rules and practices, which allow bureaucracy to be expedited. These powerful groups occur at all levels; some cross over into the formal organization. The most dramatic example is the *zaibatzu* of Japan.

Parliamentary law evolved from the English parliament and adaptations made by legislative bodies of the United States. It is designed to protect democratic principles and the rights of group members. Basic rules are one subject at a time, alternation of viewpoints, calling for the negative vote, avoidance of personalities, confining debate to the merits of the question, and dividing questions that allow for split opinions. In committees and small groups (twelve or fewer members) rules are much less formal in the parliamentary sense. Parliamentarians make a distinction between "order of business" and "agenda." The order of business is the overall procedure of a meeting; an agenda is a list of items of business to be brought before a group for consideration at a specific meeting. The way in which the parent organization conducts business, solves problems, and makes decisions implies norms and practices for the subgroups to follow. Policies are more definite rules that govern group behavior, especially communication and decision making. Contracts, job descriptions, labor agreements, and promotions are usually serious matters of policy. Past practices are critical in that they may interpret or condition labor contracts and policies handed down from outside the organization (EEOC, Title VII, IRS, EPA).

The basic forms of discussion are dialogue, panel, and symposium. Four techniques that may be used with any of these forms are buzz groups, role playing, brainstorming, and nominal group technique. A forum is simply that part of a discussion in which an audience may speak. These forms of discussion may be used for information sharing, problem solving, and instruction. Information-sharing groups include staff meetings, study groups, and workshops. Problem-solving groups include committees, conferences, and boards or councils. Instructional formats include case conferences, role playing, and, to some extent, all the forms and techniques.

Failure to listen adequately has interaction implications. We can unintentionally put someone down by our failure to listen. The key to communicative competence and good listening is in being a participant observer—that is, observing one's own behavior as well as others' behaviors while at the same time being an active participant. Most people believe they are good listeners when in fact many are not. Listening has been ranked the most perplexing problem during (1) meetings, (2) performance appraisals, and (3) superior–subordinate communication. The Ross listening model includes four steps: (1) environmental inputs, (2) sensory inputs, (3) message interpretation, and (4) feedback. Seven conversational rules for relating explain appropriate behaviors for (1) disagreeing, (2) stating opinions, (3) dismissal, (4) questioning, (5) criticism, (6) using open questions, and (7) perceiving free information.

Ethics involves moral responsibility in our interactions with others. A communicator is morally responsible for telling the truth and for the social consequences that result if the truth is not told. If mental restrictions are involved, fair and sufficient clues must be present regardless of context. Honest clues protect the receiver's fundamental right of choice. ''Morally good communications are those which best preserve the integrity of the ego, contribute to personal growth, and harmonize relationships [Nilsen].'' The intent of the sender is critical to the morality of his or her message. Equally important is the role or status of the sender. A person qualified to serve and serving in a leadership role has special ethical obligations. We expect such people to be responsible regardless of intent. We should show tolerance and an effort at understanding intent. If we are involved at all, we have a moral obligation to give fair hearing. As senders all of us have some obligation to get our facts straight before encoding messages that might capriciously misinform or injure the receiver. Moralists call this culpable ignorance—that is, ignorance from carelessness deserving blame.

PROJECTS AND CASES

PROJECTS

1. Write a two- to three-page evaluation of an out-of-class ''contemporary form of discussion'' you have observed or in which you were involved.

2. Describe a personal interaction that involved the four *levels* of communication (cultural, group, interpersonal, intrapersonal) described in Figure 5.3.

3. Attend a meeting of a relatively ritualized group (for instance, a church service, an award ceremony, a graduation, or a funeral service), and write a short report on its influence on human interaction.

4. Identify symptoms of a communication problem within a group or an organization of which you are a part.

5. Do big organizations do a poor job of communicating with young people as has been charged? Explain and discuss.

6. What kind of organization do you think facilitates good interpersonal and group communication?

7. Create a seven- or eight-word message and whisper it to one class member who, in turn, whispers it to the next person. Have the last class member repeat the message aloud and compare it to the original. Discuss the results.

8. Develop your own group verbal-pictorial model of the listening process. (See model in the chapter.)

9. Apply the Ross model to a specific group you have observed or were part of and evaluate the listening behavior. Report verbally and/or pictorially what lessons this exercise yielded. Pay special attention to the *bad* listening habits.

10. *Rogerian feedback exercise.* Divide into groups of three. Two converse and the third serves as a reporter-observer. After each short communication, the listener attempts to paraphrase the message to the satisfaction of the sender. For example:

> **Sender:** One of every four persons has been sexually abused.
> **Listener:** I heard, ''One of every four women has suffered wife abuse.''
> **Sender:** No, not quite. Let me try again . . . (and so on until the sender is satisfied with the paraphrase).

The reporter explains what he or she observed.

11. Try *really* listening to your parents the very next time you have an opportunity. Report, in 100 words or less, what you have learned about your listening habits (or theirs).

12. Discuss the listening quiz that follows. Compare yourself with others. Think of a specific person who you feel is a bad listener. Check the inventory in a way that best describes that person's behavior. Discuss.

LISTENING QUIZ

As a listener, how often do you find yourself engaging in these ten bad listening habits? First, check the appropriate columns. Then tabulate your score using the key below.

LISTENING HABIT	Frequency					Score
	Almost Always	Usually	Some-times	Seldom	Almost Never	
1. Calling the subject uninteresting						
2. Criticizing the speaker's delivery or mannerisms						

3. Getting *over*stimulated by something the speaker says						
4. Listening primarily for facts						
5. Trying to outline everything						
6. Faking attention to the speaker						
7. Allowing interfering distractions						
8. Avoiding difficult material						
9. Letting emotion-laden words arouse personal antagonism						
10. Wasting the advantage of thought speed (daydreaming)						

Key

TOTAL SCORE [ ]

For every "Almost Always" checked, give yourself a score of 1.
For every "Usually" checked, give yourself a score of 2.
For every "Sometimes" checked, give yourself a score of 3.
For every "Seldom" checked, give yourself a score of 4.
For every "Almost Never" checked, give yourself a score of 5.
Average is around 31.

From Sperry Corporation, Listening Program materials by Dr. Lyman K. Steil, Communication Development, Inc. for Sperry Corporation, © 1979. Reprinted by permission of Dr. Steil and Sperry Corporation.

13. How do group influence and ethics relate? Must receivers of influence operate in a "free marketplace of ideas"? How much choice must we give people we are trying to influence? What is free choice? How is it different from perceived free choice?

14. Discuss a real or hypothetical "allowable" mental reservation. Explain when it becomes a lie.

15. Locate a case of culpable ignorance, describe it, and explain how it might have been avoided.

CASES

1. Mr. Conway Communicates

Mr. Conway, the industrial relations director, took pride in his ability to adapt his communications to his listeners. In fact, in explaining the new pension plan to employees, he would start his conversation, "In your language. . . ." The plant supervisor reported to Conway that there was considerable ill will toward him among the workers.

WHICH ONE OF THE FOLLOWING COMMENTS ON THIS SITUATION SEEMS MOST SOUND TO YOU?

1. The tone of voice rarely offends the employees; it is usually language.
2. It is usually a combination of language and tone of voice that offends employees.
3. It is usually neither tone of voice nor language that offends employees.
4. It is possible to adapt a communication to the listener without seeming to talk down to him.
5. The danger of "talking down" to a listener is almost always involved in audience adaptation.

2. The Haberdashery Shop

A college student was employed during a summer vacation as a salesman in a retail haberdashery shop. He gave the following account of the experience:

I liked Mr. Bass, the boss, very much personally. He was very friendly, sometimes bought us drinks, and occasionally took us to a ball game. However, I had not been in the store long before I began to wonder at some of the things I saw. Once when a customer came in to pick up a hat the store did not have in stock but had agreed to order for him, Mr. Bass told him, "Come back Saturday. It hasn't arrived yet." When the customer left everyone laughed, and I learned that they had forgotten to order the hat and now had no intention of ordering it. "The next time he comes in," Mr. Bass said, "we'll tell him we couldn't get it, and since we have taken so much trouble he'll feel obligated to buy one from stock. There are a lot of angles to the selling game."

Mr. Bass liked to tell about the family of "hicks" who came in to buy a burial suit for their father. Before they knew what had happened, he had sold them a suit with two pairs of trousers. Pajamas are sized by the letters A, B, C, D, and E, but most customers give their chest measurement and leave it to the salesperson to translate this into the letter size. If the stock in C was a little low, the salesperson would give the customer a D and say nothing about it. I suppose the customer cut them off if they were too long. Once a boy came in for swimming trunks. We didn't have the right size, but the clerk held up a pair that, with a little stretching, looked as if it might fit. "How do these look?" the salesman asked. Deferring to the salesman's judgment, the boy said they looked all right, and thus made himself responsible for having chosen the size. If, after trying them on at home, he returned them, he would be reminded that he had chosen them and that the law forbids exchanging a bathing suit that has been worn.

Discuss.

3. A.L.K., Ph.D.

Dr. A.L.K., Ph.D., a consulting research psychologist, was asked by an advertising agency to conduct a consumer study pertaining to one of their advertised products. The agency had already prepared an interview questionnaire for him to use. The psychologist found that the questionnaire contained questions that appeared to bias the inquiry in favor of the brand of goods advertised by the agency. He pointed this out to the executive with whom he was dealing. The executive insisted that the questions be used as they were and indicated that if the psychologist did not care to do the job, some other market research agency would be willing to undertake it.

WHAT SHOULD THE PSYCHOLOGIST DO?

1. Since the study would be biased, report the agency to the Better Business Bureau, which deals with fraudulent business practices.
2. Refuse to do the study.
3. Report the company's proposal to the Committee on Ethics of the American Psychological Association.
4. Do the study and in reporting the findings to the company, point out that since the questionnaire was biased, no conclusion can be drawn.
5. Do the study on condition that his name will not appear publicly in connection with it.

4. The Washington Post Story

Discuss the following case in terms of where the ethics broke down interpersonally. Or did they? Is there also culpable ignorance here?

REPORTING FICTION

When a newspaper publishes a fabricated story, a lie, it betrays the trust of the community it serves, and apologies simply aren't enough to rescue its credibility.

All news organizations are vulnerable to dishonest or disturbed reporters. And, while safeguards exist at most newspapers for checking facts, few editors would claim that falsehoods *couldn't* slip into their news columns.

That said, there are some particularly disturbing questions raised by the Janet Cooke case. Miss Cooke, as you know, was awarded a Pulitzer Prize for a feature story about "Jimmy," an 8-year-old heroin addict. Her employer, the *Washington Post*, later returned the prize after discovering the story was a hoax.

We won't speculate about Miss Cooke's motives. But we can't help wondering how a distinguished newspaper was so easily victimized.

Most papers, including the *Post*, require reporters to document their stories for their editors, especially if the stories involve undisclosed sources and sensitive material. This wasn't done in the Cooke case.

The graphic portrayal of a preteen addict provoked one of the most elaborate police hunts in Washington history. No child was found. Still, as the months went by, the editors failed to demand any documentation from the reporter.

Incongruities in the story were noted by police, educational authorities, and even Miss Cooke's colleagues at the *Post*. Police were convinced that no drug dealer would supply "Jimmy" with free heroin for three years, as the story alleged. Educators noted it would be impossible for a public school student to attend math class only, as "Jimmy" was reported to. Finally, both the police department and the mayor declared the story fictitious. Still, Miss Cooke's editors not only made no attempt to check the veracity of the story, they submitted it for a Pulitzer Prize.

An investigation is underway at the *Post*, and editors throughout the country may benefit from it. But they will benefit a good deal more from the devastating reminder the Cooke case provides.

An invented news story in the journalism business is, ethically, the equivalent of embezzlement at a bank. Indeed, it is much worse than that, because it undermines public confidence in the whole mechanism by which free people are informed about their society and their world.

Janet Cooke has inflicted a grievous wound upon the *Washington Post*, but journalists everywhere are jolted by the pain.[35]

For one reporter's opinion, see and discuss the following article.

ONE REPORTER'S LIE SHAMES ALL OF US

It turns out that Janet Cooke won the wrong Pulitzer Prize. Instead of taking the gonfalon, as the hacks say, for feature writing, the lady from the *Washington Post* entered the wrong category.

She should have tried for the coveted prize in fiction.

I have no truck with liars, or sympathy for them, in any profession. When they pop up in the newspaper business, I really boil.

Ms. Cooke, in case you missed it, was awarded a $1,000 Pulitzer Prize last week for a story which appeared last year about an 8-year-old Washington child who allegedly had been hooked on heroin by his mother's boyfriend.

IT WAS A TEAR jerker, guaranteed to raise hackles and make your skin crawl. Nobody could make up a kid like little Jimmy.

The D.C. authorities were appalled that that sort of thing could go on in their city. They asked Ms. Cooke and her bosses at the *Post* to tell them where this poor child was so that he could be helped.

The *Post* refused, claiming First Amendment protection. Besides, said Executive Editor Ben Bradlee, the last thing the boyfriend did when Ms. Cooke left little Jimmy's home was threaten to carve her a new whatchamacallit if she dared to reveal where Jimmy lived.

Well, it turns out that somebody COULD make up a kid like little Jimmy. Janet Cooke did. She made up some other goodies as well.

ACCOMPANYING HER entry in the annual Pulitzer contest was a biography which was laced with more fiction. She was graduated with honors, she said, from Vassar and had earned a master's degree from the University of Toledo.

A real diamond in the rough. What a find.

But after the award was announced, somebody at Vassar said whoa. She only spent her freshman year there, then finished up an undergrad degree at Toledo.

Bradlee became suspicious, Ms. Cooke was grilled and finally admitted it all was a hoax; schools, degrees and, tragically, even little Jimmy.

The Pulitzer and the G-note were returned, to be given to the runner-up. Ms. Cooke resigned. An embarrassed Bradlee apologized profusely on behalf of the *Post*.

SO NOW, WHO do we blame? I've been in the newspaper business more than 30 years and I'll tell you who I hold solely responsible: Ms. Cooke.

A lot of people in this profession were ready to jump on the *Post* when the hoax story broke. That stems mostly from jealousy because it's such a good paper and has won so many prizes before.

Bradlee apparently is cocky and not well revered by his peers, i.e., other editors, especially those who think they broke the mold when they made Lou Grant.

The *Post* should have checked Cooke's credentials, they said. Her editors should have demanded that she identify her sources.

Baloney. There isn't a business or profession in the country that doesn't get a curve ball slipped past it once in a while. How many hysterectomies do you suppose have been done by guys with Latin degrees on the wall who've never been closer to an operating table than the butcher block at the neighborhood grocery store?

AS FOR DEMANDING the sources, they obviously had to trust Ms. Cooke's story of the threats. I've never had an editor kill a story because he didn't trust my source. There's a mystic leap involved, I guess. That's what we peddle in this business. Trust.

At one time or another, every good journalist gets into a trick bag. Maybe we get careless. Maybe we believe the wrong source. It's demeaning and embarrassing and it scars us because we have been used to propagate a hoax.

But any journalist who knowingly lies to the people who buy the paper isn't worth the powder to blow her to Kingdom Come. She leaves and it's over.

The rest of us have to live with the shame.[36]

NOTES

1. Stephen W. Littlejohn, *Theories of Human Communication* (Columbus, Ohio: Charles E. Merrill, 1978), p. 204.

2. Rensis Likert, *New Patterns of Management* (New York: McGraw-Hill, 1961), p. 104.

3. Reprinted from *Communication: The Social Matrix of Psychiatry* by Jurgen Ruesch, M.D. and Gregory Bateson with the permission of W. W. Norton & Company, Inc. Copyright © 1968, 1951 by W. W. Norton & Company, Inc.

4. O. Martyniuk and others, "Effect of Environmental Lighting on Impression and Behavior," in *Architectural Psychology: Proceedings of the Lund Conference*, ed. R. Kuller (Stroudsburg, Pa.: Dowden, Hutchinson & Ross, 1973); P. A. Bell, J. D. Fisher, and R. J. Loomis, *Environmental Psychology* (Philadelphia: W. B. Saunders, 1978).

5. N. W. Heimstra and L. H. McFarling, *Environmental Psychology*, 2nd ed. (Monterey, Calif.: Brooks/Cole, 1978).

6. W. Griffitt, "Environmental Effects on Interpersonal Affective Behavior: Ambient Effective Temperature and Attraction," *Journal of Personality and Social Psychology*, 15 (1970), 240–44.

7. D. C. Glass, J. E. Singer, and J. W. Pennebaker, "Behavioral and Physiological Effects of Uncontrollable Environmental Events," in *Perspectives on Environment and Behavior*, ed. D. Stokols (New York: Plenum, 1977).

8. Elton Mayo, *The Human Problems of an Industrial Civilization* (New York: Macmillan, 1933).

9. Excellent accounts of these studies may be found in Elton Mayo, *The Human Problems of an Industrial Civilization*; F. J. Roethlisberger and W. J. Dickson, *Management and the Worker* (Cambridge, Mass.: Harvard University Press, 1939); George C. Homans, "The Western Electric Researches," in *Fatigue of Workers: Its Relation to Industrial Production*, by the Committee on Work in Industry of the National Research Council (New York: Reinhold, 1941), chap. 4; Stuart Chase, *Men at Work* (New York: Harcourt Brace Jovanovich, 1945).

10. Chase, *Men at Work*, p. 19. For a scientific analysis, see T. N. Whitehead, *The Industrial Worker* (Cambridge Mass.: Harvard University Press, 1938).

11. For a full account, see Roethlisberger and Dickson, *Management and the Worker*; also, for a current reworking of the data and a model of social network development, see R. D. McPhee, "A Model of Social Network Development in Organizations," *Central States Speech Journal*, 37, no. 1 (Spring 1986), 8–18.

12. R. Steinberg, *Man and the Organization* (New York: Time-Life, 1975), p. 101.

13. Ibid., p. 103.

14. Henry M. Robert, *Robert's Rules of Order Newly Revised* (Glenview, Ill.: Scott, Foresman, 1981), p. 2.

15. Ibid., p. xlii.

16. Ibid., p. xxi (paraphrased for brevity).

17. Ibid., pp. 405–6.

18. James A. McMonagle and Emil R. Pfister, *The Membership Manual* (New York: Vantage, 1970), p. 35.

19. Robert, *Robert's Rules of Order*, p. 21.

20. For an interesting discussion of physical arrangement, see Paul Bergevin, Dwight Morris, and Robert M. Smith, *Adult Education Procedures* (Greenwich, Conn.: Seabury, 1963); see also Robert Sommer, *Personal Space* (Englewood Cliffs, N.J.: Prentice-Hall, 1969), pp. 58–73.

21. Alex F. Osborn, *Applied Imagination: Principles and Procedures of Creative Thinking* (New York: Scribner's, 1963).

22. See A. L. Delbecq, A. H. VandeVen, and D. H. Gustafson, *Group Techniques for Program Planning* (Glenview, Ill.: Scott, Foresman, 1975).

23. For another interesting adaptation of brainstorming called "synectics," see F. L. Ulschak, L. Nathanson, and P. G. Gillian, *Small Group Problem Solving* (Reading, Mass.: Addison-Wesley, 1981).

24. Gary T. Hunt and Louis P. Cusella, "A Field Study of Listening Needs in Organizations," *Communication Education*, 32 (October 1983), 393–401. See also Andrew D. Wolvin, "Meeting the Communication Needs of the Adult Learner," *Communication Education*, 33 (July 1984), 269.

25. For a detailed description of the Ross listening model, see R. S. Ross, *Speech Communication: the Speechmaking System* (Englewood Cliffs, N.J.: Prentice Hall, 1989), Chap. 2. Other excellent models of the listening process are Wolvin-Coakley (RECEIVING, ATTENDING, ASSIGNING MEANING, RESPONDING) in Andrew D. Wolvin and Carolyn Gwynn Coakley, *Listening* (Dubuque, Ia.: Wm. C. Brown Publishers, 1988); and Sier (SENSING, INTERPRETATION, EVALUATION, REACTION) in "Your Personal Listening Profile," © 1980 Sperry Corporation, p. 4. See also Lyman K. Steil, Larry L. Barker, and Kittie W. Watson, *Effective Listening* (Reading, Mass.: Addison-Wesley, 1983).

26. *Bureau of National Affairs*, vol. 1 (October 1983), 237.

27. M. Knapp and M. Comadena, "Telling It Like It Isn't: A Review of Theory and Research on Deceptive Communications," *Human Communication Research*, 5, no. 3 (Spring 1979), 270–85.

28. See J. Jaksa and S. Rhodes, "A 'Content-ethic' for Interpersonal Communication," *Michigan Speech Association Journal*, 14 (1979), 80–88.

29. J. F. Sullivan, S.J., *Special Ethics* (Worcester, Mass.: Holy Cross College Press, 1948), pp. 26–27.

30. See L. Flynn, "The Aristotelian Basis for the Ethics of Speaking," *The Speech Teacher*, VI, no. 3 (September 1957), 179–87; see also R. Johannesen, *Ethics in Human Communication*, 2nd ed. (Prospect Heights, Ill.: Waveland Press, 1983), p. 30.

31. T. R. Nilsen, *Ethics of Speech Communication* (Indianapolis: Bobbs-Merrill, 1974), pp. 88–89.

32. Henry Lee Ewbank and J. Jeffery Auer, *Discussion and Debate* (New York: Appleton-Century-Crofts, 1951), p. 258.

33. F. Haiman, "Democratic Ethics and the Hidden Persuaders," *Quarterly Journal of Speech*, XLIV, no. 4 (December 1958), 385–92; see also Johannesen, *Ethics of Human Communication*, pp. 124–26.

34. T. J. Larkin, "Humanistic Principles for Organizational Management," *Central States Speech Journal*, 37, no. 1 (Spring 1986), 36–44.

35. *The Detroit News*, April 19, 1981, sec. A, p. 14.

36. Pete Waldmeir, *The Detroit News*, April 19, 1981, sec. B, p. 3.

6

CONFLICT

The distinguished professor Clyde Coombs helps set the tone for this chapter: "War is not inevitable but . . . conflict is." So does Professor Kelly: "Perfect organizational health is not freedom from conflict. On the contrary, if properly handled, conflict can lead to more effective and appropriate adjustments."[1]

TYPES OF CONFLICT

All typing systems cross over, combine, and transform and hence are somewhat artificial. However, they do help explain what is probably happening. One durable explanation was suggested by Franklyn Haiman: *extrinsic* and *intrinsic*. "Extrinsic conflict is the psychological or emotional element. Intrinsic conflict is the rational, ideational, or intellectual content . . . resolving intrinsic conflict requires analytical keenness, whereas . . . extrinsic conflict requires social tact and diplomacy."[2]

A similar explanation is offered by Lewis Coser: *realistic* and *nonrealistic* conflict.[3] Realistic conflict, like Haiman's intrinsic, is a mostly rational task or goal-centered confrontation. Nonrealistic conflict is an end in itself having little to do with group or organizational goals. It is projected frustration or emotion. "My wife is cheating, and I'm going to take it out on the group."

For Harold Guetzkow and John Gyr, group conflict again has two basic dimensions, which they call *substantive* and *affective*.[4] Substantive refers to conflicts primarily related to task, and affective refers to socio-emotional or interpersonal relations. We will refer to the nontask conflicts as *psychological*.

Conflicts of both kinds also tend to occur over special types of issues. Morton Deutsch suggests five: (1) *resources*, control of such things as money, property, space, and power; (2) *preferences* and *nuisances*; (3) *values*; (4) *beliefs*; and (5) the nature of *relationships* between parties.[5] Deutsch also supplies a useful list of types of conflict that can occur across the issues at any time and in combination.[6]

TYPES OF CONFLICT

1. *Veridical* This type of conflict "exists objectively and is perceived accurately." Honest but difficult difference of opinion.
2. *Contingent* The conflict is resolvable but the parties are not aware of it. A larger perspective helps.
3. *Displaced* The parties sublimate the real issue and argue over secondary things.
4. *Misattributed* The assigning of invalid causes, often unconsciously, to conflicts. ("The job caused my divorce.")
5. *Latent* A failure to consciously recognize that a true conflict exists.
6. *False* A conflict without basis caused by misunderstanding and poor communication.

TASK CONFLICT

Groups can have honest differences of opinion (veridical conflicts) and generate healthy task conflicts—that is, arguments about substantive issues without letting the socio-emotional, personality, or psychological dimension intrude. "You're all wet on this, George—and don't forget, golf at seven tomorrow." It is also possible for such differences to generate emotionally harsh language, which can be taken personally. We then have both task and psychological conflicts occurring at the same time.

Louis Pondy sees group conflict episodes going through a five-stage process.[7] These stages are especially helpful in assessing task conflicts. If you can locate your group in the process you may be able to predict where it will go next and perhaps find ways of better managing the conflict.

FIVE STAGES OF A CONFLICT EPISODE

1. *Latent conditions* Unspoken causes exist that may surface at any time.
2. *Perceived conflict* One is now aware that a conflict exists (cognitive).
3. *Felt conflict* One feels stress, anxiety, and hostility (affective).
4. *Manifest conflict* Open, observable conflict (behavioral).
5. *Conflict aftermath* Ranges from resolution to group dissolution; perhaps a return to stage 1.

Ellis and Fisher, focusing on task conflict that they call ideational, found a three-part development pattern in their research.[8]

1. *Interpersonal* exchange
   Differences are expressed on the issues.
   Individual opinions predominate.
   Opinions are unaffected by group information.
2. *Confrontation*
   Members seek information from other members.
   Information is generated.
   Members react with polarized opinions.
   Opinions focus on specific issues.
3. *Substantive* conflict
   Information is integrated to decrease abstractness.

Information is used to modify issue stands.

Information is used to modify proposals.

Consensus is approached.

They suggest that groups tend to generate information as a means of managing conflict during periods of interpersonal difference and confrontation. Integration of existing information and discussion of specific issues are the principle means of managing conflict during the substantive period. This behavior arises from the group's belief that the group already has enough information to deal with the specific proposals before it.

In an impressive study of conflict management in over 100 business and governmental groups, Guetzkow and Gyr found several positive, forthright factors that led to success and consensus in task (substantive) conflicts.[9] (The factors were not nearly as helpful with the psychological, or affective, conflicts.) Their findings led to the following summarized factors and suggestions useful in managing task conflicts:

1. An availability of facts
2. A utilization of facts
3. Efficient, orderly problem solving
4. An active, information-seeking leader
5. Warm, friendly, nonrestrictive relationships

Other factors that helped manage both task and psychological (affective) conflict were

1. An absence of strong, self-oriented needs
2. An effort to satisfy self-oriented needs
3. A positive, affective group atmosphere
4. A knowledge of problem-solving techniques
5. Concentration on one issue at a time

Thomas Scheidel and Laura Crowell offer five more widely accepted suggestions for handling task conflicts.[10]

1. *Attempt to manage, and do not suppress task conflict.*
   Clarify the disagreement; see if it is veridical or one of the other types.
2. *Keep any developing conflicts at the task level rather than permitting them to become interpersonal.*
   The substantive is usually easier to discuss than the psychological and has fewer negative consequences.[11]
3. *Increase the leader's central, direct role if the task conflict intensifies.*
   Seek facts through probing questions; actively support an open atmosphere.
4. *Increase the quality of listening done in the group.*
   Listen for specific differences, and try to link them to the thought line of the group.
5. *Facilitate the management of task conflict by clear statement.*
   Coordinate your meanings; request clarifications; check understandings.

PSYCHOLOGICAL CONFLICT

The most recent and promising typing of general psychological conflict is a tri-part division called *Preference Theory* introduced by Clyde Coombs in a "Distinguished Scientific Contributions" address at the 1986 meeting of the American Psychological Association.[12] It has application to the psychological problems frequently found in small groups.

Coombs's Type I conflict is *intra*personal, that is, within oneself. One is faced with a single inner choice between two or more incompatible options or goals. Coombs suggests that " . . . good things satiate and bad things escalate." Auto racing is both exhilarating and threatening. Increasing your speed may satiate your desire for enlivenment while at the same time increase the threat of injury. Confronting your boss on her decision making may not only help you reestablish your waning self-concept but also further threaten your deteriorating rapport with authority.

Type II conflicts are *inter*personal, that is, relationship centered. Type II occurs because people want different things but must settle for the same thing. You may want a larger salary raise than the personnel committee is offering, but both parties must resolve the conflict by agreeing on a mutually acceptable outcome. Coombs speaks of four levels of distance between adversaries with the fourth being the most serious. At the fourth level, changing the status quo is recommended: " . . . as the status quo deteriorates, previously undesirable options become more acceptable. In effect the parties come closer together and the conflict becomes easier to resolve."[13]

Type III conflict is also interpersonal, but in this case people want the same thing, but must settle for *different* things. There is no mutually acceptable outcome. There will be winners and losers. Type II conflicts, remember, have a common, general goal or bond that allows them to compromise and settle for the *same* thing. To not settle a serious labor dispute threatens the common desires of both labor and management to preserve the company and the jobs it creates. A Type II can, it is clear, escalate into a Type III. "In Type III conflict, self-interests dominate mutual interests, and the exercise of power dominates the process of persuasion."[14]

Arbitration, the courts, government interventions, and power are the hallmarks of resolutions of Type III conflicts. Negotiation, mediation, compromise, and change are the hallmarks of Type II conflicts.

In these typing models, much depends on *who* is looking at the problem and *how* it is defined. In short, a Type I and a Type III conflict might be part of the same problem. Coombs uses the example of two men courting the same woman. It is a Type I, intrapersonal conflict for the woman since she is torn between Gary for excitement and George for security. For the men it is a win-lose, Type III conflict.

Some property settlements are mixed types; the individuals involved may want the same thing but have to settle for different things. If self-interest and intransigence dominate, then what might have been a Type II is now transformed into a Type III conflict. According to Coombs, if this goes to the courts for resolution, it becomes a Type II conflict if a jury deliberates and a Type I if a judge makes the decision.

These typing theories suggest that we are driven in most social conflicts by several strong forces, not the least of which are self-interest and common interest.

Donelson Forsyth offers a five-stage, descriptive model of conflict resolution that has utility in the task area, though primarily directed at psychological conflicts. Characteristics of each stage follow.[15]

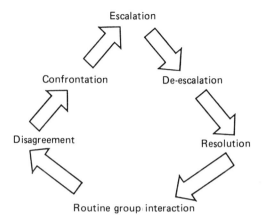

Figure 6.1

From An Introduction to Group Dynamics by D. R. Forsyth. Copyright © 1983 by Wadsworth, Inc. Reprinted by permission of Brook/Cole Publishing Company, Pacific Grove, California, 93950.

1. *Disagreement.* Differences surface. Minor ones are clarified: discussion rules, procedures, seating, and so on. False ones are set straight: "No, I have an open mind on the problem." "I have changed my opinion since 1985." Minor differences are sorted out from major ones. Some less immediate differences are deferred. Differences perceived as real and substantive are acknowledged.

2. *Confrontation.* One or more members find their actions or beliefs incompatible with others and encounter clear resistance. True *conflict* now exists. Debate follows. Commitment to one position or the other intensifies. Debaters tend to dissuade themselves from public commitment and self-observation. Tension builds, emotions harden, communication becomes less logical. Coalitions form in this stage; neutrals must commit themselves.

3. *Escalation.* The conflict spirals into more conflict. Hostility, threats, and verbal attacks replace persuasion. Misunderstanding reaches a new high and trust is lost. Frustration leads to still more aggressive behavior. Negative norms of reciprocity arise at this stage and feed the escalation. "You'll get what you give." "An eye for an eye."

4. *Deescalation.* Time and energy run down. With the resulting drop in intensity, members "cool down" and some rationality and understanding start to emerge. Group protection norms surface and force the taking of larger perspectives about the bones of contention. Trust may or may not return depending upon how serious and personal the disagreements and confrontations may have been. Negotiation, bargaining, and perhaps some conciliation occur here. If all else fails third-party interventions may be called: mediators, consultants, lawyers, higher authorities, and so on. Third parties may help make conciliations less embarrassing. However, if they are called upon prematurely, they may be viewed as intruders. If the conflict intensity is unusually high, they may do even more harm than good.[16]

5. *Resolution.* At this stage something has to give even if resolution means dissolution of the group or casting out an uncompromising, minority subgroup. On the more positive side, one faction can withdraw, concede, or be genuinely persuaded. Negotiations may resolve the conflict through compromises. Depending upon the role your group leader has been given and the rules and norms of your organization, a vote may resolve the matter. In some groups, as discussed previously, a leader may have the authority to mandate a decision and resolve things in that way.

Scheidel and Crowell again offer practical advice on handling conflict, this time in the psychological area.[17]

1. *Alter an appropriate factor in the task work.*

   Translate psychological conflicts into task-related differences in thought or information; task conflicts have fewer negative consequences.[18]

2. *Treat an interpersonal problem as a group—not an individual—problem.*

   Conflicts are interactional; all are involved; try to stay group centered.

3. *Strengthen the general feeling of security in the group.*

   Increase member support; avoid impatience and defensiveness.

4. *Expect some conflict . . .*

   Psychological conflicts ebb and flow; be tolerant—go with the flow.

5. *Mind your language* (from Gouran and Fisher).

   The messages and how we send them have much to do with how they are received or decoded. Message factors found to generally promote intergroup conflict are: "Ambiguous and emotional language, personally oriented conflict, disruptions [especially those stimulated by the destruction of trust], irrelevancies, opinionatedness, lack of direction, leaders' expressed preferences, inadequate collection and assessment of pertinent information, and rigidity. . . ."[19]

SOCIETAL CHANGE

Mass media, the computer, instant communications from all corners of the world—these and ever-increasing technology have put intergroup hostilities center stage. We talk now of groups in the largest sense: capitalist, socialist, Muslim, Christian, races, nations, social classes. Dealing with these powerful and conflicting groups and their very specific yet frequently contradictory goals has no simple and obvious solution, no simple or singular cause. For Muzafer Sherif world order and survival depend on our finding workable ways of dealing with such intergroup hostilities. While supporting our current, conflict-reduction techniques such as pleasant contacts, positive information programs, conferences, and training, Sherif contends that for any of these measures to be truly effective there must be one precondition: the awareness of superordinate goals.[20] A superordinate goal is one that is compelling for both groups and that can be achieved only through cooperation. Peace, freedom, personal dignity, these are the stuff of such global goals. If groups can relate to such lofty goals, information is better received, communication lines improve, and hostilities lessen.

In a pluralistic and democratic society like ours, the problems of very different groups trying to accommodate one another is very real indeed. The new migrations of people to America from all parts of the world have brought the whole "melting pot" notion of a uniform society into serious question. Kenneth Boulding asks, "Can we invent a 'mosaic' society, composed of many small subcultures, each of which gives its participants a sense of community and identity which is so desperately needed in a mass world, and which can at the same time remain at peace with its neighbors and not threaten to pull the society apart?"[21]

The *mosaic* society has arrived in most American organizations. Many universities no longer require identical program curricula for *all* students. Examples are Black Studies, Chicano-Boricua Studies, and other special ethnic and minority programs in law and theater. Churches have reevaluated long-standing traditions to better accommodate and attract these new and diverse groups. Business organizations are clearly aware of our mosaic society, as we learned in the early chapters of this book. Being aware is the first step. The second step—the integrating, maintaining, and managing of these different subcultures, life-styles, and value systems—is the stuff of which the inevitable conflict is made. As small-group members we should expect to meet the mosaic society in ever increasing diversity. According to Kast and Rosenzweig, organizations must be prepared for more of the following:

1. . . . a turbulent environment that requires continual change and adjustment.
2. . . . an increasing diversity of cultural values in the social environment.
3. . . . emphasis on technological and social forecasting.
4. . . . increases in size, complexity, and domain.
5. . . . differentiation of activities causing increased problems of integration and co-ordination.
6. . . . major problems in the accumulation and utilization of knowledge.
7. . . . work life concerns will increase and will impact on productivity.
8. . . . more need for persuasion rather than coercion based on authority.
9. . . . a power-equalization rather than a power-differentiation model.
10. . . . a mosaic, psychosocial system as the norm.
11. . . . organizational interface problems will increase.
12. . . . computerized information-decision systems will have increasing impact.
13. . . . more professional and scientific inputs and influence, most of whom will be part of the organization.
14. . . . a diversification of goals rather than a maximization of just one.
15. . . . more problems of performance evaluation, and many new techniques for measuring same.
16. . . . planned programs of institutional change with widespread participation in same.[22]

INTERORGANIZATIONAL GROUP FACTORS

COMPETITION AND COOPERATION

In any healthy organization some competition between small groups is inevitable. Sometimes the groups in competition are horizontal on the organizational chart and at other times vertical. Representatives of horizontal groups meet at the call of their common, next level leader. The goal is cooperation and healthy competition. Vertical groups are usually quite different and often do business through standing committees responsible for cooperation in search of larger, organizational goals. Personnel committees, industrial relations committees, and administrative policy committees are examples. Members of an administrative committee seek coordination of activities from groups that often have built-in, competitive, parochial goals: engineering and sales, production and accounting, and so forth.

In addition to these competing horizontal and vertical intergroup goals, there are informal groups that not only shadow but also cross over these horizontal and vertical lines. These shadow groups are not just the classic ones discussed in Chapter 5 but are often unusual personal contacts. In one case a student representative had unusual knowledge of faculty business and no little influence. Her source of special knowledge was a routine, informal walk from the parking lot every morning with a vice-president of the university, who was also a friend of her family. A still more bizarre case of student power took place in a private school where the student's family had just donated a new building to the liberal arts college. It is probably impossible to avoid occasionally "jumping the organizational chart," that is, going over somebody's head. However, if one does or feels one must, the person "minding the store" should be informed. One professor who didn't get along with many of his colleagues routinely buttonholed members of the board as they arrived on campus for their monthly meeting. That action made for some interesting conflicts that bounced through several levels of the organization before totally exasperating the small group of which he was a part—for a while . . .

BARGAINING AND NEGOTIATION

The formal rules and practices of union/employee–management bargaining and negotiation are better left to another book and another time, but clearly these are matters with which organizations must cope. However, much less formal but no less important bargaining and negotiating go on in intergroup communication. The committees that bridge several, related small groups are made up of people who must not only represent but also protect the groups that sent or elected them. They must at the same time look at superordinate system goals and protect the larger organization. When these groups are dealing primarily with group grievances and sources of dissatisfaction, one can expect more conflict and more bargaining and negotiation to achieve resolution. Coalitions often form to press a particular solution; often pragmatic strategies of a harsher nature emerge. Some of the vocabulary used by professional negotiators to describe these practices follows.[23]

> *Bad guys.* Members of the negotiation team who take a harsh stance toward members of the other group. They make unreasonable demands and behave obnoxiously, refusing to make even the smallest concessions. Others on their team then put on a show of trying to reason with them.
>
> *Dancer.* Member of the negotiation team who can speak for long periods of time without saying anything.
>
> *Heckling.* "Shaking up" members of the other group by insulting them, making excessive noise while they speak, joking around, or threatening them.
>
> *Last-chancing.* A standard negotiation tactic in which one announces "All right, this is my last and final offer. Take it or leave it," before the middle ground is even reached.
>
> *Log-rolling.* When negotiators on each side have a list of grievances, they make concessions back and forth; when A gives in on one issue, B gives in on the next.
>
> *Scrambling eggs.* When negotiations go poorly, teammates may deliberately try to confuse the issue by misinterpreting others, expressing themselves badly, and dragging in irrelevant issues.
>
> *Tiger teams.* A squad made up of experts that is brought in to unfreeze deadlocked negotiations or to try to reclaim ground lost earlier.

When intergroup conflicts reach this intensity, trust and cooperation may suffer badly, and tension and conflict reduction will take time and patience. If communication can be maintained it should largely be used to establish rules by which the bargaining and negotiating may continue. Such rules must be carefully followed in order to demonstrate good-faith bargaining and to help build trust.

THIRD PARTY INTERVENTION

Another way of coping with intergroup conflicts is to call upon a third party. In some cases, especially grievances, contracts may require it. In other cases the conflicting groups may or must appeal to higher organizational authority: the superintendent intervenes to help solve a conflict between two production groups. When unions have jurisdictional conflicts (whose work is it?), there may be two interveners—the business agents from both unions. Some organizations have third party professionals on staff to assist groups or individuals adjudicate problems, and interpret rules—ombudsmen, inspector generals, legal counselors, communication managers, and chaplains are examples. Also available are outside consulting firms that specialize in all manner of task conflicts: industrial and production engineers, organizational structures, accounting, and so forth.

When intergroup conflicts are due to long-standing differences or perhaps confusion about how to interact with special members of the mosaic society, intervention may be in the form of training.

Third party negotiations or mediators can often help take the heat out of intergroup conflicts by helping regulate the meetings, structuring the agenda, fact-finding, restating arguments in less emotional language, providing facesaving opportunities for those who retreat, and perhaps finding areas of compromise overlooked in the heat of battle.[24]

COMMUNICATION DIMENSIONS

CONSTRUCTIVE AND DESTRUCTIVE BEHAVIORS

Interpersonal, affective, personal attacks seriously limit a group's decision making. Task disagreements become confused with personal hostility, and our *task* irritations grow into a perception of *personal* attack. If we respond in that "face," an honest difference of opinion may suddenly become a conflict of personalities. Group rules and norms may sometimes be so rigid that a more democratic member may seethe and a free spirit may rebel. A single group member may also be causal if he or she is so nonconformist, deviant, or difficult that the group loses its patience.

A very large part of psychological or *interpersonal* conflict involves our concern for the *relationship* with another person. Will the *message* or content part of our interaction threaten the relationship?

To blurt out your strong political feelings to a dorm acquaintance is one thing. To do the same with an employer of a different persuasion (but with whom you have a satisfactory relationship) might be quite another matter. Much depends on the employer. Some people seem to have a greater tolerance for differences of opinion and conflict. So much depends upon the situation. Are you blurting out your feelings in or out of the group? Are these shows of feeling job relevant or recreational? The message content might concern an issue or goal of varying importance to you and the receiver.

Perhaps you've used strong language on an issue of only minor concern to you but of major concern to the receiver. I was once reported to the ombudsman for using the word *damn* in class. Two religious-sect students were very concerned about obscenity and had a narrower definition of obscenity than I. I made my peace with them, enabling us to continue our student–teacher relationship. We also must consider the content and relationship concerns in terms of *others* who may be involved. In this case the others were the rest of the class, some of whom would have forgone the relationship; most sensed the multiple conflict and adapted.

Conflict is inevitable but, as we shall see, not always the end of the world. So much depends on how we manage it. Some experts even think conflict is part and parcel of real intimacy.[25] What causes close relationships to fall apart is an unwillingness to face conflicts constructively. They are faced destructively or simply avoided for as long as possible.

Conflict almost always involves perceptions of incompatible goals and/or threats to a relationship.[26] That communication is at the heart of the matter is clearly stated by Simons: '' . . . communication, . . . is the means by which conflicts get socially defined, the instrument through which influence in conflicts is exercised, and the vehicle by which partisans or third parties may prevent, manage, or resolve conflicts.''[27]

Destructive behaviors tend to be self-centered, while *constructive* behaviors are relationship centered. If the issue means absolutely everything and the relationship means very little, perhaps the message strategy doesn't really matter. If the conflict escalation isn't completely destructive, it might at least clarify the issues.

Message strategies that include name calling, threats, deception, sarcasm, and other similar behaviors are clearly destructive and elicit reactions of hurt, fear, confusion, and distrust. They expand and escalate the conflict, as Deutsch would say.[28] Sometimes these behaviors are aimed more at the relationship than at the issue. ''He irritates me so much that I'll vote the opposite way,'' whatever the issue. The bumper sticker, ''Draft my ex-wife, PLEASE'' has little to do with the draft.

Behavior even concerning a relatively unimportant issue (for you) involving a relatively unimportant relationship might inadvertently turn out to be destructive. A young professor was moving to Detroit. This fact was unknown to a third person joining the two old friends.

New person:	Did I hear you say Detroit?
Young professor:	Yes, I'm . . . (interruption)
New person:	Boy, that place is the pits.
Old friends:	See you around.
New person:	Hey, don't leave. I need your help . . .

Constructive and socially sensitive approaches to conflict (or any other interaction) involve some context and situation analysis before proceeding. Some topics are, after all, superficial and bereft of rhetorical impact anyway. The new person above described Detroit in terms of gut feelings and first impressions, which are not necessarily communicative fare. More will be said of sensitivity in the next section.

Constructive conflict is open, but it is *relationship* centered as well as *issue* centered, and it seeks an atmosphere of trust.[29] It also seeks a forthright but supportive, rational, problem-solving kind of issue confrontation. At the same time it is sensitive to psychological adjustment mechanisms used by all people to take the heat out of frustration and conflict.

Messages intended to seek another's opinion, state one's own opinion, or obtain or give restatement reflect such an orientation (problem-oriented) and were positively associated with conflict resolution.[30]

In a sense, you get what you give. "Just as hostile behavior is likely to draw a hostile response, positive (favorable) messages are likely to elicit positive responses . . . positive messages by either member of a dyad are likely to prevent or reduce a potentially destructive cycle of conflict."[31]

Adjusting to Frustration and Conflict

Part of the constructive coping approach to interpersonal conflict is to first understand the psychological nature of frustration and conflict and how we humans normally adjust to it. *Frustration* results when an external barrier stands squarely between you and your need or goal.

The barrier may be a thing or condition which you can literally attack. For instance you can kick the tire that goes flat on your way to an important meeting, swear at the parking ticket that calls for a court appearance, break the putter that "makes" you bogie the hole, blow the horn as you are hopelessly caught in a gigantic traffic jam. There is a suggestion that frustration may lead to aggression in the preceding examples. Indeed, a frustration-aggression hypothesis has been postulated.[32]

When the barrier is a person such as a police officer, a boss, a teacher, parents, or groups who are typically difficult to attack physically or socially, then we have the problem of what to do with our aroused emotion and aggression. Since direct confrontation of the barrier is not always possible, this aggression is often taken out on or displaced to an innocent group, person, pet, or object. Barriers inherent in all groups, such as rules, norms, and customs, often lead us to displaced aggression. Sometimes a nonsense telephone call or an unloved, uninvited guest in the middle of a favorite television program causes this phenomenon to occur. A classic example of displaced aggression is reported by Miller and Bugelski: Boys at a camp had their weekly night at the movies interrupted by a long testing session. Pre- and post-rating showed significantly increased hostility toward minority groups, when in fact the testing had nothing to do with the minority groups.[33] There is even historical evidence that lynchings increased when the farm value of cotton decreased.

Of course frustration does not always lead to aggression. When people are involved, a lot depends on how we attribute the intent of the deed that irritated us. Rough shoves by a berserk fan at a big game may be aggravating, but not as intensely aggravating as it would have been if it had happened in a small-group environment. With experience we hopefully go through a more sophisticated process of attributing intentions and analyzing situations.

Communications and information that redirects our attributions of intentional irritations or barriers usually reduce our aggressive inclinations. Even children sort some of this out when appropriate communications are forthcoming. When third graders building block towers had them unceremoniously kicked over by a sixth grader, they quickly developed aggressive feelings. However, they were less hostile when they were told that the culprit was sleepy and upset, a *constructive* approach.[34]

When personal limitations make one's self the barrier, frustration may become very intense and lead to disillusionment and regression, as well as aggression. The would-be nuclear physicist who has no aptitude for equations, the would-be basketball player who doesn't have the necessary height, the would-be artist who simply doesn't have any talent—all are examples of frustration born of personal limitations or perhaps in-flated levels of aspiration. When we encourage or persuade people to assume unrealistic levels of aspiration and achievement completely beyond their capabilities or the realities of the environment, we can expect them to fill the gap with a great deal of frustration. To be self-motivating, plans, promises, and goals must be pragmatically realistic. Oth-erwise, we may find people actually regressing in terms of their goals or becoming so disillusioned that they simply give up.

Some psychological *conflict* besets all of us with varying levels of intensity. It typically takes place when we have to make choices between needs that are incompatible or mutually exclusive. Two or more motives block each other as it were. You hate your boss, but you need the job. You want to play golf, but you have to go to class to pass the course. You love your husband *and* your boss. The last example is a case of what is called "approach-approach" conflict, a choice between two or more positive, usually incompatible goals. A second form is called "approach-avoidance" conflict and is il-lustrated by the man who loves his wife but can't stand his children, or the paper lion who wants to play football but is terrified at the thought of getting hurt. A third form is called "avoidance-avoidance" conflict; you give your hard-earned money to the thief or risk getting hurt. Whenever we are coerced into doing something disagreeable through threats or punishment, the method is only as good as the strength of the psychological barrier (self-preservation—avoiding bodily harm), and we experience conflict and frus-tration.

Forms of Escape: Mental Paralysis, Alternation, Literal Escape   When the choices are not only incompatible but also intensely fear provoking (attack the enemy or suffer a coward's fate), people may resort to various forms of psychological escape. One way of adjusting is a mental paralysis, which leads to no action at all. For example, a man freezes on the battlefield, appears to be in a stupor, or actually collapses from emotional fatigue. In less-critical situations a person may simply appear disinterested, terribly tired, or lazy, when in fact that person is going through intense emotional con-flict. Thus, *no* decision or *no* action is a form of adjustment (avoidance). Choosing the lesser of two or more evils is conflict producing for even the best of us. This form of escape is neither uncommon nor typically successful in the long run.

A second way of adjusting to conflict is *alternation*, a kind of psychological plas-ticity involving vacillation and irresolution in which one alternately tries to satisfy each of the conflicting goals or needs. This kind of adjustment often explains unpredictable and contradictory human behavior. A priest who believes in birth control may find himself trying to appease the needs of the papal encyclical one moment and the needs of his assumed social conscience the next. A black person who has had enough of forced busing but who deeply feels a need for black unity may find himself or herself being contradictory or speaking out of "both sides of his or her mouth." Adjusting to intense conflict is a sticky, complex business.

A third way of adjusting to psychological conflict is *escape* in the *literal* sense. You walk away from a marital confrontation by going fishing; you resign from the church; you quit school. These actions avoid an outward or even physical conflict tem-porarily in some cases, permanently in other cases. Sometimes we escape by pretending a need is nonexistent. What discrimination? What problem? What contradiction in my behavior? We repress one or more of our need systems, which usually have a way of reemerging as all real needs do. This is not to say that we cannot profit emotionally from a stolen day on the golf links when the demands of the daily grind exhaust the best of us.

Adjustment Mechanisms *Adjustment mechanisms* are unconscious defense systems used by the mind to relieve ego tensions caused by conflict and frustration. They help us believe that a need does not exist or that it has been satisfied. They distort reality to defend and to take pressure off the ego.

Only when a particular defense mechanism is used consistently and becomes a chronic pattern of behavior should it be considered abnormal. Most of us could not get through a normal week without resorting to some mild defense mechanisms. They are like pressure valves that take the steam and heat out of failure, guilt, insecurity, and general stress. They are thus normal in mild degree, unconscious, and important considerations for those who would constructively cope with conflict. Some of the more important mechanisms follow.

Rationalization *Rationalization* is a less painful explanation or alibi for unacceptable behavior. The classic example is Aesop's fable of the fox and the grapes. After repeated leaps at the succulent, hanging grapes, the defeated, frustrated fox remarks that they are sour grapes anyway. ''Sour grapes'' has become an idiom for rationalization. Undoubtedly the fox was better able to live with himself after this mild distortion. Many people who receive deserved traffic tickets for moving violations have been known to offer lengthy explanations of how they were victims of circumstances. As long as these alibis do not become chronic behavior, and as long as they are not heatedly given to the arresting officer, they probably take the sting out of a trying and frustrating experience. It is, of course, modest self-deception. We can recognize this internal conflict in people who use contradictory evidence to justify their beliefs, see nothing wrong with oftimes blatant inconsistencies, often become irritated when their arguments are questioned, or are eternally seeking or inventing alibis for their beliefs or behaviors.

It is often temporary or special-issue related, but it complicates group communication. Good listeners cope best with this defense mechanism. If you know you are in a ''sour grapes'' or defeated mood, it is probably a good idea to seek friends who will understand.

Compensation *Compensation* is the process of substituting one goal-seeking pattern of behavior for another pattern that has been frustrated. Demosthenes, frustrated by stuttering, worked very hard (recall the pebbles in the mouth) to overcome his disorder and eventually became the premier Greek orator. When people substitute new need-satisfying patterns for frustrated ones, it is important to their personal adjustment and to society's adjustment that the new endeavor is not equally or more frustrating than the first. Had Demosthenes been equally frustrated in his oratory, he might have become even less secure and compensated in less useful ways. Some people compensate by seeking attention for its own sake, engaging in excessive fantasy, and even eating too much.

Since defeats and failures are part of living, we can expect to meet compensatory behavior in our interactions. We may quickly recognize compensatory communication when the source of the conflict or frustration is obvious. A student frustrated by a failed exam may pour out criticisms of the course, the instructor, the exam, and so forth in an effort to ease the pain. He or she might also brag about other glories and brilliant behaviors in an effort to substitute superiority for inadequacy. In some cases, and frequently because of intense inferiority feelings, compensatory behavior takes the form of verbal or even physical aggression. Communication and persuasion become most difficult.

Projection   The Store security guards had been secretly observing a woman who they were convinced was shoplifting. They had not detained her because they were not quite sure they could make their case stick. While pondering their next move, they were shocked to have the woman approach them and proceed to upbraid them for not arresting the several shoplifters she had observed in the store.

Projection is the attributing or transferring of guilt and unpleasant motives to others. Other typical cases are the loafer who accuses others of loafing, and the cheater who accuses others of cheating. Perhaps certain ''do-gooders'' are projecting onto others the sin that tempts them. Typically, the negative traits being projected to others are unrecognized by the guilty person. Projection helps explain much apparent contradictory behavior in people. It is a psychological mask that lets us hide behind accusations against others that are the same as the guilt-laden defects we are not always consciously aware of in our own behavior.

Repression   *Repression* is the excluding from consciousness or screening of those motives or desires considered unacceptable, repugnant, or threatening. We escape an emotionally difficult situation by pretending it does not really exist. In psychoanalytic theory repression also refers to the ejecting from consciousness of painful or guilt-laden experiences. We don't *really* remember mildly crunching somebody's fender in the parking lot. We weren't *really* cheating—just kind of checking the other person's procedures. We didn't *really* shout at Mom—well anyway, she knows we love her.

It was once written that the two most prevalent causes of repression in our society related to aggression and sex. We seem to suffer less from these taboos in the 1980s. In all probability that is not entirely due to release offered us by X-rated movies and televised professional football. All repression isn't bad. Some modest ''counting to ten'' when faced with an interpersonal conflict may save you embarrassment or perhaps the interaction itself. We all repress some anxiety in tense situations. Beginning speakers do this, and it works for a while, perhaps long enough for experience and success to offset it. However, constant repression is seldom a satisfactory psychological adjustment. Realistic confrontation and compromise of our conflicts and frustrations are pragmatically the best policies.

Contraposition (Reaction Formation)   *Contraposition* refers to a mechanism whereby repressed desires are replaced by their direct opposites. This mechanism is demonstrated by the person who ''protests too much.'' An example is the father who can't stand his mentally retarded stepson and unconsciously wishes to be rid of him, but expresses this negative wish through lavish gifts and unusual concern for the child's well-being. Freud calls this behavior *reaction formation.* Freud also suggests that romantic notions of chastity and purity may mask crude sexual desires, that piety may conceal sinfulness, and that altruism may hide selfishness.

It is evident that some interpersonal communication analysis that misjudges the interactants' motives can be 100 percent wrong.

Regression   *Regression* is a return to past behavior that was once satisfying or at least attention getting. When Rick is born, five-year-old Jack finds his status shaken and returns to thumb sucking or even bed wetting. When 50-year-old Ed is suffering leadership anxiety, we notice an almost imperceptible stamping of the foot. Seventy-year-old George handles conflict by referring to the ''good old days.'' My first automatic transmission made my new car a real joy until the first giant traffic jam threatened my new car. Suddenly I was trying to shift again. Double panic set in when the old, friendly clutch was missing. Now that we're back to straight sticks, I occasionally forget to shift. The fellow with the lampshade on his head is usually exhibiting some kind of regressive behavior whether from conflict, frustration, or too much boilermaker punch—a kind of returning to the womb.

More seriously, regression frequently translates interpersonally into a louder voice, faster rate, verbosity, and an unwillingness to give up the floor. There is, however, a beta hypothesis involved. One may do exactly the opposite, particularly if there is a role or status difference in the interactants. This is not to say that every verbal, aggressive person is suffering from some kind of latent frustration or conflict. One must take into account the people, the situation, and the context.

Other Defense Patterns In addition to the adjustment mechanisms discussed above, there are several others worthy of mention.

Identification—a form of status seeking or protection through overidentification with a group.

Fantasy—daydreaming or seeking imaginary satisfactions in place of real ones.

Negativism—a chronic state of opposition, often to all kinds of authority.

Conversion—the changing of mental conflicts and frustrations into physical symptoms.

Acting-out—permitting the expression of forbidden desires.

Participant Role Stereotypes

We use the term *stereotypes* because people do play different roles—they change. A "playboy" in one phase of a small-group interaction might play a more serious, evaluator role in another phase. It is true that some personalities are more consistent in their interactive roles, and the stereotypes come closer to fitting.

Roles can be related primarily to the task or problem with which a group is faced, as well as to the socio-emotional or psychological tensions that occur. There are also negative or disruptive roles that all of us play on occasion, such as flat disagreement with almost every idea a group has. These roles are often compensatory behaviors for personal problems that may or may not be related to the group. It can, of course, affect cohesion or togetherness. A true incorrigible can really disrupt a group's productivity.

The above role categories have been described and explained by Benne and Sheats.[35] The *task* roles tend to advance group goals. The *group maintenance* (socio-emotional) roles help morale and reduce tension. The *individual* roles are the negative or disruptive ones. See Tables 6.1, 6.2, and 6.3.[36]

For all the roles we play, some individuals seem to lock onto one role that makes it very difficult for people to disagree with them. This is particularly true if one crosses into "taboo" areas where they take every difference of opinion as a personal affront. These are difficult, rhetorically-insensitive group members. Psychologists have referred to this behavior mechanism as *reactance*, "a form of negative influence that comes about when someone is afraid that his freedom and individuality may be threatened by the attempt to influence him."[37] This often leads to nonconformity, a desire to be difficult just for the sake of being different, and a resistance to group influence, which becomes an end in itself.[38]

There are no clear and effective behaviors for coping with such radically deviant group behavior. Such deviance usually results in rejection and then ejection of the member or even the dissolution of the group. Wenburg and Wilmot[39] suggest that there are

TABLE 6.1 Group Task Roles

ROLE	DESCRIPTION
a. initiator-contributor	. . . suggests or proposes to the group new ideas or a changed way of regarding the group problem or goal.
b. information seeker	. . . asks for clarification of suggestions made in terms of their factual adequacy, for authoritative information and facts pertinent to the problem being discussed.
c. opinion seeker	. . . asks not primarily for the facts of the case but for a clarification of the values pertinent to what the group is undertaking or of values involved in a suggestion made or in alternative suggestions.
d. information giver	. . . offers facts or generalizations that are "authoritative" or relates his or her own experience pertinently to the group problem.
e. opinion giver	. . . states his or her belief or opinion pertinently to a suggestion made or to alternative suggestions.
f. elaborator	. . . spells out suggestions in terms of examples or developed meanings, offers a rationale for suggestions previously made, and tries to deduce how an idea or suggestion would work out if adopted by the group.
g. coordinator	. . . shows or clarifies the relationships among various ideas and suggestions, tries to pull ideas and suggestions together, or tries to coordinate the activities of various members of subgroups.
h. orienter	. . . defines the position of the group with respect to its goals by summarizing what has occurred, points to depatures from agreed upon directions or goals, or raises questions about the direction that the group discussion is taking.
i. evaluator-critic	. . . subjects the accomplishment of the group to some standard or set of standards of group functioning in the context of the group task.
j. energizer	. . . prods the group to action or decision, attempts to stimulate or arouse the group to "greater" or "higher quality" activity.
k. procedural technician	. . . expedites group movement by doing these for the group—performing routine taks, e.g., distributing materials, or manipulating objects for the group, e.g., rearranging the seating or running the recording machine.
l. recorder	. . . writes down suggestions, makes a record of group decisions, or writes down the product of discussion.

TABLE 6.2   Group Building and Maintenance Roles (Socio-emotional)

ROLE	DESCRIPTION
a. encourager	. . . praises, agrees with, and accepts the contribution of others.
b. harmonizer	. . . mediates the differences between other members, attempts to reconcile disagreements, relieves tension in conflict situations through jesting or pouring oil on the troubled waters, and so forth.
c. compromiser	. . . operates from within a conflict in which his or her ideas or position is involved.
d. gatekeeper/ expediter	. . . attempts to keep communication channels open by encouraging or facilitating the participation of others or by proposing regulation of the flow of communication.
e. standard setter	. . . expresses standards for the group to attempt to achieve in its functioning or applies standards in evaluating the quality of group processes.
f. group-observer	. . . keeps records of various aspects of group process and feeds such data with proposed interpretations into the group's evaluation of its own procedures.
g. follower	. . . goes along with the movement of the group, more or less passively accepting the ideas of others, serving as an audience in group discussion and decision.

TABLE 6.3   Negative and Disruptive Individual Roles

ROLE	DESCRIPTION
a. aggressor	. . . may work in many ways—deflating the status of others, expressing disapproval of the values, acts or feelings of others, attacking the group or the problem it is working on, joking aggressively, showing envy toward another's contribution by trying to take credit for it, and so on.
b. blocker	. . . tends to be negativistic and stubbornly resistant, disagreeing and opposing without or beyond reason and attempting to maintain or bring back an issue after the group has rejected it.
c. recognition seeker	. . . works in various ways to call attention to himself or herself, whether through boasting, reporting on personal achievements, acting in unusual ways, struggling to prevent being placed in an ''inferior'' position, and so forth.
d. self-confessor	. . . uses the audience opportunity that the group setting provides to express personal, nongroup-oriented ''feeling,'' ''insight,'' ''ideology,'' and so on.

TABLE 6.3 *(cont.)*

ROLE	DESCRIPTION
e. playboy	. . . makes a display of his or her lack of involvement in the group's processes.
f. dominator	. . . tries to assert authority or superiority in manipulating the group or certain members of the group.
g. help-seeker	. . . attempts to call forth "sympathy" response from other group members or from the whole group.
h. special interest pleader	. . . speaks for the "small business man," "the grass roots" community, the "homemaker," "labor," and so on usually cloaking his or her own prejudices or biases in the stereotype that best fits his or her individual need.

four conformity-pressure steps that most groups go through before ejecting such a difficult member:

1. Delay action. Ignore the member, do nothing, and hope he or she "comes around."
2. Group members talk among themselves indirectly offering light or humorous suggestions to the deviant.
3. Open ridicule of the deviant.
4. Serious persuasion using severe criticism and even threats.
5. Isolate, reject, and finally eject.

More will be said on these matters under Perceptual Mapping in Chapter 7.

COMMUNICATIVE COMPETENCE

Mark Ross relates the following story on "Saving Face." On a recent Friday night Jean, a friend of mine, and I went to a tavern owned by another friend, Joe. He had specifically invited us because he was featuring a live musician. When we arrived, Joe was waiting at a table with a full pitcher of beer for us. He was obviously enjoying his hired talent. The music was not exactly my cup of tea, but it was played with precision and finesse. After we sat down, our group interaction went something like this.

LINE

1. **Joe:** (smiling) Quite a sound, huh? You gotta go to New York to hear stuff like this.
2. **Me:** He does play with precision, Joe.
3. **Joe:** I know. He's cheap too.
4. **Me:** Where did you find him?
5. **Joe:** He plays on Sundays at our church. Jean, what do you think?
6. **Jean:** I think he stinks . . .
7. **Joe:** (mouth drops open . . . silence)
8. **Jean:** He's playing too slow . . . needs to step up the tempo. The selection of material itself is wrong. This is a bar, Joe, not Sunday school.

9. **Me:** Uh, Joe, you've gotta understand. Jean and I have been arguing about art and aesthetics all night; we're kind of hypersensitized.

10. **Jean:** That's true, but this stuff obviously is not for here.

11. **Me:** Have another beer, Jean (laughing and rolling my eyes at Joe).

12. **Joe:** (hurt) I'm really sorry.

My latter utterances were designed to *save face* for Jean. I was trying to put her *lines* into a context for Joe (an episode). In line 9, I was telling Joe that Jean's lines were occurring within the episode of a "good argument over art" rather than within the episode of an "insult." That attempt failed to work because of Jean's line 10. I then tried to integrate Jean's behavior within the episode of "drinking too much" for Joe. I don't think that worked either.

Goffman talks about self-presentation in terms of "face work."[40] Goffman would say Jean was in *wrong face* because her line was inappropriate. It failed to coordinate with the episode that Joe was creating. Joe can be said to be *out of face* because he doesn't have a line that can coordinate with Jean's. He says nothing and apparently feels hurt. My communicative work can be classifed as an attempt to save face for Jean by creating an episode for Joe that might allow him to voice a line that would coordinate.

Doing "face work" in self-presentation is just what we mean when we talk about coordinating meanings. The competent communicator needs to be sensitive to his or her self-face and others' faces. Having communicative competence obviously doesn't assure us that our lives will be stable and conflict free. Communicative competence lies partially in realizing the complexities in our communicative lives—the multitude of meaning structures that we and others create. The other part of interpersonal competence lies in action—our ability to present ourselves and our ability to *mesh* (coordinate) our self-presentation with others.

Self-presentation is really a meaning management process. We encode symbols that are illustrative of *our* personal meanings for phenomena. Our personal meanings for things are functionally related to our *selves*. The encoding of symbols, in this sense, is actually a presentation of self. When we read the words of Ernest Hemingway, for example, we learn something about the man (self). How can this be? The symbols we use are reflective of our selves.

When people interact, there are two or more self-presentations. To the extent that these self-presentations mesh or coordinate, they create a common episode. The episode could be argument, endearment, compliment, conflict, or confusion. Our ability to coordinate our self-presentation in such a fashion as to create common episodes clearly relates to our communicative competence. In talking about communicative competence, Wiemann says that "the primary function [of conversational encounters] is the establishment and maintenance of self and the social identities of the participants.[41]

Perspectives on Experience

R. D. Laing argues that our interpersonal behavior is largely a function of how we experience or perceive the communicative relationship.[42] Laing contends that a person experiences a communication encounter in two ways—from a direct perspective and a metaperspective. If we are talking, I experience your language and actions (behavior) directly. We can see other people's behavior but not their experiences. If I am sensitive, I can also infer your direct experience of me. When I infer *your* experience of me, I am working at the metaperspective level. For example, when my business agent sends me a letter demanding copy for the publisher and I think she's being pushy (direct perspective), and she realizes that I think she's being pushy (metaperspective), we have understanding. If we don't have this understanding or conjunction between direct and metaperspectives, it becomes difficult to coordinate our meanings or negotiate the episode.

Communicative competence requires understanding (the coordination of direct perspectives and metaperspectives). In the "face work" example Jean lacked understanding of Joe. Joe was hurt by Jean's comments (direct perspective), and Jean failed to realize the impact of her lines on Joe (metaperspective); hence Jean lacked understanding.

Role Taking and Role Enactment

We all play roles in the episodes within which we operate. I play one role when listening to music with friends and another when I am in the classroom.

The social contexts within which we operate vary along a continuum that goes from very informal to very formal. (See Figure 6.2.)

A night on the beach with friends might be very informal and unstructured: "See you when it's convenient." A job interview, on the other hand, might be very formal and very structured: "You'll meet the chairman at 9:00, the dean at 10:00, and vice-president at exactly 12:10." In general, the more informal the social context the more *interpersonal* the communication experience. Informal social contexts require more face work and more coordinated meaning management.

Our role playing within contexts is made up of two parts—role taking and role enactment. *Role taking* refers to the internal process we go through in making inferences about self and others.[43] As we become sensitive to a particular episode, we begin to categorize self and others. This categorization leads to expectations of behavior. Sensitive role taking aids the communicator in assessing the range and nature of the communication obligations of any particular interaction. In our earlier example Jean was not sensitive to nor willing to take a role that complemented the episode Joe was developing in relation to the music in his bar. What resulted was a lack of coordination, poor face work, and a shorter, more difficult evening.

Dynamic role taking operates in an adaptive context. In interpersonal communication there is a lot to give and take as we coordinate our actions. Therefore, we must be adaptive. We must adapt to the context, situation, or episode. We need other people's cues to assess ourselves. Our ability to self-assess enhances our ability to take roles appropriate to an episode. That even the best of us occasionally take on inappropriate roles is clear from the following letter to the editor.

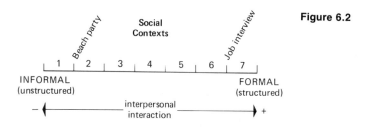

Figure 6.2

"I APOLOGIZE"

To the Editor:

> To the referees, coaches, teams and fans of Saturday's 8th-grade basketball tournament in Suttons Bay: I wish to apologize for my loud, obnoxious behavior at the championship game. While my comments about the officiation of the game were not profane in content, yet my conduct displayed unsportsmanship, a poor example to our youth, and unChristian action arising from the desire to take glory for myself instead of giving glory to God. Such public display deserves a public apology. I am most ashamed and truly sorry. It shall not occur again.

Rev. Morris Jones[44]

Role enactment is the verbal and nonverbal behavior that results from our role taking. It is the essence of interpersonal communication. In our Jean and Joe example, Jean's role enactment (lines) was not appropriate for Joe's episode. What resulted was misinterpretation, or at best a meaning mismatch. Jean was in wrong face and Joe was out of face. The Rev. Morris Jones was just red faced.

On Becoming a Participant Observer

Careful Listening   Many times it's better to be quiet for a while and listen. It's surprising how clear things become when you're not so busy talking. Observe your listening habits.

Reflexivity   *Reflexivity* refers to looking back on previous communication behaviors. If we will delay and take the time to think back and review what's been said, we often see a structure or regularity to our interaction that was previously overlooked. This structure/regularity can give us some clues about the types of episodes we've been enacting and perhaps the types of episodes we should enact in the future.

It is a common experience that a problem difficult at night is resolved in the morning after the committee of sleep has worked on it.

John Steinbeck

Empathy   *Empathy* is the essential part of what Laing calls understanding. It refers to putting yourself in the experiential stance of the other. It's taking the metaperspective. "Put yourself in the other person's shoes."

Adversity has the effect of eliciting talents, which in prosperous circumstances would have lain dormant.

Horace

Perspective Taking We can ask people about our direct perspectives: "What do you mean when you say that?" We can also ask people about our metaperspectives: "How am I coming off to you? Am I getting across?" Sometimes we should simply ask for clarification or confirmation; sometimes we should analyze how we're communicating.

Words of the Wise

In a controversy, the instant we feel anger we have already ceased striving for the truth and have begun striving for ourselves.

Thomas Carlyle

Learning to become a good participant observer is the beginning of perspective taking and the heart of building communicative competence. *Doing* participant observation is no easy task. It takes practice. It requires listening, reflexivity, and empathy to accomplish the *observation* part, and it requires an adaptive and responsive posture to do the participant part. One secret of the participation observation strategy is to let your physical being become a type of gauge. Your body must, in effect, take readings on your participation. Then you are ready to reflect on or *observe* these readings and use them adaptively to create new, coordinated participation behaviors.

Rhetorical Sensitivity

Types of Sensitivities: Rhetorically Sensitives, Noble Selves, Rhetorical Reflectors

Rhetorical sensitivity is a particular attitude toward encoding spoken messages. It represents a way of thinking about what should be said and then a way of deciding how to say it.[45]

It is, according to Hart and Burks, " . . . that type of . . . sensitivity which . . . makes effective social interaction manifestly possible."[46]

It is our view that rhetorically sensitive (RS) people are interpersonally attractive. They judge encounters carefully before taking a stand on an issue, they distinguish between "content" and "relational" communication, and they know when to "speak up" or to "shut up." They deal with conflict forthrightly *and* with sensitivity.

People not rhetorically sensitive have been described as "noble selves," (NS) and "rhetorical reflectors" (RR). The noble selves have been characterized as difficult persons who see "any variation from their personal norms as hypocritical, as a denial of integrity, as a cardinal sin."[47] Rhetorical reflectors have been described as persons who "have no self to call their own. For each person and for each situation they present a new self."[48] They empathize with (or at least appear to empathize with) and reflect each situation in which they find themselves.

Rhetorically sensitive people seek to moderate these extremes. They are not braggarts but neither are they chameleon like, fearfully reflecting and hiding in each encounter. The attitude might be scaled as shown in Figure 6.3.

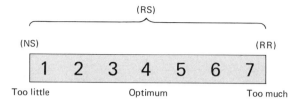

Figure 6.3 Sensitivity toward host interactions, where (NS) is Noble Self, (RR) is Rhetorical Reflector, and (RS) is Rhetorically Sensitive.

Situations and Contexts   The research into rhetorical sensitivity suggests that the notion captures the special situations and contexts in which people find themselves. For example, nurses with high rhetorically sensitive scores tend to work in rehabilitation programs, outpatient clinics, and psychiatric wards. The rhetorical reflectors work, as one might predict, with extended care and intensive care patients. The nurses with higher noble-self scores tend to be the supervisors.[49]

In a study of military personnel, officers were found to be more rhetorically sensitive than sergeants. The sergeants tended to be noble selves; the enlisted men were mostly rhetorical reflectors.[50]

Rhetorical sensitivity, then, is an effective matching of message sending to the requirements of the receivers *and* the situation and context. In a study of hundreds of students in a speech fundamentals course where audience analysis was heavily stressed, rhetorically sensitive scores were significantly higher at the end of the semester. This was not true of control subjects in other university courses.[51] Rhetorical sensitivity is a measure of a person's group-analysis efforts and willingness to carefully consider the psychological environment before encoding messages. It is the ability to accurately judge group and interpersonal encounters and to sense when to be a reflector and when to be a noble self.

It is our position that a rhetorically sensitive person will have more satisfactory group experiences. The specific attributes of such a person should be especially valuable in heading off unnecessary conflicts or coping with them when necessary. Our first suggestion is to take as your general perspective one of being rhetorically sensitive.

Adapting to Specific Audiences, Receivers, Contexts, and Situations   The rhetorically sensitive person appreciates that his or her self-concept is understood by others through interaction with others in contexts and situations that are meaningful to them. The RS know that "talk is not everywhere valued equally."[52] To adapt is to be an appropriate social actor, one who can live with reasonable role taking.

Evaluating Message Relevance   A prudent evaluator of message relevance, the RS evaluates the purpose of his or her information in any interaction. If it has little rhetorical purpose and threatens the relationship, the RS will consider silence. The RS assesses when to speak up and when to shut up. The RS does not run from a fight, but considers whether the issue is relevant and worth the effort. If so, the RS works diligently to couch it prudently and persuasively.

Considering Content and Relational Dimensions   As one who considers the content and relational dimensions of his or her communications, the RS is aware that *how* you say something is sometimes more important than *what* you say. The RS is not opposed to "straight talk" but is opposed to "letting it all hang out." The RS is opposed to manipulation, but not to ethical strategies that enhance an interaction. In the words of Hart and Burks,

> Is it inappropriate to choose carefully among alternate strategies so that my words will have the greatest social impact possible? Or is it really so wrong to stop a moment, to sift through the myriad verbalizations that can make social an idea, and to choose those rhetorical forms that appear best suited to the situation at hand?[53]

MANAGING CONFLICT FAIRLY

Conflict often spells danger but it also spells opportunity. "Give the urge to blast a chance to pass" and search for the opportunity. Realize that conflict necessitates change. Either (1) you must change, (2) the group or other person must change, or (3) the environment must change. Perhaps it will be some combination of these but change there will be.

RECOGNIZE ADJUSTIVE BEHAVIOR

It's easy to be unfair, unkind, and unobjective. In discussing the adjustment mechanisms we learned how we all occasionally succumb to conflict and frustration. We expect some tolerance from others when we temporarily "lose it," and we usually intend to extend it to others. The problem is that we don't always take the time or have the time to painstakingly analyze every interpersonal interaction or every hidden hang-up, real or fancied, that confronts us.

However, before we can get to the issue or *content* of a conflict, we often have to deal with the *relationship* dimension. We need not ignore all rationalizations, compensations, regressions, and so forth. We cannot and, as we shall see, sometimes should not. Nevertheless, an objective and sensitive analysis often calls for considerable discounting, since its message is more ventilation than substance.

If communication is the means by which conflicts become socially defined, then it is imperative that we don't let normal adjustment tendencies misdefine the real conflict. This coping perspective includes the ability ideally to know when to take a person *literally* and when not to. The situation often helps locate the tolerance line. The political arena seems to allow more adjustive shouting. When black and white Michigan Democrats came into conflict about support for a gubernatorial candidate and seats on the national party caucus, the charge of racism was loudly and quickly made. After some cooling off it was no longer heard. The same shout in an automobile plant has been, on some occasions, the cause of long, bitter legal conflicts.

Being tolerant of adjustive behavior even when it provokes anger is perhaps what Christ meant by turning the other cheek or what the old adage of "counting to ten" means. The advice of a popular communication teacher Irving Lee was to "stay angry, but look again at what you are responding to." Don't just count to ten or turn the other cheek, but rather look again objectively to see if your anger is justified. According to Lee, three out of every four times a person becomes angry, a second look will show that he or she is overreacting or is not justified in feeling angry. "When angry look again."

During a long, hot summer a young police officer weary and angry over innumerable car thefts in his precinct saw a person removing a wheel from a car. His blood boiled as he reached for his gun. He called upon all of his training and experience to pause and look again; he knew the man, it was the man's own car, and he was replacing a flat tire! A possible tragedy was avoided because a young police officer fought his emotions long enough to "look again." Before you blow your cool, run it through one more time. Is it what it appears to be? Is it really worth the extent of your anger?

A forthright problem-solving approach to conflict doesn't work well until you get past the relationship problems, many of which are intensified by insensitivity or lack of knowledge about the adjustment mechanisms. From a sender's perspective the problem is essentially the same. It's just as easy initially to overlook how our overcompensation might make a mess of an interaction and contribute to the real conflict.

Managing conflict fairly calls for an understanding and a tolerance of the defense systems used by others to protect their self-concepts and to relieve ego pressures. It also calls upon us to manage our own defense mechanisms so that we don't compound an already difficult interaction.

UNFAIR FIGHTING

One way to know what is fair is to discuss what is unfair. In their book *The Intimate Enemy: How to Fight Fair in Love and Marriage*, psychotherapist George Bach and colleague Peter Wyden review a great many unfair fighting techniques or "crazy-makers."[54] Several are relevant to the kinds of interpersonal conflicts we are talking about. Even after appropriate excuses for adjustment behavior these are really unfair.

Kitchensinking

Kitchensinking throws every argument into the fight but the kitchen sink. These are the sort of insult exchanges made famous in Neil Simon's *California Suite*.

Billy:	Shouldn't we kiss or shake hands or something?
Hannah:	Let's save it for when you leave . . . I love your California clothes.
Billy:	They're Bloomingdale's, in New York.
Hannah:	The best place for California clothes. You look so . . . I don't know—what's the word I'm looking for?
Billy:	Happy?
Hannah:	Casual. It's so hard to tell out here—are you dressed up now, or is that sporty?
Billy:	I didn't think a tie was necessary for a reunion.
Hannah:	Is that what this is? When I walked in, I thought we were going to play tennis.
Billy:	Well, you look fit enough for it.
Hannah:	Fit? You think I look fit? What an awful shit you are. I look gorgeous.
Billy:	Yes, you do, Hannah. You look lovely.
Hannah:	No, no. *You* look lovely. *I* look gorgeous.
Billy:	Well, I lost about ten pounds.
Hannah:	Listen to what I'm telling you, you're *ravishing*. I love the way you're wearing your hair now. Where do you go, that boy who does Barbra Streisand?

Billy:	You like it, you can have my Thursday appointment with him . . . If you're interested, I'm feeling *very* well, thank you.
Hannah:	Well, of course you are. Look at that tan. Well, it's the life out here, isn't it? You have an office outdoors somewhere?
Billy:	No, just a desk near the window . . . Hey, Hannah, if we're going to banter like this, give me a little time. It's been nine years, I'm rusty.
Hannah:	You'll pick it right up again, it's like French. You see, that's what I would miss if I left New York. The bantering.
Billy:	San Francisco's only an hour away. We go up there and banter in emergencies.
Hannah:	Do you really?
Billy:	Would I lie to you?
Hannah:	I never liked San Francisco. I was always afraid I'd fall out of bed and roll down one of those hills.
Billy:	Not you, Hannah, You roll *up* hills.
Hannah:	Oh, good. You're bantering. The flight out wasn't a total loss . . . Aren't you going to sit down, Bill? Or do they call you Billy out here? Yes, they do. Jenny told me. Everybody calls you Billy.
Billy:	(shrugs) That's me. Billy.
Hannah:	It's adorable. A forty-five-year-old Billy. Standing there in his cute little sneakers and sweater. Please, sit down, Billy, I'm beginning to feel like your math teacher.[55]

Gunnysacking

Gunnysacking saves up all manner of grievances and complaints that are "toted along quietly in a gunny sack . . . (till) they make a dreadful mess when the sack finally bursts." Bach and Wyden catch this crazy-maker with the following episode.

A woman arrives twenty minutes late for a meeting with her husband and an important friend. The husband is furious.

He:	Why were you late?
She:	I tried my best.
He:	Yeah? You and who else? Your mother is never on time either.
She:	That's got nothing to do with it.
He:	The hell it doesn't. You're just as sloppy as she is.
She:	(getting louder) You don't say! Who's picking whose dirty underwear off the floor every morning?
He:	(shouting) I happen to go to work. What have you got to do all day?
She:	(shouting) I'm trying to get along on the money you don't make, that's what.
He:	(turning away from her) Why should I knock myself out for an ungrateful bitch like you?[56]

Some conflict was legitimate; she was late. But check the gunnysacking and some kitchensinking—the mother-in-law complaint, the masculinity grievance, the money complaint . . .

Beltlining

Beltlining, as in boxing, strikes a blow at or below the beltline—a foul in some cases, painful at best. We all have a psychological beltline or tolerance level for *some* interpersonal pain. Communications can be more prudently transmitted when we know where those beltlines are. If a boxer had his trunks up around his neck, we'd think it an unfair fight, yet some people face conflict situations in much the same way, making a low blow out of the mildest of admonitions. For some the trunks are around the ankles masochistically inviting low blows. Unless you are in therapy, it's a sure way to become embroiled in a dirty fight (or to be ignored).

All of us need to check the beltlines of others and perhaps adjust our own from year to year and situation to situation. In dealing with intimates and friends we are advised to give some clue indicating where our beltlines are so we do not deceive others. If Mom and Dad don't want your visiting girl friend in your bedroom in their house, they should make that beltline clear before she arrives at the door. Conflicts are easier to cope with when we know what they are about and where the sensitivities lie.

Monologuing

Monologuing is incessant talking, a verbosity that tolerates no real feedback. Wendell Johnson in discussing the "Language of Maladjustment" describes an extreme case.

> One of the most striking cases I have ever known is that of a lady who seems to have no terminal facilities whatever. It is quite probable that she could talk all day; I have never felt up to making the experiment. An interesting thing about her speech is that a little of it is not unpleasant. Listening to her talk is somewhat like watching a six-day bicycle race; the first few laps are even a little exciting, perhaps. It is the five-hundredth lap that gets you. She seems to be motivated by a profound sense of frustration in her social and professional activities; in any prolonged monologue she eventually settles down to a steady outpouring of criticism and pained astonishment concerning her real and imagined rivals. In common parlance, she is a "cat." Her denunciations of other people, given usually in confidential tones, seem to serve as a crutch with which she supports her own tottering self-esteem.[57]

Certainly all verbose people are not monologuers. Even the more quiet among us can become overtalkative given the right issue or frustration. The normally verbose know they talk a lot, and they therefore work at being and frequently are excellent listeners. The persistent and chronic monologuers may have a more serious maladjustment problem according to Johnson. His descriptions may help us recognize in ourselves and others when we are reflecting a personal quandary and fighting unfairly.

> The disorienting language of verbose individuals will usually be found to express, in more or less conspicuous degrees, idealism, frustration, and the varieties of aggression that take the form of criticism, vengefulness, and vigorous self-defense. It expresses, also, a naive faith in words, something quite remindful of primitive word magic.[58]

According to Bach and Wyden monologuers are enormously resented. They have only limited constructive advice for victims of monologuing: walk out, cover your ears, hold up your hand, reward acknowledgments.[59] They have found that the best training for monologuers is to let them see and hear themselves and their victims on television. It's one way to get them to absorb feedback.

Sandbagging

Sandbagging sets up or traps someone into saying something that is later held against him or her. It is often a phony plea for openness. You comply by laying out the administrative heads in your organization and are subsequently attacked by the sandbagger who supports Uncle Lou and the administration. Sometimes sandbagging can be more subtle: A con man listens patiently and attentively until you put your foot in your mouth or buy the swamp land and essentially sandbag yourself. Women used to complain loudly about being sandbagged (or compromised) by unfair men. Of course, with enlightenment it's impossible to be sandbagged in these matters. . . .

RATIONAL PREPARATION

Preparation Perspectives

Sometimes conflict is dumped in your lap. You arrive at the office and an act of God has cut off all of the power and heat. Now that's not an interpersonal conflict. However, if you are in a leadership role, it can quickly become one if people feel that you should have anticipated such a calamity and had auxiliary power and heat available. Interpersonal conflicts are sometimes like that too. They catch us by surprise, but perhaps they shouldn't as often as they do. "I didn't know she was unhappy." "I had no idea I was being unkind." "He just up and left me." All are familiar lines to marriage counselors.

This is not a recommendation to seek or create conflicts, but it is a suggestion to be alert to small ones and to confront them before they become large ones. If you have some kind of comprehension of an interpersonal conflict and are convinced that you must confront, then consideration of the following general questions should help you prepare for such an encounter.

How Critical Is the Conflict?   Must it be confronted immediately? Should it be? Has your irritation magnified the problem? Is it really your business? Have you "looked again"? Remember Irving Lee's findings that when we are emotional and angry, three out of every four times a "look again" proves we were wrong or at least not totally justified in our anger.

Is It Primarily Relational or Content Oriented?   All interpersonal conflicts are in part relational, but some are entirely so. Other times an issue is the primary cause of conflict with some relational consequences. An argument over twin or double beds may be content for some, but lovers would, we're sure, find it relational as well. In fact, the beds may be a secondary issue from the start. It is not always easy to assign weights to content and relational matters, but we should try. If a friend is constantly monologuing using the same tired issues, it is probably relational. Perhaps you have taken the issues too seriously and your friend hasn't; perhaps you need some new friends . . .

Is the Receiver Aware of the Conflict?   The earlier marriage counselor examples make this point of awareness. "I had no idea she was unhappy." We may be very aware of another's behavior that is bothersome and frustrating to us, but if, thanks to the silence of others and ourselves, that person is unaware of a problem, we have a conflict with a very special twist—a twist that we must consider *before* engaging in systematic confrontation. The approach to this encounter should vary depending upon whether the "other" is an intimate, a casual friend, a superior, a subordinate— in short, the way in which the relationship is important to you.

Is There a Role Difference?   In Utopia all people are equal and their roles in society make no difference. Presidents and kings are viewed in the same way as the rank and file. It is a cruel illusion. Many needless conflicts are spawned by innocents who confuse ''equal under the law'' with ''equal in all ways.'' Without arguing intelligence, it is clear that some people have better reaction times, retention skills, and abilities to abstract complicated data. That can make for a role difference, but so can the less easier to swallow assigned or elected roles. In the military it is clear—RHIP, Rank Has Its Privileges. That's why we have NCO (noncommissioned officers) Clubs and Officers' Clubs. That's why the president of a major corporation or government agency has a chauffeured car and others do not. Like it or not, role difference makes a difference. It is an issue you must address pragmatically as you assess the criticality of the conflict and the approach or strategy you will use in confronting it.

Am I Prepared to Lose?   A really mean question! You should, after all, think positively and have faith that people will see things your way after honest discussion, or if not *your* way, surely they will see some other way mutually acceptable to all. After sitting in on arbitration cases it became obvious to me that some conflicts don't get resolved at all, and that third parties sometimes simply hand down resolutions and decisions. There are winners, there are losers, and there are times when we're not sure whether we've won or lost.

It pays to calculate your risks in these matters. If I lose, will my relationship suffer? How will I maintain contact? Will I be able to confront this conflict again perhaps with more success next time? Am I destroyed? Does a loss mean my job? Can I live with it?

In small-group conflicts if rational, problem-solving and aggressive, rhetorically-sensitive arguments don't resolve anything, we frequently resort to votes. We can sometimes calculate those risks by anticipating voting behavior. We may be surprised when we lose, but we are usually psychologically *prepared* for a defeat.

Coping with conflict is serious business and calls for thoughtfulness, awareness, and a willingness to confront it intelligently, fairly, and systematically. An agenda for conflict coping or fair fighting follows.

Behavior and Practice

Personally Define the Problem   Personally define the issue or behavior that bothers you. This includes all of the perspective questions suggested in the previous section. Is it critical? Is it relational? Is it understood? Is there a role difference that matters? After these considerations you're ready to *state the conflict specifically*. Try to keep it singular; don't kitchensink or gunnysack on this one. You'll only deceive yourself. Explain to your own satisfaction *how it really affects you*. Check your thinking by *trying it out on a trusted friend*. Stand still for feedback; it may also be a test of your friends. If it washes here, you are ready to consider an appropriate style of communication as you approach the confrontation.

Decide Your Communication Style   We discussed earlier your concern for the content versus the relationship. It could also be stated as your concern for your personal goals in the conflict versus your concern for the relationship or the group (in any given conflict).

Borrowing from Blake and Mouton[60] and the Jay Hall revision,[61] we get a characterization of the styles available. The horizontal scale allows you to assess just how important your personal goals are in any given conflict. The vertical scale allows you to assess just how important the relationship is to you in any given conflict. There are eighty-one intersections, but the four styles typified by the corners plus a central compromise style are enough to make the point. Your analysis of your specific conflict

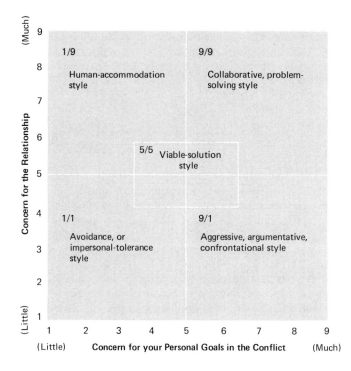

Figure 6.4

should help you choose an appropriate style. Ideally you should seek a 9/9 *collaborative, problem-solving style*, but some conflicts quickly call for backup styles when collaboration fails. Sometimes the time factor is enough. A conflict between two pilots on a damaged aircraft calls for quick assessment of what to do, but when time runs out, the senior officer turns to an *aggressive* 9/1 style: "We're going to abort. Prepare for an emergency landing." This happens despite the pilot's concern for the relationship between him or her and the crew.

The 1/1 Avoidance or Impersonal Style   In this case you have little concern for the relationship, and if the conflict impinges only slightly on your personal goals, your style might very well be a low-profile one. You can take or leave your boss as a friend, and it's a short-term relationship anyway. You are aware that he or she has matrimonial problems that you feel may be hurting his or her effectiveness as a supervisor, but they don't particularly affect your personal goals in or out of the organization. This is not much of a conflict for you, and you're not sure about the organization. This may be the time for an avoidance or impersonal style.

The 9/1 Aggressive, Argumentative, Confrontational Style   With this approach you have much concern for the conflict and minimal concern for the relationship. The senior pilot in the aforementioned example was backed into this one. His argument was a short one given the emergency.

Two union business agents representing the plumbers and the carpenters have a conflict over who has jurisdiction over the installation of bathroom wall fixtures in an apartment complex. Both groups can't do the work. One will win and one will lose if it takes arbitration, unless perchance both agents retreat to a 5/5 *viable solution style,* a viable solution of the moment. To avoid holding up the general contractor they agree for this time only that the plumbers will do the first five floors and the carpenters will do the top five floors.

The 5/5 Viable Solution Style This is a compromise style wherein your concerns are typically low or mixed. As in the jurisdictional conflict above, it is a popular backup style even when one or both concerns are very high. During the protest years of the 1960s the president of a major university was faced with ''nonnegotiable demands'' from a large group of very militant, emotional students. He commented in retrospect, ''I gave up on your rational, problem-solving approach (9/9); and I couldn't give the university away (1/1) or (1/9); confrontation (9/1) was to incite a riot . . . I sought whatever viable solutions of the moment I could negotiate (5/5).'' The compromise style is not always an easy one and not always the best long-term resolution of a conflict. In the case above, the university and the students were protected, and eventually the president was able to assume a successful, rhetorically sensitive, 9/9 collaborative, problem-solving style.

1/9 Human Accommodation Style In this situation the concern for the relationship is unusually high, and the concern for personal goals is either low to begin with or is surrendered for the sake of the relationship.

A useful but tricky style . . . sometimes. You are smitten with an incredibly attractive person who literally takes your breath away. You discover that he or she has strong political leanings that are the opposite of yours. Unless your politics are truly at the 9 on the scale, you would probably use a style that accommodates the relationship and yields on the political conflict. Depending upon how the relationship develops, you might move to any of the other styles. You might, of course, really change your politics, but you won't change the other person's if you stay at 1/9.

You love your parents and you want desperately not to hurt them, but they simply can't agree to your having a roommate of the opposite sex. You could forgo the roommate (1/9) or at least assume that style. If you try 9/9, the rational approach, and it fails, you may find yourself in an argumentative style, 9/1. Of course your parents may go 5/5, ''Okay, but not in our house,'' or perhaps 1/1, ''It's your life'' (or is that also 5/5?). We said this was a tricky style. The point is that it's just a *style* we're talking about, not necessarily perfect solutions to interpersonal conflicts.

9/9 Collaborative, Problem-Solving Style Here one has much concern for the relationship *and* much concern for personal goals. It is an enlightened style based on the assumptions that conflicts are natural in the human experience; conflicts are amenable to rational, cooperative problem solving; and a sensitive openness is the necessary first step. More will be said of these assumptions in the section on reviewing positive attitudes about conflict in this chapter.

The problem with ideal styles is that situations, contexts, and circumstances are not always ideal. The roommate problem might be amenable to this mutual-exploration style, but it could be a disaster if Mom and Dad really have strong opinions about this sort of thing. If they won't even participate in such a problem-solving discussion, you've obviously struck out.

Another set of constraints on the 9/9 collaborative approach is the ethics, oaths, agreements, and business and professional obligations to which you have previously agreed. The doctor who is asked by a friend to provide illegal drugs is going to have to be hardheaded about the law and his or her code of ethics. Professionals and others in the public eye have confrontational constraints and aggressive obligations both legally as public figures and morally in terms of their ethical codes. The organization person is tied (or ought to be) by constitutions, bylaws, labor agreements, affirmative action, the Internal Revenue Service, and other laws of the land. Some have argued that the bureaucratic constraints are so great that the synergistic (a working together) striking of a business deal is a thing of the past.

In addition to requiring participation, the 9/9 style is usually very time consuming. Don't be in a hurry.

Part of your style decision should be based on the typical styles used by the other or others involved in the conflict. If you know you are going to have to interact with a confirmed 9/1—that is, an aggressive, "tell it like it is" approach to conflict resolution—your starting point may be a little (or a lot) short of 9/9.

In one interesting study of styles (or strategies) of resolving relational conflict five types along with their representative tactics were delineated (Table 6.4). Except for empathethic understanding, they all seem a little harsh, but all were found to be used with some success across a variety of contexts.[62] We do not offer them as recommendations, however. Knowing the basic styles and being able to use those most

TABLE 6.4 Interpersonal Conflict Strategies.

1. Strategy of Manipulation	Be especially sweet, charming, helpful and pleasant before bringing up the subject of disagreement Act so nice that he or she later cannot refuse when I ask him or her for my own way Make this person believe that he or she is doing me a favor by giving in
2. Strategy of Non-negotiation	Refuse to discuss or even listen to the subject unless he or she gives in Keep repeating my point of view until he or she gives in Argue until this person changes his or her mind
3. Strategy of Emotional Appeal	Appeal to this person's love and affection for me Promise to be more loving in the future Get angry and demand that he or she give in
4. Strategy of Personal Rejection	Withhold affection and act cold until he or she gives in Ignore him or her Make the other person jealous by pretending to lose interest in him or her
5. Strategy of Empathic Understanding	Discuss what would happen if we each accepted the other's point of view Talk about why we do not agree Hold mutual talks without argument

From M. Fitzpatrick and J. Winke, "You Always Hurt the One You Love: Strategies and Tactics in Interpersonal Conflict," *Communication Quarterly*, 27, no. 1 (Winter 1979), 7.

appropriate to the requirements of each specific conflict are your best perspectives. You should also be ready to switch styles when necessary and perhaps reassess your personal concerns for certain goals and certain relationships.

Review Positive Attitudes About Conflict   Just to make sure your courage is up, your head is on straight, and you are not acting emotionally, try these attitudes for reassurance.

1. Conflict is serious business but a natural hazard of living.
2. When conflict is resolved effectively and with rhetorical sensitivity, such an experience can preserve or enhance a relationship.
3. A positive, rhetorically sensitive openness is usually the first step toward conflict resolution.
4. "When angry look again." If your anger is truly justified, it is human to admit it and to seek feedback from the appropriate respondent—but "look again."

Make an Appointment   Now that you have worked your way through your personal definition of the conflict (including the style decisions, and assuming it's still of enough concern to confront an important someone about), you are ready to get on with the discussion. But is the other person (or persons) ready? One way to find out is to test these waters by asking if there is a convenient time for your adversary or group to discuss your problem. Make a date as it were.

During one year I lost both of my parents. On my first day back to school after the second funeral an unannounced student rushed into my office literally screaming about a class schedule problem. I had to call on my last ounce of professionalism to resolve the conflict. Of course the student didn't know about *my* problems, and besides, I was paid to solve the student's problems. I really think, however, that had I a knife in my chest and blood on my shirt, this particular student would have been summarily unimpressed and would still have shouted, "Dr. Ross, I have a problem!"

Appointments can help conflicting parties arrive at a psychologically constructive time for heavy discussions. They needn't be all that formal either. "Jane, I'd like to talk to you about your problems in graduate school. Can we find a time to discuss some of these things?" To plunge in without this kind of consideration often is understood as "Jane, you're fouling up in graduate school, and we're going to talk about it right now!" It's easy to see why some people or groups never even get to a *real* confrontation of a conflict. They alienate one another in the preliminaries. Don't overlook this step in preparing your conflict-coping agenda. It's kind, rhetorically sensitive, and makes for a more systematic discussion.

Confront the Conflict   It's your day in court. *State your conflict* as you have personally defined and rehearsed it. Keep it singular and explain how it affects you. Don't monologue, keep it brief, and avoid kitchensinking and gunnysacking.

Next, *seek agreement on your statement*, not the right and wrong of it, but just the statement itself. Are you agreed that you are talking about the same problem? If you are the one on the receiving end, a good technique is to repeat it: "I hear you saying that you feel you were discriminated against in the last round of promotions because of your sex." Control your emotions and stay on the topic. If you are serious about resolution, don't trap or sandbag.

Now *allow response time*. The person or group reacting to the statement has a right to reply or in some cases to ask for a delay if more time or information is needed. If and when the discussion proceeds, don't monologue, but rather solicit feedback. Keep your analysis rational and stick with your decision on communication style unless it proves to be obviously out of sync with the situation. Be open but positive.

If you resolve or partially resolve the conflict, *review your joint understanding*. Thank your interactants particularly when there were good faith, constructive efforts made to at least try to reach a solution.

SUMMARY

''Perfect organizational health is not freedom from conflict . . . if properly handled, conflict can lead to more effective and appropriate adjustments [Kelly].'' Conflict has been typed as extrinsic and intrinsic, realistic and nonrealistic, substantive and affective, task and psychological. Conflict tends to occur over five issues: (1) resources, (2) preferences and nuisances, (3) values, (4) beliefs, and (5) relationships.

Experts see task-conflict episodes going through a multiple stage or development pattern. One five-stage process (Pondy) is (1) latent, (2) perceived, (3) felt, (4) manifest, and (5) aftermath. One three-part pattern (Ellis and Fisher) is (1) interpersonal exchange, (2) confrontation, and (3) substantive conflict. Task conflicts can be better managed through facts, orderly problem solving, information-seeking leadership, friendly relationships, clear communication, and better listening.

Coombs suggests a tri-part division of psychological conflicts: (1) intrapersonal, (2) interpersonal, (3) win-lose. Forsyth offers a five-stage model for psychological conflicts: (1) disagreement, (2) confrontation, (3) escalation, (4) deescalation, and (5) resolution. Scheidel and Crowell remind us to (1) translate psychological conflicts to task differences, (2) try to stay group centered, (3) be tolerant, (4) expect some conflict, and (5) mind our language.

Societal change is a factor in much conflict—media, computers, intergroup hostilities, and the mosaic society among others.

Interorganizational competition between groups, shadow groups, and eccentric individuals can all contribute to a lack of cooperation and conflict.

When conflicts become intense, if communication can be maintained it should be used to establish rules by which bargaining and negotiation may take place. Third-party intervention is another way of coping; some contracts may require it.

Conflict almost always involves perceptions of incompatible goals and/or threats to relationships. Destructive behaviors tend to be self-centered, while constructive behaviors are relationship centered. Name calling, threats, deception, and sarcasm are destructive and elicit reactions of hurt, fear, confusion, and distrust. Constructive conflict is open, but it is relationship centered as well as issue centered, and it seeks an atmosphere of trust. It seeks a forthright but supportive, rational, problem-solving kind of issue confrontation.

Frustration results when an external barrier stands between us and our needs or goals. Psychological conflict takes place when we have to make choices between needs that are incompatible or mutually exclusive. To escape frustration and conflict we may resort to a kind of *mental paralysis* or avoidance behavior. Another way to escape is through *alternation*, which involves vacillation and irresolution as we alternately try to satisfy each of the conflicting goals or needs. A third way is *literal escape*—that is, we simply walk away from the conflict and hope it will go away. Adjustment mechanisms are unconscious defense systems used by the mind to relieve ego tensions caused by conflict and frustration. They distort reality to defend and take pressure off the ego. They include rationalization, compensation, projection, repression, contraposition, regression, and others. They are normal in mild degree.

Goffman talks about self-presentation in terms of "face work" (as in saving face). The competent communicator needs to be sensitive to his or her self-face and others' faces. When two people interact, there are two self-presentations. If these co-ordinate, they create a common episode. A primary function of interpersonal encounters is the establishment and maintenance of self and the social identities of the participants.

Our interpersonal behavior is largely a function of how we experience or perceive the communicative relationship (Laing). We experience communication from a direct perspective and from a metaperspective. When one infers another's direct experience of oneself (my notion of what your notion is of me), one is dealing with the metaperspective level.

Role taking is the internal process we go through in making inferences about self and others. Sensitive role taking aids in assessing the range and nature of the communication obligations of any particular interaction. Role enactment is the verbal and nonverbal behavior that results from our role taking. It is the essence of interpersonal communication.

We become participant observers through careful listening, reflexivity (a looking back or reviewing), empathic understanding, and taking both a perspective and metaperspective view (What do you mean? How am I coming across?).

"Rhetorical sensitivity is a particular attitude toward encoding spoken messages. It represents a way of thinking about what should be said and then a way of deciding how to say it." It is a type of sensitivity that makes effective social interaction possible. Rhetorically sensitive (RS) people judge encounters carefully before taking a stand on an issue. They distinguish between content and relational communication, and they know when to speak up or shut up.

People not rhetorically sensitive have been described as noble selves (NS) and rhetorical reflectors (RR). The noble selves may be characterized as individuals who see any variation from their personal norms as hypocritical, as a denial of integrity. Rhetorical reflectors are described as persons who have no self to call their own. For each person and situation they present a new self. They reflect each situation in which they find themselves.

We cope with conflict better if we are rhetorically sensitive. This includes abilities to adapt to specific audiences, receivers, contexts, and situations; to prudently evaluate message relevance; and to consider the content and relational dimensions of conflict communications.

We can manage conflict fairly if we first learn to recognize adjustive behaviors. Managing conflict fairly calls for an understanding and a tolerance of the defense systems used by others to protect their self-concepts and to relieve ego pressures. It also calls upon us to manage our own defense mechanisms. Unfair-fighting techniques include kitchensinking, gunnysacking, beltlining, monologuing, and sandbagging.

Assessing a conflict situation should include the following questions: (1) How critical is the conflict? (2) Is it primarily relational or content? (3) Is the receiver aware of the conflict? (4) Is there a role difference? (5) Am I prepared to lose?

Preparation behavior for conflict situations should include the following: (1) define the issue or behavior that bothers you and state the conflict specifically, (2) decide your communication style, (3) review positive attitudes about conflict, (4) make an appointment, and (5) confront the conflict systematically.

Some useful principles to help you through trying times include (1) conflict is a natural hazard of living, (2) when conflict is resolved with rhetorical sensitivity, such an experience can preserve or enhance a relationship, (3) a positive, rhetorically sensitive openness is usually the first step toward conflict resolution, and (4) ''When angry look again.'' If your anger is justified, it is human to admit it and to seek feedback from the appropriate respondent.

PROJECTS AND CASES

PROJECTS

1. Consider the six types of conflict described by Deutsch (p. 140), and classify the last two conflicts you observed. Explain.

2. Consider the sixteen projected organizational changes of Kast and Rosenzweig (p. 145), and discuss their likelihood of happening.

3. In terms of what has been said about frustration and conflict, create a hypothetical character (or use a real one) who would be almost impossible to influence and would be a difficult group member.

4. Work up a short role play illustrating one or more of the adjustment mechanisms. Use another person as a foil. See if the class can properly assess the mechanism (e.g., an arresting officer who has just stopped you for double parking and your *rationalization*).

5. In a small group, discuss destructive conflict behaviors in terms of the coordinated management of meaning. Are name calling, threat, or sarcasm always destructive? In what kinds of contexts would they not be? Constructive conflict is both relationship and issue oriented. For example, are there ways to be sarcastic and constructive? You may want to be thinking in terms of construction systems, speech acts, and life scripts.

6. Working in a small group, develop a list with explanations for differences between content and relational conflict. What cues signal a relational as opposed to a content conflict?

7. Name two things you have done to help create a healthy communication climate. Then name two things you did (usually unintentional) that caused conflict.

8. Observe several interactions until you find a really good or a really bad one. Describe the interaction and defend your evaluation in two pages or less. Be prepared to report in class.

9. Locate a good example (it can be a short one) of one of the following kinds of unfair fighting, and prepare to share it with the class.

kitchensinking	beltlining	sandbagging
gunnysacking	monologuing	

10. Apply the ''rational preparation'' guides for conflict situations found at the end of this chapter to a current or an old personal conflict and detail your plan for resolution (or, in the case of an old experience, what might have been).

CASES

After being assigned to a group of three to six people, pick one of the following cases and prepare a 10- to 15-minute panel discussion in which you try to apply the suggestions found in this chapter. What *might* have been done? What *can* be done at this point? What decisions should be made and why? What would be an appropriate communication style (1/9, 9/1, 5/5, and so on)?

1. Allan's Promotion[63]

We were a good group until Allan came up for promotion. Before that happened Allan was about as group-minded as the rest of us were, and he was considerate. But when he found out he was being recommended for senior project analyst, he flipped. Almost overnight he changed from the good group member ready to cooperate, ready to perform his duties, to an obstinate, high-minded, egotistical jerk. He came late to group meetings, he sat back and daydreamed, yawned loudly, interrupted people, made silly comments, you know, the whole ''I am better than you are'' routine. What could we do? We were stuck with him. We needed his expertise on the project but we didn't need his grief. I tried to talk to him away from the group but it didn't work out. He wouldn't listen. A couple of the others tried to ridicule him during group meetings, but he just laughed. The leader, Vera, tried to intervene on several occasions, but he knew if he was promoted she would be technically his subordinate and didn't pay her any mind. That experience turned me against small groups. You know what happened? He got promoted and just continued to get worse. Vera quit, one guy transferred to Montana, and I returned to school. So let me ask you, professor, what do you do with someone like Allan?

2. The Coffee Break

Department *X* was a staff department with a total of eleven people on quota: a manager, an assistant, and nine staff members. The offices were all located in one aisle and were divided by glass partitions. Other members of the company were constantly in and out of Department *X*.

Several months ago, the ''coffee break'' problem became quite acute when several members of the department, and often all nine, would gather in one office to sip coffee from the machine across the hall.

The department manager held a meeting with his staff explaining that he wanted them to have their coffee break, but they must not gather in the offices as they have been doing. Furthermore, he would prefer them not to have coffee in their offices at all since it detracted from the businesslike atmosphere that was necessary to the physical setup of the department.

He suggested they use one of the conference rooms where they might have their ''break'' behind closed doors.

Unfortunately, this did not work out too well due to the following complications:

1. The receptionist now joins the group leaving the front desk unstaffed.
2. The ''coffee breaks'' are getting longer and sometimes extend to a half-hour or more.
3. With the receptionist away from the switchboard and personnel out of the offices, the phones ''ring off the hooks.''
4. The conference room is often left in a messy condition.

3. The New Form Change

The supervisor of a retail merchandise division's statistical workers is introducing an improved Order Recap Form for use by his employees. This form is quite different from what has been used before since it cuts out irrelevant detail and adds new, important information that is used daily. As with the old form, this form should be completed and handed to the supervisor every Friday.

The supervisor has decided to communicate this change to his group of ten employees during a coffee meeting.

Supervisor:	We have gotten together today to talk about an improved Order Recap Form that will be used starting today.
1st Voice:	Not another one!
2nd Voice:	You've gotta be kidding!
3rd Voice:	It's about time!
Supervisor:	Now, wait a minute. This form is vastly improved, and it is easy to fill in . . . just take a look at it. (passes out a copy of form to each participant)
1st Voice:	It looks like more work to me!
2nd Voice:	I can't see any difference!
3rd Voice:	Oh, I can see where this is better!
Supervisor:	Just like the other one, this has to be ready by Friday. If you have any questions, please let me know and I will help you individually.
1st Voice:	Why is our job always being made harder by getting new forms—no other department gets them?
Supervisor:	Now, come on, you know better than that!
1st Voice:	Well, I'm getting a little tired of all these new forms.
2nd Voice:	They don't mean anything to me one way or the other.
3rd Voice:	Oh, I think they make the job interesting.

NOTES

1. J. Kelly, "Make Conflict Work for You," *Harvard Business Review*, 48 (July–August 1970), 103–13.

2. F. S. Haiman, *Group Leadership and Democratic Action* (Boston: Houghton Mifflin, 1951), p. 181.

3. Lewis Coser, *The Functions of Social Conflict* (Glencoe, Ill.: Free Press, 1956), pp. 48–55.

4. Harold Guetzkow and John Gyr, "An Analysis of Conflict in Decision-Making Groups," *Human Relations*, 7 (1954) 367–81.

5. Morton Deutsch, *The Resolution of Conflict* (New Haven: Yale University Press, 1973, 1977), pp. 15–17.

6. Ibid., pp. 12–14.

7. Louis R. Pondy, "Organizational Conflict: Concepts and Models," *Administrative Science Quarterly*, 12 (1967), 298–306.

8. D. G. Ellis and B. A. Fisher, "Phases of Conflict in Small Group Development: A Markov Analysis," *Human Communication Research*, 1 (1975), 195–212 (characteristics outlined for clarity); see also D. S. Gouran and B. A. Fisher, "The Functions of Human Communication in the Formation, Maintenance, and Performance of Small Groups," in *Handbook of Rhetorical and Communication Theory*, eds. C. C. Arnold and J. W. Bowers (Boston: Allyn and Bacon, 1984), p. 624.

9. Guetzkow and Gyr, "An Analysis of Conflict," pp. 367–81.

10. Thomas M. Scheidel and Laura Crowell, *Discussing and Deciding: A Desk Book for Group Leaders and Members* (New York: Macmillan, 1979), p. 221.

11. K. B. Valentine and B. A. Fisher, "An Interaction Analysis of Verbal Innovative Deviance in Small Groups," *Speech Monographs*, 41 (1974), 413–20.

12. Clyde H. Coombs, "The Structure of Conflict," *American Psychologist*, 42, no. 4 (April 1987), 355–63.

13. Ibid., p. 361.

14. Ibid., p. 362.

15. Donelson R. Forsyth, *An Introduction to Group Dynamics* (Monterey, Calif.: Brooks/Cole, 1983), pp. 79–108.

16. See J. Z. Rubin, "Experimental Research on Third-Party Intervention in Conflict: Toward Some Generalizations," *Psychological Bulletin*, 87 (1980), 379–91.

17. Scheidel and Crowell, *Discussing and Deciding*, pp. 234–46.

18. Valentine and Fisher, "An Interaction Analysis," pp. 413–20.

19. Gouran and Fisher, "Functions of Human Communication," p. 631.

20. Muzafer Sherif, "A Life of Conflict and Goals," *Psychology Today*, 19, no. 9 (September 1985), 55–59.

21. K. E. Boulding, "Expecting the Unexpected: The Uncertain Future of Knowledge and Technology," *Designing Education for the Future* (Boulder, Colo.: Colorado Department of Education, 1966), p. 212.

22. Paraphrased from F. E. Kast and J. E. Rosenzweig, *Organization and Management* (New York: McGraw-Hill, 1979), pp. 605–6.

23. Forsyth, *Introduction to Group Dynamics*, p. 400.

24. For more on these matters, see S. LaTour, P. Houlden, L. Walker, and J. Thibaut, "Some Determinants of Preference for Modes of Conflict Resolution," *Journal of Conflict Resolution*, 20 (1976), 319–56.

25. A. M. Greeley, *Sexual Intimacy* (New York: Seabury, 1973). See also I. Altman and D. A. Taylor, *Social Penetration: The Development of Interpersonal Relationships* (New York: Holt, Rinehart and Winston, 1973); M. L. Knapp, *Social Intercourse: From Greeting to Goodby* (Boston: Allyn and Bacon, 1978).

26. For another view see J. L. Hocker and W. W. Wilmot, *Interpersonal Conflict*, 2nd ed. (Dubuque, Ia.: Wm. C. Brown, 1985), p. 32.

27. G. R. Miller and H. S. Simons, eds., *Perspectives on Communication in Social Conflict* (Englewood Cliffs, N.J.: Prentice-Hall, 1974), p. 3.

28. Deutsch, *Resolution of Conflict*.

29. A. C. Filley, *Interpersonal Conflict Resolution* (New York: Scott, Foresman, 1975).

30. E. R. Alexander, "The Reduction of Cognitive Conflict," *Journal of Conflict Resolution*, 23 (1979), 137.

31. W. R. Cupach, "Interpersonal Conflict: Relational Strategies and Intimacy," (paper presented at the annual convention of the Speech Communication Association, New York, November 1980), p. 7 (parentheses mine).

32. J. Dollard and others, *Frustration and Aggression* (New Haven: Yale University Press, 1939). See also R. R. Sears, E. E. Maccoby, and H. Levin, *Patterns of Child Rearing* (New York: Harper and Row, 1957).

33. N. E. Miller and R. Bugelski, "Minor Studies of Aggression: II. The Influence of Frustrations Imposed by the In-Group on Attitudes Expressed Toward Out-Groups," *Journal of Psychology*, 25 (1948), 437–42.

34. S. K. Mallick and B. R. McCandless, "A Study of Catharsis of Aggression," *Journal of Personality and Social Psychology*, 4 (1966), 591–96.

35. K. D. Benne and P. Sheats, "Functional Roles of Group Members," *Journal of Social Issues*, 4, no. 2 (1948), 41–49.

36. Ibid., pp. 42–46.

37. B. H. Raven and J. Z. Rubin, *Social Psychology: People in Groups* (New York: John Wiley & Sons, 1976), p. 513.

38. See especially J. W. Brehm, *A Theory of Psychological Reactance* (New York: Academic, 1966).

39. J. R. Wenburg and W. W. Wilmot, *The Personal Communication Process* (New York: John Wiley & Sons, 1973), pp. 34–35.

40. E. Goffman, "On Face Work," *Psychiatry*, 18 (1955), 213–31.

41. J. M. Wiemann, "Explication and Test of a Model of Communicative Competence," *Human Communication Research*, 3, no. 3 (1977), 196.

42. R. D. Laing, *The Politics of Experience* (New York: Pantheon, 1967), p. 4. See also S. W. Littlejohn, *Theories of Human Communication* (Belmont, Calif.: Wadsworth, 1983), pp. 182–85.

43. T. R. Sarbin and V. L. Allen, "Role Theory," in *The Handbook of Social Psychology*, Volume I, 2nd ed., eds. G. Lindzey and E. Aronson (Reading, Mass.: Addison-Wesley, 1969), pp. 489–99; see also R. H. Turner, "Role-Taking, Role Standpoint, and Reference-Group Behavior," in *Role Theory Concepts and Research*, eds. B. J. Biddle and E. J. Thomas (New York: John Wiley & Sons, 1966), p. 152.

44. *The Leelanau Enterprise*, February 26, 1987, sec. 1, p. 5.

45. R. P. Hart, R. E. Carlson, and W. F. Eadie, "Attitudes Toward Communication and the Assessment of Rhetorical Sensitivity," *Communication Monographs*, 47, no. 1 (March 1980), 2.

46. R. P. Hart and D. M. Burks, "Rhetorical Sensitivity and Social Interaction," *Speech Monographs*, 39, no. 2 (June 1972), 75.

47. D. Darnell and W. Brockriede, *Persons Communicating* (Englewood Cliffs, N.J.: Prentice-Hall, 1976), p. 176.

48. Ibid., p. 178.

49. Hart, Carlson, and Eadie, "Attitudes Toward Communication," p. 21.

50. D. D. Cahn and G. M. Shulman, "An Exploratory Study of the Relationship Between Rhetorical Sensitivity, Leadership Effectiveness, and Rank in Military Organization," *Michigan Speech Association Journal*, 15 (1980), 1–11.

51. L. Schoen, "A Study of the Audience Sensitivity and Rhetorical Sensitivity of Students Enrolled in Speech 0200, Basic Speech, at Wayne State University and Implications for Pedagogy," (unpublished doctoral dissertation, Wayne State University, 1981).

52. G. Philipsen, "Speaking 'Like a Man' in Teamsterville: Culture Patterns of Role Enactment in an Urban Neighborhood," *Quarterly Journal of Speech*, 61, no. 1 (February 1975), 13–22.

53. Hart and Burks, "Rhetorical Sensitivity" p. 90. For a detailed discussion of five constituent parts of a rhetorically sensitive attitude, see Hart, Carlson, and Eadie, "Attitudes Toward Communication," p. 2.

54. George R. Bach and Peter Wyden, *The Intimate Enemy* (New York: William Morrow, 1969), p. 135.

55. From *CALIFORNIA SUITE* by Neil Simon. Copyright © 1977 by Neil Simon. Reprinted by permission of Random House, Inc.

56. Bach and Wyden, *The Intimate Enemy*, p. 3.

57. Wendell Johnson, *People in Quandaries* (San Francisco: International General Semantics, 1980) p. 275.

58. Ibid., p. 278.

59. Bach and Wyden, *The Intimate Enemy*, p. 142.

60. R. R. Blake and J. S. Mouton, *The Managerial Grid* (Houston: Gulf, 1964), p. 10.

61. J. Hall, *Conflict Management Survey* (Woodlands, Tex.: Teleometrics International, 1969).

62. M. Fitzpatrick and J. Winke, "You Always Hurt the One You Love: Strategies and Tactics in Interpersonal Conflict," *Communication Quarterly*, 27, no. 1 (Winter 1979), 3–11.

63. H. L. Goodall, *Small Group Communication in Organizations* (Dubuque, Ia.: Wm. C. Brown, 1985), p. 286.

7

MEANING AND RELATIONAL EFFECTIVENESS

Meaning refers to how you are "coming across" to others, whether a single individual, a family, or a small group in an organizational setting. It involves your whole *system* of words, actions, perceptions of self and others, listening habits, and your general manner of interacting with others.

MANAGING MEANING AND LANGUAGE

GENERAL SEMANTICS

> But then they danced down the street like dingledodies and I shambled after as I've been doing all my life after people who interest me, because the only people for me are the mad ones, the ones who are mad to live, mad to talk, mad to be saved, desirous of everything at the same time, the ones who never yawn or say a commonplace thing, but burn, burn, burn like fabulous yellow Roman candles exploding like spiders across the stars and in the middle you see the blue centerlight pop and everybody goes, "Awww!"

A premier example of a run-on sentence! An eighth-grade composition teacher would "bleed" all over such writing and probably rightfully so. However, if we were to translate the sentence into standard American sentence structure and language use, some of the texture of the description would be lost and some of its richness destroyed. Jack Kerouac, a notable American writer, wrote that sentence in *On the Road*.[1]

This helps illustrate a basic tenet of general semantics theory: "An individual's assumptions, beliefs, and attitudes are a function of the structure of his language, and that his perception and behavior will be affected more or less in direct relationship to his susceptibility to influence by that language structure."[2] We are not saying that language determines thought, but we are suggesting that language ability does allow us to represent much of our world. Language arrests our world or "reality" and lets us conceptualize it, store it, and later retrieve it if we so desire. We, in effect, can "bind time."

Last semester a group argued over educational philosophy in relation to an undergraduate course. That particular instance doesn't exist anymore; it's over. It happened last February; time marches on. I am able to share aspects of that argument and that specific instance with you because I have represented it with symbols, which in this case are words. My language allows me to put the words together in a fashion that permits you to get a "picture" of a reality that existed last February. Symbols allow me to re-present an event that occurred in the past. The past isn't lost; I have, in effect, bound time through language.

Remember that my words are not the argument itself. They are a representation of it, much like a city map represents a city but is not the city itself. Ask anyone who has been lost in Chicago with map in hand.

Symbols and language allow us to represent and store realities. Our *knowledge* is a function of our language and symbols. I know what a chair is even when a chair is not present. I know what a chair is because I have stored a symbolic representation of one in my brain. What I have stored is a representation of a chair, not a real chair. The word is not the thing! Sometimes our representations of realities can cause us trouble. Remember, words (symbols) are arbitrary. There is nothing chairlike in the word *chair*; you can't sit on the word *chair*.

Line A in Figure 7.1 indicates what a person ideally perceives as a *correct* symbol, in this case the word *chair*. Line B represents the cognitive selecting and sorting of knowledge and experience that ideally represents an adequate referent. The broken line, *C*, indicates that the word *chair* and a *real* chair are not the same.

The propositional nature of language can be a problem in some language systems. Even absurd statements can be grammatically correct. Try this:

> Red is Green

Interpersonally we should be aware that different people may represent a single event (reality) differently, and a certain amount of interpersonal sensitivity may be necessary to understand another's concept of a particular event.

While still new to industrial relations, I observed a master arbitrator work out ten different cases. I heard much strong, direct language and wondered why the sophisticated representatives of labor and management spoke so harshly and if and how they would ever relate to one another outside of the hearing. I learned that part of this was a normal state of affairs, almost a ritual, and that my perceptions were in error. The union representative had to make sure his griever and/or constituency knew he went to bat on the issue. Management also played roles. The post-decision meetings were usually very cordial. An arbitrator could lose his or her credibility should the language prompt a poor decision (even a prounion decision when labor knew they should lose).

My initial confusion was caused by my different conceptualization of the reality. I viewed such strong language as intransigence and the participants as ritualistic and normal. (See Figure 7.2.)

In addition to the problem of different representations of the same reality, realities themselves can change. I recently consulted with a small machine tool company

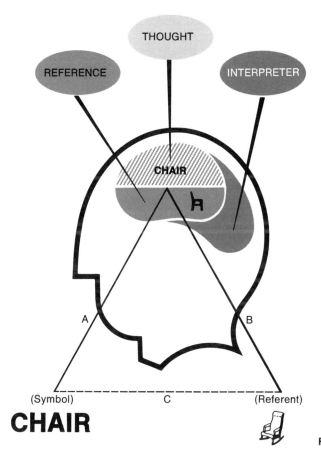

Figure 7.1 A model of meaning.

Figure 7.2 **B.C.** by Johnny Hart.

By permission of Johnny Hart and Creators Syndicate, Inc.

with whom I had worked (or tried to) ten years earlier. It had been run by an autocratic, paternalistic, 80-year-old man who had seen a lot of changes in his life and had fought every one. Ten years later, after more enlightened management prevailed, the company was indeed a different reality. Ms. Janis, the president, made that very clear to me.

Basic Premises: Nonidentity, Nonallness, Self-reflexiveness

General semantics theory provides the student of interpersonal and group communication with three valuable principles. The first is termed the principle of *nonidentity* (X is not X).[3] The principle of nonidentity corresponds to Korzybski's notion that the "map is not the territory." Remember, the word is not the thing; it is only a symbol and usually quite arbitrary at that.

The second general premise is the principle of *nonallness* (X is not all X). The idea here is that while the map may represent the territory, it cannot possibly represent *all* the territory: " . . . no matter how much you say about some 'thing,' 'event,' 'quality,' or what not, you cannot say *all* about it."

The third basic premise is the principle of *self-reflexiveness*. This premise really begins to complicate our lives because it suggests that we necessarily must use language to talk about language. We use language to reflect on language. (See Figure 7.4.)

Problems in the Management of Meaning

General semantics theorists have given us a number of working devices or warnings about how our particular language use can affect the meanings we attribute to one another interpersonally. These devices point out the potential for imprecision

Figure 7.3

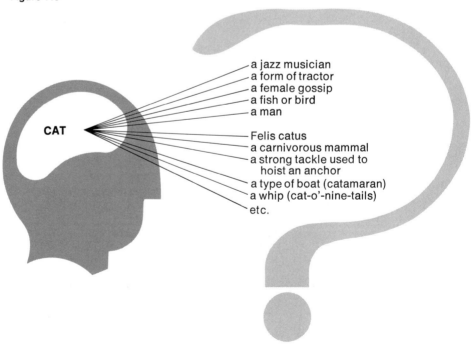

Figure 7.4   B.C. by Johnny Hart.

By permission of Johnny Hart and Creators Syndicate, Inc.

in the fit between one person's meanings for symbols and another's. Good communicators should be sensitive to these kinds of potential problems.

The *is* problem is related to the principle of nonidentity. While we usually use words to communicate, the words are not the things themselves. You can't drive around town in the word *Dodge*.

Person A:	This is love!
Person B:	What is?
Person A:	What we have.
Person B:	What's that?
Person A:	Love . . .
Person B:	Oh . . .

The ***etc.*** problem is related to the principle of nonallness. One can never have the last word on something. We humans tend to abstract. That is, we systematically leave out details when we recount experience. There is usually another angle to be explored. Don't presume you have the bottom line!

Our human capacity to abstract sometimes leads us into overgeneralization. The ***index*** rule cautions us against this. Not all used-car salespeople are alike. It's obvious that we shouldn't generalize. Sometimes we can also make generalization mistakes about groups. Recall both the small machine company and the arbitration participants.

When strong " . . . ist" words intrude in your communication ("sexist," "racist," "elitist," and so on), "the paradoxically self-reflective structure of such charges not only accounts for their power in precipitating conflict, but also precludes standard response-refutations to resolve the conflict."[4]

When a person speaks from firsthand experience in a sincere and friendly voice without being aware of faulty abstracting or generalizing, that person is creating a serious problem. The communication problems of generalization are complicated, frustrating, and often dangerous. Once you understand this clearly, you have already solved much of the practical problem, for it is when you are *aware* of abstracting and generalizing that you begin to restrain your own overstatement and reckless generalization. A practical way of using this awareness is to qualify and index your statements with great care.

Dating your language is another form of indexing worthy of a special rule. The date of an event can significantly affect the meaning of an utterance. John Lennon's line "Come together, over me," has varying degrees of semantic clout depending on the date it is uttered: January 1957 (no special significance); October 1969 (Beatles' *Abbey Road* is released); April 1970 (Paul McCartney announces he has left the Beatles); December 1980 (John Lennon dies). Try the machine company 1975 versus 1985.

The *either-or* response is a type of overgeneralization usually indicating an individual is concealing differences of degree. Absolute rulers and demagogues use the following device: "You are either for me or against me." When we routinely use words such as *all*, *nobody*, and *never*, we are probably guilty of false-to-fact language use. The person guilty of these types of exaggerations runs great risks of creating real resentment interpersonally.

CODES AND SYMBOLS

Look what happens to language when the accounting and legal groups apply their special codes.

Notice is hereby given that under supplements to tariffs filed with the Illinois Commerce Commission, all one-way and round-trip fares for distances of 38 miles or less in Chicago and Northwestern Railway Company Chicago suburban territory, and all 10 and 25 multiple-ride tickets in this territory, will be limited for passage and void on the effective date of the previously filed supplements presently suspended and subject to investigation and hearing by the Illinois Commerce Commission in its docket No. 44741 or the effective date of any further supplements filed to supersede the aforesaid supplements. In no event, however, shall any such ticket be valid for passage for a period longer than the period provided under tariff provisions under which the ticket was sold. As of the effective date of the aforesaid supplements, the refund basis for unused 10 and 25 multiple-ride tickets which have been limited for passage and rendered void as above provided will be changed from the present basis to a straight pro-rata basis. The present refund basis for one-way and round-trip tickets will remain unchanged.

Chicago and Northwestern Railway Co.

Different types of organizations or social structures tend to generate different speech systems, ways of talking, or language codes. Our particular language habits sometimes function to label us as members of certain speech communities and organizations. People often make initial attributions about us based on our particular language habits.

Attributions are made based not only on language codes but also on nonverbal codes. Gestures, dress, movements, and facial expressions tend to "place" us as members of a speech community.

Verbal and nonverbal codes usually work together—they affect one another. Sometime they are consistent with one another and thus strengthen a speaker's intended meaning, while at other times they conflict and tend to distort intended meaning. Consider the sloppy student presenting a speech on the values of personal neatness. More will be said about the interfacing of verbal and nonverbal codes later.

Restricted and Elaborated Codes[5]

Slang is a good example of a restricted code.[6] Everchanging slang really compresses meaning. Here are some examples: "Bad" formerly meant good, but now means bad or good often used in a deliberately confusing manner. "Job hunting" means sleeping or messing up on the job so persistently that you are fired and therefore presumably have to look for employment elsewhere; also that you are seeking unemployment benefits. "Tough maracas," depending on voice pitch, means either the highest compliment or the grossest insult that can be directed at Hispanics; a low-register delivery means praise; a high pitch can mean a fight.

In restricted linguistic codes experience is not verbally elaborated. Words function indexically.[7] That is, a limited number of shared words function to index a large realm of common experience. Generally, but not always, the closer we are to people the more restricted our language codes become. Have you sometimes wondered why outsiders seem awkward?

With elaborated codes, meaning is elaborated verbally in greater detail. With these types of codes the speaker must presume the listener holds a set of experiences different from his or her own.[8] Sensitive communication should be elaborative when appropriate.

Abstraction

The fact that one word can index a realm of experience (as in the previous example) relates to our ability to abstract. Without this ability to abstract, much of the interpersonal richness and fun in our lives would be missing.

The heart of the difficulty with language is the confusion of the word with the thing for which it stands. The further we are from this thing—the referent—the more problems of meaning that arise. According to Ogden and Richards meaning has three elements: a person having thoughts, a symbol, and a referent. The relationship was illustrated earlier with our chair example (Figure 7.1). The Ogden and Richards model (Figure 7.5) brings to our attention three senses of meaning: the meaning of the referent, the meaning of the symbol, and the meaning to the person (thought).

The relationship between the symbol and the thought is a direct relationship. For example I know what the word *dog* means. The relationship between the thought

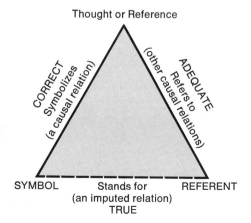

Figure 7.5 The Ogden and Richards model.

From THE MEANING OF MEANING *by C.K. Ogden and I.A. Richards. Reprinted by permission of Harcourt Brace Jovanovich, and Routledge & Kegan Paul.*

and the referent is also direct: I know what a four-legged canine is when I see one. The relationship between the symbol and the referent is indirect, though (hence the dotted line in the model). The relationship between the symbol and the referent is arbitrary. I could just as easily call a four-legged canine a "berfunkle" or a "pero." Why not? Even though *dog* (symbol) or the animal itself (referent) will elicit the thought in a person, the relationship between the symbol and referent is indirect. Again, the map (symbol) is not the territory (referent).

Abstracting is a process of thinking in which we selectively leave out details about concrete or real things. Perception has at least two elements—sensation and interpretation of this sensation. This interpretation is controlled by our individual knowledge, experience, and emotional set. For this reason, as well as because of the limitations of our language system discussed previously, all language contains an element of abstraction.

The process of abstraction occurs at different levels. For example, we have cars, sports cars, and Corvettes. The Corvette is a first-order abstraction: that is, it is a specific type of sports car, which in turn is a type of car. As we move from lower-order to higher-order abstractions, we tend to consider fewer and fewer details of the specific, original object. Another way of looking at abstraction is to consider firsthand observations as facts, but as facts that may never be described completely. If we move away from firsthand descriptions, we will be in a different order of abstraction—*inference*. Most simply, an inference goes beyond what is observed. If an ambulance is in your driveway when you return home, you may say "One of my family has been seriously hurt." This is an inference. You must go into the house to see if it is valid. Upon entering the house you may find a close friend excitedly telling your healthy family about his new business venture of converting station wagons into ambulances. The difficulty in coordinating and managing meaning between people should become apparent in relation to the abstraction process.

CONTEXTUAL INFLUENCE

TWO HEAVY-EQUIPMENT OPERATORS

Roy: Put the yellow cat in the garage; leave the other one in the yard, and let's go to lunch.

Bud: Great. Nobody will steal that old sucker.

TWO FELINE LOVERS

Sarah: Put the yellow cat in the garage; leave the other one in the yard, and let's go to lunch.

Robert: Great. I don't think that old timer will be gone when we get back.

The words are similar, but the meanings are clearly different. Roy and Bud are talking about Caterpillar bulldozers; Sarah and Robert obviously are not. Why is it obvious? Because we know the situation and context. Mix the contexts and we can have real confusion.

Sarah	Bud, you wouldn't put that sweet thing in the garage.
Bud:	Why not? Nothing that big and ugly is sweet.
Sarah:	You can go to lunch by yourself!

If Sarah and Bud are competent interpersonal communicators, they will be able to align their meanings with each other. While this example appears to be simple and straightforward, remember that you had clear clues. It is critical that we consider contextual clues before inferring meanings. Interpersonal communication operates in a multitude of contexts that are not always shared.

There are also multiple levels to meaning. And if that's not enough, there are rule systems that both constitute and regulate our meanings. If we are using different rule systems, the cat may be back in the garage! Interpersonal communication is not always simple. Unfortunately, many people assume tht it is.

When interpersonal communication is unclear or is only half clear, it is usually because we have been unable to coordinate our meanings. To communicate at all hinges upon our ability to infer meanings from contexts, signs, and symbols, and then to encode and transmit them in such a way that they coordinate or mesh with the receiver's meanings. (See Figure 7.6.)

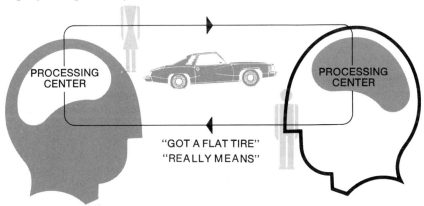

Figure 7.6 A favorite illustration of many teachers regarding coordinating meanings concerns a man staring sadly at a very flat tire. A similar farmer comes up and asks, "Got a flat tire?" If we take his words literally, his communication appears stupid indeed and we might answer, "Can't you see, birdbrain?" However, a famous psychiatrist interprets "Got a flat tire?" as follows:

> Hello—I see you are in trouble. I'm a stranger to you but I might be your friend now that I have a chance to be if I had any assurance that my friendship would be welcomed. Are you approachable? Are you a decent fellow? Would you appreciate it if I helped you? I would like to do so but I don't want to be rebuffed. This is what my voice sounds like. What does your voice sound like?[9]

Levels of Meaning (Meaning Hierarchies)

Our decoding of behaviors, events, and symbols varies along a hierarchy of meaning.[10] Our meanings change with the levels we use to interpret a symbol or set of symbols. Pearce, Cronen, and Harris illustrate the hierarchy in a manner similar to Figure 7.7.[11]

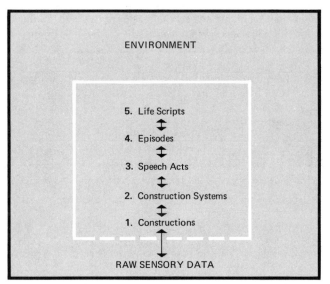

Figure 7.7 The meaning hierarchy and environment—raw sensory data.

(With apologies to Cronen, Pearce, and Harris.)

We all have hierarchies of meaning. These meaning systems aid us in ordering and regularizing our environments and hopefully in making sense out of them. The complex environments within which we all must operate are composed of a pool of raw sensory data. These data have no meaning in and of themselves. Analyzing environments may, of course, promote understanding, but environments have no inherent meanings—meanings are in us. We interpret the raw sensory data (symbols) in light of our own personal meaning hierarchies. Most of us have reasonably flexible hierarchies that allow us to move through the levels of meaning with relative ease.

The interpretation of our communication environments varies as a function of where we decide to stop within our personal set of meaning levels. A discussion of the basic levels of the meaning hierarchy should help clarify this point.

Constructions   The *construction* level (number 1, Figure 7.7) of the hierarchy is basically a perceptual level. We perceive our environment and represent it cognitively. We do more than simply respond in and to our environment; we create representations or *constructions* of it.[12] For example, I can construe (have constructions for) automobiles. I have a perceptual image of 1950s vintage Chevrolets. A 1957 Chevy (referent) need not be physically present for me to have thoughts about it. I have a cognitive construction of the car.

Construction Systems   Constructions produce belief systems. If you construe data in an environment, you generate beliefs about what has been construed. To the extent that I have a construction or constructions for 1957 Chevys, I start developing beliefs about the cars. I can even start developing beliefs about the drivers of the cars: "Mid-fifties Chevys are both engineering and design marvels ($belief_1$); therefore people who still own and drive such vehicles have both good mechanical and aesthetic senses ($belief_2$)."

What we are trying to illustrate here is a *construction system* (number 2, Figure 7.7)—a set of beliefs generated from an initial construction. Construction systems, therefore, are systems of beliefs that grow out of our constructions of raw sensory data. "Construction systems are the beliefs and purposes produced by constructs, organized into clusters which are related to particular beliefs."[13]

Speech Acts   Speech acts (number 3, Figure 7.7) are overt communicative activities. Someone saying something to someone else is a speech act. The acts need not be solely verbal; nonverbal actions directed toward another also count.

Speech acts are the first truly communicative level of the meaning hierarchy. A speech act requires a communication action between at least two people. When the owner of a Ford dealership tells an employee to "prep those two new Escorts for the sales floor," a speech act has occurred. For the person to whom the utterance is directed to understand, he or she must have at least a construction for an Escort in order to carry out the task.

Episodes   Episodes (number 4, Figure 7.7) are complexes of speech acts that are viewed as distinct entities by participants. They have been characterized as routines that have special rules for both verbal and nonverbal behavior.[14] "Checking out of the grocery store" might be called a communicative *episode*. There are rules that define and regulate the activity. We usually behave within a general set of rule parameters when purchasing groceries: standing in line, getting checks validated, stacking groceries on the counter, and so forth.

If we conceptualize the "prep those two new Escorts for the sales floor" utterance under the episode of "selling new Escorts," we realize a set of rules that govern the activity (selling Escorts). People buying their first car are sometimes not as aware of the rule parameters as they should be. They usually become wiser by the time they buy their second car!

Life Scripts   Life scripts (number 5, Figure 7-7) are sequences of episodes. These sequences function to sustain the general fabric of an individual's expectations. When going to a party composed of good friends, our expectations in terms of how the party will proceed and what will happen are related to the life script we attribute to the party.

If the episode we have termed "selling new Escorts" falls under the life script termed "running a dealership," it is one thing. It is something altogether different if it falls under the life script termed "grand theft, auto."

Coordinating the Levels

The levels of the hierarchy are related to each other in that higher levels provide contexts for understanding lower levels. For example, the speech act of a man screaming and waving his arms wildly in the middle of the street qualifies him as little more than a lunatic unless the speech act is given a context. If the episode that contextualized his speech act was jubilation over a Rose Bowl victory, the speech act makes sense; we understand. The act occurred within a context. To the degree that we as observers *don't* realize the context (episode), we see only lunacy.

People vary in their abilities to operate flexibly within hierarchies of meaning. To the extent that a person in a group communication environment fails to operate at the higher levels of the hierarchy, he or she is not communicatively competent within that particular environment. While some people seem to be very *aware* in communication settings, they are not very *responsive* in the settings. They are *aware* in that they have strong explanatory constructs and construction systems, but they fail to contextualize their construction systems within speech acts. Without an ability to operate at the speech-act level, they feel awkward and hence are not very *responsive*. They are quiet!

This is not to say that a lack of communicative competence is always at fault or due to the noncompetent person. One may be responsive but not very aware. One feels awkward interpersonally when others fail to allow one to index appropriate constructions and construction systems. Then one needs communicative competence within that particular environment. Figure 7.8 illustrates the relationship between communication environments, raw sensory data, and the hierarchy of meaning.

The two triangles in Figure 7.8 represent construct levels and communicative levels of the meaning hierarchy. Communicative levels give context to the construct levels. We get different meanings if we contextualize a construction at the speech-act level as opposed to at the life-script level.

Interpersonal communication is in large part an attempt to coordinate meanings between people. If person A is contextualizing a construction at the speech act level and person B is contextualizing at the episode level, there is room for a major mismatch. The competent interpersonal communicator is able to move through the meaning hierarchy in such a fashion as to best coordinate meanings. The two-headed arrow at the right of Figure 7.9 represents this ability to move through the meaning hierarchy. The two triangles can converge, and as they do, different communicative levels of the hierarchy give contexts to the construct levels of meaning.

It is clear that the management of meaning is no simple task. True interpersonal and group communication take effort. In the next section we will talk about two different "bands," or aspects, of communication and show how they operate within the hierarchy of meaning.

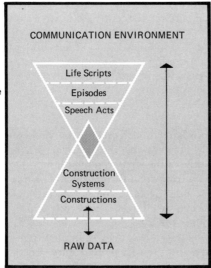

Figure 7.8   The contextual relationship within the meaning hierarchy.

Communicative Levels of the Meaning Hierarchy

Construct Levels of the Meaning Hierarchy

COMMUNICATION ENVIRONMENT

Life Scripts

Episodes

Speech Acts

Construction Systems

Constructions

RAW DATA

CONTENT AND RELATIONAL MEANINGS

One Cannot *Not* Communicate

Are you communicating when you're asleep? If you're in my classroom you are! You're saying you're bored or just worn out, or you could be ill. Even if you're sick, there's a message involved in your behavior whether I attach that meaning to it or not. Your "fatigue" may be based on the *content* of the course or on your poor *relationship* with the teacher (he's boring). Either way, you are sending a message. The old rule that "one cannot *not* communicate" is probably true.

It seems that even attempted nonbehavior has message impact. Even with silence, others will respond. You may not be communicating intentionally, but others inevitably infer or attribute intentions or meaning to your actions (or nonactions, as the case may be).[15] One of the reasons for this impossibility of not communicating lies in the fact that we use different forms or channels in our communication behavior. We use language, voice, and action. Simply stated, communication exists in both verbal and nonverbal forms. The *content*, or raw facts, of communication usually occurs within the verbal band. How we are to understand or "take" the message often occurs nonverbally.

Try this: "What a bastard."

1. A greeting between close friends
2. A reference to J.R. (in *Dallas*)
3. A file salesperson's remark (bastard file)
4. A reference to a nonstandard auto—hot rod
5. Born to unwed parents

Our understanding of the utterance is surely altered by the *relationship* dimension. The *content*, after all, is about someone born of unwed parents, isn't it? Our understanding or interpretation of the statement ranges from an endearing greeting, to a car of dubious origin, to a serious insult. In the example the content (words) remains the same. What distinguishes the utterance as a greeting or an insult is accomplished largely by voice and action.[16]

Most communication has both content and relationship aspects. It is through the manipulation of content and relationship characteristics that we can move in and through the levels of meaning in the hierarchy we presented earlier. For example, when a person uses "you old reprobate" as a *greeting*, he or she had better convince the receiver that the construction related to "old reprobate" in this case falls under the speech act called *greeting*, and a happy, friendly greeting at that! If this relationship-defining work doesn't come off as intended, there could be trouble. A reprobate is, after all, "a morally unprincipled person, one who is predestined to damnation" (Webster).

Sometimes interpersonal communication is as simple as the previous greeting. When it comes to "I love you," take care. Everything depends on how it is given context within the meaning hierarchy. If it falls within the episode of "one night stand," it is quite different from the life script of "enduring relationship." A communicologist considers the utterance "I love you" in Figure 7.9 which traces four hypothetical utterances made by two people.

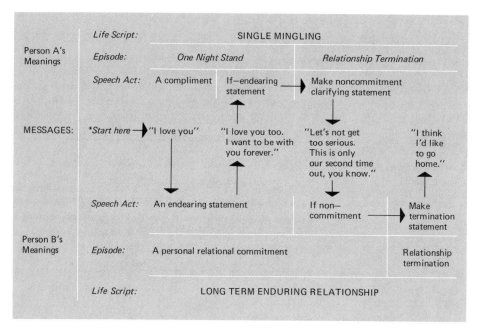

Figure 7.9 An analysis of an interpersonal relationship.

(With apologies to Cronen, Pearce, and Harris.)

As you can see, there is a clear mismatch between person A's and person B's meaning hierarchies. Their life scripts function to contextualize the message differently at first. As they begin to become aware of each other's life scripts and episodic interpretations, their meanings start to align, and in this case they realize they were not meant for each other. The ease and facility with which an individuals' meaning hierarchy is communicated to others is a major concern in interpersonal communication.

Punctuation

Mismatches between people in terms of the meaning hierarchy can result in what Watzlawick, Beavin, and Jackson call problems in *punctuation*.[17] Their classic example of the wife who nags and the husband who withdraws is a case in point. When asked, the wife says she nags *because* the husband withdraws. Her nagging (speech act) is intended to stop his withdrawing. On the other hand, the husband says he is withdrawing *because* the wife nags. His withdrawal (speech act) is in response to her nagging. Their problem is that they have both interpreted their communication at the speech-act level, but they have different personal meanings for their behaviors. The wife has *punctuated* the communication from her perspective, and the husband from his.

A glance at Figure 7.10 shows us the way out of the punctuational bind. If the couple were to both step up to the episode level of the meaning hierarchy, their punctuational differences would be made clear. Once the couple see their behaviors within the episode called "punctuation bind," their problems should cease to exist. Without moving to this level they both suffer from a case of "not being able to see the forest

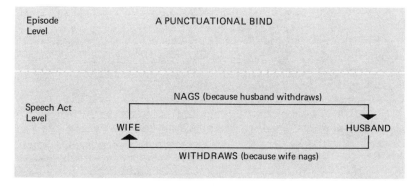

Figure 7.10   An example of a punctuation bind.

(With apologies to Watzlawick, Beavin, and Jackson, Pragmatics, pp. 54–59.)

for the trees.'' A key dimension of interpersonal communication is an openness to moving through the meaning hierarchy.

Digital and Analogic Communication

We should note that digital communication is the primary basis of semantics. Digital communication employs arbitrarily assigned symbols—words. Recall our discussion of meaning. There is nothing inherent in the word *dog* that represents the animal. In English we have a convention that relates the symbolic digit, *dog*, to a four-legged mammal that makes a good pet. We could just as easily assign the symbolic digit *pero* (Spanish) or *chien* (French). Words (digital communication) are arbitrary. They bear little resemblance to their referents.

Analogic forms of communication bear a closer resemblance to the things they stand for. The picture in Figure 7.11 is an analogic (nonverbal) form of communication. Analogic symbols are not as arbitrary as digital ones. A Spaniard, a French person,

Figure 7.11   An illustration of the difference between digital and analogic forms of communication.

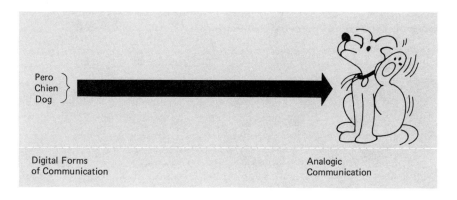

Digital Forms
of Communication

Analogic
Communication

or an American would have no trouble understanding the right half of Figure 7.11. The left half could cause some interpretational problems.

Verbal communication, because of its discrete, digital nature, is relatively easy to manipulate. We can move words around in a sentence with ease and thus create nuances in meaning. It is easy to negate facts verbally (digitally). Take the youth who has just stolen gum from the candy counter.

> **Clerk:**   Young man! Did you just steal gum from the counter?
> **Young Boy:**   What gum? I didn't steal any gum.

It is not as easy to manipulate the analogic band (nonverbal) of communication. Because analogic communication is not composed of discrete, easily manipulatable communication units, it is usually more difficult to control.[18] It functions to give context or additional interpretation to the digital band.

> **Clerk:**   Why can't you look me in the eye when you say you didn't steal gum?
> **Young Boy:**   (shuffling feet) I don't know. . . .

In the greeting "you old reprobate," the utterance can be given context analogically. If Max slaps Barry on the back, smiles, and says, "you old reprobate," Barry contextualizes (makes sense of) the verbal statement in light of its analogic context. "Backslapping" and "smiling" are analogically associated with friendship behaviors, and therefore, Barry is able to interpret the sentence as being a friendly greeting rather than an insult. Max and Barry's *relationship* has been defined analogically. Defining relationships between people and between utterances is primarily the domain of analogic communication. Analogic communication can more easily carry emotional content than it can abstract knowledge. Digital communication does better with facts, figures, and definitions of objects, which, of course, can also be critical to a relationship.

Types of Relationships

Interpersonal communication relationships can be one of at least three types: complementary, symmetrical, or transition.[19]

Complementary relationships are characterized by behaviors (verbal, nonverbal, or both) that complement each other. Complementary relationships tend to maximize relational differences. In a two-person (dyadic) complementary relationship, one person must occupy a dominant or "one-up" ($\uparrow$) position, while the other occupies a submissive, or "one-down" ($\downarrow$), position. The following set of utterances might be characteristic of a complementary relationship:

> **Boss:**   Don't leave that towel lying on the counter like that! ($\uparrow$)
> **Employee:**   Sorry, my mistake. ($\downarrow$)

Value judgments, such as good–bad, desirable–undesirable, should not necessarily be placed on either the submissive or the dominant role in complementary interaction. Submission can sometimes even function as a relationship control strategy. Submissive roles can be more powerful than dominant roles in interpersonal relations.

Symmetrical relationships are characterized by behaviors (verbal, nonverbal, or both) that reflect each other. Symmetrical relationships are based on equality rather than difference. In a two-person symmetrical relationship both persons engage in similar one-up (↑), one-down (↓), or equivocal (→) communication behaviors. We must again stress that there is nothing inherently desirable or good in symmetrical relationships. Some are quite stable, others can be overly competitive. Consider the following symmetrical utterances:

Husband:	What do you want to do tonight, dear? (↓)
Wife:	I want to do what you want, honey. (↓)
Husband:	Whatever you feel like is fine with me. (↓)

Transition relationships are characterized by communication behaviors (verbal, nonverbal, or both) that are different but not opposite. For example, if one member of a dyad tends to engage in one-up (dominant) communication behaviors, and the other member is equivocal (neither one-up nor one-down), the relationship is probably a transition relationship. Communication behaviors are different, but they are not opposite in this case. As is shown in the following utterances, it is equivocal or "one-across" behavior that allows for the possibility of the transition relationship.

Person A:	Go clean up the den, okay? (↑)
Person B:	Gee, it sure is raining hard today. (→)

Relationships can be defined by the communication behaviors that seem to occur regularly. A communication behavior within a relationship is usually one of the three previously referred to types: one-up, one-down, or one-across. The three types of interpersonal communication relationships can be defined based on the interaction of the communication behaviors that make them up. Figure 7.12 illustrates these three

Figure 7.12 Comparison of relationships based on their relational control characteristics.[20]

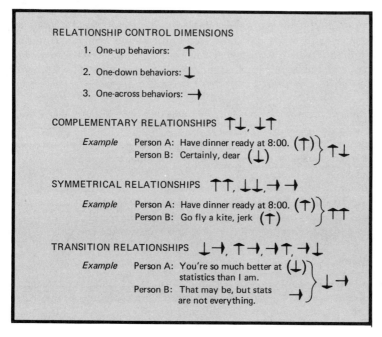

relationships (symmetrical, complementary, and transition) and their compositions.

A quick reminder: Relationships are also defined analogically. The words alone (digital communication) do not always define the relationship. We (the authors) are forced to operate in a medium (textbook) that is sometimes more digital than we would like. The point we are trying to stress is that very often an ''analogic sensitivity'' is as important to interpersonal communication competence as is rhetorical sensitivity.

RULE SHARING

Rules and Symbolic Interaction

All interaction is governed by rules. We can't even talk to one another if we don't at least know how to employ some basic grammatical rules; we have to put a noun and a verb together to make a sentence. We have seen that there are also rules that govern relationships. Rules get more complex and tentative as we move up the levels of the meaning hierarchy. ''I love you'' means one thing to a ''swinging single'' and another to a person looking for a ''long-term relationship.'' A conflation of rules is a combination or a sharing of rules between people. To the extent that people share common interpretive rules, they are better able to coordinate their meanings.

We interact with one another symbolically. Most of what we share communicatively with others are symbols. Interpersonal communication is largely a process whereby symbols are shared and exchanged for the purpose of helping us attain knowledge and understanding of ourselves and others—what Berger and Bradac call *uncertainty reduction.*[21]

We have seen that the major functional unit of interpersonal communication is the attribution of meanings to language, voice, and action. We are able to attribute meanings based on the *contexts given* and the *relationships defined.* The meaning hierarchy allows us to give context to our constructions (context giving), and the analogic aspects of our communication allow us to define and create interpersonal relationships.

It seems clear that interpersonal communication is symbolic communication. We send out symbols (words, gestures, and so forth) that are designed to *represent* things. We try to decode and give meanings to the symbols we receive. This approach can be summarized by three premises:

1. Humans act toward things based on meanings they have for them.
2. The meanings we have for things grow out of our social interaction with others.
3. Meanings are modified, contextualized, and generally manipulated through an interpretive language process used by the individual.

We create, modify, interpret, and coordinate meanings interpersonally through the use of rules. To the extent that we share common interpretive rules in making sense of symbols, we *coordinate* our meanings.[22] The rule systems we all employ are composed of at least two general types: regulative rule and constitutive rules.

Regulative Rules

Regulative rules function to regulate or guide behavior; they guide sequential communication activities. In terms of our hierarchy of meaning, regulative rules operate only at the *communicative* levels of the meaning hierarchy (see Figure 7.8). They function to regulate communication behaviors—speech acts, episodes, and life scripts. Look at the following interaction sequence in a group of three.

> **John:** How are university enrollments looking for the future, Paul?
> **Paul:** Well, I think they're dropping overall but . . .
> **Mary:** Paul, what was the . . .
> **Paul:** . . . in our area we don't seem to . . .
> **Mary:** PAUL!
> **Paul:** (irritated) What do you want?
> **Mary:** What was the name of that architect we met yesterday?
> **Paul:** Claude, Claude Davis. (looks at John) Where was I before all this?
> **John:** Enrollments.
> **Paul:** Oh yes, in our area . . .

Most people recognize Mary as the rule breaker. She's being rude. We recognize her rudeness in that her speech act violates a basic rule: Unrelated interruptions of the speaker are insensitive, if not unacceptable, behavior.

Constitutive Rules

Constitutive rules function to specify how meanings at one level of the hierarchy can be meaningful at another level of the hierarchy.[23] The speech act "thanks" can be viewed as "gratitude" (episode). However, if the utterance is done sarcastically, the episode changes to "ingratitude." (See Figure 7.13.)

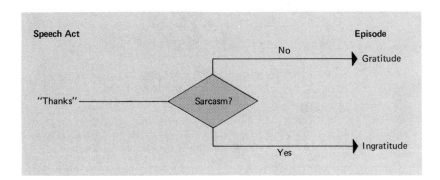

Figure 7.13 A simple constitutive rule.

Meaning Management   Suppose members of your small group seem to be in a heated argument about a subject relatively new or unknown to you, say labor contracts. Your interpretational rules for the episode "labor contracts" are not well developed, and therefore your understanding of the argument or its intensity should be tentative. This is a good time to make the boundaries of your interpretational episode *porous* and let the new incoming information fill out the rule structure. This is one of three basic ways people manage their meanings and responses.[24]

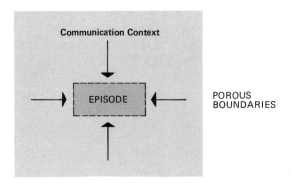

Figure 7.14 Porous boundaries.

Way 1. By allowing the boundaries of an episode to be porous. (See Figure 7.14.) That is, by allowing the rules particular to the given context to "fill out" the episode. This is sometimes the hardest way to manage meanings because it requires that we be nonjudgmental.

You could also have managed your meanings (made sense) by switching to a different but usually related episode—perhaps poor product quality. You may be in error, but you've made sense (or nonsense) out of what is taking place. Your response behaviors will differ accordingly.

Way 2. By switching episodes. That is, by bringing different episodes to bear on the given communication context. (See Figure 7.15.)

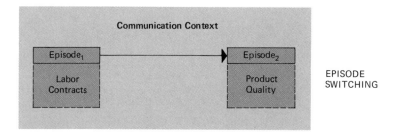

Figure 7.15 Episode switching.

You could also have contextualized the episode with a different life script: switching from your role (life script) as "dynamic, interested group member" to one of "disinterested sales manager." In the latter life script, you manage the meaning of the "labor contracts" episode by simply dismissing the whole discussion as unrelated to sales.

Way 3. By switching life scripts thereby bringing a still broader and different context to bear on the episode. (See Figure 7.16.)

The coordination of meanings is essentially an interpersonal process. We all enact episodes to explain or make sense out of communication contexts. The challenge of interpersonal communication is to get different individuals to first enact the same episodes. We have seen how the lack of coordination (episodic mismatch) can lead to

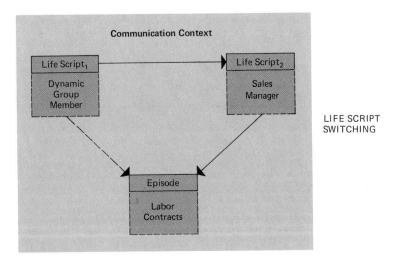

Figure 7.16 Life script switching.

potential problems. Recall the "I love you" example in Figure 7.9. Good interpersonal communication works at intermeshing communication behaviors to produce *mutually* shared episodes. Pearce discusses three methods of coordinating or sharing episodes: casting, mirroring, and negotiation.[25]

Casting A drama-based analogy can be used in explaining this method of coordination. If an actor has a role he or she wishes to play, other actors are chosen in such a way as to support the primary role. They are cast for *supporting* roles. An individual capable of interpersonally persuading others to "fill out" or operate under his or her episode coordinates meaning by casting. Casting is not always overt. It is sometimes quite subtle and sometimes even humorous.

> If you're not going to play my game, then just don't play.

Mirroring When a person coordinates conversations by mirroring, he or she "mirrors" or takes on the roles proposed by others. In this respect mirroring is the opposite of casting. "When coordinating by mirroring, persons communicate by seeking to discover what the other person wants them to do and eliciting feedback to see if they are doing well."

> I'm more than happy to play your game. Just tell me what it is.

Negotiation People who coordinate through negotiation have to be willing to compromise their personal episodes. When negotiation (as an interpersonal coordination strategy) is successful, the resulting episode is usually different from any of the initial episodes the interpersonal communicators brought with them.

> You want this game. I want that one. Let's work out a new game we both can play.

PERCEPTUAL MAPPING

PEOPLE PERCEPTION

For Carl Rogers every individual exists in a continually changing world of experience of which he or she is the center. Whether this world is called the phenomenal field or the experiential field, humans exist in a sea of experiences, both conscious and unconscious. For Rogers, this is a private world that can really be known only by the individual. The way each person perceives his or her private world is reality for that person. We do not react to absolute reality but rather to our perception of reality.

All people perception is concerned with what might be called relationship communication, since the meanings grow to a large extent from the notions we form about others while actively interacting with them.[26] There is also, of course, a content aspect, and both are ever present. Watzlawick and Beavin capture this distinction in the following:

> If woman A points to woman B's necklace and asks, "Are those real pearls?", the content of her question is a request for information about an object. But at the same time she also gives—indeed, cannot *not* give—her definition of their relationship. How she asks (especially, in this case, the tone and stress of voice, facial expression, and context) would indicate comfortable friendliness, competitiveness, formal business relations, etc. B can accept, reject, or redefine, but cannot under any circumstances—even by silence—*not* respond to A's message. A's definition may, for instance, be a catty, condescending one; B, on the other hand, may react to it with aplomb or defensiveness. It should be noticed that this part of their interaction has nothing to do with the definitions of the nature of their relationship, although they may continue to talk about pearls.[27]

Oliver Wendell Holmes explained the problems of people perception as the impressions and notions two individuals might have of each other's, and their own, personalities.[28] He labeled the personalities John and Thomas and suggested that there are *three* Johns: (1) the real John, known only to his maker; (2) John's ideal John, never the real one and often very unlike him; and (3) Thomas's ideal John, never the real John, nor John's John, but often very unlike either. There are, of course, three equivalent Toms. To Holmes's three categories we can add a *fourth*, "John's Tom's John"— that is, John's notion of what Tom's notion is of him (see Figure 7.17).

Let's analyze the explanation in more detail. The real John (or real Tom) becomes an important philosophical concept if John feels that John's John is his own reality. If John's John is John's notion of himself, his self-concept, and if self-concepts can be incorrect, then John's John can also be incorrect. The model is useful in making this point clear: The real John and John's John do not overlap completely. That the

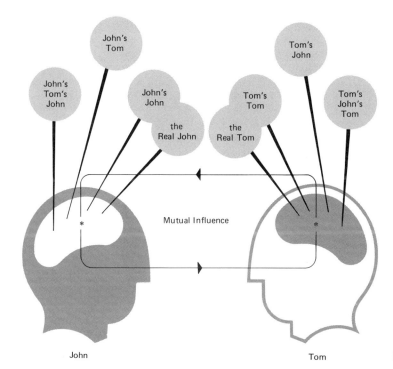

John   Tom   **Figure 7.17** People perception.

circles overlap at all indicates that John's notion of himself is, at least in part, fair to the facts. We could argue about how much the two circles should overlap for the average person. If the circles did not overlap at all, the model would suggest that John's self-concept was in no way related to reality, and psychologists would probably label John schizoid. This is not to say that all of us do not lose touch at some time or another with some topic or with some person. That brings us to John's Tom (or Tom's John), which is John's notion of Tom (or vice versa). John's notion may or may not be accurate, depending upon how well he knows Tom and how objective he is. If he does not know Tom very well, he had better pay close attention to him and seek feedback to improve his evaluation. If John did not know Tom at all, he would normally proceed with a very tentative, general, or stereotyped notion. The danger of stereotypes is now obvious! Our notions of each other certainly affect our interaction with each other.

Now let's consider what the participants *think* the other person thinks of them. As will be discussed shortly, that is an important part of how one's self-concept develops. John's Tom's John is John's notion of what Tom's notion is of him—what John thinks Tom thinks of him. From Tom's point of view it is what Tom thinks John thinks of him (Tom's notion of what John's notion is of him). If either of these notions is much in error, Tom and John may have some very unusual, confusing, perhaps even unfortunate interaction ahead of them. With this much complexity is it any wonder that we have misunderstandings with one another?

Feedback, both verbal and nonverbal, is very important to John's and to Tom's attempts to communicate and interact in an objective, prudent, and nonthreatening way. It is important that we be our best *self*, yet an honest and realistic best self, or we may quickly offend people. If a phony self is momentarily successful, it will almost always catch up with us in future interactions. We can also see in the model that John's

John is also affected by Tom's John—or at least by John's Tom's John (John's notion of what Tom's notion is of him)—and vice versa.

It is obvious that our communication with others is heavily biased and shaped by the relationship we have with others—more specifically, how we *perceive* or experience the relationship. For R. D. Laing the *experiencing* is the critical part of communication. *Experience* is the feeling that accompanies the perception of another's behavior. It is personal and involves past experiences, perceptual ability, and imagination. It is inferred and, as we discovered with John and Tom, difficult and complicated. Laing puts it bluntly: "I see you, and you see me. I experience you, and you experience me. I see your behavior. You see my behavior. But I do not and never have and never will see your *experience* of me."[29]

Laing sharpens the Holmes' example (he uses Jack and Jill) by operationally defining the three related concepts of *understanding, being understood,* and *feeling understood.*

Understanding involves one's direct perspective with the metaperspective of another. If Tom sees himself as liked by John (a direct perspective), and John's perception of Tom is one of a person who knows he is liked (by John), then we have *understanding* (see Figure 7.18).

Being understood involves the metaperspective of one person and the meta-metaperspective of the other. If Tom thinks John thinks he likes him, and if John thinks Tom thinks that he (John) thinks that Tom thinks he (John) likes him, we have Laing's notion of "being understood."

Feeling understood as opposed to being understood involves an individual's direct perspective and his own meta-metaperspective. Tom thinks he is liked by John and also thinks John knows that fact—then Tom is *feeling understood.* How good we are at *people* perception clearly has a lot to do with our relationships with others.

KNOWING OURSELVES

We have learned of our need for others; now we shall learn that we need others to discover and know who *we* are. Some social psychologists tell us that the process of inferring attributes about ourselves is much the same as the process of inferring attributes about others.

We have also learned about the tricky business of perceiving events, things, and others. Now we look specifically at how we go about perceiving ourselves and how this knowledge can help us make better perceptions of and better inferences about others. Getting to know ourselves and determining our personal attributes is what self-perception and self-concept are about. Attribution theory involves not only our personal attributes but also how we infer the personal attributes of others.

Self-perception and Self-concept

How we perceive ourselves is important because it helps control our actions. It partially determines how an individual will behave and then perceive and evaluate that behavior. For example, if an individual perceives himself or herself to be uncoordinated, then that individual's behavior will reflect that belief. The individual will shun or at least avoid athletics and may even resent physical education. In contrast, an individual with similar physical coordination capabilities who perceives himself or herself to be adequately coordinated will be more likely to enjoy athletics and display a greater athletic prowess. Thus, self-concept can affect performance, and although the

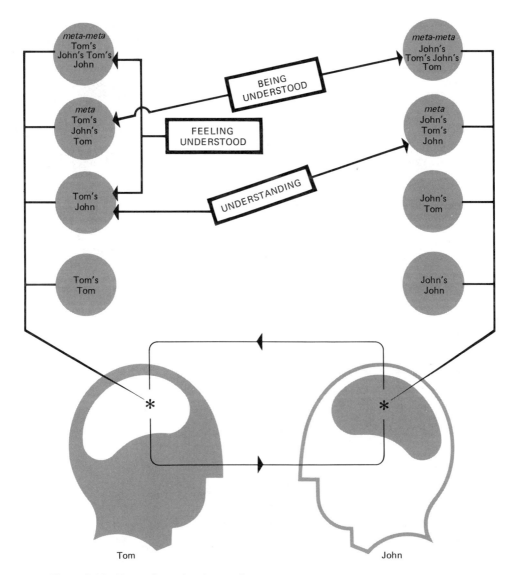

Figure 7.18 Perceptions of understanding.

For explication see R. D. Laing, H. Phillipson, and A. R. Lee, Interpersonal Perception: A Theory and Method of Research *(London: Tavistock Publications, 1966; New York: Springer Publishing Company, Inc., 1966, 1972), Chap. III, "The Spiral of Reciprocale Perspectives."*

persons possess equal ability, the second individual may appear more coordinated. Self-concept can affect not only one's attitude but also one's achievement and performance.[30]

Self-concept has been defined as "the sum total of the view which an individual has of himself. Self-concept is a unique set of perceptions, ideas, and attitudes which an individual has of himself."[31] It is both conscious and unconscious, and it changes with our most recent experiences and self-perceptions. We use words such as *self-percept*, *self-concept*, and *self-identity* to talk about one's notion of oneself. However, words such as *self-esteem*, *self-valuation*, and *self-regard* are of a slightly different order. We tend to think of these as positive or negative traits. A related term is *self-acceptance*. A person with high self-acceptance exhibits a willingness to accept both positive and negative notions as a part of his or her total self-concept. A discussion of some of the major influences of self-perception and self-concept follows. (See Figure 7.19.)

Significant Others   A large portion of our self-concept is shaped by interactions and social comparisons with others, competence, judgments, and feelings from the clues we observe or infer from others—a word or look of approval, an honest criticism, even the appearance of another. We thus develop concepts of our physical, emotional, and social selves, and we tend to perceive, respond, act, and communicate to a considerable extent using this complex self-image. For the most part we try to be consistent in our self-concept. However, when we are extremely frustrated, perhaps by too positive or too negative a self-concept, we may resort to various unrelated behaviors to compensate for our frustration. (For example, we may become overtalkative when insecure.) A realistic self-image can be a critical part of communication and perception as well as of motivation in general. Every person is the center of his or her own field of experience, and the way one perceives and responds to that field is one's own reality.

Research suggests that an unreasonable or unrealistic self-concept, particularly one low in self-esteem, may contribute to failure, thereby acting as a kind of self-fulfilling prophecy. A student who will not even discuss a math course because his or her self-

Figure 7.19   Self-concept influences.

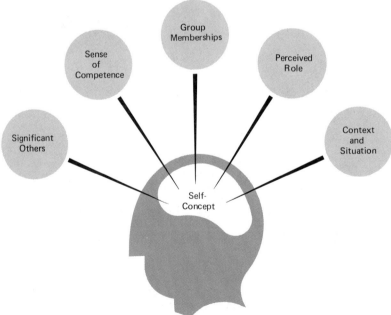

concept says that he or she is mathematically illiterate is not apt to do well in a math course. This is tragic when *only* a student's poor opinion of himself or herself stands in the way of success. However, suppose a student really has little or no math aptitude. Were this person to develop an unrealistically positive conception of his or her mathematical ability, then he or she would obviously be headed for frustration and ultimately an even poorer self-concept than the original one.

The point is that your self-concept, whether good or bad, high or low, should be within the realm of physical or social reality. Knowing what is *realistic* as well as what is unique is, of course, the eternal problem.

Competence   Your sense of *competence* is also related to your self-concept. Competence means the ability to cope successfully with the environment in which you find yourself. A self-concept that includes a feeling of incompetence may leave you in a state of helplessness and inertia and promote a sense of inferiority. You must build realistic confidence as well as competence into your self-concept. A persistent challenge to your sense of personal and social competence is a prime contributor toward frustration and, not infrequently, aggression. Your sense of competence is important to your interaction and communication with others.

Group Memberships   As stated earlier, other human beings who are significant to us form no small part of our self-concept. *Group memberships* are an important influence on us. Our self-concept reflects the society in which we live. Our family, school, and church are all thought to influence greatly our self-concept. This is not to suggest that we are all carbon copies of those having backgrounds similar to our own. Even the culture in which we live determines only what we learn as a member of a group, not what we learn as an individual. This explains in part why humans alter their behavior in what seem to be most inconsistent ways. Living in a society requires meeting certain standards or fitting into certain patterns roughly agreed on by the members of that group. Much nonstandard individual behavior is *sublimated*, expressed in constructive, socially acceptable forms in deference to these group codes. The *valuation*, *regard*, and *acceptance* individuals have of their total group—and their conceptions of the group's valuation, regard, and acceptance of them—are critical to the development of their self-concept.

Role   Role pertains in part to a more specific aspect of group membership and is also thought to have a strong influence on self-concept. Some roles are cast upon us by society because of our age, our sex, even our size, and unfortunately, sometimes our race. Some roles we assign ourselves on the basis of our life goals, and some are really disguises of our private personalities, disguises that we create in order to be accepted by certain groups. In its most important sense a role is that part we cast for ourselves on the stage of life. We may portray many roles to the world, but each of us determines, with the aid of society and its subgroups, what our particular role will be. Our self-concept is influenced by that decision.

Context and Situation   The *situational* influences upon our self-concept and our total personality include those exceptional, unpredictable, and often accidental events that happen to all of us. These are events that can alter our lives, casting us into roles that may profoundly affect our self-concept—a jail sentence, a lost love, a scholarship, a riot, an insight or perspective suddenly and never before achieved. A really good teacher probably alters the lives and careers of many unsuspecting students. An unexpected failing grade or a hard-won *A* from such a teacher can either shake or make our self-concept.

How others feel about us, or at least how we think they feel about us—particularly if they are significant others, whether reference groups, respected friends, or even those whose roles are ill defined—is probably the most important part of self-concept. What these others expect of us, how they react to us, and how socially realistic we are in evaluating these expectations and reactions form a large part of our self-concept.

Self-concept is a major part of one's personality. We may consider personality to be the sum of a person's knowledge, motives, values, beliefs, and goal-seeking patterns.

Human communication is affected by self-concept in several interesting ways. In general, we can expect others to perceive and react to us and the rest of the world in ways that are as consistent with their self-concepts as possible. Trying to "see" and understand others by understanding what their self-concepts are thus becomes a characteristic of sensitive human communication. We all should occasionally reevaluate our *own* self-concepts in terms of physical and social reality. Sometimes we either downgrade ourselves or take ourselves too seriously.

If the *self-regard* part of our self-concept is unusually negative, we might very well become difficult, negative, or even sullen communicators. An unrealistically positive *self-valuation* can, of course, make us different but equally painful communicators. A healthy, reality-centered, positive self-concept should, other things being equal, make us better and more confident communicators. Most important, it should include some willingness to accommodate change.

In review a good self-concept is objective, realistic, positive, and yet self-accepting; it can live with negative notions, too. A healthy self-concept should include some willingness to change, a tolerance for confusion, patience with disagreement, and empathy for other self-concepts. If you are a "significant other" for someone, if only for a moment, you have a special communication responsibility, for we are reasonably sure that such individuals are a key to the development of one's self-concept.

Attributions to Self and Others

I sat on a Malibu beach in 1986 reading the novel *Jaws, the Revenge.* When friends bent on water fun tried to entice me into the ocean, I found my usual enthusiasm dulled by a strange reluctance. It wasn't the people, I was sure (after all, I like them); it wasn't their manner or mode of persuasion (that had always been successful before); it had to be this scary book. I had conjured up visions of a great white shark stalking Zuma beach.

My friends were perplexed by my reluctant behavior and I'm sure went through an array of attributions of cause: Ross doesn't like us anymore; it was a bad time to interrupt him; he's had a recent bad experience with the water (they were close on that one). When they saw the book I was reading they roared with laughter. They made an attribution (a correct one) that the book had temporarily at least soured my love of the ocean.

Covariation Principle   In the story above three or four things were related to my behavior; one was obviously most responsible. H. H. Kelley said these variables covary.[32] The swimming (and the book) are called the *entity*; my friends, the *person* influence; and the way that they approached me, the *time/modality* influence.

Safely back in Michigan two of these same friends invited me to see the movie

Jaws, the Revenge. Despite all the terror in the film, we enjoyed it tremendously and had a fun-filled evening and a great reunion.

Was our fun because of the *entity* (a good movie)? Was it being with good friends—the *people* variable? Was it the beautiful and comfortable theater, or *mode*? The film could also have constituted *modality*, for the original story line was, after all, a print mode. Perhaps it was the *time*. I had been working hard and this was a needed escape or relief. All of these covariants also had something to do with our impression of the movie. As an entity *Jaws* will never be another *Gone with the Wind*, but it was a tempting attribution on that specific night.

Discounting Effect   The first lesson in all of this is that we tend to work backward from behavior to inferences about causes and we often overlook the other critical influences that covary. Was the swimming reluctance *internally* caused by an abiding fear of the water, or was it mostly or exclusively caused by a scary story about a people-eating shark? In analyzing our own behavior we go through a similar attribution process. Were we laughing during the movie because it was so funny (external) or because of our happy reunion mood (internal)? This has been referred to as the *discounting* effect. A cause should be discounted if other plausible causes are also present.

The second lesson is that we can do things that will make our impressions of others and our attributions to others more accurate.

One means of doing this is by *taking another look*. Observe *more* of a person's behavior, preferably in different contexts. Is he or she under special external pressure? Is there free choice, or does the job or the situation dictate all or part of the behavior? Does the hostage speak true treason or is there a gun at his family's head? Another, often overlooked, way of gathering more information is to ask the opinion of respected others who have observed the individual. This lesson also applies to ourselves. Check out the pressures and covariant influences that make you do the things you do. Solicited feedback from others can not only be a mind opener but also sometimes an ego shaker.

Self-disclosure

Politicians, advertisers, and students of persuasion know full well that their strategies are only as good as their information about the receivers. All interpersonal communication starts (or should start) with at least some *guesstimate* of where the other person is coming from. It would be convenient if all those people we were interested in simply disclosed everything about themselves—or would it? A first or second date might be a little less exciting without any surprises. It has been suggested that too much self-disclosure, even among married couples, causes some difficulty.[33]

Apparently a transparent openness can hurt as well as help interpersonal relations. Without any disclosure it is almost impossible to really communicate much less get to know someone. Some creative studies suggest a *reciprocity* in this matter; that is, we tend to trade information. "The more you tell me, the more I'll tell you," to a point! Appropriateness is more important than amount of reciprocity.[34] As always, so much depends on the content, the situation, the people, and the climate of trust. A stranger on the bus who pours out a line of intimate details is not apt to get the same in return unless, perchance, you have the same problem and are equally anxious about it. After all, misery likes company, especially if it's company with like misery.

There is then a *compensatory* dimension to self-disclosure. Sometimes after a difficult or frustrating experience we may withdraw and remain silent to avoid further personal hurt, but we might also pour out our problems on the first unsuspecting ear we find.[35] Good bartenders are nonthreatening listeners to lots of compensatory self-disclosure. Such compensation is not always unhealthy, but when it strains important relationships, it may be on the verge of being so.

The professional listeners—therapists, counselors, and clinicians—surely want all the disclosure they can get from people truly threatened by even the thought of self-disclosure. Some therapists define an unwillingness to disclose as a "sickness" and suggest a transparent openness to achieve adjustment and health.[36] This is, of course, a very special context. A healthy openness from healthy people is one thing, but playing therapist and expecting or demanding self-disclosure (as in some encounters) does not facilitate interpersonal communication. These demanding interpersonal encounters have been described as a "tyranny of openness" by some social psychologists.[37]

Openness   What is a healthy openness? So very much depends upon the relationship you have with the other person. Some types of relationships may be described as *necessary*, others as *discretionary*. If you have a job, it is *necessary* to relate to your boss in at least some pragmatic, job-related way. It is not necessary that you relate in matters of a more personal nature, such as your politics and your feelings toward others. You have, of course, some *discretion* here (as does your boss). Knowing when to exercise that discretion, on what topics, how much disclosure, and so forth, is a cornerstone of interpersonal relations.

Since relating and interacting is a mutual transaction, listening is part of the decision. How much should I listen to non-necessary topics? Will I build a false intimacy? Will I encourage a dependency? Will I communicate a misleading sympathy for an idea or feeling? Perhaps there are times when I should not listen. . . .

Discretionary relationships involve mostly beliefs, attitudes, and emotions. Good marriages have *necessary* topics over which there is less discretion possible—the rent, the children, the dinner schedule, and so forth. These relationships should have a much higher degree of openness and self-disclosure than the more superficial but necessary relationships on the job.

These types of relationships might also be described as levels. The *necessary* would include a level described as practical, pragmatic, biographic—an information exchange. The *discretionary* would be at a higher level, involving beliefs and the more affective feelings and attitudes. As an example, the work line stops at the box factory:

Superintendent:	What goes on here?
Foreman:	Number three glue machine wasn't reloaded properly. (A necessary information exchange)

Superintendent:	It's the union attitude toward productivity! (A belief disclosure)
Foreman:	It's those damn affirmative action hires. (Disclosures of feelings)
Big boss:	Will you stop the yacking and build some boxes! (All types and levels?)

Given the situational and context qualifications illustrated above, let's attempt to get a perspective on an appropriate amount of openness and disclosure for relationships ranging from superficial to intimate, whether they be viewed as necessary or discretionary (see Figure 7.20).

There is also a short- and long-range dimension to self-disclosure. Manipulation of this knowledge by charlatans, even to intimacy, has led to short-term gains or advantages but usually long-term relationship disasters. Unintended or weak-mo-

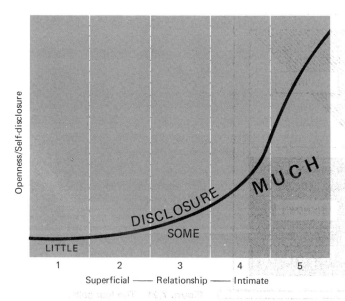

Figure 7.20 Disclosure curve.

ment disclosures can make or break relationships in both the short and/or the long term. How then should one proceed? Suggestions and systems follow in the next section.

Interactive Understanding: The Johari Window We need some level of disclosure to have any kind of relationship, even a pragmatic *necessary* one. For a long-term, intimate relationship we obviously need mutual (reciprocal) open communication and self-disclosure. How much openness is appropriate? What type of openness is appropriate for the majority of our relationships (which are not intimate)? Much depends on whether we are building a relationship, just maintaining one, or perhaps easing out of one.

One model of interactive understanding that allows you to examine your relationship with another is the Johari Window (see Figure 7.21). It is named after its creators, Joseph Luft and Harrington Ingham.[38] It gives you an intrapersonal as well as an interpersonal perspective on what may be going on. The window has four panes—one clear glass, one opaque, one mirrored on the inside (one-way glass), and one mirrored on the outside. The model panes refer to the knowledge, beliefs, attitudes, and feelings that are part of your personality. Most importantly, the model refers to the extent you desire to share or are able to share such information. A better view through the window might appear as shown in Figure 7.22.

The panes are dependent upon one another. When one changes the others change. As you disclose more (open self), you have fewer secrets (hidden self) and the panes change accordingly. Healthy relating and reacting should primarily be related to the people, the situation, and the context. Your relationship analysis should direct the appropriate interactional openness and self-disclosure.[39] Nevertheless, some people seem to be more open across a great many situations and contexts. Others are more secretive. Personality attributions without a great many observations can be spurious. However, the model creators imply that all of us have "model"-size panes (perhaps constructs) that direct our behavior.

The "blind self" is that part of yourself that you don't know about or perhaps

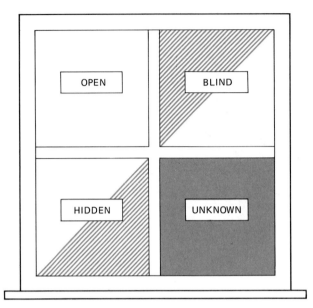

Figure 7.21   The four selfs.

don't want to know about. A lazy person may not perceive himself or herself as lazy and may even tune out communication that suggests he or she is. A person not aware of body odor might shrink this blind spot very quickly when given a bar of soap. The ''unknown self'' or ''nobody knows'' area is a little more unusual. An undiscovered prodigy may pick up a musical instrument and surprise everyone with his or her talent. You may learn in your statistics class that you have a propensity for numbers. This works both ways; you may not know that you don't know. You may think you have the patience, manipulative dexterity, and so forth to become a great surgeon, but a life

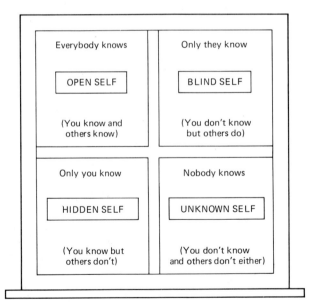

Figure 7.22   The knowledge window.

(With apologies to Luft and Ingham.)

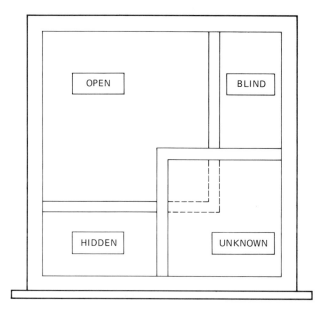

Figure 7.23 An open relationship.

experience, a dexterity test, or perhaps an organic chemistry class may help you and others know your real self.

The window panes change in size as the relationship varies or changes. A long-term, intimate relationship of the type discussed earlier would probably be characterized by openness and self-disclosure by both parties. The open-self pane would be large, and the hidden or secret-self pane small. If your true friend offers feedback on what you don't know, your "blind self" might also be smaller. The unknown area may or may not change. It is probably smaller among people who know themselves and are sensitive to the world around them. A person involved in the relationship above might be windowed as shown in Figure 7.23.

Disclosure Inventory   *Is it a "necessary" or a "discretionary" disclosure?* This is not always an easy question to answer because of the content or situation. An intimate disclosure about your estranged spouse is surely discretionary unless you are involved in therapy or counseling, in which case it may be necessary. Disclosing your income, investments, and bills is necessary disclosure when dealing with the IRS, but discretionary for most other contexts. The important thing is to sense the difference.

Is it a long- or short-term relationship? In some new encounters you may not really know. Some short-term relationships become long-term ones. Some of my students were one-course relationships that are long gone except for homecoming and other nostalgic moments. A smaller number have become lifelong friends. The short-term relationships are usually more superficial; the longer-term relationships *may* be more intimate, but not necessarily. Some long-time neighbors may enjoy a relationship that is pretty much superficial or somewhere between superficial and intimate. The guideline is that the amount of openness and disclosure usually increases as the relationship becomes more intimate. A good way to keep a short-term relationship short term is to disclose nothing; another way is to disclose too much intimate information too soon.

What are the risks? The risks are not only to yourself and the relationship, but to the other person or persons. Is there trust? Does the disclosure end here or have you told the world? Does it matter? Are you being pressured? "I've disclosed to you, now you've got to disclose." Is your disclosure compensatory? Are you apt to be sorry later? Have you disclosed enough? One may injure a relationship by appearing inscrutable.

What is the message/relationship importance? Do you value the message disclosed in the same way as the relationship involved, or in some cases is the relationship more important than the message? Perhaps we sometimes disclose more to the bartender or a stranger on an airplane because the relationship is short term and not all that important. A close and respected priest may not hear much social disclosure about your changing opinions on birth control because the relationship *is* all that important. Forthright discussions of necessary differences of opinions are to be applauded. However, if they preclude further discussions by destroying a relationship, you have need to pause. Perhaps the relationship isn't worth the effort or the constraint. Perhaps the message pertains to only a small *discretionary* part of the relationship and you are well advised not to disclose all.

INTERPERSONAL ATTRACTION AND SELF-PRESENTATION

Are you attracted by people and groups who live or work near you? For the most part do you like people like yourself? How important is physical attractiveness? Is being seen with high-status groups important to you? Do extremely competent people attract you or make you nervous? Do you most often seek out well-adjusted people? Are you attracted to blunt talk? Your answers to these questions might help you better coordinate your personality with the members of the group of which you are a part.

Research into communication encounters suggests that attraction is not haphazard but rather is shaped and strengthened by six factors related to the above questions. These factors are *nearness and exposure, similarity, physical characteristics, status and social standing, social adjustment,* and *self-presentation.*

The answers break down a bit when two or more factors overlap and conflict. For instance, forced exposure to someone of widely dissimilar attitudes does not typically lead to attraction; perhaps with luck it may lead to some better understanding. Another problem is that all people don't perceive these factors in the same way. Recall the earlier examples of people's perception.

Do we get better (more accurate) in our interpersonal perceptions as we get older? Following are some answers to this question and others like it.[40] Regarding *age,* we generally do get better as we get older. What of *intelligence?* Smarter people are usually more accurate. *Sex?* Are men more accurate than women? No, there is no good evidence of this; in fact, there is a tendency for women to be more accurate. Beyond these factors very few personality characteristics stand out. Good and bad interpersonal judges are found among a wide variety of personalities. That some people are better judges of people than others (most of the time) seems obvious.

NEARNESS AND EXPOSURE

After three years of eating Spam a young soldier was heard to say, "After a while it grows on ya, and I almost like it." Sheer exposure was getting to him. A man seeking advice about how to cut down on his alcohol intake at the social interactions that were part of his job was counseled, "Order the one drink you really can't stand and your glass will remain full.'' He ordered the hated martini and for six weeks his problem was solved. Then he related, ''Guess what? I've developed a real liking for martinis.'' The nearness or proximity finally got to him.

Is this also true of people who live near us, work with us, go to church with us, or are in some way physically near us? Other things being equal, it is. We do tend to develop ties to those who are near and to whom we are frequently exposed. A retiree observed, ''I never thought I'd miss that group of hard heads, but I do.'' After initial attraction has been established, separation or a lack of proximity will usually weaken the relationship unless other factors are strong and positive.

Persons who are both active as communicators and physically near the group action—a student government scene, a political convention, or whatever—appear to have a potential advantage in terms of attraction. Unless the person is a real boor, this is not surprising. It seems obvious that we form attractions more readily to groups near us, providing other factors are not in gross conflict and providing there is opportunity for communication.

SIMILARITY

The computer dating game tries to match people of similar traits and characteristics. Some users say that it has failed miserably. Yet the similarity-attraction notion is not all bad. It makes most sense in terms of beliefs, values, attitudes—in short, attributional agreement. We tend to like people who agree with us, that is, people who make similar attributions about any given event or attitude object. A computer programmed to seek out these agreements across factors such as educational values, social attitudes, political opinions, and religious beliefs may indeed find you an attractive date. This is not to say that other factors such as physical attractiveness or social status are ignored. These will be discussed shortly. What the computer dating service really does is reduce some of the *uncertainty* about what you're getting into.[41] It saves the time of questioning and inferring one another's attributions about these important matters. In a study in which students checked off their attributions about various social and political issues, it was clearly demonstrated that they liked most those others who agreed with them.[42]

The heavier attitudes and agreements about social, political, and religious values are more important than the more superficial opinions or even physical characteristics. While there is some evidence that racial similarity leads to attraction (superficial for some), it is probably more accurate to say that the amount of perceived prejudice against one's race leads a person to like or dislike another.[43]

Momentary feelings of anxiety or insecurity that are perceived as similar, even among total strangers, often trigger a fellowship tendency. We find it attractive to seek company, especially company of like mind or like situation. Misery not only likes company, it likes miserable company. Similar personalities as well as attitudes—despite uncertainty reduction exceptions, and old sayings to the contrary—do attract, and familiarity, other things being equal, breeds attraction, not contempt.[44]

In summary, we tend to find others more attractive when we perceive them as making attributions about issues and events similar to our own or when they can help us reduce uncertainty about what's going on. This presents an opportunity for deceit; unscrupulous persons may lead us to believe they hold attitudes similar to ours (when in fact they do not) or that their advice or ''way'' or product will resolve our uncertainties (after a cash contribution). This interesting fact of interpersonal attraction also suggests that each of us should be more objective as well as open when we listen to individuals who have attitudes that are different from our own. Such an occasion may also be a good time for us to reexamine our own attributions and the reasons behind them.

The point is that if you have really strong opinions about controversial issues such as abortion, aid to parochial schools, and God, then the attitudes you perceive in others toward these issues will affect their attractiveness to you (and your attractiveness to them). Our personal attraction, even to an old friend, may be strained if the friend suddenly discovers an attitude we hold toward race, cheating, or drugs that is quite different from his or her own. This is often true of lighter topics as well. If you like sports trivia, movies, Chinese food, or skiing, you may be attracted to someone who has those same preferences.

In the face of all these similarity arguments there are some who sincerely believe that "opposites attract." After initial similarities bring two personalities together, they may find their relationship easier (if not more attractive) if there is a complementarity.[45] A dominant wife might find a submissive husband more attractive than an equally dominant one, and vice versa. These are normal role and situation adjustments for the most part.

PHYSICAL CHARACTERISTICS

When we first see another person we are affected by what we see and how we make attributions even before we communicate orally. Large, fat, sloppy, handsome, beautiful, cool, or whatever, each characteristic will attract or repel us. Physical characteristics engender more attributions than just physical attractiveness, although in an initial or brief meeting, especially with an unusually striking face or body, we may start there.

In one "computer dance" study, individuals were randomly paired with one another. The participants were surveyed as to how much they liked their partners, how much they wanted to date their partners again, and how often they did, in fact, date their partners again. None of the personality and scholastic aptitude characteristics tested predicted couple compatibility; the largest determinant of a participant's liking for his or her date was physical attractiveness.[46] In an initial or short-term encounter in a predominantly similar group this fact must be worth something; in more serious, long-term relationships it is probably less important. I once met an extremely physically attractive person until that person talked and talked and talked.

There are sharp cultural differences of opinion about what constitutes physical beauty. Our male students from the Middle East see our lean model stereotypes as less attractive than their chunkier sisters. There are also *individual* differences about these matters in all cultures. Western art and media do continue our stereotype attributions. We tend (unfortunately sometimes) to attribute less competence, less status, and less credibility to the less physically attractive. Physical attractiveness should include the total physical makeup of an individual. This includes environmental causes of appearance, such as diet, drugs, and climate, as well as hereditary factors. People vary physically in their reaction time, energy level, and rate of learning. They also vary in hearing, sight, color, size, shape, and so on, all of which add up to and influence total personality as well as physical attractiveness. After all, beauty is skin deep only in the superficial sense. The feedback we decode over time from society about our physical makeup and the way we accommodate that feedback probably affect our attractiveness more than our superficial physical characteristics do.

Other things being equal, well-adjusted, smart young people are perceived as more attractive than those who do not possess these characteristics. There is some evidence that physical attractiveness is more important between the sexes than within each sex. That is, women tend to care more what their men friends look like than what their women friends look like (and vice versa). The roles of clothing, cosmetics, calorie counting, surgery, and other possible means of improving our appearance become critical when added to what nature gave us.

STATUS AND SOCIAL STANDING

We usually are attracted to and enjoy being with people and groups of high status and social standing because they offer us some reflected recognition. "Jack Nicklaus was seated at the next table," we report as if he were an old friend. "I belong to the exclusive Bogey Club group," we say with pride. However, when critical issues override your pride of membership as might happen with political groups, you may have some conflict.

Some status and position is earned through special skills such as athletes and actors possess; some through unusual achievement whether in sports, the arts, or business; some through superior competence, whatever the endeavor or situation. While we find people such as these attractive in general, there are moments of ambivalence that sometimes cross our minds. This is especially true of the superachiever and the extremely competent. If you perceive yourself in any kind of competition with such a person, your admiration may be tempered with some jealousy, envy, or even inferiority. If after great effort you've achieved a *B* average, your attractive roommate may lose some luster as he or she reports his or her usual *A+* grades with only average effort.

There is interesting evidence that the extremely competent may increase his or her attractiveness through what one research team describes as a *pratfall*[47]—some mishap, blunder, or clumsiness. I once stood in the mud of France waiting to be reviewed by General Dwight David Eisenhower. When the General in class A uniform stepped from his car, he tripped and fell full face into the mud of France in front of perhaps 1,000 troops. General Eisenhower flashed his famous grin, and it was "Ike" to all of us from that day forward. His pratfall hadn't hurt his station at all. He proved that despite his rank and competence he was human after all, an imperfect soldier like the rest of us. It has also been suggested that *relative* status is important. A lieutenant might not endear himself to his captain by falling in the mud.[48]

In summary, we tend to enjoy being with people who provide us with real or reflected status, position, and recognition. Manipulators be on guard; those who would play games with this factor of interpersonal attraction will fail miserably if their status is found to be unwarranted or phony.

SOCIAL ADJUSTMENT

There is good evidence that we find well-adjusted people, those with healthy self-concepts, more attractive than those who are poorly adjusted and have negative self-concepts.[49] Interestingly, people with superpositive self-concepts, people who exhibit an inconsistency in what they really are and what they *think* they are, are not perceived as attractive. *Adjustment* is, however, a relative phenomenon. A poorly adjusted or artificially stimulated group may perceive even a demagogue as well adjusted. Perhaps when one is completely lost in a cause, the degree of adjustment shown by the leader becomes irrelevant. Centuries of Hitlers and cult phenomena pay witness to this possibility. On the other hand, a normal, healthy, socially well-adjusted individual may be caught up in a moment of weakness or unusual group or physical pressure. We all lose control once in a while, but a really short-tempered person across all issues and situations is not perceived as very attractive and may even be in need of counseling.

Behaviors thought to improve another's perceptions of a person's social adjustment, and therefore attraction, include establishing rapport easily and quickly, fairness, and showing anger rarely and usually only toward those who "should know better." People who exhibit these traits are sociable and interested individuals.

Behaviors or traits found to be blocks to perceptions of good social adjustment are the personality extremes: on the one hand superiority and egoism, as exhibited by aggression, overconfidence, sarcasm, boastfulness, and a domineering attitude; on the other hand excessive inferiority, as shown by dependence, depression, withdrawal, listlessness, and excessive timidity. Either extreme can lead to defensive communication behavior by the receiver. Social adjustment is a most significant factor in interpersonal attraction.

SELF-PRESENTATION

All the world's a stage, and all the men and women merely players.

Shakespeare, As You Like It

The creative sociologist Erving Goffman puts it more bluntly than Shakespeare.

> Indeed, it seems that we spend more of our time not engaged in giving information but in giving shows. And observe, this theatricality is not based on mere displays of feelings or faked exhibitions of spontaneity or anything else by way of the huffing and puffing we might derogate by calling theatrical. The parallel between stage and conversations is much, much deeper than that. The point is that ordinarily when an individual says something, he is not saying it as a bold statement of fact on his own behalf. He is recounting. He is running through a strip of already determined events for the engagement of his listeners.[50]

The cartoon character in Figure 7.24 was, in Goffman's words, practicing "impression management." It is a large part of how you present yourself to others.[51]

Impression Management

There are three parts to one's performance: an appropriate front, dramatic realization, and a sense of mystification.[52]

Appropriate Front Hollywood worked hard on defining John Wayne through his appearance, manner, and, of course, the roles he played. It was a powerful front. Some think that John Wayne, the actor, ultimately became John Wayne, the man.

Figure 7.24   B.C. by Johnny Hart.

By permission of Johnny Hart and Creators Syndicate, Inc.

Front, then, is your general behavior, which is designed (or is natural) to better define (persuasively we hope) who you are. Parts of your personal front include factors such as appearance and manner. Your front also includes things over which you have only limited control, such as sex, age, and size. Your clothes, posture, gestures, facial expressions, and language patterns are more modifiable dimensions of your front.

Had John Wayne appeared as an unAmerican spy or a real "bad guy," we'd probably have had some very confused admirers.

Closer to home, consider a college senior preparing for an employment interview. This student may attempt an impression of maturity, self-confidence, knowledgeability, and dependability. Should this person appear for the interview wearing dirty clothes and profanely using the English language, quite a different front would be created.

Dramatic Realization   According to Goffman we must clearly realize the role expected of us and work it into the performance. We may have to be talented actors to hide our lack of confidence.

If the role calls for attentiveness, we had better give such an impression. We may be paying attention, but if we are not perceived as doing so, it is unfortunate impression management. A flippant physician who writes a fast prescription, however accurate the quick diagnosis, may be viewed suspiciously by the patient.

Mystification   This notion of impression management refers to perceptions of social distances between the actor and the audience. The physician in the previous example is more apt to be concerned with this kind of impression than the interviewee mentioned in the example before it. That is, the physician must not become too familiar lest he lose some of the mystery of the medical role. The college student, however, must accommodate the real or fancied social-distance factors in the theater in which he finds himself.

To the three dimensions Goffman proposes, we can add one more for group members: *ethical proof* in the form of (1) evidence and information and (2) communication skills and strategies.

Ethical Proof

Evidence and Information   Even highly credible sources lose some of their ethical proof or effect over time. "You're only as good as your last show." This means that there is a limit to how long you can simply assert things without citing evidence or information. Sometimes we're only as good as our information: the only navigator in a ship lost at sea, the only person with the knowledge to handle an emergency—both are examples in which *information* leads to power and influence.

The effect on source credibility of the source's use of *evidence* is a more complicated question. If one interprets early studies on the effects of evidence as McCroskey does in an excellent summary of such research,[53] one discovers a lack of close control for the variable of perceived source credibility. The question of what the group thinks, expects, and perceives is still the crux of human communication. Although McCroskey's conclusions were mixed, they did lead to the tentative conclusion that evidence had at least some impact on credibility.

An updating and rearranging of the conclusions of McCroskey's 1969 study and an accounting for the variable of perceived source credibility lead to the following generalizations:

1. Including good evidence may significantly increase immediate group-attitude change and source credibility when the source is initially perceived to be moderate-to-low credible, when the message is well delivered, and when the group has little or no prior familiarity with the evidence included or similar evidence.

2. Including good evidence may significantly increase sustained group attitude change regardless of the source's initial credibility, the quality of the delivery of the message, or the medium by which the message is transmitted.

3. Evidence appears to serve as an inhibitor to counterpersuasion.

4. The medium of transmission of a message has little if any effect on the functioning of evidence in persuasive communication.

5. Including good evidence has little if any impact on immediate group attitude change or source credibility if
   a. the source of the message is initially perceived to be high-credible;
   b. the message (when oral) is delivered poorly;
   c. the group is familiar with the evidence prior to exposure to the source's message.[54]

Communication Skills   Our use of voice and language affects our ethical proof. Studies show that people who exhibit a greater linguistic diversity in terms of verb tenses, adjectives, adverbs, and connectives are perceived as more credible. Inarticulate people are rated low in competence, dynamism, and social status.[55] Of course a showy display of language can work against a person, hurting not only credibility but also clarity. On the other hand, nonfluent, inarticulate language generally decreases one's credibility.[56] Bad grammar has been found to be an especially strong inhibitor of ethical proof and positive person perception.[57] The same can be said of poor use of voice. It has been found that receivers can detect a person's social status from voice cues alone.[58] Even an unusually slow rate of speaking (unless that is the mode of the group) has been found to negatively influence how others perceive your competence.[59] You must determine what is *appropriate* vocabulary, grammar, rate, language, and voice for your receivers in specific groups. Other communication skills such as analyzing groups, organizing messages, and reading feedback cues are also critical.

If part of self-presentation is getting people to like you, or what Robert Bell and John Daly call ''seeking affinity,'' then what communication tactics or strategies are available? Bell and Daly[60] content analyzed people's responses and produced the following typology of strategies:

1. *Altruism.* The affinity-seeker strives to be of assistance to the target in whatever she or he is currently doing.
   Example: The affinity-seeker is generally available to run errands for the target.
2. *Assume control.* The affinity-seeker presents himself or herself as a person who has control over whatever is going on.
   Example: The affinity-seeker takes charge of the activities engaged in by the target and herself or himself.
3. *Assume equality.* The affinity-seeker strikes a posture of social equality with the target.
   Example: The affinity-seeker avoids one-up games and behaving snobbishly.
4. *Comfortable self.* The affinity-seeker acts comfortable and relaxed in settings shared with the target.
   Example: The affinity-seeker ignores annoying environmental distractions, seeking to convey a "nothing bothers me" impression.
5. *Concede control.* The affinity-seeker allows the target to assume control over relational activities.
   Example: The affinity-seeker permits the target to plan a weekend that the two will share.
6. *Conversational rule-keeping.* The affinity-seeker adheres closely to cultural rules for polite, cooperative interaction with the target.
   Example: The affinity-seeker acts interested and involved in conversations with the target.
7. *Dynamism.* The affinity-seeker presents herself or himself as an active, enthusiastic person.
   Example: The affinity-seeker is lively and animated in the presence of the target.
8. *Elicit other's disclosures.* The affinity-seeker encourages the target to talk by reinforcing the target's conversational contributions.
   Example: The affinity-seeker queries the target about the target's opinions regarding a significant personal issue.
9. *Facilitate enjoyment.* The affinity-seeker tries to maximize the positiveness of relational encounters with the target.
   Example: The affinity-seeker enthusiastically participates in an activity the target is known to enjoy.
10. *Inclusion of other.* The affinity-seeker includes the target in the affinity-seeker's social groups.
    Example: The affinity-seeker plans a party for the target which numbers friends of the affinity-seeker as guests.
11. *Influence perceptions of closeness.* The affinity-seeker engages in behaviors which cause the target to perceive the relationship as closer than it has actually been.
    Example: The affinity-seeker uses nicknames and talks about "we," rather than "you and I," when discussing their relationship with the target.
12. *Listening.* The affinity-seeker listens actively and attentively to the target.
    Example: The affinity-seeker asks the target for frequent clarification and elaboration, and verbally recalls things the target has said.
13. *Nonverbal immediacy.* The affinity-seeker signals interest in the target through various nonverbal cues.
    Example: The affinity-seeker smiles frequently at the target.

14. *Openness.* The affinity-seeker discloses personal information to the target.
    Example: The affinity-seeker reveals some social insecurity or fear to the target.

15. *Optimism.* The affinity-seeker presents himself or herself to the target as a positive person.
    Example: The affinity-seeker focuses on positive comments and favorable evaluations when discussing mutual acquaintances with the target.

16. *Personal autonomy.* The affinity-seeker presents herself or himself to the target as an independent, free-thinking person.
    Example: The affinity-seeker demonstrates a willingness to express disagreement with the target about personal and social attitudes.

17. *Physical attractiveness.* The affinity-seeker tries to look and dress as attractively as possible in the presence of the target.
    Example: The affinity-seeker always engages in careful grooming before interacting with the target.

18. *Present interesting self.* The affinity-seeker presents herself or himself to the target as someone who would be interesting to know.
    Example: The affinity-seeker discreetly drops the names of impressive or interesting acquaintances in the presence of the target.

19. *Reward association.* The affinity-seeker presents himself or herself in such a way that the target perceives the affinity-seeker can reward the target for associating with him or her.
    Example: The affinity-seeker showers the target with gifts.

20. *Self-concept confirmation.* The affinity-seeker demonstrates respect for the target and helps the target to "feel good" about herself or himself.
    Example: The affinity-seeker compliments the target frequently.

21. *Self-inclusion.* The affinity-seeker arranges the environment so as to come into frequent contact with the target.
    Example: The affinity-seeker plans to have afternoon cocktails at the same time and place as the target.

22. *Sensitivity.* The affinity-seeker acts in a warm, empathic manner toward the target.
    Example: The affinity-seeker sympathizes with the target regarding a personal problem the target is experiencing.

23. *Similarity.* The affinity-seeker seeks to convince the target that the two of them share many similar tastes and attitudes.
    Example: The affinity-seeker often points out things to the target that the two of them have in common.

24. *Supportiveness.* The affinity-seeker supports the target in the latter's social encounters.
    Example: The affinity-seeker sides with the target in a disagreement the target is having with a third party.

25. *Trustworthiness.* The affinity-seeker presents herself or himself to the target as an honest, reliable person.
    Example: The affinity-seeker consistently fulfills commitments made to the target.

Polonius's advice to Laertes (*Hamlet*, Act I, Scene III) may very well fit some of the organizational settings of which you will be a part.

A double blessing is a double grace;
Occasion smiles upon a second leave.
　Pol. Yet here, Laertes! aboard, aboard, for
　　shame!
The wind sits in the shoulder of your sail,　　56
And you are stay'd for. There, my blessing with
　thee!
And these few precepts in thy memory
Look thou character. Give thy thoughts no
　tongue.
Nor any unproportion'd thought his act.　　60
Be thou familiar, but by no means vulgar;
The friends thou hast, and their adoption tried,
Grapple them to thy soul with hoops of steel;
But do not dull thy palm with entertainment　　64
Of each new-hatch'd, unfledg'd comrade. Be-
　ware
Of entrance to a quarrel, but, being in,
Bear't that th' opposed may beware of thee.
Give every man thine ear, but few thy voice;　　68
Take each man's censure, but reserve thy judg-
　ment.
Costly thy habit as thy purse can buy,
But not express'd in fancy; rich, not gaudy;
For the apparel oft proclaims the man,　　72
And they in France of the best rank and station
Are most select and generous, chief in that.
Neither a borrower, nor a lender be;
For loan oft loses both itself and friend,　　76
And borrowing dulls the edge of husbandry.
This above all: to thine own self be true,
And it must follow, as the night the day,
Thou canst not then be false to any man.　　80
Farewell; my blessing season this in thee!

NONVERBAL COMMUNICATION

IMPORTANCE

Functions

　　Consider the picture in Figure 7.25. There is no verbal message, no sound, yet we get a message. From the picture alone, we sense that *emotion* is being expressed and that attitudes are being conveyed. One scholar tells us that two of the main functions or "uses" of nonverbal behavior are for *expressing emotion* and for *conveying attitudes*.[61]

　　Study Figure 7.26. Surely there is some *conveying of attitudes*. Emotion might also be read into this picture.

Figure 7.25

By permission of Hershey Corporation.

Figure 7.26

By permission of 3M Company.

Argyle defines a third function of nonverbal communication as a kind of *self-presentation*, much as we discussed in the preceding section. The more we know about the people or the circumstances, the more attributions about the *presentation* we are apt to make.

The fourth function of nonverbal communication involves the less dramatic, but important nonverbal behaviors that usually accompany our verbal messages. We view this function as essentially that of *managing turn taking*—that is, indicating when you want to interrupt another; when you don't want to be interrupted yourself; when you want feedback, more attention, and so on. A raised-hand gesture from a listener probably indicates "hold it" to someone monologuing. Voice or paralinguistics is also a powerful nonverbal cue which we will discuss shortly.

These, then, are the four basic functions or uses of nonverbal communication: (1) expressing emotion, (2) conveying attitudes, (3) self-presentation, and (4) managing turn taking.

Amount

It has been said that only 35 percent of your communication is verbal. When you speak face-to-face with a person, that person may be receiving 65 percent of your message by means other than the words you use—by your tone of voice, by your gestures, even by the way you stand or sit and are dressed. In one view the relative ability or impact of the facial nonverbals may reach 55 percent and the vocal nonverbals 38 percent.[62] It may be that the blending of channels has more to do with meaning than the simple summing of all the channels.[63] In other words, the verbal is still critical to how we interpret the nonverbal.

When we find that a gesture that means "come here" in America means "go away" in Italy, we begin to sense the problem. There is evidence that in our own culture, black and white job applicants behave quite differently nonverbally even though their intents are the same.[64] Perhaps a culture or subculture creates its own system of nonverbal communication.[65] There is also evidence that the sexes differ in their nonverbal behaviors and that they are in line with societal role expectations.[66]

When combined with the verbal message, nonverbal signals are quite effective in conveying some ideas, particularly emotional concepts such as love and hate. People display quite different nonverbal responses to various emotional situations. One study found that some people are more sensitive than others to nonverbal signals and that such individuals tend to function better socially and intellectually. The same study also found that young people are less sensitive to nonverbal signals than are older people.[67] No wonder that in some interactions our voices and our actions speak so loudly that our words are often unheard or are not considered important.

Apparently, in the long run we cannot avoid acting nonverbally, and, therefore, we cannot avoid communicating at least nonverbally. That our nonverbal behavior may be unintentionally contrary to our verbal message is cause for concern. We express our attitudes through our body actions, our voice and articulation patterns, the objects we wear or own, our use of time and space, our language, and, of course, verbal messages. Interpersonal communication, then, includes an almost countless number of channels.

In writing about "analogic communication" (nonverbal communication), Watzlawick, Beavin, and Jackson comment clearly on the importance of context and give us, incidentally, a notion of what is included in their definition:

> We hold that the term must comprise posture, gesture, facial expression, voice inflection, the sequence, rhythm, and cadence of the words themselves, and any other nonverbal manifestation of which the organism is capable, as well as the communicational clues unfailingly present in any CONTEXT in which an interaction takes place.[68]

They footnote this comment in an amusing but telling way:

> The paramount communicational significance of context is all too easily overlooked in the analysis of human communication, and yet anyone who brushed his teeth in a busy street rather than in his bathroom might be quickly carted off to a police station or to a lunatic asylum—to give just one example of the pragmatic effects of nonverbal communication.[69]

Relationship Communication

We decide at least three important things about people largely on the basis of nonverbal communication. These are (1) personal liking or attraction, (2) evaluation of power relationships, and (3) our feelings about the response and feedback we get from others.

Let's review each of these as nonverbal codes. (1) Sometimes by nonverbal cues alone we might feel *attracted toward another*. That person seems a "likeable sort," "a good person," and easy to be with. That the opposite also happens is all too clear. (2) Power assessment is our evaluation of another person's status, influence, or clout. Nonverbal cues become important, particularly in the absence of verbal information. It has even been suggested that emergent leaders can be differentiated from other group members by their nonverbals.[70] (3) Another nonverbal area of this interpersonal decision making is our perception of a responsive listener, a person who can and will appreciate our positions or our problems. These three nonverbal decisions about people lead us in and out of a lot of group communication trouble.

GROUP AND INTERPERSONAL SPACE

Personal Space

Each of us carries a kind of space bubble around us to mark off our personal territory. It varies in size from person to person and according to the culture from which we come. More hostile people are thought to have larger bubbles. They are more easily angered and upset because it is easier to bruise their larger bubbles. People also have different bubbles for different situations. We "occupy" a certain room of the house; my room, Dad's den, and Mom's living room are pretty special at times. Invasions into another's room often make us quite unpopular. Attitudes are being conveyed here; burst a bubble and you'll find emotions being expressed.

Cultural influence is considerable. Latin Americans and Arabs tend to stand close together when they talk. Most North Americans like to talk at arm's length. What is normal distance for Latin Americans and Arabs is considered intimate or hostile by most of us. The possibility of poor, or at least confused interpersonal communication is obvious. Within our own culture, the appropriate distances change according to the message and how well we know the listeners. We tend to stand farther away from strangers than from friends. Of course, we are apt to stand closer when saying "I love you" than when saying "Hello there!" We also use our voices differently according to distance, message, and mood.[71] Figure 7.27 depicts various speech situations that a person might encounter.

Other things being equal, friendly groups made up of people with smaller space bubbles should take up less space than groups made up of strangers or hostile members. Research supports such a notion.[72] Research also suggests that larger distances between

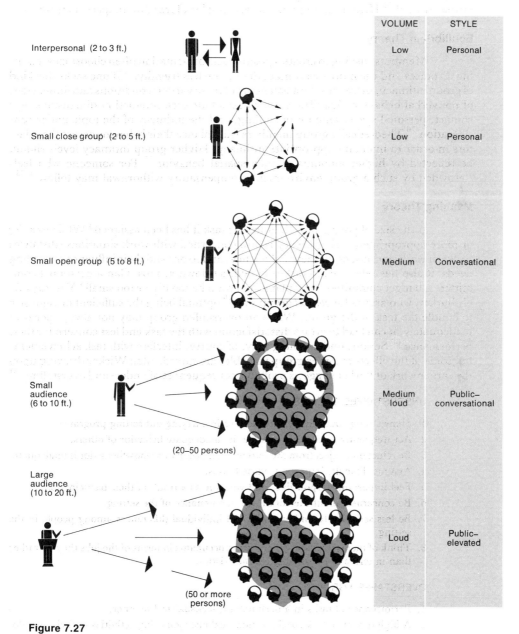

Figure 7.27

© *Raymond S. Ross*

group members occur when they face threatening situations or the members are otherwise stressed.[73] Higher-status members are usually afforded more space than others.[74]

Equilibrium Theory

Members wishing to create a positive self-presentation often choose closer seating distances and use more eye contact than those less friendly.[75] If one seeks this kind of group intimacy, there must be a balancing of these various conditions and dimensions of nonverbal behavior. *Equilibrium theory* posits four such interaction dimensions: eye contact, personal space, amount of smiling, and the intimacy of the topic under consideration.[76] Theoretically group members will balance their behavior across these factors in order to maintain appropriate intimacy. Higher group intimacy levels should be reflected by higher amounts of such spatial behavior.[77] For someone who feels "crowded by such a group environment, compensatory withdrawal may follow."[78]

Manning Theory

Is the size of your group right for the task it has been assigned? While *manning* or more appropriately *staffing* theory is also concerned with work situations (distances between work stations, equipment sufficiency, and so on) and their influence on staffing needs, it also has relevance to task-oriented, sit-down groups. Can a personnel committee, a budget committee, or a planning group be too big or too small? Yes, says R. G. Barker, who argues for *optimal* group size,[79] optimal being the sufficient or right size to handle the task of the group. While an overstaffed group may not always perform inadequately, it can lead to group dissatisfaction with the task and less concern for their performance.[80] Serious understaffing may, of course, interfere with task achievement, but some of the effects on other group variables are mixed. Alan Wicker drawing upon the earlier work of Barker suggests probable consequences of under- and overstaffing.[81]

UNDERSTAFFED GROUPS

1. Show strong, frequent, varied actions in carrying out setting programs.
2. Act frequently to correct or shape the inadequate behavior of others.
3. Be reluctant to eject from the setting other occupants whose behavior is inadequate.
4. Assume difficult, important, varied tasks.
5. Feel important, responsible, and versatile as a result of their participation.
6. Be concerned about the continued maintenance of the setting.
7. Be less sensitive to and evaluative of individual differences among people in the setting.
8. Think of themselves and other setting occupants in terms of the jobs they do rather than in terms of personality characteristics.

OVERSTAFFED GROUPS

1. Performance of tasks in a perfunctory, lackadaisical manner.
2. A high degree of task specialization, jealously guarding activities in their own domains.
3. Little concern among individuals for the quality of functioning of the setting as a whole.
4. Few efforts to help others improve their performance, and a tendency to remain aloof to see whether others "sink or swim."

5. Conversations in the setting that focus more on personalities and idiosyncracies of people in the setting than on task-related issues.

6. Cynical attitudes about the setting and its functions and about the organization of which the setting is a part.

7. Relatively low self-esteem, with little sense of competence and versatility.

Of course some size-of-group determinations in modern organizational settings are influenced by policy, rules, and legal necessities. Some democratic organizations may insist that groups or committees have equal representation from all departments. If you have nine departments your minimum size is predetermined. If, by rule or law, certain minority groups *must* be represented and they are not found among your nine representatives you may have to add more people. In short, optimal is not only decided by task considerations but also by legal, political, and social constraints.

TURNTAKING AND PARTICIPATION

Visual and Vocal Cues

Unless you are monologuing, groups take turns speaking and listening. Much of this is signaled visually, but it is also done vocally. Some of the signs are obvious, such as holding up your hand or perhaps touching the other person. Some are quite subtle—a nod of the head, a closing of the eyes, a long pause.

How you send and receive these signals are important parts of participation. Some ''fighting for the floor'' is fun in active groups, but it quickly becomes disturbing if you are constantly being rudely interrupted. Have you met the verbal person who seems to avoid looking at you (he or she can overlook your signals that way) and is eternally reluctant to give up his or her turn? If this person speaks with long, turn-inviting pauses, but his or her concentration, we presume, makes him or her temporarily deaf (your vocal signs can be overlooked that way), then you've met a real boor. Children usually handle this person better than adults. They just push and scream until they get a turn. Of course, children haven't yet learned tact and all the subtle rules and behaviors of turn taking.

We have to know (1) how to get the floor, (2) how to hold it, (3) how to yield the floor, and (4) how to signal when we would like to skip a turn. The *when* is probably more important than the *how* (but that's what this whole book is about).

Some of the visible ''I'm yielding'' signs are usually in concert with a changing pitch. If you're having trouble *yielding* the floor, try asking questions. People rarely miss that invitation to speak.

Getting the floor is often only a matter of taking advantage of invitations. However, sometimes you have to become more aggressive kinesically, just as you would have to violently wave a hand to get the attention of a monologuing professor. A pronounced nodding of the head keeping pace with the speaker's delivery can sometimes get you a turn. The raised index finger is good; the raised palm is blunt but effective if rudeness isn't a problem.

Mark Knapp captures some standard voice and kinesic behaviors as someone tries to get the floor.

When the speaker and listener are well synchronized, the listener will anticipate the speaker's juncture for yielding and will prepare accordingly—getting the rhythm before the other person has stopped talking, much like a musician tapping a foot preceding his or her solo performance. If the requestor's *rhythm* does not fit the speaker's, we might observe some stutter starts, for example, "I . . . I . . . I . . . wa . . . " Sometimes the turn-requesting mechanism will consist of efforts to speed up the speaker, realizing that the sooner the speaker has his or her say, the sooner you'll get yours. . . . The most common method for encouraging the other person to finish quickly is the use of rapid head nods, often accompanied by verbalizations of pseudoagreement, such as "yeah," "mm-hmm," and the like. The requester hopes the speaker will perceive that these comments are given much too often and do not logically follow ideas expressed to be genuine signs of reinforcement.[82]

When a speaker pauses, a would-be interrupter often has time to insert vocalizers like "um," "ah," "uh-huh," or to utilize other behaviors like sighing, coughing, clearing the throat—all clear signs to most people that you would like to interrupt. To *maintain* the floor during necessary pauses (if only to breathe), the speaker might fill up these pauses with these same kinds of vocalizations. If you are *really* serious about maintaining the floor, you would probably also increase your rate and volume and try to avoid any silent pauses.

WOMEN TALK

but men cut in

Wanda: Did you see here that two sociologists have just proved that men interrupt women all the time? They—

Ralph: Who says?

Wanda: Candace West of Florida State and Don Zimmerman of the University of California at Santa Barbara. They taped a bunch of private conversations, and guess what they found: When two men or two women are talking, interruptions are about equal. But when a man talks to a woman, he makes 96 percent of the interruptions. They think it's a dominance trick men aren't even aware of. But—

Ralph: These people have nothing better to do than eavesdrop on interruptions?

Wanda: —but women make "retrievals" about one-third of the time. You know, they pick up where they left off after the man—

Ralph: Surely not all men are like that, Wanda.

Wanda: —cuts in on what they were saying. Doesn't that—

Ralph: Speaking as a staunch supporter of feminism, I deplore it, Wanda.

Wanda: (sigh) I know, dear.

Seating Effects

If leaders can control seating patterns by using name cards they may put overtalkative group members to their immediate left or right, making it easier to overlook visual, turn-taking requests. When members can choose their own seats, Robert

Sommer found that cooperating pairs chose to sit side by side while competing pairs preferred more distant, opposite locations.[83]

It has also been observed that in groups without an assigned leader or with a minimally active leader, there is a tendency for members of a group to comment immediately after the person sitting opposite them. This phenomenon has been termed the Steinzor effect after the man who first discovered it.[84] Part of the reason is probably visual, and part may be the tendency for competitors to sit opposite one another. When a strong leader was in charge, Hearn found that the Steinzor effect weakened, and that group members made more comments to those sitting next to them.[85]

APPEARANCE AND TIME EFFECTS

Clothes and Things

Dear Mr. Molloy: I am second in command of a large management consulting firm. We send our people all over the world to consult in highly technical fields. They are mostly engineers, and the majority have several graduate degrees.

For the last few years, we've had our annual convention in Arizona, where we have found a hotel that everyone likes. The problem is, every time we show up, we each get the same gift: a free cowboy hat and a big belt buckle with the year's motto on it. Now the fellows have taken to wearing these belt buckles to work. I don't think it does much damage here in California, but I suspect that when they go East or to Europe and Japan, it gives off the wrong message.—*D.J., San Diego*

Dear D.J.: You're absolutely right. If your men are wearing these cowboy belt buckles with conservative suits, they may come across as untrustworthy. If, on the other hand, they're wearing the type of suits that go with these belt buckles, they are sending an even stronger negative message. The "cowboy look" does not travel well. In most other sections of the world, it says "rube," and it says it very loudly in Japan and Europe. I suggest you tell the fellows to leave their belt buckles back on the ranch.[86]

Research suggests that individuals who appear attractive to the receivers of communication are more successful interpersonally. In one clever study, a young woman was dressed and made up attractively for one group of receivers and then was dressed and made up to look unattractive to a similar group. The young woman was judged to be more believable and was generally found to be more persuasive and more desirable when presented attractively.[87]

We cannot change everything about our physical appearance through clothing, grooming, and "things" that we put on, hang on, glue on, tie on, or splash on. However, we can do a lot, but it is sometimes a short way from appropriate to inappropriate.

Right or wrong, many stereotypes are associated with clothes and things. Research helps us define even these. Persons who wear bizarre clothes are considered more radical, activist, and more likely to experiment with drugs. People who wear more conventional dress are associated with everyday jobs and "traditional fun."[88] The problem is in knowing what kinds of clothes and things are conventional, in style, or expected

Figure 7.28 Would you hire this woman as she appears to the left? Not if you reacted to her photo like a group of employers questioned, who gave her zero ratings. However, proving that appearances do count, the employers said they would hire the same woman (right) with the same resume, after she spruced up with a new hairdo and makeup.

Judith Waters, "Cosmetics and the Job Market," in The Psychology of Cosmetic Treatments, *J. A. Graham and A. Kligman, eds. (New York: Praeger, 1985), p. 122.*

of us. That happens to be the problem of all interpersonal communication, whether nonverbal or verbal. Some life scripts include dress codes that prescribe what it takes to be "consistent and acceptable." Some excerpts from the School of Health, Loma Linda University dress codes make clear how specific the nonverbal message is for some people in some organizations.

Your registration constitutes consent to cooperate with these policies.

ESPECIALLY FOR WOMEN

Modest dresses, sweaters or blouses with skirts or slacks, are acceptable wear for class attendance. The concept of modesty includes fit and cut as well as length. Hemlines and necklines on dresses and skirts are to be modest in both sitting and standing positions.

Levis, shorts, or short culottes are not appropriate.

Conspicuous makeup is not appropriate and jewelry should be limited to a wedding ring.

ESPECIALLY FOR MEN

Suits and slacks with sweaters, shirts, ties, sport coats, and blazers are all acceptable men's wear for class attendance. Shorts, casual jeans, dungarees and tight-fitting slacks are not appropriate.

The health professional must understand and consider his own acceptance by the community which he serves. Beards, long sideburns, and mustaches, if worn, should be neat and well-trimmed. Hair should be no longer than collar length and well-groomed.

The point is that the nonverbals of clothes and things make a big difference in the way we are seen *totally*—that is, socially, vocationally, sexually, and so on. Try this next group of seven in Figure 7.29.

Chronemics

Your treatment of time is a symbolic act. The joke is told about the Psychoanalytic School of Social Work where if you're *late* you are considered hostile, *early* you're anxious, *on-time* you're compulsive. Most, but not all Americans, are serious if not neurotic about being on time. We also take *leaving* time very seriously and are quick to attribute messages and attitudes to "time" behaviors. Some Americans have more casual attitudes about time than others. As an example, some students are routinely late for all their classes, and their reasons have nothing to do with their regard for the other students, the professor, or the course. Then again, people tend to read lateness as some kind of negative attitude.

Figure 7.29   From left are: President Zia of Pakistan, King Birenda of Nepal, President Ershad of Bangladesh, President Jayewardena of Sri Lanka, Prime Minister Rajiv Gandhi of India, King Wangchuck of Bhutan, and President Gayoomo of the Maldives.

AP/Wide World Photos, Inc.

Cultural differences point out the importance of time as nonverbal communication. Navajo Indians have great interest in immediate or *now* time but little interest in future time. Their language has no words for "future" or "late." Iranians have less interest in *now* time but great interest in past time.[89] An appointment in our culture for 10:00 A.M. on Tuesday means just that (give or take 5 or 10 minutes). However, the Navajo might hear only Tuesday; South Americans might hear the message as any time between 10:00 and 11:00 A.M. Of course, even these cultures have succumbed to more technical time demands such as airline departures, radio and television programming, timed laboratory experiments, and the like. An invitation to drop by *anytime* (rather than a specific day and time) is usually interpreted as "don't bother," unless there is a very close personal relationship that allows predictions of *appropriate* time. The same general invitation in another culture may literally mean that *any* time is appropriate.

To complicate matters even more, our meetings, and especially those in business, are usually single-issue or problem-oriented (monochronistic). Not so across the cultures. A Latin American may have several unrelated issues in mind and, in fact, have several other meetings scheduled at approximately the same time. This can be most frustrating for Anglo-Saxons, who expect to spend only a few minutes in a meeting and subsequently feel trapped for hours. We are told that this system of multiple issues in one meeting works well even for business people once everyone starts with the same assumptions. The point is that we *don't* start with the same assumptions, and it's easy to feel insulted or to insult others.

In our culture we are more time-specific, and when we don't follow the general rules we are perceived as sending a message. Others will attribute meanings to our deviant behavior. Being 30 minutes late for a 45-minute conference call invites all kinds of negative inferences from the waiting group. Seldom are we in trouble for being early, but we may get into trouble for being late! (One famous American general who had risen from the ranks claimed that one of the secrets of his success was always being 15 minutes early for meetings.) Almost every interview form includes an evaluation of the subject's dependability, which often translates into his or her attitude toward being on time. Our general culture tends to stress promptness. Television viewers complain by the thousands when a scheduled program is delayed by a news special or a game that runs into overtime.

Lateness suggests low regard for the sender, the situation, or the message. The late person who remains silent runs some interpersonal risks. If a person has no really good reason for being late and no one really cares, perhaps it doesn't matter. Students say that about some large lecture classes with no attendance requirement. However, in small classes in which relationships are more personal, a routinely late person (by 15 to 20 minutes) is inviting negative attributions about such behavior. I called one such student aside and asked for an explanation. The apologetic student explained that her previous class was across the campus and that her professor routinely went overtime. Fair enough, but why didn't she tell me? She didn't think it mattered. When I suggested that I was concerned that she was expressing low regard for me or the course, she was absolutely flabbergasted and replied that it was one of her favorite courses.

Even if an explanation for unusual tardiness is weak or nobody's business, some apology is in order. "I'm sorry, I can't explain right now." It cuts down the number of negative attributions possible and keeps the communication door ajar. We can often save strained interpersonal relations by giving good reasons when we are late.

Staying time in a classroom situation is defined by the bell at the end of the class. However, in less formal business and social settings there is more leeway. What is an appropriate amount of time for a business meeting? Usually not all day, as the case may be with the Latin Americans discussed previously. Typically we specify the time span: "Let's take an hour and discuss this matter," or "Have you got a couple of hours at lunch tomorrow?" Some of these luncheons may go on for three or four hours, I'm told, indicating that someone didn't know when to leave.

PERSPECTIVES

Our nonverbals of whatever kind, conscious or unconscious, may be characterized as follows:

1. They always communicate something.
2. They are believed.
3. They are bound to the situation.
4. They are seldom isolated.
5. They affect our relationships.

They Always Communicate Something

Assuming some kind of human interaction, *one cannot not behave*, and since behavior is nonverbal communication, *one cannot not communicate*. A blank stare communicates something to the decoder, even if it is just confusion. This is not always appreciated by less-sensitive personalities. These behaviors may be consciously or unconsciously conveyed, but one way or another they communicate. They communicate emotion and attitudes, they communicate who we are, and they help us manage interpersonal interactions.

They Are Believed

Perhaps nonverbals should not be believed, but this tendency exists. Con men have taken advantage of this fact from the beginning. Nonverbals may be hard to fake for most of us but not for good actors. When what you *say* disagrees with how you *look* or *sound*, people tend to believe the nonverbals.

They Are Bound to the Situation

Your small sales group has just heard that sales are up and that bonuses are forthcoming. "Oh, that's just great," you reply. The tone and inflection of your voice, the expression of your face, the body posture you assume—all tend to agree on the message. Your small group is informed that sales is being transferred to a more distant, less desirable location. "Oh, that's just great," you comment, only this time these identical words are accompanied by a slap to your head, a roll of the eyes, and a voice that clearly conveys displeasure. The nonverbals in this case are clearly the ones to be believed.

When it comes to basic emotions, the face is thought to be most believable. Two distinguished scholars insist it is, even across cultures and even where there is no television to teach the stereotypes.[90]

Happiness **Anger** **Fear** **Sadness**

Figure 7.30

Anger by permission of Lehn and Fink Products Group, Sterling Drug Inc. Sadness by permission of Colgate Palmolive Co. Fear by permission of Museum of Modern Art.

Figure 7.31 Cartoonist's sketches.

Our young friends in the pictures really don't need words to get their message across; neither does a cartoonist (see Figures 7.30 and 7.31).

They Are Seldom Isolated

It is very difficult for most of us to be very angry and yet control our actions and voices so that we appear calm. A glisten of perspiration, a faster eye blink, a slight tremble, a dryness in the voice—these and more give us away. Even when we are laughing on the outside (and crying on the inside), the character of our laughter probably gives us away. These other nonverbals tend to be related, consistent, and supportive of one another. When they are not, suspicions about intent are raised. Except in pictures or audiotapes, nonverbals are difficult to isolate. In addition, nonverbal behaviors can have multiple meanings, some obvious, and some very subtle indeed.

Unless you are in a laboratory looking at very limited and controlled facial expressions, you are perceiving a total impression, which includes all of the verbals as well as all of the nonverbals. It also includes the setting and psycho-environment as discussed in previous chapters. Despite all of the importance of the nonverbal messages, the lesson here should be clear. Don't ignore the verbal; it's still the major part of most interpersonal interactions. To concentrate on only one isolated movement, expression, or tone is a poor way to manage meanings.

They Affect Our Relationships

As we said at the beginning of this chapter, we decide three important things about people largely on the basis of nonverbal communication. These are personal liking or attraction, evaluation of power relationships, and our feelings about the response and feedback we get from others. Figure 7.32 catches a bit of all the nonverbal relationship decisions. Liking is expressed by the proximity of this small group of three.

Figure 7.32

AP/Wide World Photos, Inc.

Power of a sort rests with the lawyer on the left; feedback response is certainly being expressed by Senator Talmadge and the ''eye'' in the middle.

RULES FOR RELATING

For all of our group dynamics and small group research, the practical rules produced are rarely spelled out and are taught mostly by trainers outside of the academic community. Some scholars apparently think such efforts are too prescriptive and too inflexible. Well, Emily Post is still good reading for people who wish to be socially effective, Dale Carnegie has helped many frightened people, and the need for even practical conversational skills seems obvious. Donald N. McCloskey, economist, agrees and speaks eloquently of the Jurgen Habermas norms of conversation (*Sprachethik*) as being central to scholarly communication:

> Don't lie; pay attention; don't sneer; cooperate; don't shout; let other people talk; be openminded; explain yourself when asked; don't resort to violence or conspiracy in aid

of your ideas. We cannot imagine good conversation or good intellectual life deficient in these, for they are the metarules implicitly adopted by the mere act of joining what the culture thinks of as a conversation, whether among economists about how to manage the economy or between parents about how to manage the teenager.[91]

Unfortunately most people, even those well-educated, continue to make the same relating and interacting errors they made as children.[92] Some group examples and suggestions similar to those discussed in the conflict chapter follow.

DISAGREEING

> **John:** I think the new personnel director is doing a good job.
> **Paul:** Oh, no!
> **Mary:** John, why do you say that?

Paul's disagreement was a discussion stopper or an invitation for a fight. Mary's comment sought information and reasons for John's opinion. Rule: *Get reasons before disagreeing.*

STATING OPINIONS

> **Paul:** The new personnel director is a jerk.
> **John:** You're nuts!
> **Mary:** You're both nuts!
> **Ray:** Now hold it . . . .

Paul stated his opinion as a fact and left little room for discussion. It would have been better had he used more open-minded language, such as, "I think the new personnel director is in trouble." Discussion would then be easier. Rule: *Don't state opinions and beliefs as facts.*

ARROGANT DISMISSAL

> **Mary:** It appears that we're going to have to cooperate more with the ABC Company.
> **Paul:** I guess so, but boy, they're hard to deal with.
> **Peter:** I know their marketing guy. I could approach him . . .
> **Boss:** I refuse to listen to any more of this nonsense. We've never worked that way before and we aren't going to start now!

The boss is guilty of *arrogant dismissal*. Irving Lee, a famous communication professor called it a mood of dismissal in which a person makes it clear that he or she has had enough; more talk is just plain out of the question.

Arrogant dismissal is a sure way to impede or stop rational problem solving. Rule: *Disagree, but avoid either-or response, and give fair hearing.*

LEADING QUESTIONS

Peter: I'm not sure Jane is ready for promotion. She's only been on the job two years.

Paul: Well, let's look at the record . . .

Mary: You guys really are chauvinists, aren't you?

Were Mary a lawyer in a court of law, the judge would reprimand her for asking a leading question. Rule: *Don't ask leading questions.* Also: *When angry, look again.*

CRITICISM

Mary: We're all here but John.

Paul: Here he comes now, late again.

Boss: John, we like to start promptly at 8:30.

John: (defensively) I'm doing the best I can; did I miss anything?

John insulted his group thrice, first by being late, second by insinuating that not much was going on anyway, and third by not accepting a fair criticism. Better he had replied: I'm sorry. Our baby sitter is eternally late. Rule: *Accept deserved criticism; head it off if you can (before the boss speaks). Say, "I'm sorry."*

Mary: Paul, you're a troublemaker and I don't like your attitude.

Peter: Easy, Mary. I don't think Paul deserves that.

Paul: Thanks, Peter, but let's hear Mary out. What specific trouble and what attitude are we talking about?

Paul responded correctly. Rule: *When you feel criticism is unfair, ask for specifics to better argue (or concede) your case.*

CLOSED VERSUS OPEN QUESTIONS

Mary: I think we should support Mr. Jones for grievance representative.

Peter: What about Mr. Smith?

Paul: I like Jones but don't forget Jackson; he worked with us.

Mary: We haven't heard from Jim. Do you like Mr. Jones?

Jim: Yes.

Peter: Are you against Mr. Smith?

Jim: No.

Mary: Jim, why do you like Mr. Jones, and how does he compare to Smith and Jackson?

Jim: Well, I would say . . .

Closed questions don't encourage the undertalkative (Jim) as much as open ones: Why? How? In what way? Rule: *Use open-ended questions to promote discussion.*

FREE INFORMATION

Peter: Paul, we'd like to get your opinion on the new marketing strategy . . .

Paul: Sure, but I'm not too well informed—I've been struggling with budgets. The new strategy . . . etc., etc.

Mary: Thanks, Paul, but can you tell us more about how sales fits in?

Paul: OK, but I'm not sure of all of this . . . those doggone budgets. The sales group fits in . . .

Peter: Very helpful, Paul. By the way, is there something about budgets we should know?

Paul: Well, as a matter of fact there is . . .

Sometimes a reluctant participant or one with bad news will offer what Alan Garner calls "free information" (budgets in Paul's case) or "subtle cues seeking response."[93] Peter wisely followed the cue with an open question. Rule: *Listen for free information.*

SUMMARY

"An individual's assumptions, beliefs, and attitudes are a function of the structure of his language, . . . his perception and behavior will be affected more or less in direct relationship to his susceptibility to influence by that language structure [Budd]." Symbols and language allow us to represent and store realities. Our knowledge is a function of our language and symbols.

General semantics provides us with three valuable principles: (1) the principle of *nonidentity* (the word is not the thing); (2) the principle of *nonallness* (the word is not the entire thing); and (3) *self-reflexiveness* (we use language to talk about language). Special problems of the above may be defined as *is, etc.*, *indexing*, *dating*, and *either-or*.

Different types of social systems tend to generate different speech systems, ways of talking, or language codes. Verbal and nonverbal codes usually work together and affect one another. Sometimes they are consistent with one another and thus strengthen a speaker's intended meaning, while at other times they conflict and tend to distort intended meaning. Generally, but not always, the closer we are to people (common experience), the more restricted our language codes become. With elaborated codes the speaker must presume that the listener holds a set of experiences different from his or her own. Sensitive group communication should be elaborate when appropriate.

Abstracting is a process of thinking in which we selectively leave out details about concrete or real things. Abstraction occurs at different levels. As we move from lower to higher levels we tend to consider fewer and fewer details of the specific, original object (FIDO, Golden Retriever, dog).

Good communication depends upon people being able to coordinate their meanings. This hinges upon our ability to infer meanings from contexts, signs, and symbols, and then to encode and transmit in such a way that they mesh with the receiver's meanings.

Our meaning changes with the level we use to interpret a symbol or set of symbols. Our decoding varies along a hierarchy of meaning thought to include constructions, construction systems, speech acts, episodes, and life scripts. These meaning systems aid us in ordering and regularizing our environments and in making sense out of them. The levels of the hierarchy are related to each other in that higher levels provide contexts for understanding the lower levels. The interpretation of our communication environments varies as a function of where we decide to stop within our personal set of meaning levels. The competent group communicator is able to move through the meaning hierarchy in such a fashion as to best coordinate meanings.

Even attempted nonbehavior has message impact. People attribute intentions and meanings even to nonactions. One cannot *not* communicate. Most communication has both content and relationship aspects. Both dimensions need to be coordinated.

Digital communication employs mostly arbitrarily assigned symbols (words); *analogic* forms are not as arbitrary and bear a closer resemblance to the things they stand for (for example, pictures) and can more easily carry emotional content. Analogic symbols usually function to give context or additional interpretation to the digital band, and they help define relationships. Digital symbols do better with facts, figures, and definitions of objects.

Human communication can be one of at least three types: (1) complementary, (2) symmetrical, and (3) transition. Complementary relationships tend to maximize relational differences. Symmetrical relationships are characterized by verbals and non-verbals that reflect each other. They are based on equality rather than difference. Transition relationships are based on behaviors, both verbal and nonverbal, that are different but not opposite. Very often an "analogic" sensitivity is as important to communication competence as is rhetorical sensitivity.

All communication interaction is governed by rules. A conflation of rules is a combination or a sharing of rules between people. To the extent that people share common interpretive rules, they are able to coordinate their meanings.

Symbolic interaction may be summarized by three premises: (1) humans act toward things based on meanings they have for them; (2) the meanings we have for things grow out of our social interaction with others; and (3) meanings are modified, contextualized, and generally manipulated through an interpretive language process used by the individual.

We employ both regulative and constitutive rules. Regulative rules operate at the *communicative* levels of the hierarchy and function to regulate speech acts, episodes, and life scripts. Constitutive rules function to specify how meanings at one level of the hierarchy can be meaningful at another level of the hierarchy. "Thanks" can mean gratitude or ingratitude, depending on how the episode is interpreted.

We manage our meanings and responses in any of three basic ways: (1) we allow the boundaries of an episode to become porous—that is, we allow the rules particular to a specific context to "fill out" the episode; (2) we switch episodes—that is, we bring different episodes to bear on the specific context; and (3) we shift the level of abstraction in the meaning hierarchy—that is, we may give a new context to an episode by switching to a different life script.

Three methods of coordinating or sharing episodes include casting, mirroring, and negotiation. Good communication works at intermeshing communication behaviors to produce mutually shared episodes.

When communication fails or is only half clear, it is often because we have been unable to coordinate our meanings. To communicate at all hinges upon our ability to infer meanings from contexts, signs, and symbols, and then to encode and transmit them in such a way that they coordinate or mesh with the receiver's meanings. All people perception is concerned with relationship communication, since the meanings grow to a large extent from the notions we form about others while actively interacting with them. There is also a content aspect; both are ever present. Our communication is heavily biased and shaped by the relationship we have with others—that is, how we *perceive* or experience the relationship. Experience is the feeling that accompanies the perception of another's behavior. Three critical states are *understanding, being understood,* and *feeling understood.*

The process of inferring attributes about ourselves is much the same as inferring attributes about others. Self-concept is the sum total of the view which we have of ourselves. It affects not only our attitude but also our achievement and performance. Competence means capacity, fitness, or ability. Sense of competence is related to self-concept. Also related are significant others, group memberships, social roles we play, and the situations in which we find ourselves.

The covariation principle includes three variables: entity, person, and time/modality. We tend to work backward from behavior to inferences about causes. We often overlook the other critical influences that covary; we discount unfairly. We can improve our attributions to others by observing each person in a variety of contexts.

Openness is related to relationships, some of which are necessary, while others are discretionary. We need some disclosure to have any kind of relationship, even the necessary ones. How much openness depends on whether we are building a relationship, just maintaining one, or perhaps easing out of one. The Johari Window gives an interpersonal perspective on what may be happening. The four panes refer to the knowledge, beliefs, attitudes, and feelings that are part of an individual's personality—open, blind, hidden, and unknown. The window panes change in size as a relationship varies; they are interdependent, too. A "when to disclose" inventory includes: Is it a necessary or a discretionary one? Is it a long- or short-term relationship? What are the risks? What is the message/relationship importance?

Attraction is shaped and strengthened by at least six factors: (1) nearness and exposure, (2) similarity, (3) physical characteristics, (4) status and social standing, (5) social adjustment, and (6) self-presentation.

The four parts to one's impression management are an appropriate front, dramatic realization, a sense of mystification, and ethical proof. Ethical proof consists of (1) evidence and information and (2) communication skills and strategies.

It has been said that only 35 percent of our communication is verbal; 65 percent of our messages may be given by means other than the words we use, such as our tone of voice, our gestures, and the way we stand, sit, and dress. The four basic functions of nonverbal communication are (1) expressing emotion, (2) conveying attitudes, (3) self-presentation, and (4) managing turn taking. We decide at least three important things about relationships largely on the basis of nonverbal communication: (1) personal liking or attraction, (2) evaluation of power relationships, and (3) our feelings about the response and feedback we get from others.

Each of us carries a kind of space bubble around us to mark off our personal territory. Hostile people are thought to have larger bubbles. Cultural influence is considerable. We use our voices differently according to distance, message, and mood. Friendly groups generally take up less space than other kinds unless threatened or stressed. Equilibrium theory posits four nonverbal interaction dimensions: eye contact, personal space, amount of smiling, and the intimacy of the topic under consideration. Theoretically, group members will balance their behavior across these factors. Manning or staffing theory suggests that overstaffed groups may perform inadequately and experience group dissatisfaction. Understaffing may interfere with task achievement. Optimal size is decided not only by the task and the people but also by legal, political, and social constraints.

To help manage turn taking, we must know how to get the floor, how to hold it, how to yield it, and how to signal when we'd like to skip a turn.

In leaderless groups there is a tendency for members of a group to comment immediately after the person sitting opposite them. This phenomenon is known as the Steinzor effect.

Object language uses the influence and display of material things. It includes the clothes we wear, our jewelry, cosmetics, and so forth that make a statement. The key word is *appropriate*. Clothes and things affect how we are seen totally—socially, vocationally, sexually, and so forth.

Your treatment of time (chronemics) is a symbolic act. In our culture we tend to be time-specific. Being late invites negative attributions.

Our nonverbals of whatever kind, conscious or unconscious, may be characterized as follows: They always communicate something, they are believed, they are situation-bound, they are seldom isolated, and they affect our relationships.

Seven conversational rules for relating explain appropriate behaviors for (1) disagreeing, (2) stating opinions, (3) dismissal, (4) questioning, (5) criticism, (6) using open questions, and (7) perceiving free information.

PROJECTS AND CASES

PROJECTS

1. Collect two examples of context confusion that caused language to mean different things to different individuals.

2. In one page, list five words or short language segments that turn you off (almost regardless of context), and try to explain why.

3. Interview a person of a different race or culture (or subculture) regarding the language he or she finds most offensive. Report results in one page or less.

4. Find an advertisement or commercial that you feel is racially, sexually, or culturally debasing (linguistically), and explain your choice.

5. Working as a group, write out a short interaction sequence (two pages) to be performed by group members for the class. The interaction sequence should illustrate some aspects of language and meaning (principles of semantics, elaborated/restricted codes, abstraction processes, meaning management, and so on). After the interaction sequence is performed, the group should explain the interaction in terms of the concepts it illustrated. If, for example, the interaction is humorous, wherein lies the humor? Does it lie in varying levels of abstraction? In meaning mismatches between the characters, the misinterpretation of a restricted code, and so forth?

6. Recall a group communication event in your life that you view as significant (where you were deeply moved, embarrassed, downtrodden, or stimulated). Write a short pa-

per explaining the event in terms of your levels of meaning (construction and the like) and how they were coordinated between individuals.

7. Find and transcribe some talk between people on television or from a play. Analyze the talk in terms of the relationship-control dimensions of each utterance. Code each utterance as a one-up, one-down, or one-across behavior. Look at the general complex of behaviors in your transcript and decide if the talk is primarily composed of complementary, symmetrical, or transition relationships. See if you can then write a short description of the relationship of the communicators based on your analysis.

8. In a small group, prepare and perform a skit and introduction that illustrates one of the following:
   a. digital vs. analogic communication
   b. regulative and constitutive rules
   c. methods of meaning management
   d. punctuation principles
   e. language codes

9. You most likely formed an initial impression of your instructor. Impression formation is quite normal and sometimes aids us in our general interpersonal stance. However our first impressions do not always guide us correctly.

   Develop and write a 100-word first impression of your instructor. Be sure to include an analysis of variables like his or her motives, traits, and personality attributes. You may want to share these first impressions with your instructor and others in the class. You may be surprised!

10. Analyze one of your interpersonal-communication relationships in terms of the interpersonal needs the relationship fulfills. Analyze the relationship in terms of the inclusion, affection, and control needs the relationship serves.

11. Explain how interpersonal relationships develop in terms of person perception. Use examples from your own experiences. You may want to explain developing relationships in terms of Laing's three concepts: understanding, being understood, and feeling understood.

12. Select a person who attracts you, and assess your evaluation of that person in terms of the factors of attraction discussed in this chapter. (Or do the same for a person whom you find unattractive). Be prepared to discuss it in class.

13. Our understanding and interpretation of the interpersonal events and encounters is often a function of our particular self-perceptions and attributions. Explain an encounter or event of your choice in terms of the entity, the person influence, the time dimension, and the modality influence.

14. "All the world's a stage, and all the men and women merely players." (Shakespeare)
    We all attempt to manage other's impressions of us. Analyze your instructor's impression management in terms of his or her front, dramatic realization, and mystification.

15. In a small group, explore your feelings about self-disclosure. How much? Under what circumstances? When? In what kinds of relationships? Advantages? Disadvantages?

16. Try deliberately using one of the seven "rules for relating" at the end of Chapter 7 (free information, disagreeing, and so forth). Write down your observations as soon as you disengage. Prepare to report.

17. Try an experiment in *object language*. Wear something unusual (for you) and interact with family or friends. Write a one-page report of what happened to the communication. Discuss it in class.

CASES

1. Consider the case of "Mainstream Data Systems" (the first case in Chapter 1).

2. June Brown, a black columnist, has some forthright advice on nonverbal communication, especially *time* and *clothes*. Discuss.

JOBS AWAIT APPLICANTS WHO REALLY CARE[94]

Here's some good news about jobs: I've found an employer who will hire 10 unskilled people, maybe more, for jobs paying $3.35 to $3.55 per hour.

The only requirements are that applicants must present a voter registration card and a letter from their last employer showing a good record on absence and tardiness. Instead of an employment letter, high school graduates can substitute a report card or a letter from school showing the number of absences or tardiness.

Anyone presenting records showing no absences or tardiness for one year will be hired on the spot.

BUT, BEFORE anyone rushes out to claim the job, let me tell you more about it. The job involves working in a facility that not only cares for old people but also children with birth defects.

Any person working there will need a great love for damaged human beings. . . . Most of them will live a long time, spending their years unspeaking, unlearning, unmoving.

Some of these children, I was told, were born with defects because their mother experimented with drugs. Will you help love and care for them?

One more thing: Some men job seekers come barefoot, wearing cut-off jeans. Some women come dragging three or four babies with them. Don't be like that; come fully clothed and ready for work.

3. *Role playing session* (from an assignment by Nancy Barkly, Ph.D., Wayne State University).

Situation   A man (a woman) in the class died leaving $250,000 to the class.

Stipulations

   I. You cannot divide the money. All must participate in spending the money.
   II. The class must agree by consensus within a time limit (one class period).
   III. If the class does not decide within the time limit, the money goes to charity and no one in the class gets a penny.

Instructions   The following male, female, and androgenous roles will be assigned by your instructor (secretly by number). Your role is not revealed until the discussion starts. Your instructor will act as a lawyer and answer questions related only to the stipulations.

MALE ROLES

1. You are very quiet, shy, and "wishy washy." You agree with anyone who asks you anything even if your statement is a direct contradiction of a previous view. You are strictly a follower and offer very little of yourself to the group.

2. You are an avid bird watcher. You know everything there is to know about birds and delight in arising promptly at 4:30 A.M. every morning to make the five-mile hike to your bird-watching loft. You dislike competitive sports although you are very much for physical fitness. In fact, physical fitness is almost a fetish of yours. You would like to gain the alliance of some woman as you are lonely and would like a companion.

3. You are an ex-pro fullback, a real sports nut, and an outdoors man. You dislike being inside, have no use for culture and the fine arts, and enjoy "getting out with the boys" at every chance. You also consider yourself quite a lady's man and are a bachelor (so far the field is much more appealing than any ties). You like soft-spoken women but admire money.

4. You are the preacher type although not a preacher. You are sure some of the people in this group are in "serious trouble with the Lord" and need to reform. This is particularly true of the woman who is a "swinger." You like her and would like to reform her. You don't smoke, drink, or gamble, and have never been to a night club as you can't stand to witness the sinful goings-on there.

5. You dislike the outdoors but like to travel visiting cultural centers, museums, and the like. You have traveled extensively and feel Tibet was the most interesting place you have ever been. You feel superior to this group, however, and aren't too active in their discussions. You like strong women.

6. You are a hypochondriac (always complaining about your health, taking pills, and so on). You are shy, are afraid of everything including your own shadow, and whine a lot. Your idea of a real great time is to play Mozart records after returning from a Bach concert.

7. You love the outdoors, sports, and have always wanted to go on an African safari with a group of men. You enjoy the company of women if it's a "woman's place" type activity. You are chauvinistic and against equal rights for women in every way.

8. You are a loudmouth and a braggart. You feel superior to everyone in this group and want to be the leader. Try to become the leader. You also feel the opposite sex finds you irresistible.

9. You love to gamble and brag about your skill with cards. You also love to flirt as you need women's attention and approval. You especially need the approval of the one woman in this group who is an ex-general, as she is a challenge to you. You do not drink or smoke.

10. You are rich, lazy, and have a big mouth. You name drop and point out your financial skills every chance you get. You would like to control this discussion because it is a threat to your ego to have anyone else control a discussion involving you and money.

11. You are a health-food fanatic. You like to frequent health spas and think you are absolutely "body beautiful" and irresistible to women. You need women's attention and try constantly to get it. You do not like parties, however, unless they are outside in a clean and healthy environment.

FEMALE ROLES

1. You are a real "swinger." The wilder the idea the better. Life to you is one big party after another. You are a big flirt, especially with shy men. The shyer the man or the more frightened he appears, the more you see him as a must to conquer. Ham it up!!! You try to convert *anyone* you think is "missing" life.

2. You are afraid of your own shadow and see yourself as a helpless female whom men *must* help. You take part shyly and ask pointless questions to gain attention. You con-

stantly build up men's egos. You dislike sports, travel, or outdoor activities though you like "outdoorish" men. You like to get all dressed up and go dining and dancing or something romantic and glamorous.

3. You are an ex-general of the WACs. You are tough as nails, dislike men, and think little of the women in this group. You dislike any form of entertainment except movies and TV (especially war movies). You live in a mobile home and have built your furniture. You are very *loud* and outspoken. Be tough and ham it up.

4. You are wealthy, a name dropper, and a socialite. You also think of yourself as superior to this group but would like to make sure that *their* discussion does not affect "your position in society." You are loud and rude. Keep supporting the leader and try to get people to be quiet and listen to him.

5. You have traveled extensively and enjoyed Tibet the most. You have lots of money but do not show it and dislike anyone who does. You are not afraid to help others out by giving facts about various places in the world as you have been just about everywhere.

6. You are rather shy but if you find someone (especially of the opposite sex) who shares your interests, you'll take a chance and get out of your shell to explain yourself though in a shy way. You love to read and enjoy fine art. You also have become very interested in charcoal painting, especially in sketches of animals and birds.

ANDROGENOUS ROLES

1. You want to be leader and will do anything including appointing yourself to become the leader. If someone else is leader, try to take over. You try to be a democratic leader but can't help but try to sway the group to your view at times. You always speak in a loud voice as it seems to you to be a sign of your power.

2. Although you do not wish to be the leader, you do everything you can outside of assuming leadership to see that everyone gets a chance to give his or her viewpoint. Try to get order and keep the group on the task at hand. Try to get the group to follow the discussion process.

3. You are domineering and like to hear yourself talk. You do *not* want to do any work but keep offering suggestions and ideas. You think the group should have a money-making project. If anyone asks you to do anything that may involve work, delegate it to someone else. You are a health-food nut and admire the wealthy. Yoga is the extent of your physical activity.

4. You are very wise, knowledgeable, and philosophical. You read constantly. You do not enjoy any sports, even as a spectator. To you competitive sports are base, vile, and animalistic. You do enjoy travel for the sake of culture.

5. Noise drives you nuts. You want quiet but keep asking for it in a noisy way. If others ask your opinion, try to get them to express their own, or try to get people to follow the discussion process. *Don't* be too active in the discussion.

6. You are a "middle of the road" type as far as interests go. You like just about everything and would like very much to help the group get a solution. You are patient but dislike people who dominate. Try to bring the quiet ones in the group to express themselves.

7. Although ordinarily good natured, you are in a bad mood today and anyone who seems to be talking too much irritates you to the point that you make caustic remarks. Say nothing helpful but contribute disruptive remarks occasionally.

8. You are a "swinger" but have kept it from this group. Now you see a chance to see if any of the "duds" in this group really know how to live it up. You support ideas that lead to a wild idea without being obvious.

NOTES

1. Jack Kerouac, *On the Road* (New York: Viking, 1957), p. 8.
2. Richard W. Budd, "General Semantics: an Approach to Human Communication," in *Interdisciplinary Approaches to Human Communication*, eds. Richard W. Budd and Brent D. Ruben (Ro-

chelle Park, N.J.: Hayden, 1979), p. 71; see also B. L. Whorf, *Language, Thought, and Reality* (New York: John Wiley & Sons, 1957).

3. See Wendell Johnson, *People in Quandaries* (San Francisco: International General Semantics, 1980); see also S. I. Hayakawa, *Language in Thought and Action* (New York: Harcourt Brace Jovanovich, 1978).

4. Julia T. Wood and W. Barnett Pearce, "Sexists, Racists, and Other Classes of Classifiers: Form and Function of ' . . . ist' Accusations," *Quarterly Journal of Speech*, 66, no. 3 (October 1980), 250.

5. See Basil Bernstein, "Elaborated and Restricted Codes: Their Social Origins and Some Consequences," in *Communication and Culture, Readings in the Codes of Human Interaction*, ed. Alfred G. Smith (New York: Holt, Rinehart & Winston, 1966), p. 429.

6. Raymond S. Ross, *Speech Communication*, 7th ed. (Englewood Cliffs, N.J.: Prentice-Hall, 1986), p. 32.

7. Bernstein, "Elaborated Codes," pp. 436–37.

8. Ibid., p. 437.

9. Karl Menninger, *Love Against Hate* (New York: Harcourt Brace Jovanovich, 1942), pp. 268–69.

10. Vernon E. Cronen, W. Barnett Pearce, and Linda M. Harris, "The Logic of the Coordinated Management of Meaning: A Rules-based Approach to the First Course in Interpersonal Communication," *Communication Education*, 28, no. 1 (January 1979), 23–28.

11. Ibid., p. 25.

12. George A. Kelley, *A Theory of Personality: The Psychology of Personal Constructs* (New York: W. W. Norton, 1963).

13. Cronen, Pearce, and Harris, "Management of Meaning," p. 25.

14. J. J. Gumperz, "Introduction," in *Directions in Sociolinguistics: The Ethnography of Communication*, eds. J. J. Gumperz and Dell Hymes (New York: Holt, Rinehart & Winston, 1972), p. 17.

15. Robert L. Scott, "Communication as an Intentional Social System," *Human Communication Research*, 3, no. 3 (Spring 1977) 258–68.

16. See Paul Watzlawick, Janet H. Beavin, and Don D. Jackson, *Pragmatics of Human Communication* (New York: W. W. Norton, 1967), pp. 51–54.

17. Watzlawick, Beavin, and Jackson, *Pragmatics*, pp. 54–59.

18. See Mark L. Knapp and Mark E. Comadena, "Telling It Like It Isn't; A Review of Theory and Research on Deceptive Communications," *Human Communication Research*, 5, no. 3 (Spring 1979), pp. 279–82.

19. Frank E. Millar and L. Edna Rogers, "A Relational Approach to Interpersonal Communication," in *Explorations in Interpersonal Communication*, ed. Gerald Miller (Beverly Hills: Sage, 1976), p. 96.

20. Adapted from Millar and Rogers, "A Relational Approach," p. 97.

21. See Charles R. Berger and James J. Bradac, *Language and Social Knowledge* (London: Edward Arnold Publishers, 1982); also see Benjamin J. Broome, "The Attraction Paradigm Revisited: Responses to Dissimilar Others," *Human Communication Research*, 10, no. 1 (Fall 1983), 137–51, and William B. Gudykunst and Tsukasa Nishida, "Individual and Cultural Influences on Uncertainty Reduction," *Communication Monographs*, 51, no. 1 (March 1984), 23–36.

22. W. Barnett Pearce, "The Coordinated Management of Meaning: A Rules-Based Theory of Interpersonal Communication," in *Explorations in Interpersonal Communication*, ed. Gerald Miller (Beverly Hills: Sage, 1976), p. 25.

23. Cronen, Pearce, and Harris, "Management of Meaning," p. 26.

24. Ibid., p. 23. See also G. Kelley, *A Theory of Personality* for a detailed discussion of personal constructs in relation to sense making. Of course, other persons who are part of the episode had also better be "coordinated."

25. Ibid., p. 25.

26. See John Stewart, *Bridges Not Walls* (New York: Random House, 1986), p. 27.

27. Paul Watzlawick and Janet Beavin, "Some Formal Aspects of Communication," in *The Interactional View*, eds. P. Watzlawick and J. H. Weakland (New York: W. W. Norton, 1977), p. 61.

28. Oliver Wendell Holmes, *The Autocrat of the Breakfast Table* (Boston: Phillips, Simpson, 1858), p. 59.

29. R. D. Laing, *Politics of Experience* (New York: Pantheon, 1967), pp. 4–5; see also Dudley D. Cahn, Jr., *Letting Go* (Albany, New York: State University of New York Press, 1987), p. 11.

30. See Shirley C. Samuels, *Enhancing Self-Concept in Early Childhood* (New York: Human Science Press, 1977), p. 36.

31. Donald W. Felker, *Building Positive Self-Concepts* (Minneapolis, Minn.: Burgess, 1974), p. 2.

32. H. H. Kelley, "Attribution Theory in Social Psychology," in *Nebraska Symposium on Motivation*, ed. David Levine (Lincoln: University of Nebraska Press, 1967), 15, pp. 192–240.

33. G. Simmel, "The Secret and the Secret Society," in *The Sociology of Georg Simmel*, ed. K. Wolff (New York: Free Press, 1964), p. 329.

34. L. A. Hosman and C. H. Tardy, "Self-disclosure and Reciprocity in Short- and Long-Term Relationships: An Experimental Study of Evaluational and Attributional Consequences," *Communication Quarterly*, 38, no. 1 (Winter 1980), 20–30.

35. L. Rosenfeld, "Self-Disclosure Avoidance: Why I Am Afraid to Tell You Who I Am," *Communication Monographs*, 46, no. 1 (March 1979), 63–74.

36. See Sidney Jourard, *Self-Disclosure: An Experimental Analysis of the Transparent Self* (New York: John Wiley & Sons, 1971); see also S. Jourard, *The Transparent Self* (New York: Van Nostrand Reinhold Co., 1971).

37. I. Altman and D. A. Taylor, *Social Penetration* (New York: Holt, Rinehart & Winston, 1973).

38. Joseph Luft, *Of Human Interaction* (Palo Alto, Calif.: National Press, 1968), p. 6.

39. J. Delia, "Some Tentative Thoughts Concerning the Study of Interpersonal Relationships and Their Development," *Western Journal of Speech Communication*, 44, no. 2 (Spring 1980), 101.

40. See Mark Cook, *Interpersonal Perception* (Baltimore: Penguin, 1971).

41. See C. R. Berger, "Task Performance and Attributional Communication as Determinants of Interpersonal Attraction," *Speech Monographs*, 40, no. 4 (November 1973), 280–86. See also Broome, "Attraction Paradigm Revisited," pp. 137–51.

42. See Donn Byrne, *The Attraction Paradigm* (New York: Academic, 1971).

43. G. Lindzey and E. Aronson, eds., *The Handbook of Social Psychology*, Vol. 2, 2nd ed., (Reading, Mass.: Addison-Wesley, 1968), pp. 498–500.

44. R. S. Ross, *Understanding Persuasion*, 2nd ed. (Englewood Cliffs, N.J.: Prentice-Hall, 1985), p. 41.

45. George Levinger, David J. Senn, and Bruce W. Jorgensen, "Progress toward Permanence in Courtship: A Test of the Kerckhoff-David Hypothesis, *Sociometry*, 33 (1970), 427–43.

46. Elaine Walster and others, "Importance of Physical Attractiveness in Dating Behavior," *Journal of Personality and Social Psychology*, 4 (1966), 508–16.

47. Elliot Aronson, Ben Willerman, and Joanne Floyd, "The Effect of a Pratfall on Increasing Interpersonal Attractiveness," *Psychonomic Science*, 4 (1966), 227.

48. David R. Mettee and Paul C. Wilkins, "When Similarity 'Hurts': Effects of Perceived Ability and a Humorous Blunder on Interpersonal Attractiveness," *Journal of Personality and Social Psychology*, 22 (1972), 246–58.

49. J. McCroskey and others, "The Effects of Communication Apprehension on Interpersonal Attraction," *Human Communication Research*, 2, no. 1 (Fall 1975), 51–65.

50. Erving Goffman, *Frame Analysis: An Essay on the Organization of Experience* (Cambridge, Mass.: Harvard University Press, 1974), p. 508.

51. Erving Goffman, *The Presentation of Self in Everyday Life* (Garden City, N.Y.: Doubleday and Company, 1959), p. 208.

52. Ibid., pp. 22, 30, 67.

53. James C. McCroskey, "A Summary of Experimental Research on the Effects of Evidence in Persuasive Communication," *Quarterly Journal of Speech*, 55 (1969), 169–76.

54. James C. McCroskey, "The Effects of Evidence as an Inhibitor of Counterpersuasion," *Speech Monographs*, 37 (1970), 188–94; conclusion 3 from McCroskey, "Summary of Experimental Research," 175.

55. James J. Bradac, Catherine W. Konsky, and Robert A. Davies, "Two Studies of the Effects of Linguistic Diversity Upon the Judgments of Communicator Attributes and Message Effectiveness," *Communication Monographs*, 43 (March 1976), 70–79. See also J. J. Bradac, R. A. Davies, J. A. Courtright, R. J. Desmond and J. I. Murdock, "Richness of Vocabulary: An Attributional Analysis," *Psychological Reports*, 41 (1977), 1131–34.

56. Eldon E. Baker, "The Immediate Effects of Perceived Speaker Disorganization on Speaker Credibility and Audience-Attitude Change in Persuasive Speaking," *Western Speech*, 29 (1965), 148–61; and Gerald R. Miller and Murray A. Hewgill, "The Effect of Variations in Nonfluency on Audience Ratings of Source Credibility," *Quarterly Journal of Speech*, 50 (1964), 36–44. See also Anthony Mulac, "Evaluation of the Speech Dialect Attitudinal Scale," *Speech Monographs*, 42 (1975), 184–89; and Tamara Carbone, "Stylistic Variables as Related to Source Credibility: A Content Analysis Approach," *Speech Monographs*, 42 (1975), 99–106.

57. See H. C. Triandis, W. D. Loh, and L. A. Levin, "Race, Status, Quality of Spoken English and Opinions About Civil Rights as Determinants of Interpersonal Attitudes," *Journal of Personality and Social Psychology*, 3 (1966), 468–72.

58. James D. Moe, "Listener Judgments of Status Cues in Speech: A Replication and Extension," *Speech Monographs*, 39 (1972), 144–47. See also William Goldman and Philip Lewis, "Beautiful Is Good: Evidence That the Physically Attractive Are More Socially Skillful," *Journal of Experimental Social Psychology*, 13 (1977), 125–30.

59. See Richard L. Street and Robert M. Brady, "Speech Rate Acceptance Ranges as a Function of Evaluative Domain, Listener Speech Rate, and Communication Context," *Communication Monographs*, 49 (December 1982), 290–308.

60. Robert A. Bell and John A. Daly, "The Affinity-Seeking Function of Communication," *Communication Monographs*, 51 (June 1984), 96–97.

61. M. Argyle, *Bodily Communication* (New York: International Universities Press, 1975). See also M. Argyle, *The Psychology of Interpersonal Behavior*, 2nd ed. (New York: Penguin Books, 1972), p. 47.

62. Albert Mehrabian, *Nonverbal Communication* (Chicago: Aldine-Atherton, 1972), p. 182.

63. Timothy G. Hegstrom, "Message Impact: What Percentage Is Nonverbal?" *Western Journal of Speech Communication*, 43, no. 2 (Spring 1979), 134–42.

64. William Kloman, "E. T. Hall and the Human Space Bubble," *Horizon*, 9 (Autumn 1967), 43.

65. Frances S. Dubner, "Nonverbal Aspects of Black English," *Southern Communication Journal*, 37, no. 4 (Summer 1972), 366.

66. Marianne LaFrance and Clara Mayo, "A Review of Nonverbal Behaviors of Women and Men," *Western Journal of Speech Communication*, 43, no. 2 (Spring 1979), 96–107.

67. Robert Rosenthal and others, "Body Talk and Tone of Voice—the Language without Words," *Psychology Today*, September 1974, pp. 64–68.

68. Watzlawick, Beavin, and Jackson, *Pragmatics*, p. 62.

69. Ibid., p. 62.

70. John E. Baird Jr., "Some Nonverbal Elements of Leadership Emergence," *Southern Speech Communication Journal*, 42 (1977), 352–61.

71. E. T. Hall, *The Silent Language* (New York: Doubleday, 1973), pp. 208–9.

72. J. J. Edney and M. J. Grundmann, "Friendship, Group Size, and Boundary Size: Small Group Spaces," *Small Group Behavior*, 10 (1979), 124–35.

73. M. Dosey and M. Meisels, "Personal Space and Self-protection," *Journal of Personality and Social Psychology*, 11 (1969), 93–97.

74. M. Giesen and H. A. McClaren, "Discussion, Distance, and Sex: Changes in Impressions and Attraction During Small Group Interaction," *Sociometry*, 39 (1976), 60–70.

75. G. W. Evans and R. B. Howard, "Personal Space," *Psychological Bulletin*, 80 (1973), 334–44.

76. M. Argyle and J. Dean, "Eye-contact, Distance, and Affiliation," *Sociometry*, 28 (1965), 289–304.

77. M. L. Patterson, "Compensation in Nonverbal Immediacy Behaviors: A Review," *Sociometry*, 36 (1973), 237–52.

78. S. Saegart, "High-density Environments: Their Personal and Social Consequences," in *Human Response to Crowding*, eds. A. Baum and Y. M. Epstein (Hillsdale, N. J.: Erlbaum, 1978).

79. R. G. Barker, "Ecology and Motivation," in *Nebraska Symposium on Motivation*, Vol. 8 ed. M. R. Jones (Lincoln: University of Nebraska Press, 1960). Also see Barker, *Ecological Psychology: Concepts and Methods for Studying the Environment of Human Behavior* (Stanford, Calif.: Stanford University Press, 1968).

80. A. W. Wicker, S. L. Kirmeyer, L. Hanson, and D. Alexander, "Effects of Manning Levels on Subjective Experiences, Performance, and Verbal Interaction in Groups," *Organizational Behavior and Human Performance*, 17 (1976), 251–74.

81. A. W. Wicker, *An Introduction to Ecological Psychology* (Monterey, Calif.: Brooks/Cole, 1979), pp. 145–46.

82. Mark L. Knapp, *Essentials of Nonverbal Communication* (New York: Holt, Rinehart & Winston, 1980), p. 133.

83. Robert Sommer, "Further Studies of Small Group Ecology," *Sociometry*, 28 (1965), 337–48.

84. Bernard Steinzor, "The Spatial Factor in Face to Face Discussion Groups," *Journal of Abnormal and Social Psychology*, 36 (1950), 552–55.

85. G. Hearn, "Leadership and the Spatial Factor in Small Groups," *Journal of Abnormal and Social Psychology*, 54 (1957), 269–72.

86. *Detroit Free Press*, July 20, 1980, p. 2.

87. J. Mills and E. Aronson, "Opinion Change as a Function of the Communicator's Attractiveness and Desire to Influence," *Journal of Personality and Social Psychology*, 1 (1965), 73–77. See also R. N. Widgery and B. Webster, "The Effects of Physical Attractiveness upon Perceived Initial Credibility," *Michigan Speech Journal*, 4 (1969), 4–15.

88. Knapp, *Essentials of Nonverbal Communication*, pp. 113–19.

89. For more on cultural differences see Hall, *The Silent Language*.

90. Paul Ekman and Wallace V. Friesen, *Unmasking the Face* (Englewood Cliffs, N.J.: Prentice-Hall, 1975), p. 23.

91. Herbert W. Simons, "Chronicle and Critique of a Conference," (The Rhetoric of the Human Sciences), *Quarterly Journal of Speech*, 71 (1985), 55.

92. For an excellent discussion of conversational skills see Alan Garner, *Conversationally Speaking* (New York: McGraw-Hill, 1981).

93. Garner, *Conversationally Speaking*, pp. 47–49.

94. June Brown, "10 Jobs Await Applicants Who Really Care," *The Detroit News*, a Gannett newspaper, May 24, 1981, B. 9.

8

LEADERSHIP

SOURCES OF POWER

Consider the organizational setting shown in the TV series *L.A. Law*. Who has power in their frequent group meetings? Where or how did they get it? Does their power sometimes change? How and when is it used? The program is about a small but very successful law firm in Los Angeles. For those unfamiliar with positional designations in a law firm, *partner* translates into owner and an *associate* is a new lawyer in the firm seeking partner status. That effort takes seven to twelve years. For story-line reasons some cast members are specifically identified as Jewish, Hispanic, black, and retarded. The cast follows:

1. *Leland* (Richard Dysart). Senior partner and remaining cofounder of the law firm. His name is on the door. *Pater familius*. General and corporate law.
2. *Douglas* (Alan Rachins). Full law partner; the firm's business manager; son of the deceased co-founder. General and criminal law.
3. *Mike* (Harry Hamlin). Full law partner; the firm's most successful trial lawyer with a wide range of legal specialties.
4. *Arnie* (Corbin Bernsen). Full law partner; one of the best divorce lawyers in Los Angeles.
5. *Stewart* (Michael Tucker). Newly elected junior law partner; tax, bankruptcy, and estate planning law; recently married to Ann, new law partner. Jewish.
6. *Ann* (Jill Eikenberry). New junior partner; wife of Stewart; criminal and general law.
7. *Victor* (Jimmy Smits). Third newest associate; trial lawyer; personal injury law. Hispanic.
8. *Abby* (Michele Green). Second newest associate, recently promoted from temporary status; assistant to Ann; criminal and general law.

9. *Jonathan* (Blair Underwood). Newest associate of firm; recent Harvard Law graduate; assistant to Arnie; divorce and personal injury law; aggressive; highest starting salary. Black.

SUPPORT CAST

1. *Roxanne* (Susan Ruttan). Arnie's legal secretary; started in firm at age 19, now in early thirties.
2. *Grace* (Susan Dey). Not a member of the firm; assistant district attorney; Mike's love interest.
3. *Bennie* (Larry Drake). Office gopher; mid-thirties. Retarded.
4. Law clerks, students, interns as needed.

ORGANIZATIONAL POSITION POWER

Douglas, the firm's business manager, opens the meeting, makes announcements, chides people on expenses, and then follows any report that suggests things are confused or not going well. Douglas has a special right to procedural and management leadership by reason of his *position*. If the meeting is proceeding poorly due to unreasonable behavior by Douglas, Leland, the founder and *pater familius*, may exercise his considerable position power. "Enough criticism, Douglas, move on to the next case." This is also referred to as *legitimate* power. It is also clear that partners have more position power than nonpartners.

INFORMATION POWER

If the discussion turns to a particularly sticky divorce case involving a wealthy, long-time client, Arnie has the information power, that is the expertise and competence, and may become the task or content leader. Since Leland knows the client as a long-time, personal friend, he also has information power. If the topic under consideration were a tax case, then Stewart, the tax expert, has special power and no little leadership responsibility. Information power is sometimes abused by withholding it for personal gain.

The secret of business is to know something nobody else knows.

Aristotle Onassis

EXPERIENCE POWER

These sources of power are not mutually exclusive. Clearly, experience may overlap information and position power. If, however, the agenda involves discussion of a discrimination case, and if a firm member has had both personal and legal experience in related matters, he or she may be called upon to exercise group leadership. It might be Victor, who is Hispanic; Jonathan, who is black; Stewart who is Jewish; and so on. It's like the battlefield replacement lieutenant who goes to the veteran combat sergeant for help and leadership. Seniority is not always the same as experience. In some organizational groups it is more closely related to position power.

COMMON GROUND POWER

All of the nine group members are lawyers. A nonlawyer joining the group would generally be at a disadvantage. However, the group commonality does not exist in sex, ethnic background, racial origin, and so on. Jonathan, the new, highly paid black lawyer, had to establish power through his considerable ability, not because he was black (one hopes) but because he was new and being paid more than other new firm members. One gains power as one is more clearly perceived and identified as one of the group. One may acquire leadership as one is perceived as an especially attractive or desirable group member. This has also been called *referent power*.

Within the firm there are common ground subgroups who exercise their power. The partners are an exclusive power group who vote on new partners, adjust salaries, and so on. There are also subgroups of law clerks, interns, and students who have common ground power within their own groups but little in terms of the firm's deliberations. These matters also relate to position power. Common ground power also frequently involves political power. Douglas, the procedural leader, is also the son of the firm's co-founder. He has a special linkage with Leland, the boss, and his father's friend.

COMMUNICATION SKILLS

These include one's ability to relate to others, to manage interpersonal conflicts between group members, to reason, to argue, and to generally coordinate the group with its decisions. One wishes that Douglas was better at his relational skills, but the group is used to his bluntness and senses that he is a good administrator, has position power, and that the group needs some reprimanding once in a while. What Douglas lacks in interpersonal skills he makes up for in task coordination and procedural leadership. A group member truly capable in all of the communicational and relational skills is a real asset to any group and usually wields considerable power. This person is often a candidate for more positional power.

LEADERSHIP AND LEADERS

The five sources of power just discussed do not stand alone nor are they the only possible power sources. Furthermore, they change over time. Power generally translates into influence and *leadership*, not necessarily into the position of *leader*.

In general, *leadership* should be thought of as any significant action by any member that influences group achievement. Your group may have an assigned leader whose duties may range from a modest regulation of participation to near domination and control. It is possible to be in a leaderless group (that is with no appointed leader) and still have considerable leadership should this leadership emerge in some way from the group. By the same token, one could be in a group with a poor assigned leader; if no good leader(s) emerged, this group would really have no leadership. The distinction, therefore, between leader and leadership and leaderless and leadershipless is a critical one. All group members have a stake and often a part in leadership. Thus, these matters apply to all group discussants, whether they happen to be assigned group leader, chairperson, moderator, or whatever.

We can define a *positional leader* then as someone in a legitimate role position who influences and directs others in conformance with their expectations for that role. It usually takes time and effort to earn respect and appropriate role expectations, especially when new situations arise.

Other communication-related sources of power and leadership are suggested by Marvin Shaw in an excellent summary of the research in the field of group dynamics. He calls these deductions "Hypotheses About Leadership."[1]

HYPOTHESES ABOUT LEADERSHIP

1. Persons who actively participate in the group are more likely to attain a position of leadership than those who participate less in the group's activities.
2. Possession of task-related abilities and skills enhances attainment of a position of leadership.
3. Emergent leaders tend to behave in a more authoritarian manner than elected or appointed leaders.
4. The source of the leader's authority influences both the leader's behavior and the reactions of other group members.
5. Effective leaders are characterized by task-related abilities, sociability, and motivation to be a leader.
6. Democratic leadership results in greater member satisfaction than autocratic leadership.
7. Leaders tend to behave in a more authoritarian manner in stressful than in nonstressful situations.
8. The degree to which the leader is endorsed by group members depends upon the success of the group in achieving its goals.
9. A task-oriented leader is more effective when the group-task situation is either very favorable or very unfavorable for the leader, whereas a relationship-oriented leader is more effective when the group-task situation is only moderately favorable or unfavorable to the leader.

STYLES, ATTITUDES AND FUNCTIONS

One's style depends in large part on the kinds of power one has and of course the power of others in the group. It also depends on the organizational climate and how prescribed some group goals may be. However prescribed matters may be, your group is still essentially an open system. System variables beyond power and the immediate situation include organizational intentions, group expectations, political considerations, and member personalities.[2] First we will look at style variables attendant upon the larger organizational views of leadership. Then we will address leader style adaptations more closely related to small groups within these larger settings.

ORGANIZATIONAL LEADERSHIP

Style refers in part to method and in part to philosophy. Many times the style characteristics are preset by the system of organization in which one operates. For example, the Marine Corps drill instructor (D.I.) understands full well the autocratic style expectations of the Corps, and the recruits put up with this highly directive style because, after all, that was what they expected. If their role expectations for their D.I. were something less, they shouldn't have volunteered. Styles vary with organizational expectations or with situational expectations as well as with personal and receiver expectations. Styles of leadership are variously described as laissez-faire, nondirective, permissive, democratic, supervisory, authoritarian, and autocratic. These styles may be ordered on a control continuum as shown in Figure 8.1.

The Marine Corps in the previous illustration was the *organizational leadership* in the heading above, and their attitudes (policies, and so on) were represented by their (the Corps') role expectations for a D.I. A *leader* attitude is more personal and may or may not reflect the organization of which he or she is a part. Religious leaders tend to reflect their churches' role expectations, but not always. They sometimes reflect the role expectations of their parishioners, which may be different from the diocese or larger unit of which they are a part. Then again, a pastor may elect to go his or her own way apart from either, in which case the pastor is usually seeking a new career.

Our *L.A. Law* firm had no large, corporate leadership policy and practice with which they had to coordinate and conform. However, in one episode *L.A. Law* considered (as a group) the wisdom of joining a large, national law firm with offices in forty states. Each partner would receive a huge bonus should they agree to the takeover. They turned it down after lengthy discussion. The main reasons were disagreements with the highly authoritarian leadership and heavily ritualized procedures. The organizational climate and the style of organizational leadership were not to their liking. They liked their independent power roles. Even Douglas looked better.

The point being made is that the role one plays in leadership or as a designated

Figure 8.1 Styles of leadership.

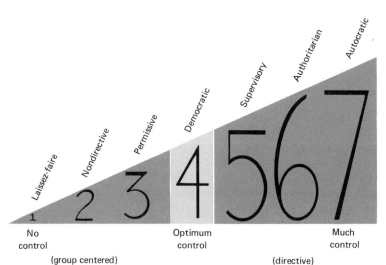

No control

(group centered)

Optimum control

Much control

(directive)

group leader is dependent to a large degree on all of these different organizational expectations.

Likert's Theory

Rensis Likert's research was mainly concerned with leadership in large organizations. The principles described are interesting and occasionally relevant to small-group, interpersonal influence. He suggests two basic kinds of operating characteristics in the organizational environment, namely authoritative and participative. These two are further divided into four specific leadership styles. They are charted as shown in Figure 8.2.

Research by Likert and his colleagues at the University of Michigan Institute for Social Research makes their case for "system 4," particularly where productivity is the dependent variable.[3] Systems 1 and 2 are thought to be more "job centered," and 3 and 4 more "employee centered."

As early as 1961 Likert wrote, "The trend in America, generally, in our schools, in our homes, and in our communities, is toward giving the individual greater freedom and initiative. There are fewer direct, unexplained orders in schools and homes, and youngsters are participating increasingly in decisions which affect them."[4]

In studies done by the Institute for Social Research (I.S.R.) the usual design was to take high-producing work groups and contrast them with matched low-producing groups. The groups and their leaders were then asked their attitudes in rather direct ways. They would be asked, for example, if they felt much job pressure or little, if they felt their supervisor was punitive or not when they had done a poor job, "On what basis do you judge your standing with your immediate supervisor?" and so on. The I.S.R. researched organizations such as the Prudential Insurance Company, General Electric, IBM, Lever Brothers, and many more.

A typical study is reported by Likert in which first-line supervisors who are "employee centered" have the best records of performance. In the high-producing groups six or seven supervisors were found to be "employee centered." In the low-producing groups seven out of ten supervisors were "job centered." The "system 4" supervisors " . . . focus their primary attention on the human aspects of their subordinate's problems and on endeavoring to build effective work groups with high performance goals."[5]

Likert concedes that supervisors must also have high production goals as well as what he calls a contagious enthusiasm for the importance of achieving these goals. When the pressure for performance becomes unreasonable, productivity falls off. After measuring attitudes toward "pressure" in thirty-one similar departments of an or-

Figure 8.2 Systems of organizations.

From Rensis Likert, The Human Organization: Its Management and Value *(New York: McGraw-Hill Book Co., 1967), p. 14.*

ORGANIZATION LEADERSHIP

Authoritative		Participative	
Exploitive Authoritative	Benevolent Authoritative	Consultative	Participative Group
1	2	3	4

ganization, the I.S.R. teams reported the interesting results shown in Figure 8.3. It was also reported in this data that unreasonable job-centered pressure is associated with a low level of confidence and trust in the supervisor. The implications for group leadership are interesting.

A study of clerical workers showed that a loose or "general" form of supervision will ordinarily yield better performance and productivity than "close" supervision. Nine out of ten supervisors in high-producing sections were under general supervision while eight out of twelve supervisors in low-producing sections were under close supervision. Similar results reportedly were found for nonsupervisory employees.[6]

Our experience in organizational research suggests that one should *expect less* pressure, *less* close supervision in units that are producing well, and expect *more* of everything in units that are performing poorly. With due respect, it may be that we have cases here in which correlations are indeed high, but not necessarily causal. An industrial psychologist, Victor Vroom, expresses similar concerns.

> It would be naive to think that group decision making is always more "effective" than autocratic decision making, or vice versa; the relative effectiveness of these two extreme methods depends both on the weights attached to quality, acceptance, and time variables and on differences in amounts of these outcomes resulting from these methods, neither of which is invariant from one situation to another. The critics and proponents of participation management would do well to direct their efforts toward identifying the properties of situations in which different decision-making approaches are effective rather than toward wholesale condemnation or deification of one approach.[7]

In any event, a good manager apparently provides an environment where a subordinate is clear on objectives and what needs to be accomplished and yet feels a freedom to do the job in his or her own way at his or her own pace. Low-producing supervisors tend to spend more time with subordinates, but the time is apparently spent on very specific, close supervision. Better supervisors apparently know when to ignore mistakes, letting experience be the teacher, or when to use mistakes as helpful training opportunities.

There is also evidence in the I.S.R. studies that a leader's skill and style in relating to his or her group through consistent, meaningful interpersonal and group communication is a significant aspect of influence and success. The greater a leader's skill, the greater the productivity and job satisfaction of his or her subordinates. "A supportive attitude . . . as well as the constructive use of group meetings, is necessary to develop group pride and loyalty."[8]

In terms of interpersonal influence, supervisors in a large utility were asked

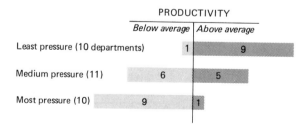

PRODUCTIVITY

	Below average	Above average
Least pressure (10 departments)	1	9
Medium pressure (11)	6	5
Most pressure (10)	9	1

Figure 8.3 Attitudes toward "pressure."

From Rensis Likert, New Patterns of Management *(New York: McGraw-Hill Book Co., 1961; Garland, 1987), p. 8.*

the basis on which they judged their ''standing'' with their immediate supervisor. Their answers were as follows.[9]

BASIS FOR JUDGMENT	PERCENT CHECKED "YES"
1. From the amount of responsibility and authority he gives me.	74%
2. He asks my opinion frequently.	58%
3. Because I still work for him.	58%
4. I infer it from lack of criticism.	58%
5. From the number of raises I received.	46%
6. He tells me where I stand.	42%
7. From the number of promotions I received.	25%
8. No real basis.	6%

In sum, the supervisors determined their ''standings'' with the bosses primarily in terms of how much responsibility and authority they were given, how often their opinion was sought, and to a lesser extent, on the number of raises and promotions received. In trying to integrate these various employee-centered findings, Likert suggests a principle of *supportive relationships*.

> The leadership and other processes of the organization must be such as to ensure a maximum probability that in all interactions and all relationships with the organization each member will, in the light of his background, values, and expectations, view the experience as supportive and one which builds and maintains his sense of personal worth and importance.[10]

McGregor's Theory

In Douglas McGregor's view the attitudes leaders hold toward and about the cosmos or universe, the nature of man, and the nature of influence and communication are the basic determinants of personal style and role expectations. For McGregor these attitudes worked like a self-fulfilling prophecy in influencing groups, organizations, and the behavior of the people in them. By cosmology McGregor meant a person's fundamental concept of cause and effect, of physical and social reality, of one's ability to bring some semblance of order to life's experience: '' . . . at a deeper level, his beliefs, however implicit, concerning 'the meaning of it all.' ''[11]

For McGregor the nature of man was ''rational-emotive.'' To self-actualize one must recognize and come to terms with one's emotional and human side. He felt the rational and emotional were inextricably interwoven: '' . . . it is an illusion to believe that they can be separated.''[12] Organizations concentrate on the rational side and try to ignore or avoid the emotional influences. For McGregor human loyalty, enthusiasm, drive, commitment, acceptance of responsibility, and self-confidence are all emotional variables. ''Motivation is an *emotional* force . . . if a human being existed who was completely unemotional, objective, and logical, he would by definition have no *interest* in the success of any organization.''[13]

In all of his writing McGregor was most concerned with *integration*, by which he meant a creative invention of how the individual and the group come to terms with each other regarding power and influence. Influence, persuasion, and interpersonal communication to be effective must be "transactional." They must possess a high degree of mutuality: ". . . influence in any form is a two-way process."[14] Effective communication is interactional in influence.

To dramatize the importance of managerial cosmologies or attitudes toward people and organizational life, McGregor postulated two now famous hypothetical theories, *Theory X* and *Theory Y*.

Theory X   McGregor postulated three principles of what he considered a traditional and not uncommon view of organizational direction and control.

1. The average human being has an inherent dislike of work and will avoid it if he can.
2. Because of this human characteristic of dislike of work, most people must be coerced, controlled, directed, threatened with punishment to get them to put forth adequate effort toward the achievement of organizational objectives.
3. The average human being prefers to be directed, wishes to avoid responsibility, has relatively little ambition, wants security above all.[15]

It is McGregor's opinion that as long as these assumptions pertain, leadership will never fully assist in motivating the average human being.

Theory Y   In this theory McGregor postulates six assumptions that he describes as dynamic rather than static. In his view these are the appropriate assumptions if leadership is to be maximally motivating.

1. *The expenditure of physical and mental effort in work is as natural as play or rest.* The average human being does not inherently dislike work. Depending upon controllable conditions, work may be a source of satisfaction (and will be voluntarily performed) or a source of punishment (and will be avoided if possible).
2. *External control and the threat of punishment are not the only means for bringing about effort toward organizational objectives.* Man will exercise self-direction and self-control in the service of objectives to which he is committed.
3. *Commitment to objectives is a function of the rewards associated with their achievement.* The most significant of such rewards, e.g., the satisfaction of ego and self-actualization needs, can be direct products of effort directed toward organizational objectives.
4. *The average human being learns, under proper conditions, not only to accept but also to seek responsibility.* Avoidance of responsibility, lack of ambition, and emphasis on security are generally consequences of experience, not inherent human characteristics.
5. *The capacity to exercise a relatively high degree of imagination, ingenuity, and creativity in the solution of organizational problems is widely, not narrowly, distributed in the population.*
6. *Under the conditions of modern industrial life, the intellectual potentialities of the average human being are only partially utilized.*[16]

According to McGregor, Theory X offers easy rationalization for poor leadership. It leads to an overemphasis on *telling* people what to do (directing) and seeing that they have done it (controlling). If things go poorly, it is because of the human resources. Theory X assumes people must be made to do what is necessary for the success of the organization.

Theory Y puts a priority on human relationships, using control selectively. It stresses collaboration and leadership skill in achieving it. It seeks a climate that provides opportunities for group-related initiative, ingenuity, growth, and self-realization.

More than anything else, it seeks the principle of integration—that is, "... the creation of conditions such that the members of the organization can achieve their own goals *best* by directing their efforts toward the success of the enterprise."[17]

In review, the cornerstones of effective leadership and team effort in providing a motivating climate involve a mutual understanding and identification of goals, a flexible structure, a system of mutual trust and support, and, above all, a system of open, but prudent transactional communication. McGregor had an antipathy toward one-way communication programs.

McGregor's assumptions are paraphrased in Figure 8.7 page 270. The control chart attempts to show how his style suggestions compare to others.

Theory Z

In Chapter 1 we discussed William Ouchi and his notion that Japanese success is due to an extension of *Y* or "4" into a form of egalitarian, team-oriented, participatory management which he calls *Z*.[18] Cragan and Wright suggest that successful assimilation of individuals into an organization relates to their understanding of the prevailing management climate or culture.[19] They contrast *X*, *Y*, and *Z* across a dozen issues that organizational groups typically face. The four below help clarify the *Z* approach.

ISSUE	X	Y	Z
Group meetings	Meetings are held primarily for telling subordinates about management decisions and expectations.	Meetings are sometimes held to solicit information from workers for management decision making.	Participatory decision-making meetings are held that include management and workers.
Decision making	Decisions are made by those in charge.	Managers seek the advice of subordinates before making decisions.	Workers participate with managers in group decision making.
Quality control	Management is solely responsible for seeing that work is done correctly.	Management encourages workers to take responsibility for quality of their work.	The organization is quality-control conscious through the use of QC groups.
Attitude ("corporate hero")	Manager is assertive and task oriented (has task skills).	Manager is friendly, compassionate, and understanding (has people skills).	Manager is open minded and committed to participatory management (has group skills).

Behavioral Style Typologies

One interesting study of organizational leaders in a *Residence Life Program* at a major university identified four behavioral patterns used by these leaders.[20] Some of the nineteen leaders studied used mostly one pattern; others varied their use of patterns. The conclusion was that organizational demands, role definitions, and evaluations influenced leader behavior. Also note that these leaders spent 60 percent of their time working with subordinates, almost half of that time in small groups.

The behavior patterns or types identified are as follows:

TABLE 8.1 Summary of Behavioral Patterns of Bureaucratic Organizational Leaders

POSITIONAL LEADER	The central features of the activity of positional leaders were the evident concern for control and establishing of well-defined procedures, structures, and guidelines. Relationships with subordinates were highly rule- and role-bound. There was a high degree of centralization and limited participation by subordinates in decision making and other leadership processes. The power of the position was a major source for control, and the attainment of organizational goals. Relationships with subordinates was characterized by impersonalness and task-relatedness. Communication tended to be position-centered.
POLITICAL LEADER	The central features of the activity of political leaders were the evident concern for control and the highly personal nature of the relationships established with subordinates. There was a high degree of centralization and limited participation by subordinates in decision-making and other leadership processes. Control was exercised through the interpersonal relationships established. Both power and influence were used in combination to achieve high control and the attainment of goals. Communication tended to be both position and person-centered.
ADMINISTRATIVE LEADER	The central features of the activity of administrative leaders were the evident concern for establishing well-defined procedures, structures, and guidelines and the decentralization of decision-making and other leadership processes. There was a high degree of participation by subordinates in the leadership process. Relationships with subordinates tended to be task-related but not impersonal. Personal influence was the primary source for control and the attainment of goals, although the power of the position was used when deemed necessary. Communication tended to be both person and position-centered.
RELATIONAL LEADER	The central features of the activity of relational leaders were the evident concern for establishing personal relationships with subordinates and the decentralization of decision-making and other leadership processes. There was a high degree of participation by subordinates in the leadership process. Relationships with subordinates tended to be highly personal and not necessarily task-related. Personal influence was the major source for control and goal achievement; the power of the position was used rarely. Communication tended to be person-oriented.

V. H. Vroom and P. W. Yetton offer another interesting classification of five leadership methods ranging across three basic leadership styles: *autocratic*, *consultative*, and *group*. In the group style the members have the greatest amount of influence.

LEADERSHIP METHODS[21]

1. *Autocratic I*   The leader makes the decision using information available at that time.

2. *Autocratic II*   Group members provide only information rather than generating or evaluating alternative solutions. The leader then makes the decision.

3. *Consultative I*   The leader shares the problem with group members individually, getting their suggestions without bringing them together as a group. Then the leader makes the decision independently.

4. *Consultative II*   The leader shares the problem with the members as a group obtaining their ideas and suggestions. Then the leader makes the decision, which may or may not reflect the group input.

5. *Group*   The leader and members as a group generate and evaluate alternatives and attempt to reach consensus on a solution. The leader is willing to accept and implement any solution that is supported by the group.

Vroom and Yetton offer seven organizational *rules* designed to protect the quality and acceptance of decisions and to help a leader decide which method to use.[22]

1. *The information rule.* Don't make any unilateral decisions if you are short on information or expertise.
2. *The trust rule.* Eliminate the group method if the decision is critical and the group cannot be trusted to protect larger organizational goals.
3. *The unstructured problem rule.* Go to the group or consultative group method for information and structure.
4. *The acceptance rule.* If group acceptance and group implementation are critical, go to the more democratic group methods.
5. *The conflict rule.* When members are apt to be in conflict and an autocratic decision may not be readily accepted, go to the more democratic group methods.
6. *The fairness rule.* When commitment and acceptance are critical and quality of decision is less so, let the group decide as fairly as possible.

Figure 8.4   Matching leadership style to stages of the product life cycle.

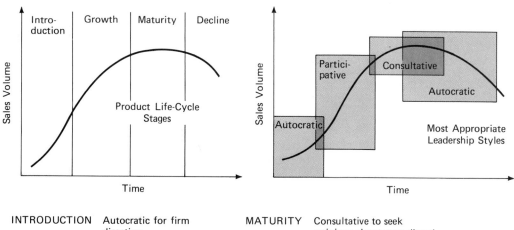

| INTRODUCTION | Autocratic for firm direction | MATURITY | Consultative to seek opinions about new directions |
| GROWTH | Participative to exploit market opportunities | DECLINE | Autocratic to exert maximum control |

7. *The acceptance priority rule*. When acceptance is critical and not assured by autocratic decisions, and if subordinates can be trusted, use the "equal partnership" group method.

More recently Lester Bittel observed that these decisions and resulting styles are often related to the life cycle of a company's main product line. He recommends the following leadership styles using "participative" instead of "group."[23] (See Figure 8.4.)

SMALL-GROUP LEADERSHIP

Contingency Theories

A Leadership Role Dilemma   "Prepare to come about! OK crew, let's do it—I want everybody on the starboard side [pointing] NOW!" "Oh come off it, Uncle Jim. What's with the Captain Bligh?" responded John, a 13-year-old landlubber. Fortunately the air was light and the maneuver was well executed—this time. Was Uncle Jim's style of leadership too directive for his crew of two children and their parents? Were the group's expectations (John was representative) for Uncle Jim's captain role wrong?

These are not easy questions; a lot depends upon the situation. A sturdy keel boat on an oversized pond would probably condition your answers one way; a nineteen-foot *Lightning* with a centerboard on a thirty-mile bay of Lake Michigan perhaps another. The scene is the latter. The air was light at first. Five miles out it became a stiff fifteen-to twenty-mile-an-hour wind. The green crew sensed that things were a little more urgent now; so did Uncle Jim. "Look, people, since I'm the only one who knows rough water sailing, you're going to have to follow directions or we're apt to have problems. John, please put on your life jacket." Uncle Jim's style is different now; so is the situation. Perhaps this latter style would have been better at the start.

The crew is also part of the situation. The young boys were Uncle Jim's nephews; their father was his brother-in-law. Jim explained later that his crew orientation had been nonexistent because his brother-in-law had resisted such explanations, stating he'd been on boats before—but not like this one, we discover later. Here in one sense was a tough leadership role. Jim didn't want to insult his brother-in-law, yet he had a tremendous situational responsibility for the lives of all aboard. One's personal relations are a critical part of leadership. So, too, is the task at hand or the potential task in this case. Uncle Jim didn't have any real or legitimate power such as a captain on a coast guard cutter would have. However, it was his boat . . .

"Prepare to come about. Keep your heads down—coming about! John, get down!" Too late, for the boom took Johnny overboard, but the life jacket kept the dazed youngster afloat. Uncle Jim threw the coiled spring line at him, secured the end, and commanded, "Hang on!" The boat had come about and the heavy air filled the sails. John held on with a tenacity born of panic. His white-faced father slowly pulled him toward the hard-charging *Lightning*. Uncle Jim tied the tiller and dropped the jib. The boat slowed; to come about was to capsize. John was pulled aboard, and a silent crew headed briskly home on the mainsail. They did what they were told to do. Uncle Jim had no more role dilemma. In the future, he resolved, there would be crew orientation and there would be acceptance of the leader's role or there would be no sailing. We don't always have Uncle Jim's options.

According to Fred Fiedler, prime mover toward this highly regarded contingency model of leadership, there are three basic components in any relationship that give a person control and influence: (1) personal relationships, (2) task structure, and (3) position power.[24]

For Fiedler the *relationship* factor is the most important, whether for a work group or a sailing crew. Do they like you? Will they trust your judgment? Can you rely on their support and understanding? Do they perceive you as "a good man speaking well"? Do these judgments and perceptions cross different situations? Leland, the *pater familius* of *L.A. Law*, had that kind of respect, and it did indeed turn out to be critical to the fortunes of his group. Uncle Jim apparently never had it from the start, or was the situation so novel that it overrode any personal regard or ethical proof he may have had?

The *task structure*, according to Fiedler, has to do with " . . . the degree to which the goal is clearly defined, the degree to which there is only one way of doing a task, or the degree to which you can clearly specify how something is to be accomplished."[25]

Uncle Jim thought he had a rather unstructured task—"laze around the bay in light air." The structured part of sailing he could handle himself in light winds. When times become urgent the sailor's task becomes highly structured, and there aren't too many options. Evaluation of success is quick and clear. Task structure became a critical contingency in Uncle Jim's leadership style.

Position power is one of the power sources we discussed at the opening of this chapter. The coast guard captain has great position power. His crew has appropriate role expectations, and he has considerable authority because of his position. Uncle Jim could not hire, fire, or discipline his crew in the same way that the coast guard captain could. When we are in situations more like Uncle Jim's, we have much greater need of persuasion theory.[26]

Situational Contingencies   Life is easier for leaders, according to Fiedler, when a person has this positive regard from his or her group; when the task is clear, steady, and highly structured; and when his or her power is based on knowledge, expertise, and/or legitimate authority that is made clear.

Favorable and Unfavorable Situations   Whether a leader should be group centered or directive is then contingent upon all of the matters discussed above. Interestingly, Fiedler's research suggests that a more directive leader performs best when the three influence factors (relations, task structure, position power) are most favorable and also when they are least favorable.[27] The more permissive, nondirective leader was found to perform best under more status-quo conditions—when the bay is calm; when the war is over.

One's interpersonal effectiveness is for Fiedler a critical key to influence and leadership.

The personal relationship between the leader and key members of his group is probably the most important, single determinant of group processes which affect team performance. The liked and respected leader does not need formal power, and he can obtain compliance from his group under circumstances which, in the case of a disliked or distrusted leader, would result in open revolt. As has been shown [e.g., Godfrey *et al.*, 1959; Fiedler, 1961], the liked and accepted leader's interpersonal attitudes influence group performance to a significantly greater degree than similar attitudes of a leader who is sociometrically not accepted by his group.[28]

Another contingency or situational notion of leadership is offered by Paul Hersey and Kenneth Blanchard.[29] They suggest that an effective group leader should vary his or her style and behavior depending on the *maturity* of the followers. Maturity is not based on some personality variable but rather on (1) a group's *ability* or readiness for the task at hand and (2) the members' *willingness* or motivation to actually do it.

After maturity is determined one can draw upon four theoretical styles of leadership. These styles have been diagrammed as shown in Figure 8.5. The appropriate style should include the right combination of direction (task) and support (relationship) behavior.

A group *unable* and *unwilling* to get on with the task assigned is considered low in maturity. Whether that state is due to insecurity, incompetence, or inexperience, a highly directive, **telling** style is recommended.

A group willing but for some reason unable to achieve a task is in need of direction but of a more persuasive kind, which Hersey and Blanchard call **selling**.

A group that is able but unwilling to do what they have been charged to do needs still more persuasion or motivation. In this view such a state is best achieved through participation or **participating**.

When a group has high maturity, that is, it is *able*, *willing* and *confident*, the appropriate leader behavior is to let them alone. Responsibility for the task is delegated, the **delegating** style.

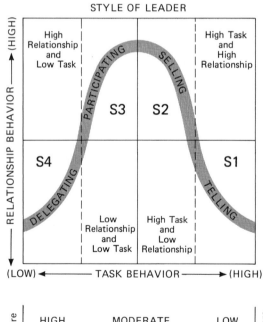

Figure 8.5 Situational leadership.

P. Hersey/K. Blanchard, Management of Organizational Behavior: Utilizing Human Resources, *4th edition,* © *1982, p. 152. Reprinted by permission of Prentice Hall, Englewood Cliffs, N.J. 07632.*

Functional Responsibilities

If your perceived leadership role does not happen to agree with most of your receivers' expectations, you may not exert much influence. In relatively informal, short-lived groups such as committees or subcommittees it usually helps all concerned as well as the emergent or assigned leader if there is some concordance about role expectations. If your role is strictly procedural and a random appointment, you may emerge as a very forceful type, but not many will be expecting that of you. If, on the other hand, you have been hand picked because of your experience and expertise, you can look for different role expectations. However, not always! Sometimes that fact is not known to the members, and sometimes they don't bother to do their homework. Interpersonal influence may call for role explanation and role assertiveness in these situations. You may risk some embarrassment in the doing, but to not do it is to risk charges of interpersonal entrapment or the embarrassment of others. "Why didn't you tell me you were a brain surgeon before I criticized high-risk medicine?" "You mean the guy (who just left) is a vice-president at Ford?" (after totally castigating the whole organization).

When people agree on position descriptions (chairperson, president, supervisor, professor), they may not agree on their role expectations. There is even antipathy toward formal leadership on the part of some; but such behavior is predictable if in your search for concordance that role expectation appears. To complicate things further, people change; roles and their expectations change. Many years ago professors wore their caps and gowns to class. Very general and pragmatic role expectations for the position of *leader* are essentially the same as the functions of *leadership* (the responsibility of all group members). In organizational settings most leaders are designated and they are specially charged to achieve the functions that follow (see Figure 8.6).

Goal Achievement or Systematic Efforts Toward the Task at Hand
Expected are elements of leadership related primarily to content, including things such as contributing and evaluating ideas, locating issues and consensus, synthesizing, cross-relating the ideas of others, and generally seeking specific contributions toward a goal. The lessons of Chapters 3 and 4 pertain here: risky shifts, groupthink, problem solving, and decision making. Depending upon the group mission, the task leader may also be expected to represent the group to others and to shoulder much of the blame when things don't go well.

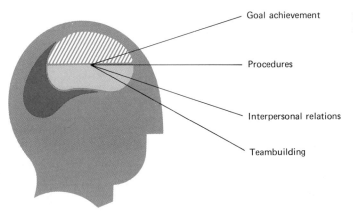

Goal achievement

Procedures

Interpersonal relations

Teambuilding

Figure 8.6 General functions of designated leaders.

Procedures   Procedural functions, such as starting the meeting, drafting and/or following an agenda, ending the meeting, and so forth, are also role expectations in the more formal interactions. These have also been called group maintenance functions. If you're planning a program of meetings, the Xerox Corporation procedural checklist may be helpful.

Three to four weeks before the meeting:

- Set date and time.
- Reserve location for meeting.
- Prepare list of attendees; mail invitations and forms for presubmitted questions.
- Order refreshments.
- Arrange for audiovisual material and/or signs, if required.

Two weeks before meeting:

- Collect presubmitted questions and route for answering.

One week before meeting:

- Prepare copies of presubmitted questions to distribute at meeting.
- Place agenda, any prepared remarks, and questions and answers in a three-ring binder and give to the speaker three days before the meeting.
- Confirm arrangements for meeting room and refreshments.

Day before the meeting:

- Get supplies ready: meeting questions, critiques, sharpened pencils, pads, ashtrays, and so forth.

Day of the meeting:

- Take supplies to the meeting at least one hour before it begins.
- Check that refreshments are ready.
- Distribute presubmitted questions before meeting; mail critiques to attendees immediately after meeting.

Within two weeks after the meeting:

- Tabulate and analyze critiques.

By permission of Xerox Corporation[30]

The communication rules and practices discussed in Chapter 5 pertain here.

Interpersonal Relations   This aspect of the leader's role involves setting psychological climate, coordinating meaning, resolving conflict, controlling emotions, regulating turn taking, and generally promoting social interaction. These are the topical areas of Chapters 5, 6, and 7.

Some rules and suggestions overlap the procedural and interpersonal functions. In one General Motors' program of small group meetings ("Number 1 Team"), a list of do's and don'ts was drawn up for assigned leaders.

DO:

1. Encourage free discussion on the general subject of our industry and what we can do individually and collectively to improve our position.

2. Maintain just enough control of sessions so that each person has an opportunity to express his or her views if they choose.

3. Let the conferees know that these meetings are for the purpose of establishing better communications and understanding among the members of the department, supervision and service personnel.

4. Approach the sessions with the idea that nothing concrete in the way of specific job improvements is expected or required to result from the employees' comments. Primarily interested in feedback to plan future programs based on employee needs and desires.

5. Limit the size to a comfortable number—5 to 7, more if you can handle them.

6. Select groups of employees in your department that work together as units. Analyze your group rather than scheduling by convenience.

7. Be firm, but not overbearing if company policy is called into question.

8. Follow up on any specific requests for information made by an individual—seek help from No. 1 Team Coordinator when you cannot accomplish on your own.

9. After several sessions, try to analyze discussions for common interests—any desire on part of employees to correct or change a condition that exists.

DON'T:

1. Don't try to hold a controlled formal meeting with opening speech or lecture, but be prepared to start the discussion by requesting employees' ideas on how we can plan future programs that will be mutually beneficial.

2. Don't argue or take sides during a discussion on controversial issues—don't ridicule others' opinions.

3. Don't assume a superior or condescending attitude toward the group—you are part of it.

4. Don't make general policy statements if you are not positive that you are correct.

5. Don't allow any one member to monopolize the discussion—including yourself.

6. Don't assign values to the meetings either positive or negative—"These meetings will solve our problems" or "I don't know why we're here—let's have coffee and get back to work." Until some discernible pattern evolves, treat initial meetings as rap sessions.

7. Don't take a "stab" at answers to questions that may come up—write them down and get the correct answers later.

8. Don't have such loose control that the meeting resembles a small mob.

By permission of General Motors Corporation[31]

Teambuilding This involves group unity and coordination of members' activities. It is the practical application of systems theory. The notion is catching on in our largest industries. Pre-1986 American cars were typically designed sequentially.

First, appearance was decided by marketing and the stylists. Engineers then adapted their efforts to fit into the design; manufacturing then tried to accommodate the engineers; and, finally, service was handed the problem of repair. With this separate effort approach, it is no wonder that we had design and engineering dilemmas such as spark plugs that were all but impossible to reach for replacement.

Ford Motor Company went to the systems approach with the Taurus–Sable project and established a *team* representing styling, engineering, manufacturing, marketing, and service to assure coordination. This group (team) or any member could delay the project should he or she detect a design flaw.[32] "You've made the fuse panel inaccessible." "The spare will have to go on the roof." "There's no room for the rear seat in the rear wheel drive model." The teamwork seems to be paying off as Taurus–Sable become hot sellers.

In the new General Motors plant at Van Nuys, California, a "team concept" has been installed that much resembles the quality circles discussed in Chapter 1. "'Workers Circles' composed of four to eight team members help solve problems, monitor product quality, and determine how the assembly line should run."[33] New innovations like this sometimes run afoul of past practices and union contracts. While national UAW leaders have endorsed such changes, some locals vigorously have not.

Any small group that seriously analyzes its procedures, seeks a coordinated interdependence, and works at establishing rapport through communication is practicing teambuilding. In the modern democratic world of work, it should be considered a leadership and a followership function and obligation. Chuck Kormanski and Andrew Mozenter[34] observed the following behaviors in effective team members:

- Understand and are committed to group goals.
- Are friendly, concerned, and interested in others.
- Acknowledge and confront conflict openly.
- Listen to others with understanding.
- Include others in the decision-making process.
- Recognize and respect individual differences.
- Contribute ideas and solutions.
- Value the ideas and contributions of others.
- Recognize and reward team efforts.
- Encourage and appreciate comments about team performance.

When a group has serious problems clarifying member duties, responsibilities, expectations—in short, *role* obligations—organizational development (OD) specialists may be asked to intervene. One such technique is called "Role Analysis Technique" (RAT), which uses structured meetings where all persons with the help of the group hammer out what is expected of them individually and what they should or should not expect of others. Each member leaves the program with a written summary of his or her team role.[35] Workshops and retreats have also been used for such role analysis, team spirit, and teambuilding efforts.

EPILOGUE

At the risk of undoing all of the systems theory advocated throughout this book, it does seem obvious that among leaders and followers there are some mostly *X* types and some mostly *Y* types in our workaday and social groups. Perhaps *X* types prefer more direction—"Don't confuse me with all the explanations. What the heck do you want done?" A direct order for a *Y* type might be an anathema—"Ye gods, I'm not a galley slave!" Perhaps, "We've got a problem in aisle two. Can you help untangle it?" Perhaps another reason both *X* and *Y* leaders appear to be successful is because they have a tendency to collect their own kind. The deviate simply moves on. *X*s seek out *X*s and *Y*s seek out *Y*s.

The Likert, McGregor, and Ouchi group-centered models are ideal or perhaps idealistic, but, as we have seen, they are not always the most appropriate style. Perhaps we have to play the contingencies and blend our styles as Fiedler would suggest. Or perhaps we should assess our power, the group's ability, experience, and willingness and then decide to tell, sell, involve, or let 'em alone, as Hersey and Blanchard tell us. The control chart (see Figure 8.7) shows *XY* and contingency at the bottom. It represents the notion that a leader, particularly in a more formal situation, has reason to be somewhat *X* in some situations and *Y* in others.

The important thing is to be aware of a range of leadership styles. Understand that one can be a consistent leader and still have a flexibility based on all of the contingencies just discussed. It is an adaptive process, according to Julia Wood, who argues that

> . . . effectiveness in leading is most probable when a leader is sufficiently perceptive to analyze the unique situation and the group members in relation to the goals for discussion and is able to employ appropriate behaviors in light of this analysis . . .
> . . . In order to assess "the forces that determine his most appropriate behavior," a leader must analyze group members and the situation. Understanding what members need, want, and expect from their work and their leader has direct bearing on a leader's ability to act effectively.[36]

Professor Wood capsulizes her adaptive approach to leading as follows:

> The focus, then, of the adaptive approach to leading is on (1) analyzing the unique group members and situation requiring leadership so that (2) the leader may adjust his or her personal behaviors or self-presentation to meet the requirements of the circumstances. A primary implication of the adaptive approach is that the behavioral strategies of an effective leader must *vary* according to the particular situation, task, and members with which he or she must deal.[37]

As with most general adaptation styles, virtue usually lies near the middle. Experience advises that a *democratic* style is generally superior to an absolute or nonresponsible style. However, in some groups in which *goal achievement* becomes unusually pressing, leadership should go up the scale if such an action can help. On the other hand, to achieve sincerely healthy *interpersonal relations*, particularly when emotions are strained or personalities are in conflict, the best strategy may be to go down the scale. In unusually hostile or confrontational groups, *a viable solution of the moment*, beyond style considerations, is all one can hope for.

The most practical leadership style for small groups in most organizational settings is probably a functional one. Concentrate on the task, procedures, interpersonal relations, and teambuilding. Power should be dealt with democratically but also real-

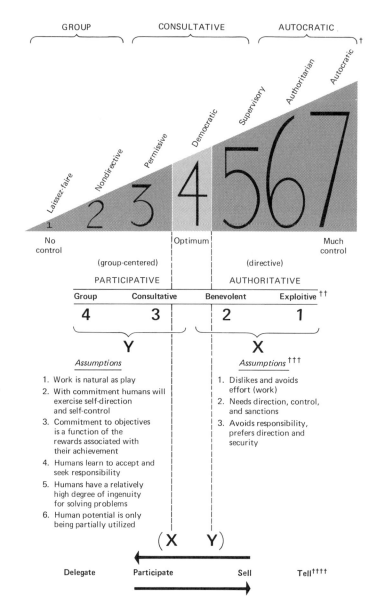

Figure 8.7 Control continuum.

†*V.H. Vroom and P.W. Yetton,* Leadership and Decision Making *(Pittsburgh: University of Pittsburgh Press, 1973); see also V.H. Vroom and A.G. Jago,* The New Leadership *(Englewood Cliffs, N.J.: Prentice Hall, 1988).*

††*Rensis Likert,* The Human Organization: Its Management and Value *(New York: McGraw-Hill Book Co., 1967).*

†††*Douglas McGregor,* The Human Side of Enterprise *(New York: McGraw-Hill Book Co., 1960).*

††††*Fred Fiedler and M.M. Chemers,* Improving Leadership Effectiveness: The Leader Match Concept *(New York: John Wiley & Sons, 1984); see also P. Hersey/K. Blanchard,* Management of Organizational Behavior: Utilizing Human Resources, *4th edition (Englewood Cliffs, N.J.: Prentice Hall, 1982).*

istically. The two newest able members of Ford Motor Company's Board of Directors did not make it on ability alone (Edsel Ford, 39, and William Ford, 30).

According to H. Lloyd Goodall, the best way to learn functional leadership skills is to develop analysis-type *questions* aimed at improving the responses made to others in group situations.[38] He suggests the following:

1. *What is the goal of my group?*
   —How does this goal relate to the organization's objectives?
   —Who will determine whether or not we have reached our goal?
   —Have I provided the group members with an adequate awareness of our goal and the tasks needed to accomplish them?
   —Are there any obstacles that may prevent us from reaching our goal?
   —What can be done to overcome these obstacles?
2. *What are the goals of the individual group members?*
   —How do these goals enhance our ability to attain the objective?
   —How might these personal goals conflict with our ability to attain the objective?
   —How can I be instrumental in overcoming these potential or real sources of conflict?
   —What factors outside of the immediate group setting may influence the statements or actions of my group members?
   —Are there hierarchical or territorial problems that may affect our discussions?
   —Are there interpersonal problems that may affect our discussions?
   —What can I do to help overcome these potential sources of difficulty?
3. *What are the patterns of influence generated by my group?*
   —Who says what to whom with what effect?
   —What are each member's sources of personal power?
   —How do these sources of power conflict? How may they be coordinated?
   —What is my authority with the group?
   —What are my sources of power within the group?
   —How do the individual group members perceive my authority and power? How do they respond to it?
4. *What are the equities and inequities within this group?*
   —What rewards are pursued by individuals in the group?
   —What punishments are meted out by or to individual group members?
   —What are my group's standards for apportioning resources among members?
   —Who regularly feels distress during group meetings? What is the source of the distress?
   —How can I be instrumental in alleviating the distress of group members?
5. *How effective are the agendas and procedures used by this group?*
   —Are group members well prepared for group meetings?
   —Do group members have an active role in shaping the agenda?
   —Do I provide adequate understanding of the uses of the agenda and procedures involved in making decisions and in solving problems?
   —What can be done to improve the efficiency of the group?
   —How can I be instrumental in improving the efficiency of the group?

A newsletter message from an anonymous school counselor entitled ''A Memorandum from Your Child'' perhaps offers the most poignant suggestions for those who would lead.

Don't spoil me . . . I know quite well that I ought not to have all that I ask for . . . I'm only testing you.

Don't be afraid to be firm with me. I prefer it . . . it lets me know where I stand.

Don't use force with me; it only teaches me that power is all that counts . . . I will respond more readily to being led.

Don't make promises you may not be able to keep; that discourages my trust in you.

Don't fall for my provocations when I say and do things just to upset you . . . then I'll try for more such victories.

Don't be so upset when I say I hate you. I don't mean it but I want you to feel sorry for what you've done to me.

Don't make me feel smaller than I am. I will make up for it by behaving like a big shot.

Don't do things for me that I can do for myself; it makes me feel like a baby and I may continue to put you in my service.

Don't let my bad habits get me a lot of your attention; it only encourages me to continue them.

Don't correct me in front of people; I'll take much more notice if you talk quietly with me in private.

Don't try to discuss my behavior in the heat of conflict: for some reason my hearing is not very good at this time and my co-operation is even worse. It's all right to take the action required but let's not talk about it until later.

Don't try to preach to me; you would be surprised how well I know what's right and wrong.

Don't make me feel that my mistakes are sins. I have to learn to make mistakes without fearing that I am no good.

Don't nag or I shall have to protect myself by appearing deaf.

Don't demand explanations for my wrong behavior . . . I really don't know why I did it.

Don't tax my honesty too much; I'm easily frightened into telling lies.

Don't forget I love and use experimenting; I learn from it, so please put up with it.

Don't protect me from consequences. I need to learn from experience.

Don't take too much notice of all my small ailments. I may learn to enjoy poor health if it gets me a lot of attention.

Don't put me off when I ask honest questions; if you do you'll find I may stop asking and seek my information elsewhere.

Don't ever think it is beneath your dignity to apologize to me; an honest apology makes me feel surprisingly warm toward you.

Don't ever suggest you're perfect or infallible; it gives me too much to live up to.

Don't worry too much about the little time we spend together: it's how we spend it that counts.

Don't let my fears arouse your anxieties; then I will become more afraid; show me courage.

Don't forget I can't thrive without lots of understanding and encouragement, but I don't need to tell you that, do I . . . Treat me like you treat your friends; then I will be your friend.

REMEMBER I LEARN MORE FROM A MODEL THAN A CRITIC.

SUMMARY

Sources of power include organizational position, information, experience, common ground, and communication skills. The sources of power do not stand alone, and they change over time. Power generally translates into influence and *leadership*, not necessarily into the position of leader. Leadership is any significant action by any group member that influences group achievement. A positional leader is someone in a legitimate role position who influences and directs others in conformance with their expectations for that role.

Style of leadership refers in part to a leader's methods and in part to the philosophy about leadership. Styles vary with organizational and situational expectations as well as with personal and receiver expectations. General styles of leadership are variously described as laissez-faire, nondirective, permissive, democratic, supervisory, authoritarian, and autocratic. The role one plays as a leader and the style one affects is dependent in large part on these various role expectations. Of course, one's power, as discussed earlier, can also affect a leader's role.

Rensis Likert argues that a person's style of leadership is a large part of the psycho-environment. He suggests two basic kinds of operating characteristics, namely authoritative and participative. He makes a strong case for participative management, which he describes as "employee centered." The usual design by Likert's Institute for Social Research was to take high-producing work groups and contrast them with matched low-producing groups. A great many famous organizations were so tested. Various studies report that (1) "employee centered" first-line supervisors have the best records of performance, (2) unreasonable job-centered pressure is associated with a low level of confidence and trust in the supervisor, (3) a loose or "general" form of supervision yields better performance and productivity than "close" supervision, (4) 60 percent of the high-producing foremen were "nonpunitive" and helpful, and (5) a supportive attitude, as well as the constructive use of group meetings, is necessary to develop group loyalty, among many other factors. To integrate these various employee-centered findings Likert formulated a principle of *supportive relationships*.

Likert also views an ideal organization as involving overlapping or linking group memberships. The superior in one group is a participating subordinate in the next.

Leadership style is considered more important to the psycho-environment than attitudes toward the organization and interest in the job itself. The appropriate style for Likert is, of course, employee-oriented rather than job-oriented.

In leadership attitude theory the view is that the attitudes organizational leaders hold toward the cosmos, the nature of man, the nature of influence, and the nature of communication are the basic causes and determinants of the psycho-environment. For Douglas McGregor these attitudes worked like a self-fulfilling prophecy in influencing organizations and the behavior of the people in them. By *integration* McGregor meant the way in which the organization and the individual might come to terms. For McGregor, influence, persuasion, and communication must be transactional to be effective. By this he meant an interactional two-way process with a high degree of mutuality. To dramatize extremes of management attitudes, McGregor postulated two hypothetical theories, *X* and *Y*. *Theory X* was the more common theory, which held that (1) people hate work and seek to avoid it, (2) people need to be coerced to work, and (3) people prefer direction and security and avoid responsibility. *Theory Y* is the appropriate one for maximal motivation. It holds that (1) work is natural, (2) people will exercise self-direction and control in the service of objectives to which they are committed, (3) achievement is a significant reward, (4) people seek responsibility when the climate is right, (5) most people have a high degree of imagination and creativity, and (6) human potential is being only partially utilized. It is the notion of Ouchi that Japanese success is due to an extension of Y or "4" into a form of egalitarian, team-oriented, participatory management, which he calls Z.

Behavioral typologies of organizational leaders are described by Husband as (1) positional, (2) political, (3) administrative, and (4) relational.

Vroom and Yetton offer a classification of five leadership methods ranging across three basic leadership styles: autocratic, consultative, and group. They offer seven organizational rules designed to protect the quality and acceptance of decisions and to help a leader decide which method to use. Lester Bittel observes that these decisions and resulting styles are often related to the life cycle of a company's main product line: autocratic during introduction and decline; participative and consultative during growth and maturity.

According to one contingency model of leadership, there are three basic components in any relationship that give a person control and influence: (1) personal relationships, (2) task structure, and (3) position power. The *relationship* factor includes attributes and impressions of liking, trust, and personal support. The *task structure* has to do with the degree to which the goal is defined, the number of different ways of reaching the goal, and how specific the methods are. *Position power* has to do with legitimate authority and receiver role expectation as discussed earlier. Life is easier for leaders, according to Fiedler, when they have positive regard from their groups; when the task is clear, steady, and highly structured; and when their power is based on knowledge, expertise, and/or legitimate authority. A more *directive* leader performs best when the three influence factors are most favorable and also when they are least favorable. The more *group-centered* leader performs best in more status-quo, routine conditions.

Another contingency notion of leadership by Hersey and Blanchard suggests varying one's style according to the maturity of one's followers, based on their ability and willingness. They suggest four styles: (1) telling, (2) selling, (3) participating, and (4) delegating.

Functional leadership includes: *goal achievement* or systematic efforts toward the task at hand, *procedures, interpersonal relations*, and *teambuilding*.

A range of leadership styles is available. One can be a consistent leader and still have a flexibility based on all of the contingencies. A democratic style is generally better than an absolute or nonresponsible style. However, when goal achievement is critical, going up the scale may be appropriate. When emotions are strained or personalities are in conflict, better interpersonal relations may be achieved by going down the scale. The most practical leadership style in organizational settings is a functional one.

PROJECTS AND CASES

PROJECTS

1. Watch an episode of *L.A. Law*. Pay special attention to the group meetings. Make notes on all examples of the following power sources that are discussed in the text. Prepare to report in class.

Organizational position
Information
Experience
Common ground
Communication skills

2. Recall a group where you or someone else had considerable power, influence, and leadership. Describe that influence in terms of the five sources of power discussed in the text.

3. Observe a radio or television discussion and attempt to classify the various leadership functions that emerge (goal achievement, interpersonal relations, procedural, or team-building). Be alert for changes in function by the participants. Assess their effectiveness.

4. Consider all the groups of which you have been a member. Who was the best leader? Why? Compile a list of roles or behaviors that your ideal leader plays or enacts. How does your group-related behavior differ from your ideal leader?

5. Discuss the relationship between role, role expectation, situation, and leadership style. Are there situations that demand certain leadership styles regardless of role expectations? Give some examples. Are there role expectations that demand certain leadership styles regardless of situation? Give examples.

6. In contingency theory the three sources of interpersonal influence are (1) personal relationships, (2) task structure, and (3) position power. Discuss in two pages or less an incident similar to our sailboat story that illustrates how these components are contingent.

7. Review Vroom and Yetton's leadership rules and write a short supporting illustration (real or hypothetical) for each one. Prepare to report.

8. *Leadership style assessment (Task and People).*

T–P Leadership Questionnaire

Name_____ Group_____

Directions: The following items describe aspects of leadership behavior. Respond to each item according to the way you would most likely act if you were the leader of a work group. Circle whether you would most likely behave in the described way: always (A), frequently (F), occasionally (O), seldom (S), or never (N).

A F O S N   1. I would most likely act as the spokesperson of the group.

A F O S N   2. I would encourage overtime work.

A F O S N   3. I would allow members complete freedom in their work.

A F O S N   4. I would encourage the use of uniform procedures.

A F O S N 5. I would permit the members to use their own judgment in solving problems.

A F O S N 6. I would stress being ahead of competing groups.

A F O S N 7. I would speak as a representative of the group.

A F O S N 8. I would needle members for greater effort.

A F O S N 9. I would try out my ideas in the group.

A F O S N 10. I would let the members do their work the way they think best.

A F O S N 11. I would be working hard for a promotion.

A F O S N 12. I would tolerate postponement and uncertainty.

A F O S N 13. I would speak for the group if there were visitors present.

A F O S N 14. I would keep the work moving at a rapid pace.

A F O S N 15. I would turn the members loose on a job and let them go to it.

A F O S N 16. I would settle conflicts when they occur in the group.

A F O S N 17. I would get swamped by details.

A F O S N 18. I would represent the group at outside meetings.

A F O S N 19. I would be reluctant to allow the members any freedom of action.

A F O S N 20. I would decide what should be done and how it should be done.

A F O S N 21. I would push for increased production.

A F O S N 22. I would let some members have authority that I could keep.

A F O S N 23. Things would usually turn out as I had predicted.

A F O S N 24. I would allow the group a high degree of initiative.

A F O S N 25. I would assign group members to particular tasks.

A F O S N 26. I would be willing to make changes.

A F O S N 27. I would ask the members to work harder.

A F O S N 28. I would trust the group members to exercise good judgment.

A F O S N 29. I would schedule the work to be done.

A F O S N 30. I would refuse to explain my actions.

A F O S N 31. I would persuade others that my ideas are to their advantage.

A F O S N 32. I would permit the group to set its own pace.

A F O S N 33. I would urge the group to beat its previous record.

A F O S N 34. I would act without consulting the group.

A F O S N 35. I would ask that group members follow standard rules and regulations.

T _____   P _____

SCORING INSTRUCTIONS

1. Circle the item number for items 8, 12, 17, 18, 19, 30, 34, and 35.
2. Write the number 1 in front of a *circled item number* if you responded *S* (seldom) or *N* (never) to that item.
3. Also write a number 1 in front of *item numbers not circled* if you responded *A* (always) or *F* (frequently).
4. Circle the number 1s that you have written in front of the following items: 3, 5, 8, 10, 15, 18, 19, 22, 24, 26, 28, 30, 32, 34, and 35.
5. *Count the circled number 1s.* This is your score for concern for people. Record the score in the blank following the letter *P* at the end of the questionnaire.
6. *Count the uncircled number 1s.* This is your score for concern for task. Record this number in the blank following the letter *T*.

DETERMINING YOUR STYLE

Directions: To determine your style of leadership, mark your score on the *concern for task* dimension (*T*) on the left-hand arrow below. Next, move to the right-hand arrow and mark your score on the *concern for people* dimension (*P*). Draw a straight line that intersects the *P* and *T* scores. The point at which that line crosses the *shared leadership* arrow indicates your score on that dimension.

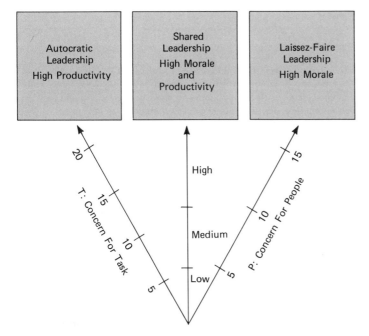

Autocratic Leadership
High Productivity

Shared Leadership
High Morale and Productivity

Laissez-Faire Leadership
High Morale

Reproduced from J. William Pfeiffer, Reference Guide to Handbooks and Annuals (San Diego, CA: University Associates, Inc., 1985). Copyright 1969, American Educational Research Association.

CASES

1. The Wildcatters

During World War II a steel plant was engaged in work of crucial importance to the war effort. In one department responsible for an essential process in manufacturing the product, seventy-five middle-aged women were employed as tin turners. Most of them had family members in the war and were zealously patriotic and bitterly resentful of anyone they considered a "slacker." All employees were required by the firm's contract with the government to be members of the Metal Workers Union.

Among the women, however, were two members of the religious sect known as Witnesses. Members of the sect are pacifists, and while the two women had no objection to working in the plant, they refused on religious grounds to attend patriotic meetings, to subscribe to war bonds, to stand at attention and salute the flag during public patriotic observances, and the like. They were excellent workers with high seniority in their jobs and were loyal and active members of the union.

The other women gave the two offending workers the "silent" treatment, which the two took without complaining. Finally, the other women staged a wildcat strike and insisted they would not return to work as long as the two "slackers" were on the job with them.

Further facts in the situation were the following: The union was under pledge not to strike while the war was in progress. The union constitution contained a clause forbidding the union to discriminate against a worker because of religion. The management was under obligation to the government to meet its production quota. Under its contract with the union, the management could not dismiss a worker without cause especially if the worker had seniority.

QUESTIONS

1. What "group" procedures can be used to solve this problem?
2. What leadership style would you use? Remember: We were in danger of losing the war; we were under martial law; we drafted striking railroad workers . . .

2. The Modern Manufacturing Company

For forty-seven years Frederick Schmidt was the principal owner and dominant figure in the management of the Modern Manufacturing Company, which had been a family business for four generations. He prided himself on knowing all of his several hundred employees by name and on taking a warm, personal interest in their welfare. "Every employer is his brother's keeper," he once said, "and such factories as ours realize this fact."

The record indicates that Mr. Schmidt's interest in his employees was genuine and that for a lifetime it had dominated his relations with them. As early as 1897 an Employee's Aid Society was established. In 1920 a Foreman's Club was set up and in the following year a technical library was provided for employees who wished to improve themselves. From the beginning of the Schmidt regime, liberal awards were made for length of service; in 1925 employees who had been with the firm for thirty years were given a two-month vacation with pay, given a bonus of $1,000, and provided with travel money that enabled some of them who had been born abroad to visit their birthplaces. An elaborate company picnic was held each summer, and the annual Christmas party was accompanied by the liberal distribution of bonuses and food baskets. As early as 1938 the forty-hour week with time and a half for overtime was standard. A bank account was set up by the firm for each child born to an employee, and the parents were provided with the use of a baby's crib without cost. When a child graduated from high school, he or she received a cash gift. Other activities and facilities provided free by the firm included a band, a playground, an athletic association, a park and clubhouse, a gymnasium, and a skating rink. As the years of his service drew near an end, Frederick Schmidt looked back on a lifetime of service to the firm and its employees with pride and satisfaction.

During the Vietnam War, a union attempted to organize the plant for the first time and began to distribute handbills at the factory gate. The management was frankly amused. What could the union offer their employees that they didn't already have? But the union won the election by an overwhelming majority.

Soon after, Mr. Schmidt retired, a bitter and broken man. He died the following year, his death hastened, some felt, by the shock.

QUESTIONS

1. Did leadership style have anything to do with this turn of events?
2. What incentives are *not* mentioned?

NOTES

1. Marvin Shaw, *Group Dynamics* (Hightstown, N.J.: McGraw-Hill, 1981), pp. 343–45.
2. See especially M. M. Chemers, "Leadership Theory and Research: A Systems-Process Integration," in *Basic Group Processes*, ed. P. B. Paulus (New York: Springer-Verlag, 1983), pp. 9–39.
3. Rensis Likert, *The Human Organization: Its Management and Value* (New York: McGraw-Hill, 1967), pp. 3–24.
4. Rensis Likert, *New Patterns of Management* (New York: McGraw-Hill, 1961; Garland, 1987), p. 1.
5. Ibid., p. 7.
6. Ibid., p. 9.
7. Victor H. Vroom, "Industrial Social Psychology," in *The Handbook of Social Psychology, Vol. V: Applied Social Psychology*, 2nd ed., eds. Gardner Lindzey and Elliot Aronson (Reading, Mass.: Addison-Wesley, 1969), p. 239.
8. Likert, *New Patterns*, p. 28.
9. Ibid., p. 54.
10. Ibid., p. 103.
11. Douglas McGregor, Caroline McGregor, and Warren G. Bennis, eds., *The Professional Manager* (New York: McGraw-Hill, 1967), p. 4.
12. Ibid., p. 18.
13. Ibid., p. 23.
14. Ibid., p. 15.
15. Douglas McGregor, *The Human Side of Enterprise* (New York: McGraw-Hill, 1960, 1985), pp. 33–34.
16. Ibid., pp. 47–48.
17. Ibid., p. 49.
18. W. G. Ouchi, *Theory Z* (Reading, Mass.: Addison-Wesley, 1981).
19. John F. Cragan and David W. Wright, *Communication in Small Group Discussions* (St. Paul, Minn.: West, 1986), p. 284.
20. Robert L. Husband, "Toward a Grounded Typology of Organizational Leadership Behavior," *Quarterly Journal of Speech*, 71, no. 1 (1985), 103–18.
21. Paraphrased from V. H. Vroom and P. W. Yetton, *Leadership and Decision Making* (Pittsburgh: University of Pittsburgh Press, 1973), p. 13.
22. Paraphrased from Vroom and Yetton, *Leadership and Decision Making*, pp. 32–35. For more on these matters also see V. H. Vroom, "Leadership," in *Handbook of Industrial and Organizational Psychology*, ed. M. D. Dunnette (Chicago: Rand McNally, 1976); V. H. Vroom and A. G. Jago, "On the Validity of the Vroom/Yetton Model," *Journal of Applied Psychology*, 63 (1978), 151–62; V. H. Vroom and A. G. Jago, *The New Leadership* (Englewood Cliffs, N.J.: Prentice Hall, 1988).
23. Lester R. Bittel, *Leadership: The Key to Management Success* (New York: Franklin Watts, 1984), p. 156.
24. F. Fiedler and M. M. Chemers, *Improving Leadership Effectiveness: The Leader Match Concept*, 2nd ed. (New York: John Wiley & Sons, 1984). See especially F. Fiedler, "A Contingency Model

of Leadership Effectiveness," in *Advances in Experimental Social Psychology*, Vol. 1, ed. L. Berkowitz (New York: Academic, 1964), pp. 150–90.

25. Debra J. Stratton, "How to Be a Successful Leader: Match Your Leadership Situation to Your Personality, an Interview with Dr. Fred Fiedler," *Leadership*, (November 1979), p. 27.

26. For information on these matters, see R. Ross, *Understanding Persuasion*, 2nd ed. (Englewood Cliffs, N.J.: Prentice-Hall, 1985).

27. L. Berkowitz, ed., *Advances in Experimental Social Psychology*, pp. 155–58.

28. Ibid., p. 159.

29. Paul Hersey and Kenneth H. Blanchard, *Management of Organizational Behavior: Utilizing Human Resources* (Englewood Cliffs, N.J.: Prentice-Hall, 1982), p. 151.

30. "Procedural Checklist," (Rochester, N.Y.: Xerox Corporation, 1987).

31. "Number 1 Team," (Detroit: General Motors Corporation, 1987.)

32. Mark Tapscott, "Ford's Bullish on Its $3 Billion Bet," *Insight*, 2, no. 33 (August 18, 1986), 46.

33. David Kushma, "GM Plant Divided in Team Plan," *Detroit Free Press*, June 4, 1987, sec. A, p. 19.

34. Chuck Kormanski and Andrew Mozenter, "A New Model of Team Building: A Technology for Today and Tomorrow," in *The 1987 Annual: Developing Human Resources*, ed. J. William Pfeiffer (San Diego: University Associates, 1987), p. 257. See also E. J. Ends and C. W. Page, *Organizational Team Building* (Cambridge, Mass.: Winthrop, 1977); also see A. Zander, "Team Spirit vs. the Individual Achiever," *Psychology Today*, 8, no. 6 (1974), 64–68.

35. See I. Doyal and J. M. Thomas, "Operation KPE: Developing a New Organization," *Journal of Applied Behavioral Science*, 4 (1968), 473–506.

36. Julia Wood, "The Leader's Brief: Teaching an Adaptive Approach to Leading," *Communication Education*, 26, no. 4 (1977), 355. See also Warren G. Bennis, "New Patterns of Leadership for Adaptive Organizations," in *The Temporary Society*, eds. Warren G. Bennis and Phillip E. Slater (New York: Harper Colophon, 1969), pp. 97–123; and Robert S. Tannenbaum and Warren H. Schmidt, "How to Choose a Leadership Pattern," *Harvard Business Review*, 36 (March–April 1958), 101.

37. Wood, "The Leader's Brief," pp. 356–58. Wood describes a leader's brief that should prove useful to training leaders.

38. H. L. Goodall, *Small Group Communication in Organizations* (Dubuque, Ia.: Wm. C. Brown, 1985), pp. 147–48.

9

BOARDS: THE POWER GROUPS*

The Visiting Nurse Corporation (VNC) is a large, metropolitan home health-care agency with 500 employees who work out of nine district offices in a tri-county area. Its annual budget is over $17 million. The corporation has a board of thirty-three distinguished citizens, each of whom brings a special expertise to the organization. As a past president of that board I recall my first six weeks as the new president. I met separately with all of the twenty-seven special staffs associated with the VNC. These two-hour meetings were held on their grounds, in their district offices, and included nursing staff, management, and support staff. Our general goals were to educate the new president of the board and discuss agency problems. I was surprised to learn how little the organization knew about the board that had so much power over their organizational destiny. I heard the same honest questions over and over again:

What really is a board?
Are they all alike?
How are boards selected?
What do boards do?
How are board members trained?
What does the president do?
How should we handle our board?

I would add, "How should the board interact with the staff?" Over the years I've spent much lecture and training time trying to answer these questions for people in organizations, especially new or prospective board members. This chapter will at-

*This chapter was written by Jean Ricky Ross, former Chairperson of the Board, Visiting Nurse Corporation of Metropolitan Detriot.

tempt to answer most of these same questions. No, all boards are not alike, but first some general definitions and observations.

WHAT IS A BOARD?

Frank Sinatra has often been referred to as Chairman of the Board. Why? To suggest importance and power. So too with the ongoing force of citizen boards in our everyday lives. Their decisions affect our communities culturally, governmentally, educationally, and financially. Libraries, museums, art galleries, and zoos operate under policies set by their boards. Most churches have very active boards. Our governing city councils function as boards representing those of us living in the community. Your pre-college education was controlled by a school board. Today your college or university is board controlled. Perhaps you are currently a member of the ski team board, your dormitory board, or the student government board.

According to estimates by the U.S. Department of Commerce, the service sector accounts for seven out of every ten jobs in this country. Many of these service industries are nonprofit such as home health care, hospitals, schools, United Way, and other fund-raising organizations—each is governed by a board of directors. All states legally require that one to three people be listed as on the board of directors in the original incorporation application. A list of board members must also be included in an application for tax-exemption status from the Internal Revenue Service. To legally function and supply services (and jobs) in the community, a nonprofit organization *must* have a board of directors. Publicly held corporations are required to establish boards that are elected by the shareholders. Rules abound—the system is not as open as most other small groups in organizational settings.

To be recognized as an official campus organization, most colleges require (1) a statement of charter or purpose, (2) a current list of officers, (3) membership lists, and (4) an approved sponsor. In other words, boards of organizations don't just happen.

Mandated boards are here to stay; their jobs and rules are becoming more complex as problems in health, welfare, and education escalate. An efficient, effective board of directors will enhance the efforts of all agencies dealing in these arenas. To this end many major industries are encouraging their employees to contribute their expertise. Time is allocated for board service; recognition is given to employees for their service; participation is considered in an employee's evaluation.

As citizens we must become knowledgeable volunteer participants in the board process. As staff members employed by an organization controlled by a board, understanding the nature and function of that board becomes crucial to personal success and the success of your employer.

For all the constraints on these very special groups, their deliberations are open-system, and previous small-group suggestions still very much apply. However, certain procedures and practices tend to become heavily rule governed and even ritualized in an effort to avoid running afoul of the laws of the land, the bylaws, and the organizations' policies, which govern much of their efforts. If some of the rules that follow sound prescriptive, it's because, in most cases, they *are prescribed.*

Robert's Rules of Order defines a board as an "an administrative, managerial, or quasi-judicial body of elected or appointed persons which has the character of a deliberative assembly with the following variations:

1. boards have no minimum size . . .
2. . . . its operation is determined by responsibilities and powers designated to it by authority outside itself.''[1]

Members of the board may be referred to as directors, trustees, regents, or governors. In this chapter we will be using the title ''Board of Directors.''

Cyril Houle defines a board as ''an organized group of people collectively controlling and assisting an agency or association which is usually administered by a qualified executive and staff.''[2] His definition is built upon a number of common board characteristics.

1. *A board is always related to an institution, service, or association*—a William Beaumont Hospital, a Lions Club, or an American Heart Association.
2. *The board relationship to its parent group is one of both control and assistance.* The hospital board, comprised of thirty-two volunteers and eight medical and administrative staff, has the responsibility of *control* by making policies and seeing that they are carried out. If the hospital's new Physician Referral and Information Service program needs interpreting and publicizing in the community, board members should utilize their talents and contacts in the community to *assist* the hospital.
3. *A board is made up of individuals but is collective in its nature.* Board decisions are not made by a single individual but are determined through an effective group process. The Lions Club board may have many fine individual ideas for their seeing-eye dog program fund raiser. However, before the group adjourns, a majority opinion must prevail or planning for the money raising event cannot continue. The board of your college ski club must collectively decide if the slopes at Squaw Valley, Snowmass, or Vail better suit the skiing abilities of its members.
4. *A board must work with an executive and staff who have rights and responsibilities of their own.*[3] Board and staff formulate policy together but the board is responsible for setting policy and reviewing its implementation; a staff is responsible for implementing policy set by the board.

One of the major responsibilities of most boards is the hiring and, if necessary, firing of the executive officer. The executive officer is usually responsible for hiring the staff. Good board–staff balance produces a team working as partners, each understanding the other's role, rules, and responsibilities. Board–staff roles will be discussed later in this chapter.

ARE ALL BOARDS ALIKE?

TYPES

They are not all alike. Their functions vary and they are selected quite differently, but they do have many things in common. There are four major types.

Controlling Board

Ford, General Motors, and even Lee Iacocca have boards that control funds, programs, and Mr. Iacocca. These are governing boards that have the immediate and direct legal responsibility for setting the policies for a company, agency, university, hospital, or a Blue Cross/Blue Shield organization.

In the private sector the typical *corporation* board of directors has responsibilities (1) for establishing broad corporate policies and (2) for the overall performance of the company. In larger organizations the board is rarely involved in day-to-day operating details. Some directors receive an annual retainer and/or an additional fee for meetings attended. AT&T directors receive a retainer of $22,000 and a fee of $1,000 for each board, committee, or shareholder meeting attended. AT&T directors who chair committees receive additional stipends of $3,000 to $5,000. There is controversy about these matters in the public sector (e.g., school boards); other community boards, except for perhaps a professional coordinator, are unpaid.

As we discussed in Chapter 5, *policy* is an established course of action to be followed in recurring situations. It provides a written framework for carrying out the work. "A policy is a statement of management's intent with respect to matters of broad and long-range significance to the company."[4] Policies should be developed for long-term usage. A new policy statement should not be required every time a new service is developed. However, just as strategic planning has been reduced from five to three years in many organizations, so too must policies be reviewed and kept up to date.

Policy recommendations should come from an organization's staff going first to the executive director or chief executive officer (CEO) for assessment. Perhaps a current policy already addresses the situation but is not being implemented; perhaps management can utilize new methods to handle the problem. If not, the policy recommendation should be brought to the board with all necessary documentation and information for their consideration.

Policies are not easy to formulate. They are subject to rules of law, protocol, budget, personnel, interlocking with other policies, time constraints, and so forth. Here again we see the need for good staff–board balance and teamwork.

Auxiliary Board

The auxiliary board is one created to carry out certain agreed upon responsibilities such as fund raising, special programs in the community, or volunteer services. Its power and authorization for functioning comes from the controlling board, which has the right to review and approve auxiliary programs. It may recommend but does not set or review policy.

A good example is the Volunteer Service Committee of William Beaumont Hospital, a 1,000-bed institution in Royal Oak, Michigan. It was created thirty years ago to provide the hospital with volunteers working in various areas of the hospital. Its board is responsible for seeing that 1,200 volunteers are trained to perform the duties assigned to them in hospital departments such as emergency, X-ray, pharmacy, or outpatient surgery. Volunteers must also be knowledgeable about their hospital to direct patients and visitors; they must wear the correct uniform; they should have the current information about hospital developments to interpret to their community. All of this is accomplished through an extensive program of service committees—small groups in an organizational setting. Thirty-five committee chairpersons plus twelve executive-committee members make up the auxiliary board, another small group. The president of this board is a member of the controlling board, the hospital's board of directors. When a new service is requested by hospital staff (staff–board teamwork), the auxiliary board considers its applicability to their program, pilots it for a month, and they may or may not recommend it to the hospital board for approval.

Your campus organizations are typically led by auxiliary boards serving under the controlling university or college board of directors, trustees, governors, or regents. They are an extension of the university and subject to the principles and regulations governing the university. There have been exceptions . . .

Association Board

Association boards control the affairs of voluntary membership groups. Fraternal bodies, Leagues of Voters, community action groups, women's resource centers, community musicales, and special interest organizations such as the American Cancer Society or the Arthritis Foundation are examples of groups having association boards. Their responsibility is to their membership. Some have an executive and staff. The work of others is done by the boards and the association members.

Most professional and trade organizations have association boards that determine the direction and policies of the association. Some examples are the American Medical Association, American Psychological Association, National Education Association, Speech Communication Association, Plumbing and Heating Association, and the National Association for Home Health Care. Some of these, such as the American Psychological Association (APA) with a membership of 87,000 and a budget of $42 million, are very large groups with a correspondingly large staff to handle their business. The APA policies are decided by an elected council of representatives comprised of 115 association members. Twelve board members serve as the executive committee of the council. Much of the work of the association is done by the ninety-plus boards, committees, and task forces, all composed of volunteer members.

Community Boards

Community boards are responsible for community-based organizations that provide a variety of social services in the areas of health, education, culture, recreation, rehabilitation, youth, and senior citizen services. The local organization may be affiliated with a national group such as the Red Cross, Salvation Army, or YWCA/YMCA. Usually these are very large boards, giving them a wide community representation. In a large metropolitan area, a Red Cross or United Foundation board may have 100 or more members. An executive board of 10 to 15 typically meets monthly to develop policy and program. Auxiliary boards such as Women for United Foundation have special assignments within the U.F. framework. They represent the U.F. in their own community and reflect the issues and needs of that community.

Fund raising and development of new services are often primary missions of community boards. Large board size is then a valuable asset. Dean Schooler, director of the University of Colorado Development Center, lists the following board member roles:[5]

1. Giving time and money
2. Raising funds
3. Working with staff on grants
4. Leading fund-raising campaigns
5. Working with development staff on contacts and fund-raising programs
6. Developing existing and new constituencies
7. Recruiting volunteers
8. Maintaining accountability and responsibility to donors.

MEMBERSHIP

''The process by which an organization is managed successfully cannot be limited only to its management. The process must also include the role and function performed by the board of directors. The enormous economic, financial, social, legal, regulatory, international, and other pressures which exist today have greatly complicated the environment in which institutions must function. They have forced multiple and changing demands upon organizations which hope to survive and prosper.''[6]

How Does One Become a Board Member?

In a small organization you may be invited to join by those who are already on the board. In a larger organization a nominating committee may invite you after assessing current needs of the board and studying recommendations from board, staff, and community members. In some cases board members are elected or appointed. If recommended by the nominating committee, a board vote may be mandated by organization bylaws.

Some board consultants consider the nominating committee to be one of the most crucial organizational committees. As such, it should meet on a year-round basis. A nominating committee I chaired for several years met four to six times a year. At its first meeting the committee members were oriented to their responsibilities, goals, and procedures. An assessment was made of the board's current strengths and future needs. Possible candidates, their backgrounds, and areas of expertise were discussed. Recommendations were made for the chairperson to contact the candidate to determine interest and availability. Copies of bylaws, the annual report, the board membership list, and other pertinent data were sent to the prospective member. An interview with the chairperson (or a committee member) followed. The interviewer's data was then presented to the committee to determine if the candidate should be presented to the board for election.

Board members may be appointed by an outside authority. The governor of a state appoints members to a myriad of state boards. A city mayor may have the same responsibility and legal power. Typically these appointments are made upon recommendation of current board members, staff, or constituents.

Members may be elected by the people or, in the case of corporations, by the stockholders. In the state of Michigan boards members of the state universities are elected by the people. Corporation boards are elected at the annual meeting after a slate of candidates has been mailed to the stockholders presenting the members' names and qualifications. AT&T, for example, has a committee on directors that makes recommendations to the board on nominee selections. Shareholders may also suggest qualified candidates for committee consideration. The board-approved slate is mailed to the stockholders with the notice of the annual meeting and a proxy statement.

The need for different board expertise changes from year to year. An organization considering restructuring will need people with vision, organizational skills, and legal expertise. An agency expanding its program and services into another geographical area will need membership from that area, public relations and advertising experts, and finance professionals.

If an organization derives any funding or payment for their services from the federal government (Medicare/Medicaid), United Foundation/United Way, grants, and so forth, board composition will be examined closely. Demographic, racial, and ethnic makeup of the board must be representative of the total community served as a matter of law.

RESPONSIBILITIES

Board responsibilities vary among organizations but generally can be divided into eight broad categories. Boards must

1. Establish program policies, standards, and decide the management structure.
2. Administer the affairs, business, and properties of the organization.
3. Employ an executive officer who administers the program, maintains standards, and executes the policies of the board.
4. Participate in strategic planning.
5. Satisfy all legal responsibilities and requirements for a board under state and federal law.
6. Ensure the organization's financial stability, including authorization of the budget and selection of an auditor.
7. Conduct continuous evaluation of program, staff, and board effectiveness.
8. Inform the public about the organization and its programs and services.

Many boards are also responsible for electing their officers and members of the nominating committee and approving the creation of advisory and special committees of the board.

COMMITTEES

Not all boards have a committee structure. Some prefer to work as a committee of the whole and appoint task forces as needed. Others are too small to be divided. However, for a board with twenty-five or more members that meets monthly for two to three hours, committees become the working machinery of the organization. In very large community and association boards, the committee structure is a necessity. The American Psychological Association, for example, has two major committees: (1) administrative, with five subcommittees, and (2) governance, with seven subcommittees, plus a nominating subcommittee.

Committees are an organizational device, an action arm, for getting work done through the group process. It is at the committee level where the real work transpires. Here the problems are defined, researched, and possible solutions are developed and discussed. Staff should be asked to contribute their perspectives and knowledge. A finance committee should have a member of the finance department present at their meetings who has a working knowledge of the organization's financial operation. If an investment portfolio is one of the committee's responsibilities, outside consultants may be invited to report at some meetings. During labor negotiations the personnel committee needs a direct report from the organization's negotiator. Current human resource development programs within the organization should be reported to the committee by a personnel staff member. After thorough screening a committee recommendation can be brought to the board for their consideration and appropriate action.

Effective committees don't just happen. Successful committees use a combination of elements and techniques in their operation. They should

1. *Know and understand their task or goal.* What is their purpose for meeting? Are they to plan a community celebration of the agency's eighty-fifth anniversary? Are they to meet regularly to oversee the organization's fiscal operation?

2. *Know their organizational limitations.* What are their responsibilities? What are the policies affecting their operation? What authority do they have? Will their recommendations be considered and acted upon?

3. *Adhere to a time schedule.* Work should be accomplished in a timely fashion during regularly scheduled meetings. Prepared agendas and all necessary information should be distributed prior to the meeting.

4. *Use a chairperson who can successfully operate as a leader, counselor, facilitator, and presiding officer and who understands when to use each role.*

5. *Utilize members with good decision-making ability who are willing to give the time necessary for meetings and adequate study of documents beforehand.* Ideally they should be reasonably compatible and able to work as a team.

6. *Encourage a key staff person to be present if appropriate to the work of the committee.* Having professional expertise and knowledge of the day-to-day operations available at meetings facilitates the work of the committee.

Executive Committee

The executive committee has a coordinating function and can meet regularly or on special notice to handle emergencies. It is a "board within a board" composed of the officers and chairpersons of the standing committees. The immediate past president is often a member. This committee has the right to exercise the powers of the full board in the management of the organization between meetings of the board, if so specified in the bylaws. It must report its actions at the next meeting of the board.

The executive committee of the Michigan Hospital Association meets regularly the evening before the monthly board meeting to coordinate and prepare for an efficient meeting. As we mentioned earlier, extremely large boards with many functions in the community need an executive committee that meets regularly to handle routine board activities.

Some problems call for preliminary consideration by a special, smaller group from the whole board. Discussion of an executive officer's poor performance and what should be done about it would be the type of problem an executive committee would handle in the early stages.

Standing Committee

This type of committee performs a continuing function on a permanent basis with duties specified in the bylaws. It should have clearly defined boundaries of activity and responsibility. For example, a finance committee is responsible for the financial affairs of the organization, not for fund raising. Standing committees usually report directly to the board and are a scheduled part of the regular board-meeting agenda.

Some typical standing committees are finance, personnel, community relations, bylaws, nominating, program, and strategic planning. Their chairpersons may be members of the executive committee. As mentioned earlier, staff representation on these committees is vital.

Special Ad Hoc Committee

A special ad hoc committee is appointed as the need arises to carry out a specified task. Upon completion of the task, the committee is automatically dissolved. Chairpersons of these committees are not members of the executive board for theirs is a temporary post. Planning for a new service of meal delivery to homebound senior citizens would be done by an ad hoc committee and brought to the board for approval. Here again staff participation would be a welcome addition.

Professional Advisory Committee

This type of committee is composed of nonboard, professional workers from the community who represent the scope and activities of the organization together with some selected board members. They serve as advisors to the board and staff, formulating and reviewing specific procedures and recommending changes as needed. They also assist in identifying community needs for the agency. Committee members serve as a communication link between the organization and the professional groups they represent. If the chairperson of such a committee also is a board member, committee recommendations can be reported to the board for approval in a timely manner.

The professional advisory committee of the Visiting Nurse Association of Metropolitan Detroit is composed of thirteen representatives from the disciplines of medicine, nursing, speech pathology, occupational therapy, physical therapy, and social work plus three board members. It meets quarterly and is a mandated board committee for agency fulfillment of accreditation requirements.

Organizations differ in their structures and bylaws. They may use a combination of the four just described or add others such as consultative, review, and executive-search committees should the need arise. All of these have very specific goals and may use outside consultants working with board members. Corporation boards may have additional committees such as public policy, proxy, pension, and audit.

HOW ARE BOARD MEMBERS TRAINED?

How are they oriented, prepared, and evaluated? Careful selection of board members is only the beginning; nurturing their initial interest and enthusiasm to produce high performance is the real goal. Certain actions help accomplish this goal.

PREPARATION OF NEW MEMBERS

As a college student you may be a member of a board controlling specific college activities. How were you introduced to the job ahead of you? Did you feel prepared for the first board meeting? Were you friendly and comfortable with at least a few of the members? If yours is a leadership role, you have an extra duty to see that new board members are knowledgeable about the organization and aware of their responsibilities as board members. Let's look at some ways to accomplish this.

Welcome

Immediately after selection the new member should receive a welcoming letter or phone call from the president of the board, the nominating committee, or the corresponding secretary. Prospective members, knowing their names are being submitted to the board for election, may be wondering whether they have been approved when notification is not received promptly.

Orientation

Orientation has several purposes: to give the new members specific information about the organization; to acquaint them with all facets of board activities and how they may fit into them; to help gain confidence; and to promote high standards of performance.

The amount of time necessary for orientation or briefing will depend on the size of your organization, the scope of its activities, and the type of board–staff involvement. A small group will call for a less formal briefing. If copies of the bylaws, annual report, and membership roster were distributed during the initial contact, our new member already has some knowledge. A meeting with the executive board or the whole board, if a small one, may be in order. A discussion of board procedures and the board of directors' roles and responsibilities can give the new member some added insights. The opportunity to meet informally with board members prior to the first meeting is helpful. A board manual can be given at this time. More will be said about this valuable tool shortly.

In large organizations a more structured orientation may be necessary. Agency staff will present information related to various aspects of operation; the table of organization may be explained; the organization's relationship to the community will be discussed. An experienced board member may present the role of a board member in the agency. Pertinent articles, brochures, and past minutes will be distributed together with a board manual. A tour of the physical plant may be in order. A follow-up orientation is sometimes scheduled after new members have a chance to gain some experience and have further questions.

The Detroit Visiting Nurse Corporation schedules two or three orientations over a two-week period to accommodate the work schedules of busy members. A three-hour informative briefing given by staff and board is held in the morning. Individual field visits with nursing staff in patients' homes are undertaken in the afternoon. In this way the board member receives vital information about the organization, health care, financial restrictions, and so forth and develops a general understanding of the work and services offered by the organization. Because of this organization's complexity, board members requested reorientations. Many opted for another field visit in a different area of the city. Some form of reorientation can and should become a regularly scheduled, continuing part of any board's education.

Board Manuals

When you buy a VCR you receive an instruction book, a manual, which tells you how to connect, program, and adjust the VCR. It becomes a standard reference tool and so does a board manual. Some basics that can be included are

- historical profile
- statement of philosophy and purposes
- bylaws
- organizational chart of the board
- list of board members with addresses and titles
- responsibilities and functions of board members
- responsibilities of chairpersons
- responsibilities of elected officers
- description of board committees
- committee assignment listing
- policies of the board
- description of current programs, services, or subsidiary organizations
- explanation of relationship of the organization to a parent corporation, if applicable
- sources of funding
- budget
- strategic plan summary
- organizational chart of agency
- list of personnel with addresses and titles

COMMITMENT

Agreeing to serve on a board indicates interest and, hopefully, some commitment. Our goal is to enlarge that commitment and obtain an even more productive board member.

Offering specific and challenging assignments that show progress and change as a result of a board member's work is one method. Few people resign from a board because of overwork or being overly challenged. However, extra thought and care should be given to these first assignments. Examine the capabilities and interests of the new director. Be sure the job is something the person really wants to do. It should not be too wearing or time consuming; ideally it can be done by working with other board members; it should have a better than average chance of success; and it should be an activity that will warrant public recognition and praise upon completion.

Early retirees with their wealth of knowledge and leadership experience have been an excellent source of board material. For them board work often provides a continuing stimulus. This, coupled with leadership opportunities, may increase their commitment.

COMPETENCY

Board members are chosen for their proven competency, capability, and past experience, vital ingredients for a strong and powerful board. Previously however, these skills may have been utilized in quite different settings. The process of focusing the new member's attention on the needs of this particular organization begins with orientation and continues throughout his or her board activity.

Various methods can be used to develop capabilities tailored to a specific board. One is a program of reading in which new books in the field or excerpts from them are circulated. Pertinent articles and pamphlets can be distributed. An executive report given at the regularly scheduled board meeting should deal with current industry happenings as they affect the organization or institution. Staff can be given the opportunity to present case studies illustrating new programs or services. Visits to similar organizations or sharing a meeting with them may be illuminating. Workshops, retreats, and city, state, and national conferences can be an important part of an ongoing educational program for board members.

Some board authorities feel an evaluation or self-assessment of the board should be done at least once every two years. The purpose is to better utilize the individual competencies of board members and to make changes if needed.

A rating scale for boards was developed after asking a large number of experienced board members what they considered to be the most important characteristics. (See Figure 9.1.) After a board has been rated on each of the twelve characteristics, a line should be drawn from one mark to another resulting in a board profile. Ideally, a straight line should connect all of the dots in the *excellent* column. There is room for board improvement on any falling to the right of excellent. Later on, a new profile can be drawn, which hopefully will indicate progress. See how it applies to your current board affiliation.

GROUP PROCESSES

Picture our board group composed of strong personalities, all successful leaders within their individual work environments, now placed in a situation where they have only the power granted to them collectively. Individual control over the work of the organization occurs only when the board group is in session or when it specifically requests that a certain task be done.

In the preceding chapters we have discussed the ways to achieve group cohesion. An experienced, sensitive chairperson can do much to facilitate the blending of diverse personalities and more will be said about this shortly. However, each board member has responsibilities for his or her attitude and actions. An effective member

1. brings perspective to the issue at hand,
2. is receptive to new ideas,
3. expresses ideas clearly and succinctly,
4. can be tactful and diplomatic in times of disagreement,
5. insists upon full discussion of each issue,
6. supports the final board decision even if it differs from his or her recommendation.

Thomas Whisler says it more succinctly in *The Wall Street Journal*:

1. No fighting.
2. No crusades.
3. Do your homework.
4. Participate.
5. Serve your apprenticeship.[7]

WHAT DO BOARD LEADERS DO?

Our emphasis here is on the president, chairman, or chairperson (whichever title applies) of the board, but all rules and practices described also pertain to the board com-

CHARACTERISTICS	HOW THE BOARD RATES				
	Excellent	Good	Average	Poor	Very Poor
A. The board should be made up of effective individuals who can supplement one another's talents.	•	•	•	•	•
B. The board should represent the interests that are to be consulted in formulating policy.	•	•	•	•	•
C. The board should be large enough to carry all necessary responsibilities but small enough to act as a deliberative group.	•	•	•	•	•
D. The basic structural pattern (board, board officials, committees, executive, and staff) should be clear.	•	•	•	•	•
E. There should be an effective working relationship between the board and the executive and staff.	•	•	•	•	•
F. The members of the board should understand the objectives of the agency or association and how those objectives are achieved by the activities undertaken.	•	•	•	•	•
G. The board should have a feeling of social ease and rapport.	•	•	•	•	•
H. Each member of the board should feel involved and interested in its work.	•	•	•	•	•
I. The board should formulate specific goals to guide its work.	•	•	•	•	•
J. Decisions on policy should be made only after full consideration by all parties concerned with the decision.	•	•	•	•	•
K. The board should be certain that effective community relationships are maintained.	•	•	•	•	•
L. The board should have a sense of progress and accomplishment.	•	•	•	•	•

Figure 9.1 A rating scale for boards.

By permission of the National Board of Young Men's Christian Association.

mittee chairpersons. This is not to suggest that board members in whatever assignment will not emerge as leaders when the task is in their area of expertise.

The president of the board has important power throughout the entire organization. In some instances the president or chairman of the board and the chief executive officer may be the same person. As president of an auxiliary board, power extends only to that part over which you have domain. Specific duties are listed in the bylaws and usually state that the president shall (1) be the principal officer of the organization, (2) preside at all meetings of the membership, of the board, and of the executive committee, (3) perform all other duties incident to the office and such other duties as the board may authorize or direct, and (4) appoint all standing and special committees and serve as an ex-officio member of all such committees.

PREPARATION FOR LEADERSHIP

Board presidents usually have served on a board for several years before they are elected to the presidency. Valuable experience can be gained during this period in matters of the organization, the staff, and the board itself. Many organizations have a board president-elect who works closely with the president, assuring a smooth transfer of leadership. Some auxiliary boards have paid professional staff assigned to help the board president.

The best presidents are rarely expert in all areas; special expertise comes from the board members. The best ones are the good organizers, the strong leaders, the motivators. A good president is a catalyst for needed change, but also a defender of a satisfactory status quo.

PLANNING

Necessary for any officer or committee chairperson is a well-drawn-up plan of work—a time-flow sheet indicating what procedures must be followed and when. Regularly scheduled meeting dates are entered; so too are community appearances, publication deadlines, meetings with the executive officer, committee appointments, budget hearings, executive evaluations, and so forth. Appropriate lead time is factored into the plan. Additional dates may be entered for each month and revised as necessary. At the end of your assignment, you may want to refine your master plan, a system you found useful in doing the job efficiently. This should be turned over to your successor to help orient him or her.

COMMITTEE APPOINTMENTS

Appointing committees may be one of the most important jobs of a board president. All committees have several universal functions: they offer a vital mini-education about the organization for new members; they develop future leadership; and they act as a trainer and showcase for existing leadership. The real work is done in board committees.

The appointing officer often confers with the president-elect, past president, executive officer, and other board members. In some organizations in which I have participated, members were asked to list several committees in which they were interested with the understanding that everyone, for example, could not serve on the finance or strategic planning committees. The committee chairperson will probably be drawn from the previous committee's roster; however, a good board president is always considering future committee leadership when making appointments.

Successfully matching a member's interest and competence with the right committee can make the day of any board president. I complimented the chairperson of the finance committee, a partner in an international accounting firm and one of my appointments, on his ability to explain very intricate financial matters in an understandable way. He appeared pleased with my commentary and responded, "Ricky, that's the only business I know. I'll handle the number problems; you take care of the people problems."

As we mentioned earlier, ideally all committee members should be compatible. This does not mean we shouldn't have dissenting opinions during committee discussions. However, if there is a history of serious, interpersonal conflict between two members that the other committee members or the chairperson cannot neutralize, pause—a board needs *task* conflict to avoid groupthink, but it also needs mature personalities who can rise above petty, interpersonal differences. Perhaps they should be assigned differently to protect the organization and its goals.

STRUCTURING MEETINGS

This would be a good time to reread Chapter 5 for overall information on committees, order of business, agendas, policies, and parliamentary law. The Appendix has additional material on parliamentary procedure. The material in this chapter will deal more specifically with board situations.

Some board meetings must be open to the public by law. Others may be closed by choice or open by invitation or permission.

Agendas/Order of Business

Board agendas are usually developed jointly by the board president and the executive officer. The agenda, together with supporting documents, is sent out prior to the meeting allowing board members time to study the information. The order of business is typically included indicating the persons responsible for presenting each report. Usually the committee chairperson summarizes the committee's work and recommendations. Board questions, a discussion, and then a vote follows the report. A detailed, written copy should be given to the recording secretary. If a critical motion is to be made, it should be written out ahead of time in a businesslike manner. Some organizations have forms for this procedure to ensure accuracy in the minutes.

Even though the order of business may be somewhat prescribed in your organization, you may be able to adjust it to strengthen your meetings. Here are a few suggestions I've found to be useful:

1. Separate complicated task items so that they do not follow one another.
2. Avoid placing organizationally emotional items back to back. (Adrenalin may be flowing; let your members catch their breath.)
3. Routine, time-consuming, dull business items should be spaced throughout the order; otherwise you may find yourself looking out at a very important, but very bored constituency.

4. Place crucial items in the middle of the business order. If placed too early, some busy latecomers will miss it; if late in the order, some members may have to leave beforehand or the interest level of those remaining may be ebbing.

5. Alternate items that you think will necessitate a longer period of time for discussion with those that can be handled quickly.

6. Have a unifying item at the end; close on a note of achievement if you can.

Location

Regularly scheduled board meetings are customarily held in the same location, often in the organization headquarters. Staff attendance can be conveniently arranged. Busy board members know which freeway to travel and where their allocated parking space will be upon arrival. However, I have served on individual boards that represented a variety of agencies in the community where we met in a different agency office each month. Even though this was not as time efficient, it gave board members an opportunity to learn more about each specific agency by visiting its physical plant.

Facilitate Discussion

Anthony Jay, chairman of Video Arts Ltd. and a producer of industrial training films, recommends that the board president see himself or herself as the servant of the board group rather than the master. The role becomes one of assisting the group in achieving the best possible solutions. This can be done by interpreting and clarifying, by moving the discussion forward, and by hopefully resolving it in such a way that all understand and accept it as the will of the majority, a *consensus* as defined earlier.

Let's assume you are the president of a board or the chairperson of an important committee. As president (or chairperson) you have a definite right, often an obligation, to speak. If you want a particular point to be emphasized, it is customary to have someone else begin the discussion. Your commentary and summary can come later. If you keep hearing the sound of your voice in a discussion, you are probably being a self-indulgent president. Several years ago I served as president-elect of a state organization. The president was brilliant, intense, and somewhat impatient with those of us who did not recognize a problem or solution as quickly as he did. In explaining the problem or solution, he monopolized the meeting leaving a turned-off, uncooperative board. Fortunately our working relationship was such that he and I could discuss his problem and work out a series of nonverbal indicators to let him know when this situation was arising. Good board members welcome *constructive* criticism.

Enthusiasm is contagious; so is the lack of it. Just because board work is crucial to an organization's success doesn't mean the board can't enjoy what they're doing and most do. Having a president who instills not only knowledge but also enthusiasm gives the group a sense of accomplishment and momentum.

HOW DOES THE STAFF BUILD A WORKING RELATIONSHIP WITH THE BOARD?

How does the board interact with you as staff? What are these board/staff roles, and how do they relate? Board experts William Conrad and William Glenn observed that:

> the vitality and effectiveness of a voluntary organization is in direct proportion to the strength of its volunteer/staff relationship. This relationship is the key—the one com-

ponent that holds it all together. The role of the board and the role of the staff must be clearly defined, accepted, and honored for the ultimate success and growth of the organization.[8]

ROLE OF THE CHIEF EXECUTIVE OFFICER (CEO)

The organization's CEO directs and controls the organization's operations and activities. He or she selects, employs, supervises, and dismisses other staff in accordance with policies approved by the board and determines salaries of nonunion personnel. In most organizations the CEO attends board meetings and certain, specified committee meetings.

If you recall, the executive officer is hired (and fired) by the board and is under direct supervision of the board. When a board hires an executive officer, it is obligated to support that person, short of incompetence, in good times and bad. Hopefully the person selected by the board is experienced and competent enough to manage a diverse organization and also is knowledgeable about small group communication and has the skills to develop a smooth functioning relationship with the board.

All matters pertaining to the executive officer should go through the president of the board. Routine requests from board members are easy to handle. However, when a controversial issue is brought to the attention of the board president, he or she must take it to the executive officer for discussion. A good rapport between these two principals is a necessity for a smooth functioning organization. Trust in each other and open-system communication are essential. Regularly scheduled meetings between the two help in building strong agendas as well as good relationships.

Review evaluations of the executive officer, including salary, are done annually by the board president and specific board members if so stipulated in the bylaws. The president is responsible for notifying and discussing the evaluation results with the executive officer.

STAFF ROLES

Board committee chairpersons and the staff assigned to them should also work toward a high-quality relationship. The presence and contributions of a board president who everyone knows has a good working relationship with the executive officer is a catalyst for the whole organization.

Listed below are suggestions I have received from experienced staff personnel who have worked with board members.

1. *Be familiar with the board bylaws and basic parliamentary procedure.*
2. *Recognize that board members are often unpaid volunteers whose time is valuable.* Meetings requested by the staff should be set at convenient times for board members who often must leave paid jobs. Indicate how long a meeting will take and adhere to that schedule.
3. *Request feedback from board members on the issues at hand.* These people are experts in a variety of fields; use their expertise and abilities. For example, one new staff assistant hired to develop and operate a home helpers' service in the community was given a board committee composed of a vice president of marketing; a lawyer; an accountant; a partner in a national, financial consulting firm; the past president of the board; and the current board president. The job was a big one and was suc-

cessfully implemented because this staff person wisely used the unusual pool of knowledge and expertise available to her. The board members themselves were excited about working on the project and felt duly rewarded upon its success.

4. *Be prepared with facts and figures.* Circulate such information beforehand if at all possible. Attempting to read new material, listen to a staff report, and offer a valuable insight at the same time is an almost impossible task for the best of board members. A well-done, professional presentation complete with visual aids is also recommended. Anticipate questions and have the answers or offer further information and get the answers to the board as soon as possible.

5. *Define terms specific to a certain field that may be unfamiliar to the committee.* Keep jargon to a minimum. Prepare to supply definitions; board members will demand them. In some organizations like health care, where there is technical language and diverse board membership, a glossary of terms is a good idea.

6. *Listen actively even if you feel threatened by what you hear.* Avoid the impulse to give a speech defending yourself too quickly; the board is only doing its job. Your objective is to get input from board members and to discuss it rationally.

7. *Keep yourself up-to-date professionally. Read your specialty publications and attend professional conferences.* Most organizations encourage workshop and conference attendance, often allocating work time for them and paying registration fees. Continuing education hours or units are mandatory for certification in many professions. And remember, your board members are reading too so you must be knowledgeable and current in your field.

8. *Stay within the organization's chain of command.* Items for discussion at committee or board meetings should be fully explored beforehand with your supervisor. Don't approach individual board members for support of your pet project; if your boss approves, discuss it with the entire committee. Don't maliciously gossip about agency personnel with board members; these are "proper channel" people.

The staff interacts with the board mostly as part of a specific committee. Board members expect staff to handle physical arrangements for meetings, including scheduling, notification, catering, and disbursement of the meeting results. They expect to receive concise, up-to-date information several days prior to a meeting. If a board person has a presentation to make at the board meeting or in the community, be sure he or she is adequately prepared with all necessary facts about the organization.

Phone calls should be returned promptly and personally. If you request a meeting with a board member, be sure to indicate its purpose and its approximate length.

Recognize board members by name (and reputation) if possible when they are in your buildings and offices. They expect that.

As a staff member you also have a right to expect certain things from your board members; in some organizations you can vote them out of office. Staff personnel has the right to expect a board member to apply his or her knowledge and expertise to the problems of the organization and even to individual staff members. Board accessibility by phone or an appointment should be possible. Prompt response should be made when contacted by staff. Agreed-upon deadlines should be observed.

Board members should be aware of staff organizational problems and give support and counsel when needed. However, this does not mean overlooking the organization's chain of command. Staff should expect a board member to have an overview of the total agency and to support the organization and the executive officer.

Like the board, staff are individuals who enjoy recognition for their achievements. An announcement at a meeting with the staff person present not only recognizes that individual but also informs the board that their staff is among the best. Strong staffs and strong boards honor their roles and their expectations.

SUMMARY

Decisions made by boards affect our communities culturally, governmentally, educationally, and financially. Libraries, museums, zoos, churches, schools, hospitals, corporations, and others operate under policies set by their boards. Nonprofit organizations are legally required to have boards. Publicly held corporations also are required to establish boards that are elected by the shareholders. Rules abound; the system is not as open as other organizational small groups.

Members of a board may be referred to as directors, trustees, regents, or governors. A board is defined as ''an organized group of people collectively controlling and assisting an agency or association which is usually administered by a qualified executive and staff [Houle].''

There are four major types of boards: (1) controlling, (2) auxiliary, (3) association, and (4) community. Members may be nominated by a board, appointed by outside authority, or elected by the public or by shareholders. Selection procedures vary with the type of board.

Board responsibilities include the following: establishing policies, the management structure, hiring the CEO, strategic planning, budget, organizational evaluation, and public information. On larger boards major committees do the work: administrative or executive, governance, and so forth. Subcommittees assist the major committees. Staff personnel are often asked to assist. The administrative or executive committee is composed of the officers of the board and the chairpersons of the standing committees. Depending upon bylaws, the executive group has the power of the full board. Typical standing committees are finance, personnel, community relations, bylaws, nominating, program, and strategic planning. Corporation boards may have additional committees such as public policy, proxy, pension, and audit. Outside consultants are often retained by all boards to assist with special or technical problems.

Effective board members are advised to serve an apprenticeship, participate, and avoid crusades and fighting. The president, chairman, or chairperson of the board has real and important power throughout the organization and is expected to preside at all meetings and be an ex-officio member of all board committees. The president also formally appoints all committees.

Agendas and orders of business are usually developed jointly by the board president and the CEO. In most organizations the CEO attends board meetings and certain specified committee meetings. Review evaluations, including salary of the CEO, are done annually by the board president and others as specified in the bylaws.

Staff personnel who must interact with the board are advised to

Know the board bylaws and procedures.
Know who the board members are.
Know their expertise and how to use it.
Carefully prepare facts and figures.
Define special or technical terms.
Listen before speaking.

Avoid becoming defensive.

Keep up to date in their specialty.

Follow the chain of command.

Board members are advised to be aware of staff problems, to listen, but to follow the chain of command in giving support and counsel. Staff should expect a good board member to know the organization, to support it and its CEO.

PROJECTS AND CASES

PROJECTS

1. Locate and interview a board member. Ask your friends, parents, relatives, and so on. Ask if they are on any boards. You may be surprised at the number of people you know who are on one of the board types described. Find out everything you can about the organization the board controls and how they operate. Write a short, descriptive report using Chapter 9 as a guide. Prepare to report in class.

2. Attend a board meeting and write a description of how members operate as a group. (Some board meetings are closed; some are closed for certain agendas; some must be open by reason of law; some require permission or invitation.)

3. Locate an annual report from a major organization with a listing of its board members and sketch out the backgrounds of the board members. Why are they on the board? Prepare to report.

4. Review the rules and members of your college or university board (regents, trustees, governors, directors), and prepare to role play their deliberations on a current agenda item. Select a nonroutine, more complex issue.

5. In some cases the president or chairman of the board and the CEO of the organization are the same person (e.g., AT&T). How does this happen? What are the advantages and disadvantages? Discuss.

CASES

1. The Dethroned President

When President Frank Marant gained control of Great Southern Foods from his uncle five years ago, one of his primary goals was to impose a system of financial controls over the $500 million processed foods conglomerate. The 38-year-old Marant was able to accomplish his initial objective. His controls were of some value in salvaging the company when it lost $26 million four years ago. Paradoxically, Marant's tight controls led to his recent downfall.

Insiders say controls were an obsession with Marant. He centralized his management to the point of frustrating leading executives in the company. His insistence upon checking and re-checking caused many a delay in decision making. Operations were virtually strangled in paperwork. One good example: Great Southern's most recent annual report claimed that the company would spend $5 million this year to open twenty-five more processing operations. Six months into the fiscal year, insiders report that little work has been done on the projects; because of Marant's insistence upon such a thorough analysis for each project, decisions have been postponed.

Such delayed decision making can be particularly harmful to the fast-moving field of processed foods. The continuous parade of new products in the processed foods field makes quick reaction time a necessity. An anonymous personnel director said that "Marant's situation is a textbook example of how a bungling president can mess up a company and bring about his own demise." The same personnel executive was among the fifteen people participating in a palace revolt last month when Marant was stripped of his authority.

The end for Marant came when two inside directors, Joe Palaggi and Dean Wilson, had become upset about the company's lethargy in the fall. During the same time span, a number of key managers in Great Southern had complained to Palaggi and Wilson that Marant's managerial style had been demoralizing. When it seemed that Marant was about to fire two key general managers, Palaggi and Wilson blew the whistle. They went to an outside director to explain how the company was headed toward a rapid decline. Palaggi and Wilson headed a drive to build a dossier of Marant's shortcomings as a company president.

The end for Marant came when Palaggi, Wilson, and three outside directors met in Atlanta. A special board meeting was called. Three dozen operating executives threatened to quit unless Marant was deposed from his chief executive position. The board moved swiftly, stripping Marant of his president and chief operating executive titles. He was reassigned as vice president of special projects at a $100,000 cut in pay.

Marant informed a business reporter that the whole affair was a conspiracy to remove him because he wanted to run a sophisticated, finely tuned business. A confidant of Marant said that what Marant's antagonists really objected to was his plan to bring in two new marketing-oriented executives from the outside. A countercharge issued by one of the inside directors active in Marant's dethroning was, "Frank just wasn't willing to accept the fact that you can't run a business by reading computer printouts and writing memos. If you don't get out and visit the troops, they'll eventually get rid of you."

QUESTIONS

1. What do you think of the board's behavior?
2. What should Frank Marant do now?
3. What could have been done to resolve this conflict before it reached such drastic proportions?
4. Do you think appointing Frank Marant as vice president of special projects will prove to be an effective compromise? Why or why not?

2. Bay View High School

You are a member of the school board of a medium-sized Western city. It is September and the high school must immediately replace a very fine history teacher who died quite suddenly, since school starts next week. You have to choose from among four applicants—Frances, Harry, Jim, and Bill.

1. Frances had an exceptional academic record in a teachers' college. She is bright and hardworking, well liked and well mannered. However, she is a very stubborn young woman—also a confirmed atheist—and does not hide her lack of religious belief. When asked if she intended to teach atheism to her pupils, she replied that she would teach what she believed, and no one had the right to ask her not to. The principal contends that a school owes a duty to the public not to approve a new teacher who holds fanatical ideas about atheism, which, if impressed upon the minds of the young, might work to their detriment and injury. Frances appealed that you cannot discriminate against a person for her religion or lack of religion in the United States. She maintains that if she is qualified, she should be hired.

2. Harry had an average academic record at a small church school. His recommendations are just adequate, with the clear indication that some question of competence remains in the minds of his teachers. When the principal asked how well his practice teaching had gone, Harry replied that he did not get through all the material he was supposed to cover. The principal contends that Harry would be incompetent; Harry contends that he is willing and able to learn as he teaches.

3. Jim had an exceptional academic record at a large, well-respected private university. His recommendations were excellent as far as academic training was concerned. Although well liked and well mannered, Jim is very uncomfortable around women and definitely seems to prefer the company of men. Jim admitted that this was true and replied that he was a homosexual but had the situation in full control. Jim said that he would not teach any of his homosexual views but if asked would admit that he preferred the company of men to that of women. The principal contends that the school has a responsibility to protect its students and that exposure to Jim might be a detriment and an injury. Jim contends that this is his private life; he has his own circle of friends in a town fifty miles away and has never been in trouble with the police, nor was he in any trouble during four years of undergraduate work. He maintains that he is well qualified and that his qualifications should be the basis for employment.

4. Bill had a sporadic academic record from a large public university. The principal reports that he is neat, clean, and well dressed. He had been a campus radical and took part in several protests, on one occasion spending eighteen days in jail because of his activities. His record also shows that Bill has strong political leanings toward communism. Upon questioning, Bill admitted his association with violent factions but assured the principal that he was now ready to settle down and that he would like to teach. Bill said that he would not teach communist doctrines but would not lie to the students if asked about his beliefs. The principal contends that the school cannot afford to subject its students to a communist; Bill maintains that his qualifications are good and that he should be considered for the position.

THE PROBLEM

Which candidate should the board select to fill the teaching position in the high school history department?

What other options does the board have?

3. Crosscraft Corporation

Mr. Appley is the founder of Crosscraft Corporation and now maintains a seat on the board of directors as president of the firm. For the last three years the corporation has been losing a quarter of a million dollars a year. Mr. Appley has been asked to bring in outside help to solve the situation; he refuses. It has been suggested that some of the products are outdated and should be discontinued; he refuses to address this as well. The chairman of the board has asked him to retire as he is 65 years old; however, no set retirement policy has prevailed at the corporation; Mr. Appley also refuses to retire. His doctors have also stated that he would not live a year after he retires.

Your position is that of a member of the board of directors.

FIVE PROPOSALS HAVE BEEN SUGGESTED; ON WHICH SHOULD YOU CAST YOUR VOTE?

1. Keep Mr. Appley on as a member of the board, but disregard his opinions and do what is best.

2. Since Mr. Appley founded the corporation, nothing should be done that would affect his life, since this would also be morally wrong.

3. Retire Mr. Appley even though it will probably mean his death.

4. Demote Mr. Appley from the board of directors, and give him another position of less authority.

5. Do nothing at the present, since Mr. Appley is probably the oldest and wisest member of the board and knows what is best for the corporation.

4. Anytown Hospital

An Anytown jury last week found Dr. John Smith guilty of manslaughter for performing what was first presumed to be a legal abortion. The verdict appeared to conflict, at least in part, with the landmark Supreme Court decision 16 years ago that barred states from interfering with abortions carried out before the fetus is old enough to survive outside the womb.

Since the High Court's ruling, most doctors have felt free to perform abortions during the first 24 to 28 weeks of pregnancy. The fetus in the Smith case was said to be 20 to 24 weeks old, but the state charged that Smith had not given it an adequate chance to live once it was removed from the womb of its unmarried teenage mother. After a review of the conflicting evidence, Judge George Justice told the jurors that to find Smith guilty, they had to consider the fetus a living person. After seven hours of deliberation, they did just that.

Smith plans to appeal the verdict, which could throw the issue back to the Supreme Court for clarification. "Everything I did was in accordance with law and with good medical practice," said Smith, who predicted that other doctors might be discouraged from performing abortions while the Anytown verdict stands.

Your position is that of a member of the board of directors of Anytown Hospital.

QUESTIONS

1. What action will you take in regard to the Smith case now and during the appeal process?
2. What recommendations will you make to your other doctors in light of this case?
3. Will this incident affect the hospital's public relations and how will you cope with that?

5. The Kidney Machine

The board of General Hospital must consider applicants for the use of its kidney machines. Each of the patients described below has been evaluated by the medical staff, and it has been determined that each will probably die in six to eight weeks without the constant use of the machine. Unfortunately, there are only four machines available for home use. What options does the board have?

1. John Hallbright. Age 31. Married. One child, a daughter 4. College graduate. Works as teller in a bank. Wife employed as an elementary school teacher.
2. Maria Villareal. Age 39. Unmarried. College graduate. Holds master's in physical therapy. Employed at VA hospital for 14 years. Is head of physical and occupational therapy treatment center.
3. Pamela Watson. Age 23. Married, no children. College graduate. Teaches social studies and is cheerleader advisor in junior high school. Husband is teacher in the high school.
4. Avery Smith. Age 51. Married. Three children, daughter 19, sons 17 and 15. High school graduate. Owner and operator of Smith Industries, Inc., a machine shop that employs 150. City councilman for 12 years; member of library board of directors for 6 years. Has suffered several heart attacks (last one 3½ years ago). Medical bills plus lack of health insurance cause him to make application for the free machine.
5. William Work. Age 11. One of seven children of Mr. and Mrs. Ralph Work.
6. Walker Red Cloud. Age, about 40. Ojibwa, Indian. At least four children by two wives. Fourth-grade education. No occupation.
7. Nancy Adams. Age 34. Divorced, three children, daughter 7, twin sons 6, all in her custody. Employed as secretary in a real estate office.

NOTES

1. Henry M. Robert, *Robert's Rules of Order Newly Revised* (Glenview, Ill.: Scott, Foresman, 1981), p. 399.

2. Cyril O. Houle, *The Effective Board* (New York: Association, 1960: Battle Creek, Michigan: W. K. Kellogg Foundation, 1983), p. 12.

3. Ibid., pp. 5-7.

4. Diane J. Duca, *Nonprofit Boards* (Phoenix, Ariz.: Oryx, 1986), p.38.

5. Dean Schooler, "Diverse Roles and Broader Involvement," *Voluntary Action Leadership* (Winter 1980), p. 22.

6. James G. Lagges, "The Board of Directors: Boon or Bane for Stockholders and Management?" *Business Horizons* (March–April 1982), p. 50.

7. Thomas L. Whisler, "Some Do's and Don'ts for Directors," *The Wall Street Journal*, March 21, 1983, p. 3.

8. William R. Conrad and William E. Glenn, *The Effective Voluntary Board of Directors* (Chicago: Swallow Press, 1976), p. 10.

10

OBSERVING AND IMPROVING GROUP EFFECTIVENESS

HEURISTIC OBSERVATION METHODS

By *heuristic* we mean "aids to learning," which in this case involve mostly analysis of feedback based on structured observations. In the classroom these observations can range from self-analysis, sociograms, and rating charts to critics, consultants, and elaborate interaction analysis systems—even television.

In the organizational setting these same observational techniques will be found in the various training programs you will encounter. These and more will also be found in some performance appraisal, promotion, and review systems; some will be done in small groups. In all organizations there is also a more subtle, unstructured, but omnipresent form of observation, feedback, and evaluation. The review of the more standard techniques that follows should help you gain insight into the more subtle forms as well as into your own small-group behavior.

BASIC SYSTEMS

Category

These are descriptive observations in frequency data form. That is, one counts various observed behaviors according to preestablished classifications. Category observations may range from the "number and time" of each member's contributions, to the character of their contributions (i.e., informative, task, interpersonal, and so on). Some border on evaluation, but the emphasis is on frequency data that can be analyzed and evaluated later. With the use of videotape and frequent replays, category observations can become very detailed: vocabulary, grammar, nonverbals, interruptions, and so forth. Illustrations of structured category systems will follow shortly.

Frequency data can also be collected diagrammatically, that is, the participation of each member is charted by observers (who spoke to whom, for how long, and the like). These diagrams or *sociograms* often provide graphic insights into group be-

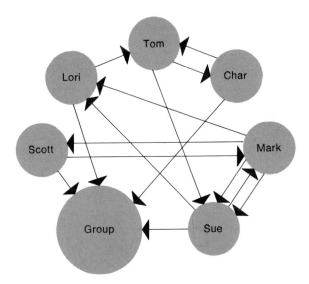

Figure 10.1   Sociogram.

havior. Most observers draw circles representing the discussants and then diagram the flow and amount of interpersonal communication. One can often find graphic evidence to show to the overtalkative (see Figure 10.1). If you're describing assigned leaders, some simple form of network analysis as discussed in Chapter 2 also could be used diagrammatically.

TABLE 10.1   The Wright Group Satisfaction Index

Group Numbers_____
Group Name_____
Group Size_____

Directions: At the conclusion of your group's discussion, please mark each scale according to *how you think* the group *feels* about itself. None of the scales are necessarily "good" or "bad," "high" or "low." Please mark the space on each scale that you think identifies how the group *feels.* Make certain to answer all scales.
    Thank you.

1. Relaxed	:____:____:____:____:____:____:____:	Pressured
2. Tension inducing	:____:____:____:____:____:____:____:	Tension releasing
3. Conformity	:____:____:____:____:____:____:____:	Nonconformity
4. Dissimilar	:____:____:____:____:____:____:____:	Similar
5. Unsatisfied	:____:____:____:____:____:____:____:	Satisfied
6. Constrained feeling	:____:____:____:____:____:____:____:	Casual feeling
7. Coordinating	:____:____:____:____:____:____:____:	Noncoordinating
8. Incompatible	:____:____:____:____:____:____:____:	Compatible
9. Gratifying	:____:____:____:____:____:____:____:	Nongratifying
10. Withdrawing	:____:____:____:____:____:____:____:	Contributing
11. Accord	:____:____:____:____:____:____:____:	Discord
12. Contention	:____:____:____:____:____:____:____:	Harmony

TABLE 10.2 Group Evaluation Form

Group Identification_____

Directions: Check the evaluative term that best describes the group's performance on each of the following aspects of the symposium or the panel discussion. Turn this form in to your instructor at the conclusion of the group presentation.

SYMPOSIUM	Excellent	Good	Average	Fair	Poor
Definition of problem					
Limitation of problem					
Analysis of problem					
Information sharing in question and answer period					

PANEL DISCUSSION	Excellent	Good	Average	Fair	Poor
Summary of Def. & Anal. of Problem					
Establishment of Criteria					
Evaluation of Solution					
Group Productivity					
Group Cohesion					
Group Leadership					

Directions: Circle the evaluative term that best describes the group's effectiveness on the symposium or the panel discussion.

Excellent	Good	Average	Fair	Poor

ROSS DISCUSSION EVALUATION FORM

1-2-3	4-5-6	7-8-9
Weak	Average	Strong

Criteria for evaluating discussion participation include the following:

A. Task Contributions	Information, breadth and accuracy Ideas, number and merit Problem analysis Reasoning from the data
B. Procedural Behavior	Participating proportionately Agenda seeking and following Leadership contributions Idea synthesis and classification
C. Relational Effectiveness	Attentive listening Communication adaptation Cooperative thinking Emotional control
D. Teambuilding Efforts	Climate setting Consensus seeking Interaction promotion Group involvement
E. Overall Effect	General impression of how the member related, interacted and contributed to the group

Members Names

	1	2	3	4	5	6	7	8	9	10	11
Project											
Class Hour											
Date											
A. Task Contributions											
B. Procedural Contributions											
C. Relational Effectiveness											
D. Teambuilding Efforts											
E. Overall Effect											
Total Scores											
Rank Order of Participants											

General comments on the group as a whole (Use back of sheet as needed):

Figure 10.2

© *Raymond S. Ross.*

Rating

These are descriptive observations in degree form. Member contributions are not so much classified, isolated, and counted, as they are estimated according to one or more continua. How cooperative was member 1 or how cooperative was the group? Weak? Strong? Some rating charts are the product of factor-analyzed research. Others are simply based on veteran teachers' experience. John Cragan and David Wright offer examples of each.[1] (See Tables 10.1 and 10.2.) The satisfaction index was derived from an original list of over 100 items. The Wayne State University rating chart also asks for members to be ranked (see Figure 10.2). That, of course, forces evaluation and is threatening for some.

Category systems, sociograms, and rating systems can be combined and frequently are in more structured, global group analysis and evaluation. Such general systems are usually divided into two basic observations of *task* and *socio-emotional* (or interpersonal); sometimes other observations like *procedural* are added. Several structured, proven systems will be discussed shortly.

Critics and Consultants

Your instructor or a guest "expert" may critique your group's efforts in terms of your interaction, your reasoning, your decisions and their quality, and so on. Other members of your class may also serve as critics. These observations may stem from specific criteria suggested in some rating charts and your text. We will discuss task experts and other types of trained critics in the next section, Structured Analysis.

SELF-REPORTS

Earlier we wrote about your role as a participant observer, that is, the monitoring of your personal group behavior and the group itself, while participating. This takes recall at the end of the discussion or perhaps during a TV replay, if it was recorded. You observe and analyze your own participation and perhaps your feelings about the group of which you were a part.

These participant-observer reports can be oral, essay, or various kinds of checklists and self–group rating systems. The more elaborate member and group evaluation schemes will be discussed later. We speak here of a less formal look at how you *think* you did. A discussion of your thoughts and a report to others of the group can often be an eye opener and a shaker; it also can be an aid to self-improvement. The emphasis in these reports is usually on interpersonal interactions rather than on the task. The suggestions on coordinating your meanings and improving relational effectiveness found in Chapter 7 should provide an outline for your oral report or written essay. If interpersonal conflict was part of your group experience, the material in Chapter 6 should augment your outline. Choose those headings in the chapter outlines that you feel pertain to your experience, reread them, put them in appropriate outline form, then write a personal essay of your participant observations. Those interpersonal parts of the rating charts discussed previously should also offer ideas for your introspective reports.

If your report emphasis is to be on the task—how well you and your group did in its problem solving and decision making—then Chapters 4 and 5 should be particularly useful.

These self-reports may then be primarily introspective and intrapersonal in emphasis. They can be interpersonal and group centered if you report your own observations of those dimensions. Some instructors and trainers may ask you to keep a diary of a group project or series of discussions of which you were a part. Text citations may be required to help you integrate theory and practice in your diary reports. Field observations of community groups, family groups, business groups, or church groups also make good fare for self-reports, which can be shared with your classmates.

The VCR and the Camcorder have opened new observation techniques not only for the field groups discussed above but also for the analysis of previously recorded movies, TV shows, and training sessions. The staff meetings that usually open the *L.A. Law* TV program are rich in classic rules and practices for small groups in organizational settings. So too are such movies as *The Right Stuff, The Poseiden Adventure, Platoon,* and many others.

STRUCTURED ANALYSIS

INTERACTION

Unlike the self-reports, a structured observation and analysis makes a more determined and scientific effort to break down the group process into its component parts function, acts, or content.[2] That there is a difference of opinion about which are the most important components or units is clear from the instruments available. Some, as we shall see, emphasize functional roles; others concentrate on decision emergence; still others on social problems. Some structured systems are more interpersonal–interaction oriented; some more task oriented. Most of the research instruments attempt to structure observations of both dimensions. All are *interaction* centered, that is, how acts, task or interpersonal, are interstructured during group discussion. This unit will be divided into *interaction* analysis for those discussed above, and into *task–outcome* for those analyses based on the quality of the decision, the reasoning, and the way a group's overall *outcome* measures up to expert opinion, criticism, or perhaps a ''school'' solution.

Interaction Process Analysis (IPA)

In Chapter 4 we referred to this instrument as it was used by researchers to locate phases that most problem-solving groups go through. The whole system of observation and analysis, which is called *interaction process analysis*, is a classification of communicative acts; *act* is defined as verbal and nonverbal behavior. An observer is responsible for three areas of observation: positive social-emotional acts, task acts, and negative social-emotional acts. The categories of acts are shown in Table 10.3.

Observers' tabulations of acts in various research studies (usually of college students) indicate an average group profile of 25 percent positive reactions (category *A* in Table 10.3), 56 percent attempted answers (*B*), 7 percent questions (*C*), and 12 percent negative reactions (*D*).

Observation record sheets can be set up as shown in Figure 10.3. The interacts between members can be recorded by coupling their numbers. If 1 speaks to 4, it's (1-4). If 1 speaks to the group as a whole, it's (1-0).

TABLE 10.3 Categories for Interaction Process Analysis

MAJOR CATEGORIES	SUBCATEGORIES	ILLUSTRATIVE STATEMENTS OR BEHAVIOR
Social-Emotional Area	A. Positive (and Mixed) Reactions	
	1. Seems friendly	Jokes, gives help, rewards others, is friendly
	2. Dramatizes	Laughs, shows satisfaction, is relieved
	3. Agrees	Passively accepts, understands, concurs, complies
Task Area	B. Attempted Answers	
	4. Gives suggestion	Directs, suggests, implies autonomy for others
	5. Gives opinion	Evaluates, analyzes, expresses feeling or wish
	6. Gives information	Orients, repeats, clarifies, confirms
	C. Questions	
	7. Asks for information	Requests orientation, repetition, confirmation
	8. Asks for opinion	Requests evaluation, analysis, expression of feeling
	9. Asks for suggestion	Requests direction, possible ways of action
Social Emotional Area	D. Negative (and Mixed) Reactions	
	10. Disagrees	Passively rejects, resorts to formality, withholds help
	11. Shows tension	Asks for help, withdraws, daydreams
	12. Seems unfriendly	Deflates other's status, defends or asserts self, acts hostile

Reciprocal or Opposite Pairs: a b c d e f

a. Problems of communication
b. Problems of evaluation
c. Problems of control
d. Problems of decision
e. Problems of tension reduction
f. Problems of reintegration

Based on Robert F. Bales, *Interaction Process Analysis* (Cambridge, Mass.: Addison-Wesley 1950), p. 9; A. Paul Hare, *Handbook of Small Group Research* (New York: Free Press of Glenco, 1962), p. 66; and Robert F. Bales, *Personality and Interpersonal Behavior* (New York: Holt, Rinehart & Winston, 1970), pp. 91–97. By permission of Robert F. Bales and the University of Chicago, © 1950. All rights reserved.

ACTS	1	2	3	4	5	6
Jokes, gives help, rewards others, is friendly						
Laughs, shows satisfaction, is relieved						
Passively accepts, understands, concurs, complies						
Directs, suggests, implies autonomy for others	(1-4)					
Evaluates, analyzes, expresses feeling or wish	(1-0)					
Orients, repeats, clarifies, confirms						
Requests orientation, repetition, confirmation						
Requests evaluation, analysis, expression of feeling						
Requests direction, possible ways of action						
Passively rejects, resorts to formality, withholds help						
Asks for help, withdraws, daydreams						
Deflates other's status, defends or asserts self, acts hostile						

Figure 10.3

SYMLOG

More recently Bales has produced another system of coding and observing group interaction called SYMLOG, which stands for *System* for the *Multiple Level Observation* of *Groups*.[3] This more complicated model attempts to catch more of the personality characteristics of the interactants. The behaviors to be observed are based on the following personality dimensions: (1) dominance/submission, (2) friendly/unfriendly, and (3) instrumentally controlled/emotionally expressive. Instrumentally controlled refers to behaviors thought to be work oriented or value controlled, a higher order of intellectual control than the emotional.[4]

These three dimensions can each be classified as (1) upward, downward, or neutral, (2) positive, negative, or neutral, and (3) forward, backward, or neutral. This yields twenty-seven possible and theoretically observable roles (minus one for the neutral found in all three conditions). The system is modeled in three-dimensional space as a cube.[5]

The original rating form[6] had five adjectives. A newer form collapses the polar adjectives and a three-term rating chart has proved effective (not often, sometimes, often).[7]

One can rate a group member's disposition toward any of the twenty-six roles along each dimension. These three scores, computed for each member, can then be compared. While this complicated system is more useful in research observations than in the classroom, it has heuristic value in that its theoretical underpinnings are reasonable and understandable. It is a large part of what people observe in your behavior, whether they understand the model or not. That it has some encouraging face validity is shown in a study by Isenberg and Ennis in which people rated the social behavior of sixteen well-known public figures, thought from pilot studies to tap all areas of the SYMLOG space. When charted, the line of polarization extended from Yassir Arafat, UNF (authoritarian, controlling, disapproving) to Charlie Chaplain, DPB (quietly happy just to be with others). Hitler was UNF, Jesus, PF (works cooperatively with others), as one would predict.[8] More recently a study by Wall and Galanes encourages its application for research into group conflict.[9]

Interact System Model (ISM)

This model of structured analysis makes the *interact* between persons the behavior to be observed. In the Bales IPA model, the emphasis was on individual *acts*. An *interact* is the observable verbal or nonverbal act of one member followed by a reaction from another. It is really an interactive behavior model that studies pairs of contiguous acts.[10]

ISM concentrates on the decision dimension and classifies statements in terms of how they respond to a decision proposal. Recall that in our earlier discussion of Fisher's decision-emergence theory, it was his hypothesis that almost all communications in a task-oriented group are related to a decision proposal. The same kinds of categories used in the decision-emergence model are used here. They provide a list of functions performed on a potential decision. Fisher's outline of the categories follows:[11]

1. Interpretation
   f. Favorable toward the decision proposal
   u. Unfavorable toward the decision proposal
   ab. Ambiguous toward the decision proposal, containing a bivalued (both favorable and unfavorable) evaluation
   an. Ambiguous toward the decision proposal, containing a neutral evaluation
2. Substantiation
   f. Favorable toward the decision proposal
   u. Unfavorable toward the decision proposal
   ab. Ambiguous toward the decision proposal, containing a bivalued (both favorable and unfavorable) evaluation
   an. Ambiguous toward the decision proposal, containing a neutral evaluation
3. Clarification
4. Modification
5. Agreement
6. Disagreement

Fisher explains the language and the application of his system to observation as follows:

> A comment that is classified as favorable is a comment that functions on the decision proposal by expressing a favorable attitude toward it and, thus, implicitly attempting to influence the perceptions or opinions of other members toward a favorable position regarding the proposal. Similarly, a comment that is unfavorable toward the proposal attempts to influence other members to reject the proposed idea.
>
> It is possible, however, to interpret or *substantiate (that is, to interpret with evidence)* a decision proposal ambiguously. An ambiguous comment is one in which the speaker's attitude or opinion is not explicit in the act itself, either because it is neutral (for example, "That's interesting") or because it contains both a favorable and an unfavorable evaluation (for example, "That's a good idea, but it needs a lot of work before it is acceptable").[12]

To observe, one creates a matrix with 12 rows and 12 columns, reflecting the 12 categories in Fisher's system. This provides for 144 potential interacts. An observer classifies the first act and the second act placing a mark in the appropriate cell between the two. An analysis of such data allows an observer to see better the frequency and character of act pairs or interacts in group discussion.[13] As with SYMLOG, unless you are a researcher the most useful parts of this model are the insights provided in its theoretical base, particularly those related to interpersonal interacts and decision proposals.

OUTCOME MEASURES

The emphasis here is on the task, that is, the problem or case you're discussing and the quality of your analysis and solution and also the group *outcome* or decision. Of course a manager, an instructor, or a training director may have a lot to say here, but guest experts or consultants are also occasionally invited to offer experience, ideas, critiques, and criticism. This is a popular and effective training procedure; such guests are also used to assist and advise ''working'' small groups in real-life outcomes involving problem solving and decision making. Interpersonal interaction critics (like your instructor) may also have task-related comments, but their emphasis is typically on communication behaviors. Their criticisms are usually more helpful and less threatening if they work with data generated by some kind of objective observation scheme.

Peer Group Observers

Peer or student observers are frequently used for analysis and some criticism. They usually restrict themselves to task and process analysis—at least early in a group's experience. Personal communication criticisms are very threatening for some people, but blunt process and task criticisms are also interpreted by some sensitive members as insults to their reasoning ability or their intelligence.

Our emphasis here is on the task, the outcome or decision, and the process used to solve the problem. As a peer-group observer you may be asked to serve as a consultant or critic and to comment, post discussion, in such areas as (1) group product or outcome, (2) how efficiently the group proceeded in its problem solving, (3) how likely the group is to support and implement the solution, and (4) the effectiveness of procedural leadership. What follows is meant to assist you in your observations, analysis, and commentary, as well as to prepare you for such criticism, whether from peers or guest observers.

Process Observers

John Brilhart offers a comprehensive checklist of questions to assist observers. Those most related to the *process* follow:[14]

1. Are there clear and accepted group goals? Has the committee a clear understanding of its charge? Is there an understanding of the type of output needed?
2. Are all members aware and accepting of limits on their area of freedom?
3. Are any environmental problems disrupting the group, such as poor seating arrangements, noise, or other distractions?
4. Do members seem to be adequately prepared with information?
5. Are information and ideas being evaluated, or accepted at face value?
6. Has some procedure, or agenda for the discussion been provided or developed by the group? If so, how well is this being followed? Does it serve the group's needs?
7. In a problem-solving discussion, has the group defined and clarified the problem thoroughly, or has it become solution-centered too soon?

8. How creative is the group in generating potential solutions to its problem? In interpreting information?

9. Has judgment been deferred until solutions have been listed and understood by all members?

10. Do members seem to share the same values and criteria in making decisions, or do they need to clarify their criteria?

11. When evaluating ideas and opinions, is the group making use of the information brought out during earlier discussion?

12. How are decisions being made?

13. If needed, has the group made adequate plans to implement its decisions, including member responsibilities, future meetings, and so forth?

14. Are periodic summaries needed to help members recall and maintain perspective on the discussion and move the group to new issues without undue redundancy?

15. If needed, is the discussion being adequately recorded (and possibly charted)?

16. If there is a designated leader, what style of leadership is he or she providing? Does this seem appropriate to the group?

17. Does the role structure provide optimal inputs from all members? Are any needed behavioral functions missing?

18. Are special procedural techniques such as brainstorming or parliamentary procedure being used in ways that are productive? Could procedural changes benefit the group?

A group observation report based on the Bales IPA subcategories described earlier can provide group members with valuable descriptive information. See FORN in Figure 10.4.

The *problem-solving* part of process observation and evaluation has also been addressed by Brilhart in the following *group* rating chart (Figure 10-5).[15]

Consultant Observers

These are typically *task* specialists as we discuss them here. Interpersonal-relationship consultant observers are the communication or interaction specialists discussed earlier.

Organizationally, a task specialist may be invited from personnel, accounting, labor relations, marketing, public relations, engineering, and so on. Task specialists and consultants from outside the organization are also used when extra help is needed, or perhaps for a fresh view when organizational stress is running high. As a student ''consultant'' you may be assigned such observational duties according to your major or your experience (e.g., health care, criminal justice, management, public relations, counseling, and so forth).

A small group of organizational communication majors discussed the following incident and totally missed the task dimensions. To make matters worse their problem solving was singularly unsystematic. A tactful but forthright task consultant's comments follow the discussion. Our consultant was a management specialist with training in accounting and small-group procedures.

Miss Winkler has been employed by the River Manufacturing Company under the supervision of Mr. Wilson, as the bookkeeper in charge of accounts receivable. Her work has been exceptionally good, and Mr. Wilson often has commended the accuracy, neatness, and currency of her records.

Insert appropriate letter:

(F) Frequently   (O) Occasionally   (R) Rarely   (N) Never

Descriptive Terms

	1	2	3	4	5	6	7	8
PROJECT CLASS HOUR DATE								
1. SEEMS FRIENDLY								
2. DRAMATIZES								
3. AGREES								
4. GIVES SUGGESTION								
5. GIVES OPINION								
6. GIVES INFORMATION								
7. ASKS FOR INFORMATION								
8. ASKS FOR OPINION								
9. ASKS FOR SUGGESTION								
10. DISAGREES								
11. SHOWS TENSION								
12. SEEMS UNFRIENDLY								

General Comments on the Group:

Figure 10.4   FORN group report.

Instructions: On each scale indicate the degree to which the group accomplished each identified behavior. Use the following scale for your evaluations:

Poor	Fair	Average	Good	Excellent
1	2	3	4	5

Circle the appropriate number in front of each item.

1   2   3   4   5   1. The concern of each member was identified regarding the problem the group attempted to solve.

1   2   3   4   5   2. This concern was identified *before* the problem was analyzed.

1   2   3   4   5   3. In problem analysis, the present condition was carefully compared with the specific condition desired.

1   2   3   4   5   4. The goal was carefully defined and agreed to by all members.

1   2   3   4   5   5. Valid (and relevant) information was secured when needed.

1   2   3   4   5   6. Possible solutions were listed and clarified before they were evaluated.

1   2   3   4   5   7. Criteria for evaluating proposed solutions were clearly identified and accepted by the group.

1   2   3   4   5   8. Predictions were made regarding the probable effectiveness of each proposed solution, using the available information and criteria.

1   2   3   4   5   9. Consensus was achieved on the most desirable solution.

1   2   3   4   5   10. A detailed plan to implement the solution was developed.

1   2   3   4   5   11. The problem-solving process was systematic and orderly.

Figure 10.5   Problem-Solving Process Scale

     Mr. Watson, a C.P.A. and field representative of the accounting firm of Smith and Company, was auditing the River Manufacturing Company's books. When he came to the accounts receivable, he wished to examine the ledger cards and to run an adding machine tape on them for the purpose of checking the total against the control ledger. After engaging Miss Winkler pleasantly in conversation, he asked if he might see her ledger cards. "What do you want them for?" she asked sharply. He explained that he would need to run a tape on them in connection with his audit of the books. Miss Winkler took a tape from her desk and handed it to him with these words: "I have already run the figures on this tape, and you can use it. It will save you a lot of time and bother." Her manner made it clear that she expected him to be appreciative of her having gone so far beyond the call of duty to help him.

     Mr. Watson thanked her but added that it was his practice to run a tape himself and added: "It will be nice to be able to use your figures to check my own accuracy.

May I have the cards now?'' Her reply was an explosive ''NO!'' And she immediately stormed into the office of her supervisor, Mr. Wilson.

''That man doesn't think I do my work accurately,'' she said. ''He refused to use my figures. I did all that work to help him and then he turns up his nose at it.'' After listening to her patiently, Mr. Wilson said: ''Well, everyone knows how snoopy these auditors are. And after all, if they do not want to accept such generous favors as you thoughtfully provided for them, it is their business. Not everyone appreciates human kindness and consideration and maybe auditors are in that class.''

Miss Winkler returned to her desk and with icy politeness handed Mr. Watson the ledger cards.

The consultant observer comments:

You have missed a major issue in the problem, namely, the nature of an audit or the job of an account auditor. If you had started by defining the key terms, or exploring the felt difficulty, I believe you would not have missed the boat. I know that one of your group knows about audits . . . I gather that John either thought everybody did, or felt constrained from speaking up. An auditor routinely comes unannounced and book-keepers should know that. That's another term (''bookkeeper'') you should have de-fined, along with ''C.P.A.,'' ''machine tape,'' ''ledger cards,'' ''accounts receivable,'' and others. When an auditor is refused access to the records (the cards), he becomes suspicious as he is paid to be. Minimally he will record such reluctance in his report; maximally he will suspect fraud or embezzlement. The case suggests many felt diffi-culties from Winkler's explosive ''NO'' to Wilson's reaction. What do you think Wil-son's boss will say about all this?

Just this much defining and preliminary analysis suggests several criteria with which the group might have worked:

1. Cooperate with auditors.
2. Protect the company.
3. Protect and train employees.
4. Control the work force.
5. Prepare employees like Miss Winkler for change and shock.

Consider the hypotheses about what might be coming down based on what I've said so far:

1. Winkler is a crook.
2. Wilson is a crook.
3. (Be creative) Winkler loves Wilson.
4. Wilson is a poor money manager.
5. Winkler is sick. . . .

I've left Watson, the auditor, out of this. I feel he was simply doing his job— or trying to; I think your speculations about Watson were not germane.

As you evaluate the facts in the case against the criteria I've suggested, you should have been able to reach consensus on the following: (1) Watson is out of this, (2) Winkler was wrong—eccentric at best, and (3) Wilson handled it poorly.

Winkler did not cooperate fully with the auditor even though she finally gave him the cards. Incidentally, a bookkeeper worth the name should know about audits. She did not, therefore, protect the company. Wilson did get Winkler to give up the cards, but what did he teach Winkler? He reinforced her confusion about auditors; he did not control her behavior; he put the company at unnecessary risk. If Winkler is simply a difficult personality who does the work of ten, then Wilson should prepare her for audits and other interruptions that she may find foolish or threatening. Winkler deserved a blunt reprimand not the baloney Wilson gave her. If I were Wilson's boss I'd want to talk to him real quick.

So much for the case. I feel that if you had stuck with some standard problem-solving agenda like Dr. Ross suggests in his textbook, you would not have missed critical definitions and issues, that the criteria would have been clearer, your analysis more to the point—but then I wouldn't have had much to say as a consultant observer.

"School" Solutions

Some small group outcomes can be measured against known facts, known policies, and successful past practices and procedures. Most of you have probably discussed or heard about such synergy games as "Lost at Sea," "Desert Survival," "Subarctic Survival," "Management Survival," and the classic NASA problem "Lost on the Moon." Experts in these task matters have scientifically (for the most part) figured out what decisions are most appropriate and are prepared to explain their rationales in great detail. *Their* answers or decisions are the "school" solutions, that is, the outcomes desired. How well your group did is measured by simply matching your decisions against the school decisions. A short version of the NASA problem illustrates the procedure. You should, for example, rank the compass and matches last since there is no magnetic pole and no air on the moon.

NASA PROBLEM

INSTRUCTIONS: This is an exercise in group decision making. Your group is to employ the method of Group Consensus in reaching its decision. This means that the prediction for each of the fifteen survival items *must* be agreed upon by each group member before it becomes a part of the group decision. Consensus is difficult to reach; therefore, not every ranking will meet with everyone's *complete* approval. But try, as a group, to make each ranking one with which *all* group members can agree.

You are a member of a space crew originally scheduled to rendezvous with a mother ship on the lighted surface of the moon. Due to mechanical difficulties, however, your ship was forced to land at a spot some 200 miles from the rendezvous point. During re-entry and landing much of the equipment aboard was damaged, and, since survival depends on reaching the mother ship, the most critical items available must be chosen for the 200-mile trip. Below are listed the fifteen items left intact and undamaged after landing. Your task is to rank order them in terms of their importance for your crew in allowing them to reach the rendezvous point. Place the number 1 by the most important item, the number 2 by the second most important, and so on through number 15, the least important.

RANK

a. Box of matches _____

b. Food concentrate _____

c. 50 feet of nylon rope _____

d. Parachute silk _____

e. Portable heating unit _____

f. Two .45 caliber pistols _____

g. One case dehydrated pet milk　　　　　_____

h. Two 100-pound oxygen tanks　　　　　_____

i. Stellar map (or moon's constellation)　　_____

j. Life raft　　　　　　　　　　　　　_____

k. Magnetic compass　　　　　　　　　_____

l. Signal flares　　　　　　　　　　　_____

m. First-aid kit containing injection needles　_____

n. Solar-powered FR receiver–transmitter　_____

o. 5 gallons of water　　　　　　　　　_____

CLASSIC TRAINING METHODS

The most prevalent in small group training are case studies, critical incidents, propositional discussions, and simulations and games. Several of these have already been illustrated in discussing outcome measures, especially ''consultant observers'' (a critical incident) and ''school solutions'' (a game).

CASE STUDY DISCUSSIONS

Length, detail, and structure are the principle differences between *cases* and *critical incidents* as we use them in small-group teaching. The ''Fournier Clock Company Case'' involving quality-control problems is almost five single-spaced pages in length, and includes details about such things as raw materials, parts, manufacturing departments, operations, and even the executive personnel. The ''Dashman Company Case'' and other cases from the Harvard Business School are equally lengthy, often including questions and outlines to aid in one's analysis. The Dashman case even included letters that were exchanged by the principal characters. Many of these cases are taken from real-life experiences. Lawrence comments on the advantages of case discussions:

> A good case is the vehicle by which a chunk of reality is brought into the classroom to be worked over by the class and the instructor. A good case keeps the class discussion grounded upon some of the stubborn facts that must be faced up to in real-life situations. It is the anchor on academic flights of speculation. It is the record of complex situations that must be literally pulled apart and put together again before the situations can be understood.[16]

When detailed cases such as these are used for instruction, they are typically given to you well before the class or classes in which they will be discussed. Sometimes a group (team or task force) is given such a case to work on outside of class and then to report only their procedures and their decisions at a future class period.

Professors Cragan and Wright comment that the cases that work best for them have clear learning objectives and tend to center on key small-group communication behaviors. They suggest that cases with actual dialogue help get the learning outcomes desired. They will also have some groups act out or role play a case.[17]

If you're asked to research and write a case of your own, Denise Mier discovered that professionally written cases tend to outline as follows:[18]

1. A clear and precise statement of the type of organization involved
2. A general description of the organization's background, such as the organization's philosophy for doing business, the size and structure of the organization, its products, and markets, and so on
3. A brief account of the immediate circumstances responsible for the apparent issue
4. Presentation of those facts in detail that appear related to the communication problem
5. An analysis of how the organization's management handled the situation and suggestions for improvement of the communication problem.

CRITICAL INCIDENT DISCUSSIONS

These are mini-cases that usually revolve around a specific incident such as the auditor who ran into the reluctant bookkeeper, discussed previously. Each incident features only one or two learning outcomes instead of several as in the longer cases. The learning outcomes should relate to small-group and communication behaviors, and also, in our emphasis, to organizational dimensions. Some incidents offer choices for you to consider; others do not. They are typically read, discussed, and critiqued on the same class day.

The critical incident that follows has primary learning objectives related to group problem solving, specifically, analysis and establishing criteria. Its equally important, secondary lessons deal with management.

CRITICAL INCIDENT

While watching a baseball game among the employees during the lunch period, Mr. Moore, the new employment manager, noticed one player, a young man of 20 who was a new employee, whose movements seemed extremely awkward and inaccurate. He noticed also that the employee had a speech defect. Later, in an interview with him, Moore became suspicious that the young man was not mentally normal. An intelligence test revealed that he was mildly retarded. The employment record showed that on his present job he had had several minor accidents, though his production rate was fairly good.

What should Moore do?

1. Keep the employee under observation and improve the selection procedure for future hiring.
2. Transfer the employee to a job he can do safely and well.
3. Talk over the problem with the employee's supervisor and check on his job assignment to make sure the present job is the one most suitable to his ability.

4. Discharge the individual on the grounds that he has no future with the firm.
5. Discharge the individual on the grounds that his presence on the work force will be bad for the morale of the other employees.

A group analysis that takes both learning objectives into account and is not too quick to assess the five choices should quickly discover that the young man's "present job" is not described. Since his production was "fairly good," we can rule that out. He did have "several minor accidents." However, that is meaningless without knowing the danger or accident potential in his job. If he's working with molten metal, it may be a good record; if he's working with powder puffs and falling down a lot, it may be a poor record. At this point it should occur to the group that they need to check on his job assignment (and find a choice with that language in it). In the incident format, that becomes a criterion measure. It should also be clear that to find out if he's suited to the job he has, they'll either have to observe him (Mr. Moore will) or talk to somebody who has another criterion measure. Since choice number 3 covers the job assignment and the employee's supervisor, and no other choice does, it follows that one must choose number 3. The lessons inherent in this short, critical incident can be extended by hypothesizing about what this choice might reveal. If the supervisor says that the young man is one of his best workers on a boring line job and that he has had fewer accidents than most, we might leave things alone and look for more people like him for such jobs. Another management lesson imbedded in the incident has to do with line of authority. Mr. Moore should have started the investigation of his felt difficulty by going to the employee's supervisor. Should the job assignment and the supervisor's report produce an opposite scenario, we might wish to consider the other four choices. In the absence of such facts, it is cavalier to choose anything but number 3. Number 1 begs the question in assuming the selection procedures are poor. He may be a good hire. Number 2 begs the question in assuming he was given an improper job assignment. Numbers 4 and 5 involve the serious business of discharge which, when done without documentation, is bad management.

The group problem-solving lessons transcend the critical incident, but since we're interested in organizational settings, the management lessons are a real bonus.[19]

Other advantages of critical-incident discussions and the case methods in general are that they

1. Provide interest and motivation in learning because they are reality centered
2. Provide theory and application lessons in specific terms
3. Afford participation experience and critique of such efforts
4. Teach and also manage complexity for more efficient learning
5. Provide reinforcement of lectures and textbook lessons.

TOPICAL OR PROPOSITIONAL DISCUSSIONS

These are the larger social issues found in organizations or society in general that call for research and systematic discussion over time. These are the subjects often used for class projects. They are typically put in the form of a question. For example: "What should be our position on quality circles and their impact on American unions and business?" They can be questions of fact, policy, or value, or some combination.

Even if your project is to run three weeks or more, some guideline limits are in order:

1. Limit the *scope* of your proposition or question. Some very broad or obtuse questions (''How can truth save American business?'') call for more time than your group has. A question on ''truth in advertising'' is more limited in scope.
2. Find a *researchable topic*. Consider your access to information and the time it takes to access it. If your topic necessitates a trip to the Library of Congress, unless you are near Washington, D.C., your research calls for more effort than the time and the learning outcomes require.
3. Make sure your topic has *interest* to all or most of the group members. Controversy can help hold interest if it doesn't preclude discussion because of members having very rigid attitudes toward the topic. Some topics are better left to the debate class. Check with your group on these matters.

It is clear that some topics that serve the learning process in one class will block it in another. One class with a large number of Pentecostal students simply refused to discuss ''What is the role of obscenity in rhetorical persuasion?'' Even topics in the organizational domain elicit some rigidity and sensitivity. A group of black students took offense at the topic ''Has affirmative action outlived its usefulness in American business?''

We should not, of course, run from controversy and conflict in our project choices. Learning to deal with it is one of the learning outcomes. However, the project as a training method does not function well if it engenders subtleness, acrimonious debate, withdrawal, or verbal attack. Organizational topics close to home, city, county, and state problems calling for solutions are good fare. One standard term-project assignment at Illinois State University calls for the group of five to seven members to work out of class. They discuss and select any small group aspect, theory, or set of skills, and then cooperatively prepare a fifteen- to twenty-minute videotape presentation that enhances the class's understanding of the principles and practices of small group communication.

ROLE SIMULATIONS

The extemporaneous acting out of assigned roles or dramatic parts in a group, often of a real or hypothetical incident, is the classic form of simulation known as role playing. As a technique, role playing is often a good preliminary to the various *forms* of discussion. A *panel* may discuss what they saw and heard. The actors may report their feelings and reactions *symposium* style. The audience may question the actors in an *open forum* style, and so on.

For example, two students were asked to simulate the following roles: *John*— the foreman in a small shop processing prefabricated parts for the automotive industry; *George*—a relatively new employee who has been coming in 15 to 20 minutes late for the past four days.

That's all *John* knows. *George* is secretly informed that he's coming in late because of doctors' appointments at the Veterans Administration where they are treating him for wounds received in the Persian Gulf. He's been trying to reschedule and has finally done so.

The lesson to be learned is that you should *first* get the facts before determining disciplinary communication.

The scene: John meets George coming in 20 minutes late at his locker.

>**John:** This is four days in a row. I've about had it. This is going in your personnel record—one more late arrival and you're fired.
>
>**George:** I've had some problems . . .
>
>**John:** (interrupting) Not like you're going to have if you're late again! Get to your work station.

In the critique it's pointed out that John should have first asked *why* George was late. Get the facts and then tailor the disciplinary communication to the factual situation for it to have maximum impact. For example,

>**John:** George, this is four days in a row. What's going on?
>
>**George:** I've had some problems . . . that I've worked out. Between the V.A. and a stupid injury to my lower back . . . etc., etc.
>
>**John:** I'm glad you've rescheduled your therapy sessions. We can't have you coming in late and screwing up the job. Next time tell me when this is going to happen so I can reschedule and protect both our jobs. I hope you're improving. How is it proceeding?

There are more lessons now. In addition to the "facts" problem, consider that George was also remiss in not informing his foreman. Of course this all presumes that George is telling the truth. A good foreman should check with personnel to see if George's problems are recorded and to generally learn more about his employee. Still one more lesson that could be pursued has to do with invasion of privacy (George's records).

The stereotype roles of group members described in Chapter 6 can also be assigned to role players. "Orienter," "harmonizer," "blocker," "playboy," "special interest pleader," and so on can be fun and also very revealing in a nonthreatening way. Cases or critical incidents can be the topic of discussion. Some members and a procedural leader should *try* to play it straight. Some roles obviously are negative, some task oriented, and so on. These exaggerations have a way of bringing member habits to a more conscious level where they can be discussed more objectively.

Role playing should have a point to it, but it should also be fun. Some role players have been known to *overact*, to confuse, and even to frighten other players. Then the lesson may be lost, and it's rarely fun.

GROUP GAMES

In a sense the "school" solution illustrations "NASA," "Arctic Survival," and "Desert Survival" are similar to games, as are some kinds of special simulations and role playing.

The *alter ego* game really involves role playing another's "second self" or the opposite side of one's personality. A circle of discussants is surrounded by a second circle of observers who are the alter egos of the person behind whom they sit. They can report post-discussion; they can interact with their counterpart on prearranged time-outs; they can whisper their feelings and ideas during the discussion; and so on. The variations of this game are many. The sometimes jolting suggestions of a contrived alter ego are hopefully easier to assimilate in a gamelike atmosphere than under direct critique.

Other games stress winning and losing and competition and cooperation *among* and *between* groups. The classic ''Prisoner's Dilemma'' or ''Win as Much as You Can'' are good examples. Pairs of individuals within a group must make a series of decisions about whether to choose an X or a Y. The combined decisions of the group members determine each person's payoff. For example:

---

4 *Xs* : Lose $1.00 each

---

3 *Xs*   *Xs* win $1.00 each
   :
1 *Y*   *Y* loses $3.00

---

2 *Xs*   *Xs* win $2.00 each
   :
2 *Ys*   *Ys* lose $2.00 each

---

1 *X*   *X* wins $3.00
   :
3 *Ys*   *Ys* lose $1.00 each

---

4 *Ys* : Win $1.00 each

The group can discuss choices and try to persuade each other. However, the rules do not bind anyone to his or her professed choice. Bonus rounds may be incorporated in which the payoffs are increased. The game is supposed to dramatize the necessity of trust if people are to work cooperatively in a competitive, organizational environment. The danger with mixed motive games like this is that, if not properly processed and explained, they can also destroy trust.

Other group games like ''Tinkertoys'' are designed to simulate businesses involved in designing, manufacturing, marketing, and selling creative products. I have seen middle managers spend two days playing with Tinkertoys and playing the game with great seriousness. Their discussions about the business lessons learned suggested that the game time was well spent. Observations on their teamwork and communications between the various product groups made for some very specific consultant commentary to which they closely listened.

Group games are less prevalent now than they were during the seventies, but be prepared for the new ones involving computers and Camcorders.

ORGANIZATIONAL DEVELOPMENT (OD) PROGRAMS

These OD programs are designed to improve organizations through training, work-shops, retreats, and consultation usually directed toward specific problems or goals. Unusually high numbers of grievances, high employee turnover, poor morale, weak supervision, or poor communication are typical problems for an OD program to assess. These training programs, often planned by organizational, small-group, and com-munication specialists, are grounded in social science theory and research. Our pro-grams at the Institute of Labor and Industrial Relations (ILIR) at the University of Michigan/Wayne State University started with a "Needs Analysis" by a two- or three-person team to assess an organization's problems and its current state of development. This analysis involved systematic observation, interviews, and often a written survey.[20] Needs and goals were then specified, complete with learning objectives and tentative lesson plans. The third step was the design of the complete program with the assistance and input of the appropriate organizational executives and the training director, if there was one. Programs ranged from on-campus, executive development (XD) programs to on-site, supervisor programs designed to improve the handling of grievances, dis-cipline, group leadership, and so on. They would range from 26 weekly two-hour ses-sions to three-day (and night) workshops. Many specialty programs are interested pri-marily in personal growth and development directed at making people better group members and more effective and sensitive interpersonally. They range from T-groups and sensitivity training to encounter and Gestalt.[21] Other training programs are more interested in behavior modification and range from Human Resources Development to Assertiveness Training. We will describe a sampling of some of these "helping" groups.

PERSONAL GROWTH GROUPS

Best known among these group programs are *T-group*, *sensitivity training*, *encounter*, and *Gestalt*.

T-group

The purpose of the T-group (*T* for training) is to improve human relations in the work place. The hoped-for developmental factors are (1) to have participants learn from their own experiences in a group laboratory setting and (2) to have participants learn about group dynamics and related skills.

The history of T-group goes back to Kurt Lewin and the start of the National Training Laboratory (NTL) at Bethel, Maine, in the 1940s. During the sixties and seventies under the direction of Leland Bradford, thousands of executives participated in their programs or similar ones. Part of the learning strategy was to get a person out of the work place and into a "laboratory" setting. Since things often became quite personal, executives from the same organization were put in different training groups. Programs often ran two to three weeks under the direction of a trained *facilitator*. It is a totally unstructured group, and at first a very frustrating experience for people used to highly structured work environments. The group works, often painfully, toward its own order and control through intensive, often blunt interactions. This is caused, in part, because the trainer refuses to take charge, and, in part, because we have a group of high-powered people who have only equal power with relative strangers. If the program works—and there are dropouts—one should learn about oneself through feedback often unavailable on the job. This often shocking revelation has been known to dramatically change a person's group interaction and interpersonal communication on the job. However, long-term effects are not clear.[22]

Sensitivity Training

T-groups that concentrate more on a person's emotional and personal adjustment problems rather than on organizational communication problems are called *sensitivity-training* groups. These often bizarre groups fluorished in the seventies under a large group of uncertified trainers, much to the consternation of the NTL.

Encounter

The T-group gave way to the encounter group. It, like sensitivity training, strays more from group dynamics and focuses on self-awareness through therapeutic feedback. It is still directed at normals, but its emphasis moved from interpersonal communication to interpersonal intimacy, often involving emotional and sensory stimulation. As the sixties and *encounter* matured, the emphasis moved to help people achieve *awareness*, *openness*, and fuller interpersonal experiences. Scholars like Carl Rogers and William Schutz brought more defensible theories and rational methods to the world of encounter.[23]

Gestalt

The 1960s also ushered in the eloquent Fritz Perls and the *Gestalt* group.[24] Gestalt methods are the heart of the Esalen Institute programs in Big Sur, California. Unlike the previous personal growth groups, the leader is central to this method. The goal is to have one overcome one's hangups, emotional conflicts, and interpersonal inadequacies. This is hopefully achieved by a wide array of methods involving psychodrama, intensive group experiences, and especially the affirming of one's own experience (existentialism). This search for one's self often centered on bodily awareness; the nude group showers were thought to be one method of overcoming one's hangups. At its best, Gestalt therapy should remind us, perhaps show us, that we are, in large part, responsible for our own group and interpersonal problems and our own growth and development.

BEHAVIOR MODIFICATION GROUPS

Behavioral Change

While some of the previously described helping groups are still with us, most contemporary groups stress observable behavioral change. One is first taught to perceive one's relating and interacting problems behaviorly. The group helps one "see," experience, and define one's problem, but always in behavioral terms. "John, you interrupted others five times in the last 30 minutes, mostly the women." "Jane, you appear attentive when others speak, but under analysis you clearly did not hear two of the four main points we've been discussing." The group provides help, support, and reinforcement, but also behavioral criticism. The leader may introduce specific exercises to help group members modify their behavioral problems.[25] Speech teachers do this in many ways from ''How now brown cow?'' to speech anxiety. Effectiveness improvement is measured by observing before and after behaviors.

Behavior modification assumes that bad habits are learned and that they can therefore be unlearned. The goals are defined in behavioral terms, whether it's to improve articulation, increase eye contact, or reduce interruptions. Behavior modification as a therapy is also popular in helping people with such problems as alcohol, obesity, and smoking.

Human Resources Development

One practical application and extension of behavior therapy groups called *human resources development* is offered by Robert Carkhuff. Carkhuff synthesized the research of Carl Rogers and others and identified helping interpersonal skills. He reasons that these specified behavioral skills (empathy, respect, and so on) can be taught in groups. His teaching model is intuitively sensible: (1) define the skill, (2) model it, (3) practice it (role play), (4) adapt to concrete feedback from the group, and (5) practice outside the group. Carkhuff and his staff have developed a very useful pedagogy text for teachers who would like to improve their own interpersonal skills in the classroom.[26]

Assertiveness Training

Assertiveness training is a special kind of behavior modification group directed at people who have trouble speaking up in situations that call for confrontation, negative feedback, saying no, admitting mistakes, resisting peer pressure, and others where there is some perceived but manageable risk.[27] Professional training groups make a clear distinction between assertiveness and aggressiveness. To assert is to state positively and forthrightly; to aggress is to state with hostility and an intent to injure. Responsible training also includes the identification of personal rights, learning to refute irrational thinking, and learning new ways of responding and communicating more assertively.[28]

The leader is central to assertiveness training groups and must establish a climate where one is willing to self-disclose. Disclosure of situations where one failed to speak up are analyzed by the group, and similar experiences are recounted by group members. Members are specifically coached by the trainer, particularly in the area of behaviors related to communication style. Sometimes we are hesitant to speak up because we don't know how to ''say'' it. In the latter part of the course, much time is spent on a very specific kind of *behavior rehearsal*. This technique involves impromptu but guided role playing of a recommended specific behavior. ''Sit straight, a little more volume, and no frowning.'' The group members help with positive feedback demonstrating their version of the behavior required and serving as actors in the behavior rehearsals. The trainer is coach, counselor, facilitator, and summarizer. Practitioners think the behavioral rehearsal technique is the single, most important factor in assertiveness training.[29]

COMMON DEVELOPMENTAL FACTORS

While many of the personal growth and behavior-modification group techniques discussed above are based on therapy models, they can and are obviously being used in nonclinical situations and in a variety of settings. The more task-centered OD programs use these techniques, as do those interested in all manner of interpersonal and communicational skills. Most of your speech communication courses are interested in behavioral modification if skills are involved, as are your courses in business administration. Clearly, personal growth based on theory and practice is also a desired learning outcome.

Confounding variables such as goals, leadership, organization, and member differences make it difficult to judge the effectiveness of these therapy models when applied to OD groups. Nevertheless Irvin Yalom, a researcher and psychotherapist, concludes that in therapy groups there are at least eleven positive group-dynamic factors (he calls them therapeutic factors) that cut across these various approaches. One hopes they are equally helpful with normal groups. The factors, edited slightly, follow.[30]

1. Instillation of hope (others are learning; there is hope for me).
2. Universality (others have problems like mine).
3. Imparting of information (I can learn new ways to cope).
4. Altruism (I can help others).
5. Recapitulation of unsatisfactory experiences (I see them more correctly now).
6. Development of social skills (I should be more sensitive to others).
7. Imitative effects (If he or she can do it, so can I).
8. Interpersonal relations (learning from the group as a social microcosm).
9. Group cohesiveness (members accept one another).
10. Catharsis (I am free to express my emotions).
11. Existential awareness (affirming one's existence despite an often unfair, painful, lonely, complex world; I am responsible for myself).

The research data together with leader evaluations of the various clinical programs suggest that most people can benefit from such programs. Some probably will not, and a small number may actually regress.[31] In the nontherapy programs regression is not as serious a matter, yet one is reminded of the necessity for professional trainers and the careful selection of participants for such training.

SUMMARY

Basic methods of observing and evaluating group effectiveness include category systems, rating chart systems, critics/consultants, and self-reports.

A *structured* observation and analysis makes a more determined and scientific effort to break the group process down into its components, functions, acts, or content. One such structured system is called "interaction process analysis" (Bales). It classifies verbal and nonverbal behavior. An observer is responsible for noting three kinds of acts: positive social-emotional, negative social-emotional, and task. Another highly structured system of analysis is called SYMLOG, which stands for *System* for the *Multiple Level Observation* of *Groups*. SYMLOG attempts to catch more of the personality characteristics of the interactants. The behaviors to be observed are based on the following personality dimensions: (1) dominance/submission, (2) friendly/unfriendly, (3) instrumentally controlled/emotionally expressive. The system generates twenty-six roles for observers to record. A third method of structured analysis is the "interact system model" (Fisher/Hawes). An *interact* is the observable verbal or nonverbal act of one member followed by a reaction from another. This model studies pairs of contiguous acts. This system has a 12 × 12 matrix on which an observer may record data with a total of 144 potential interacts.

Observation can also be done by your peers, by process experts, by consultants, and by comparing your group solution of a case or critical incident to a ''school'' solution. Checklists, rating charts, consultant observations, and school solutions are illustrated.

Classic training methods for small-group problem solving and decision making include case studies, critical incidents, propositional discussions, role simulations, and group games.

Organizational development (OD) programs are designed to improve organizations and their people through training, workshops, retreats, and consultation aimed at specific problems or goals. These programs are grounded in social science and behavioral theory. Many specialty programs are interested primarily in personal growth and development; others stress behavior modification. Sample group programs described include T-group, sensitivity training, encounter, behavioral change, human resources development, and assertiveness training. Variables that may confound judging the effectiveness of such training include leadership, the organization, member differences, and the trainers.

PROJECTS AND CASES

PROJECTS

1. Observe a discussion group and chart the flow of communication among the participants. Use arrows to indicate direction, and use one arrow for each substantial comment (a comment other than a simple exclamation or yes or no answer). A model is shown on page 306. Discuss what the model indicates about the various participants. Do there appear to be relationships between amount and duration of group members' talk and leadership? Group structure? Role members play? Attainment of group goals? Stereotypes?

   After observing several hundred similar, short panel discussions, veteran teachers advanced the following conclusions. These may suggest more things to observe.

   a. Vocal subgroups often developed.

   b. Seating was often awkward and disordered.

   c. Leaders were seldom appointed or voted upon.

   d. Time was not always well budgeted.

   e. Systematic discussion was infrequent.

   f. Some group members were allowed to dominate the discussions.

   g. Some members should have been drawn into the discussion more frequently.

   h. Initial agreement was not often challenged.

   i. Language was often too absolute and unqualified for the question at hand.

   j. With a few exceptions, the group thinking was relatively flexible.

   k. The participants seemed to enjoy their work.

l. The expert answer was generally accepted as intelligent after discussion by the entire class.

m. The groups were interested mostly in answers—not in the problems.

n. For some, the panel discussion appeared to be a new experience in flexible thinking.

2. Write a three-page personal, introspective report about the attitudes and behaviors you exhibit in group communication. What have you learned about yourself as a participant in cooperative communication? See the previous project for ideas. Prepare to share.

3. Select an organizational-development issue suitable for two or three days of research. Describe the issue as a question (e.g., what are the pros and cons of sensitivity training?), prepare a one-hour agenda, select a procedural leader, do your research, and prepare for class discussion(s). You may use combinations of the various forms of discussion. You might choose from these topics of general interest:

T-group	Assertiveness training
Sensitivity training	Supervisory development
Biodots	DTA (Developmental Task Analysis)
LEAD	Jet fuel
Situational leadership	Communicating empathy
Maturity style match	Flawless consulting
Personal stress	Assessment and interviewing
Managing conflict	Making meetings work
Timetrack	Quality circle packet
Probe	Group development
Map	Human relations
Scan	Public speaking
Speech impact	Humanus
Computer games	Storyboard
Strategic listening	Ethics in the marketplace
Encounter group	Transactional analysis
Gestalt	Behavior modification
Human resources development	Teambuilding

4. Locate and research for discussion one of the many communication and small-group "training aids": "Simulation Exercises," "Experiential Learning Aids," "Learning Resources" kits, tests, books, cassettes, films, and/or games. These are popularly advertised as Organizational Development (OD), Human Resources Development (HRD), and other titles related to personal growth and development in an organizational setting. Some recent titles follow.

Structured Experience Kit	Problem solving
The Schutz Measures	Interaction
Team Development Inventory	Communication
Nuclear-Site Negotiation	Presentation
Tape-assisted Listening test	Conference leading

Creative Growth games	Adult Personality Inventory
Bafa Bafa (Simulation)	Spectrum-1
Supervisory dynamics	The One-Minute Manager
Motivation Analysis Test	LBA (Leader Behavior Analysis)

CASES

1. "We Can't Afford Behavioral Science Around Here"[32]

Todd was happy to be hired by Bradbury Foods as a first-level supervisor in its main processing plant. It was apparent to him that being a supervisor so soon after graduation from business school would be a real boost to his career. After about one month on the job, Todd began to make some critical observations about the company and its management style. He began to wonder if the company was somewhat behind the times in its management practices.

To clarify things in his own mind, Todd requested a meeting with Adam Green, plant superintendent. The meeting between Todd and Adam included dialogue of this nature:

Adam: Have a seat, Todd. It's nice to visit with one of our young supervisors, particularly when you didn't say you were facing an emergency that you and your boss couldn't handle.

Todd: (nervously) Mr. Green, I want to express my appreciation for your willingness to meet with me. You're right, I'm not facing an emergency. But I do wonder about something. That's what I came here to talk to you about.

Adam: That's what I like to see. A young man who takes the initiative to ask questions about things that are bothering him.

Todd: To be quite truthful, Mr. Green, I am happy here and I'm glad I joined Bradbury Foods. But I'm curious about one thing. As you may know, I'm a graduate of a business college. A few of the courses I took emphasized using behavioral science knowledge to manage people. You know, kind of psychology on the job. It seems like the way to go if you want to keep people productive and happy.

Here at Bradbury it seems that nobody uses behavioral science knowledge. I know you're a successful company. But some of the management practices seem out of keeping with the times. The managers make all the decisions. Everybody else listens and carries out orders. Even professionals on the payroll have to punch time clocks. I've been here for almost two months and I haven't even heard the term *participative management* used once.

Adam: Oh, I get your point. You're talking about using behavioral science around here. I know all about that. The point you're missing, Todd, is that behavioral science is for the big profitable companies. That stuff works great when business is good and profit margins are high. But around here business is kind of so-so, and profit margins in the food business are thinner than a potato chip. Maybe someday when we get fat and profitable we can start using behavioral science. In the meantime, we've all got a job to do.

Todd: I appreciate your candid answer, Mr. Green. But when I was in college, I certainly heard a different version of why companies use behaviorally oriented management.

QUESTIONS

1. What is your evaluation of Adam's contention that OD knowledge is useful primarily when a firm is profitable?
2. To what extent should Todd be discouraged?

3. What should Todd do?

4. Based on your experience, how representative of most managers is Adam Green's thinking?

2. Consider unused cases from other chapters; most are related to observing and improving.

NOTES

1. John F. Cragan and David W. Wright, *Communication in Small Group Discussions* (St. Paul, Minn.: West, 1986), pp. 322–23.

2. See especially Ole R. Holsti, *Content Analysis for the Social Sciences and Humanities* (Reading, Mass: Addison-Wesley, 1969).

3. R. F. Bales and S. P. Cohen, *SYMLOG: A System for the Multiple Level Observation of Groups* (New York: Free Press, 1979), p. 3; see also R. F. Bales, "Overview of the SYMLOG System: Measuring Behavior in Groups," in *1988 Annual: Developing Human Resources*, J. William Pfeiffer, ed. (San Diego: University Associates, 1988), pp. 261–85.

4. Ibid., p. 178.

5. Ibid., p. 23.

6. Ibid., p. 21.

7. D. J. Isenberg and J. G. Ennis, "Perceiving Group Members: A Comparison of Derived and Imposed Dimensions," *Journal of Personality and Social Psychology*, 41 (1981), 295; see also R. F. Bales, *SYMLOG Case Study Kit* (New York: Free Press, 1980).

8. Isenberg and Ennis, "Perceiving Group Members," pp. 293–305.

9. V. D. Wall and G. J. Galanes, "The SYMLOG Dimensions and Small Group Conflict," *Central States Speech Journal*, 37, no. 2 (Summer 1986), 61–78.

10. See B. A. Fisher and L. Hawes, "An Interact System Model: Generating a Grounded Theory of Small Groups," *Quarterly Journal of Speech*, 57 (1971), 444–53.

11. B. A. Fisher, *Small Group Decision Making: Communication and the Group Process* (New York: McGraw-Hill, 1980), p. 323.

12. Ibid., p. 118.

13. Ibid., Appendix, p. 310.

14. John K. Brilhart, *Effective Group Discussion*, 5th ed. (Dubuque, Ia: Wm. C. Brown, 1986), pp. 361–62.

15. Ibid., p. 375.

16. P. Lawrence, "The Preparation of Case Material," in *The Case Method of Teaching Human Relations and Administration*, ed. K. Andrews (Cambridge, Mass.: Harvard University Press, 1953), pp. 215–24.

17. John F. Cragan and David W. Wright, "A New Pedagogy for Teaching Small Group Communication" (a paper delivered at the World Communication Associaton convention, Norwich, England, August 3–5, 1987).

18. Denise Mier, "From Concepts to Practices: Student Case Study Work in Organizational Communication," *Communication Education*, 31, no. 2 (April 1982), 153.

19. For more on these matters, see Gary Kreps, *Organizational Communication* (New York: Longman, 1986), pp. 319–26.

20. See especially Rensis Likert, *The Human Organization* (New York: McGraw-Hill, 1967), pp. 196–211.

21. For more detailed descriptions, see J. Hansen, R. Warner, and E. Smith, *Group Counseling: Theory and Process* (Chicago: Rand McNally, 1980).

22. See R. E. Kaplan, "The Conspicuous Absence of Evidence That Process Consultation Enhances Task Performance," *Journal of Applied Behavioral Science*, 15 (1979), 346-60.

23. See C. Rogers, *Encounter Groups* (New York: Harper and Row, 1970); and W. C. Schutz, *Joy: Expanding Human Awareness* (New York: Grove, 1967).

24. Fritz Perls, *Gestalt Therapy Verbatim* (Lafayette, Calif.: Real People Press, 1969).

25. See S. Rose, *Group Therapy: A Behavioral Approach* (Englewood Cliffs, NJ: Prentice-Hall, 1977).

26. Robert R. Carkhuff, D. H. Berenson, and R. M. Pierce, *The Skills of Teaching: Interpersonal Skills* (Amherst, Mass.: Human Resources Development Press, 1977); see also Carkhuff, Berenson, and Pierce, *The Art of Helping IV, Student Workbook* (Amherst, Mass.: Human Resources Development Press, 1980).

27. E. D. Gambril and C. A. Richey, "An Assertion Inventory for Use in Assessment and Research," *Behavior Therapy*, 6 (1975), 547-49.

28. See A. J. Lange and P. Jakubowski, *Responsible Assertive Behavior: Cognitive/Behavioral Procedures for Trainers* (Champaign, Ill.: Research Press, 1976).

29. R. G. Heimberg and others, "Assertion Training: A Review of the Literature," *Behavior Therapy*, 8 (1977), 953-71.

30. Irving Yalom, *The Theory and Practice of Group Psychotherapy* (New York: Basic Books, 1985), pp. 3-11 (parentheses mine).

31. M. Lieberman, I. Yalom, and M. Miles, *Encounter Groups: First Facts* (New York: Basic Books, 1973).

32. A. J. DuBrin, *Foundations of Organizational Behavior: An Applied Perspective*, © 1984, pp. 17-18. Reprinted by permission of Prentice-Hall, Inc., Englewood Cliffs, New Jersey.

Appendix

PARLIAMENTARY RULES

INTRODUCTION

If your group or class decides, for purposes of simulation to follow *Robert's Rules of Order* (parliamentary procedure) or some common practice rules, you will find the brief table of motions that follows an aid in such discussions. For very technical questions, you should consult texts post-1982 or certified parliamentarians. Courses are taught in parliamentary procedures, and tests are given for certification. However, you can learn and can conduct yourself appropriately in most situations by using the table of parliamentary law.

The 1981 revision of *Robert's Rules of Order*[1] has changed very little from the 1970 or the 1921 edition. There are, however, five clarifications based on how certified parliamentarians interpret the rules for modern times.

The Previous Question This is to close debate and force a vote, which may be put in more colloquial forms such as "I call for (or "call") the question" or "I move we vote now," and all the rules still apply. One is reminded to demand a second, and always take a vote ($\frac{2}{3}$) separately from and before the vote(s) on the motion(s) to which it is applied.[2]

To Lay on the Table This is to defer a pending question to take up something immediately urgent, which is to be strictly adhered to. It has sometimes been used illegitimately to kill rather than to simply defer. When such use is clear, it should be ruled out of order.[3]

Interruption of Votes This is also called *parliamentary inquiry* or *point of order*. It is permitted only before any member has actually voted, unless it is simply business being transacted during tabulation.[4]

If it was ordered that debate on a main motion be closed and the *vote be taken* at a specified hour, and that time has passed, *no further amendments can be offered*. One can, however, reconsider the vote that set the time limit.[5]

A-1 Table of Parliamentary Motions

QUESTIONS

TYPE OF MOTION	PURPOSE	May Interrupt a Speaker	Mover Must be Recognized	Requires a Second	Debatable	Vote Required	Amendable
PRIVILEGED MOTIONS:							
5. Adjourn to specific time	To set time of next meeting	no	yes	yes	no	maj.	yes
4. To adjourn	To dismiss the meeting	no	yes	yes	no	maj.	no
3. To take a recess	To dismiss for given period	no	yes	yes	no	maj.	yes
2. Question of Privilege	To make a request during debate	yes	no	no	no	chair	no
1. Call for orders of day	To force consideration of a postponed motion	yes	no	no	no	none	no
INCIDENTAL MOTIONS:							
To appeal a decision of the chair	To obtain vote reversing the chairperson	yes	yes	yes	limited	maj.	no
To call for a division of the house	To ascertain correct vote	yes	no	no	no	none	no
To raise a point of order	To correct a parliamentary error	yes	no	no	no	chair	no
To object to consideration	To prevent consideration of a motion	yes	no	no	no	$\frac{2}{3}$	no
To divide motion	To consider in separate parts	no	yes	yes	no	maj.	yes
To withdraw a motion	To remove from floor	no	yes	no	no	maj.	no
To suspend rules	To permit action contrary to the standing rules	no	yes	yes	no	$\frac{2}{3}$	no
To close nominations	To prevent admission of additional candidates	no	yes	yes	no	$\frac{2}{3}$	yes
To rise for parliamentary inquiry	To ascertain proper procedure	yes	no	no	no	none	no
To rise for information	To ascertain status of business	yes	no	no	no	none	no
SUBSIDIARY MOTIONS:							
8. To table	To defer action	no	yes	yes	no	maj.	no
7. The previous question	To close debate and force vote	no	yes	yes	no	$\frac{2}{3}$	no
6. To limit or extend limits of debate	To control length of time for discussion	no	yes	yes	no	$\frac{2}{3}$	yes
5. To postpone to a certain time	To defer action or to create a special order	no	yes	yes	limited	maj.	yes
4. To refer to a committee	To allow consideration for house by special group	no	yes	yes	limited	maj.	yes
3. To amend an amendment	To clarify an amendment	no	yes	yes	yes	maj.	no
2. To amend or substitute	To modify a motion	no	yes	yes	yes	maj.	yes
1. To postpone indefinitely	To suppress action	no	yes	yes	yes	maj.	no
MAIN MOTION:							
The bill or resolution	To introduce business	no	yes	yes	yes	maj.	yes
RENEWAL MOTIONS:							
To reconsider	To reopen debate and consideration	yes	yes	yes	yes	maj.	no
To reconsider, and have entered on minutes	To enter on minutes for subsequent reconsideration	yes	yes	yes	no	maj.	no
To rescind	To reverse earlier action	no	yes	yes	yes	$\frac{2}{3}$	yes
To take from table	To return to consideration previously deferred	no	yes	yes	no	maj.	no

Boards   Boards of any size are regarded as a form of assembly.[6] Small boards of a dozen or fewer members have greater rule flexibility than larger ones. They vary from deliberative assembly in that its operation is determined by responsibilities and powers delegated to it or conferred on it by authority outside itself.[7]

NOTES

1. Henry M. Robert and Sarah Corbin Robert, *Robert's Rules of Order Newly Revised* (Glenview, Ill.: Scott, Foresman, 1981).
2. Ibid., p. 170.
3. Ibid., p. 183.
4. Ibid., p. 355.
5. Ibid., p. 165.
6. Ibid., p. 4.
7. Ibid., p. 399.

INDEX